AF599225

DE' VISI MOSTRUOSI AND CARICATURES

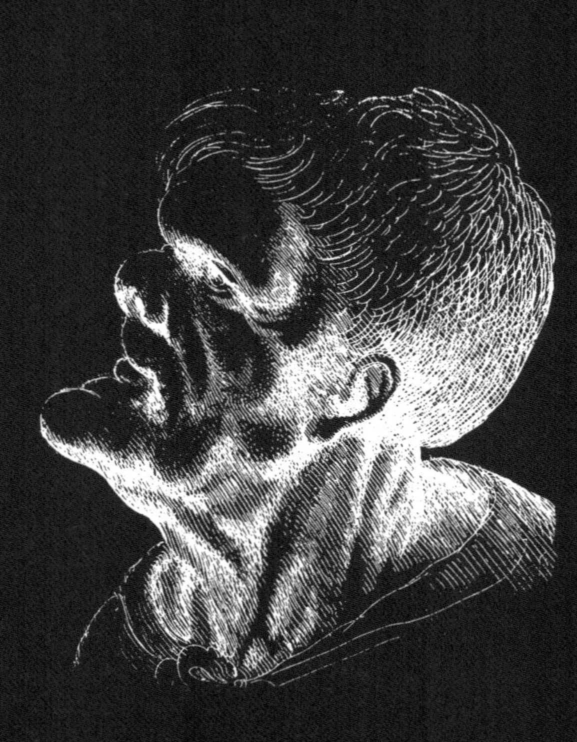

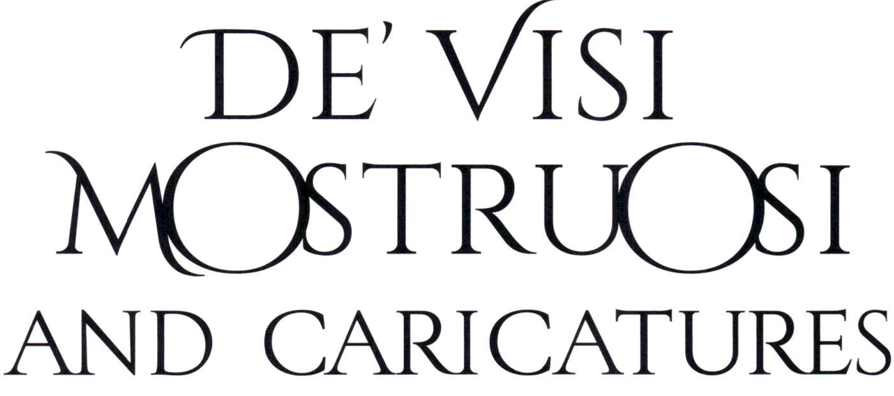

FROM LEONARDO DA VINCI TO BACON

EDITED BY PIETRO C. MARANI

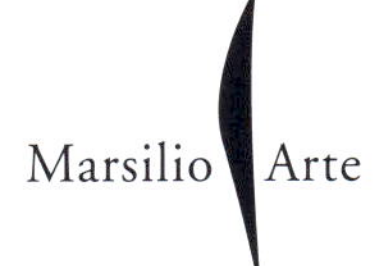

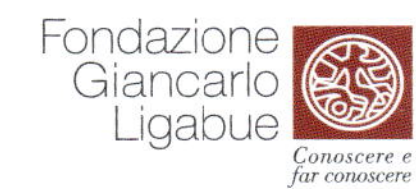

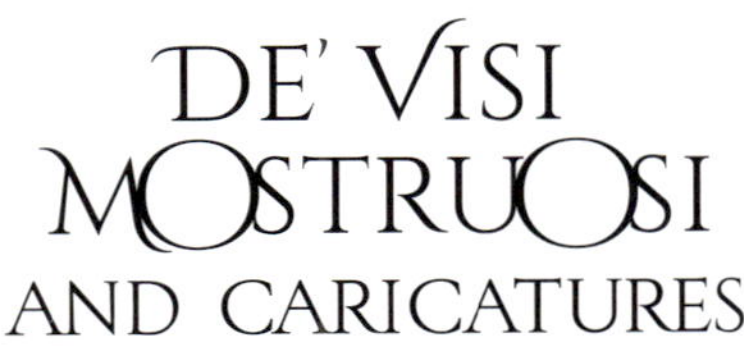

FROM LEONARDO DA VINCI TO BACON

Venice, Istituto Veneto di Scienze, Lettere ed Arti, Palazzo Loredan, 28 January – 27 April 2023

Under the Aegis of

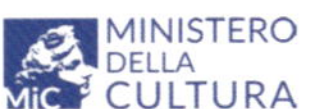

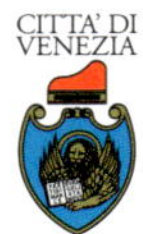

Promoted and Organised by

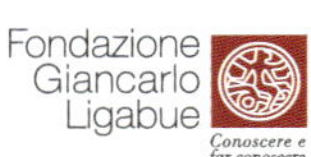

Partner

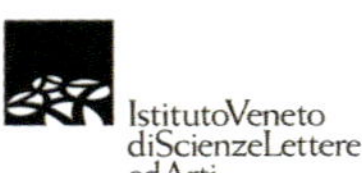

Main Sponsors

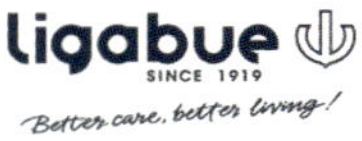

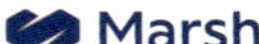

Sponsor

CAMPARI

Technical Sponsor

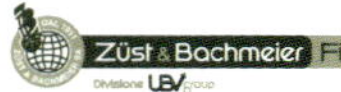

FONDAZIONE
GIANCARLO LIGABUE

President
Inti Ligabue

Honorary Vicepresident
Massimo Casarin

General Executive Secretary, Registrar
Gianluca Ferrarese

Head of Editorial and Communication
Lucia Berti

General Secretariat
Silvia Lattuada

Public and Private Loans Manager, Transport and Insurance
Elisa Bissacco

Archive, Iconography and Exhibition Set-up
Elisa Bissacco
Cecilia Riva

Communication Project
Federico Dei Rossi
Ubis Design Workgroup

Set-up Project
Luca Facchini
Ubis Design Workgroup

Multimedia Projects
Federico Dei Rossi
Nicola Facchini
Ubis Design Workgroup

Restoration
Giulia Simbula

Set-up
Dee Group s.r.l.
Interlinea Fine Art Services
OTT ART s.r.l.

Press Office
Villaggio Globale International

Insurance
Marsh

Transports and Logistics
Zust&Bachmeier SA
Gruppo Ligabue

Exhibition Curated and Catalogue Edited by
Pietro C. Marani

Scientific Committee
Alessia Alberti, *Conservator, Gabinetto dei Disegni e Raccolta delle Stampe "A. Bertarelli", Castello Sforzesco, Milan*
Luca Massimo Barbero, *Director, Istituto di Storia dell'Arte, Fondazione Giorgio Cini, Venice*
Paola Cordera, *Associate Professor, Museology, Art Critic, and Restoration, School of Design, Politecnico, Milan*
Inti Ligabue, *President, Fondazione Giancarlo Ligabue, Venice*
Enrico Lucchese, *Researcher, Dipartimento di Lettere e Beni Culturali, Università degli Studi della Campania*
Pietro C. Marani, *Curator and Full Professor, History of Modern Art, and Museology, School of Design, Politecnico, Milan*
Alice Martin, *Head of the Devonshire Collection, Chatsworth*
Mons. Alberto Rocca, *Dottore, Veneranda Biblioteca Ambrosiana; Director, Pinacoteca; Director, Classe di Studi Borromaici, Milan*
Calvin Winner, *Head of Collection, The Sainsbury Centre for Visual Arts, Norwich*

General Coordination, Executive Secretariat
Lucia Berti
Silvia Lattuada

Essays and Entries by
Alessia Alberti [AA]
Rosalba Antonelli [RA]
Rita Capurro [RC]
Paola Cordera [PC]
Laura Corti [LC]
Enrico Lucchese [EL]
Pietro C. Marani [PCM]
Sara Taglialagamba [ST]
Calvin Winner [CW]

Public Lenders
Designmuseum Danmark, Copenhagen
Devonshire Collections, Chatsworth
Ente Raccolta Vinciana, Milan
Fondazione Accademia Carrara, Bergamo
Fondazione Giorgio Cini, Venice
Castello Sforzesco, Gabinetto dei Disegni, Milan
Gallerie degli Uffizi, Gabinetto dei Disegni e delle Stampe, Florence
Gallerie dell'Accademia, Venice
Staatliche Kunstsammlungen, Kupferstich-Kabinett, Dresden
Musée du Louvre, Département des Arts Graphiques, Paris
Nuova Fondazione Rossana and Carlo Pedretti, Lamporecchio
Pinacoteca di Brera, Gabinetto dei disegni, Milan
Sainsbury Centre for Visual Arts, Norwich Research Park, University of East Anglia
Veneranda Biblioteca Ambrosiana, Milan

Private Lenders
Ligabue Collection, Venice
Private collections, Milan
Private collection

Acknowledgements
Bernard Aikema, Giulia Barcella, Katrin Bäsig, Gabriella Belli, Claudia Beltramo Ceppi Zevi, Daniele Benati, Bruno Bertaggia, Elisabetta Bianchi, Deborah Bonandrini, Giulio Bora, Paola Borghese, James M. Bradburne, Stephanie Buck, Luca Carrà, Daisy Cartwright, Taz Chappell, Martin Clayton, Luisa Cogliati Arano, Jago Cooper, Beatrice Cristini, Gigetta Dalli Regoli, Matteo De Fina, Vincent Delieuvin, Stefano De Martino, Laurence des Cars, Marzia Faietti, Maria Teresa Fiorio, Elena Fontana, Varena Forcione, Ciara Gallagher, Giuseppe Garavaglia, Marco Gislon, Anthony Hirst Vitali, Steven Hooper, Pernille Klemp, Letizia Lodi, Rodolfo Maffeis, Katherine Mager, Giulio Manieri Elia, Alice Martin, Gudula Metze, Fanny Meurisse, Giovanna Mori, Charles Noble, Giovanna Palandri, Alessia Panella, Mauro Pavesi, Sebastiano Pedrocco, Valeria Poletto, Francesco Porzio, Amber Rebecca, Furio Rinaldi, Nicoletta Rivolta, Alberto Rocca, M. Cristina Rodeschini, Xavier Salmon, Claudio Salsi, Silvia Salvini, Ida Santisi, Michela Scarpa, Eike Schmidt, Fred Schroeder, Anne-Louise Sommer, Kirsten Toftegaard, Simone Tonin, Françoise Viatte, † Enrico Vitali, Christel Winling, Filippo Zevi

A particular acknowledgement to the President of the Istituto Veneto di Scienze, Lettere ed Arti, Andrea Rinaldo, and to all the members of the Consiglio di Presidenza of the Istituto

Viewed superficially, it may appear anomalous for a Foundation such as ours to promote an exhibition of Old Master drawings by great Italian artists, when in recent years it has always presented major archaeological, anthropological and ethnographic exhibitions devoted to the art and culture of distant civilisations and peoples, or cultural connections in the evolution of concepts and ideas in the ancient world.

Yet there are topics that prompt various reflections; and caricature between the sixteenth and eighteenth centuries, the focus of the exhibition, is certainly one of these. Naturalism, physiognomy, grotesque portraiture, the exaggeration of traits, the identification and classification of human types in drawings by Leonardo and the great artists of Lombardy, Emilia but above all Venice and the Veneto who ventured into this genre prompt us to reflect in a different way on our humanity. Some did so for pastime or in a spirit of ridicule, others prompted by market demand, yet others as a way of studying or shrewdly analysing the contemporary world. It was a way of exploring the natural world in those times, examining the customs of the society that immediately preceded our own and to which we are inevitably still indebted.

It is always Humanity that is at the centre of our interests. Curiosity, the thirst for knowledge, the love of culture and art, the desire to 'know and make known' evoked in the motto of the Giancarlo Ligabue Foundation are the coordinates of our explorations. Venice, in particular, the starting point for our survey of the world, is also a point of constant return, on which we always gaze, reflecting on its dimension as a crossroads of cultures but also a place of identity, a cradle of traditions and knowledge to be studied, preserved and spread.

The great Leonardo da Vinci is the inevitable starting point for any study of the subject, in Venice as elsewhere, as seems confirmed by the most recent research. The exhibition presents an exceptional number of his 'monstrous faces' or 'grotesque heads' including the so-called 'Head of an old woman' in the Ligabue Collection. Leonardo was one of the many passions cultivated by Giancarlo Ligabue, the author of the book Leonardo da Vinci e i fossili, *while another major section of the exhibition looks at Venetian artists. Marco Ricci, a landscape painter and set designer, his friend Anton Maria Zanetti, a brilliant amateur in constant competition in creating caricatures of a varied Venetian milieu, and Giambattista Tiepolo, with his refined style, are the specific interpreters of a singular figurative genre in the artistic civilisation of Venice, which takes us back to the eighteenth-century city and its swan song.*

Then the exhibition moves rapidly forward. We decided to close it with an emblematic and extraordinary reference to contemporary art, to show that the tradition is not at an end, that physiognomy, the exaggeration of characters, and deformity return to figurative art all the more in an era of existential crisis and psychological frailty like the twentieth century.

We are very gratified to be able to present in this context one masterpiece by Francis Bacon from the Sainsbury Centre of the University of East Anglia in Norwich: sequential and syncopated images, a face disintegrated and disjointed, clearly expressing the analysis of the unconscious and the disorienting reality of modern man, urging us to further reflection.

I wish to thank Pietro C. Marani, one of the leading experts in this field and on Leonardo's work, who agreed to develop the exhibition project, the scholars who in the catalogue have helped focus on various aspects of this singular artistic and cultural phenomenon and those who, starting from the tireless staff of our Foundation, have contributed to the exhibition.
Above all, my gratitude goes to the many prestigious Italian and foreign lenders who have trusted us with the loans of some very delicate and precious works in the exhibition by important artists. The possibility to exhibit in Venice, in particular, the graphic masterpieces of Leonardo da Vinci from the Veneranda Biblioteca Ambrosiana and the Pinacoteca di Brera in Milan – for which I thank the prefetto Marco Ballarini and the directors Alberto Rocca and James B. Bradburne – and the Devonshire Collection of Chatsworth is a privilege and a source of pride.
To Sir Peregrine Andrew Morny Cavendish, 12th Duke of Devonshire, I wish to express my personal gratitude and friendship.

Inti Ligabue
President of the Giancarlo Ligabue Foundation

The Ligabue Foundation has been interacting for many years with the Istituto Veneto di Scienze, Lettere ed Arti, through remarkable exhibitions that blend artistic, scientific and social aspects. These exhibitions have found a natural place in the Institute in which the chosen artworks, always displayed with great mastery, are positioned among the ancient shelves of the historical library. Not by chance. The drive that inspires the Ligabue Foundation has much in common with the mission and the origins of our Institute, specifically the fostering of multidisciplinary research, the relentless search for unusual themes that mix traditionally separate cultural domains, the discovery of new languages in the dialogue among different cultures.

After having explored remote places' archaeology, symbols and artefacts, with his fifth exhibition in collaboration with the Institute, Ligabue Foundation is now entering the field of art with a new and different angle and experimental connotation. Here, from the grotesque spirit of the first caricatures shown, the analysis progressively becomes more and more introspective until it manifests – in particular with the work of Francis Bacon – a scream of pain and a call for destructuring the ego. Along this fascinating road we meet the grace of the Tiepolos, the naturalism of the Lombards, the curiosity for the monstrous that begins with Leonardo.

This new path has been thought of by a science committee of the highest level, yet capable of involving all kinds of public, from specialists to children who will be guided by tutors on educational paths specifically designed for them. It is a journey across the centuries and into the personalities of different artists through the taste of caricature that has always piqued the curiosity of a vast public – which deserves to be visited by many and recognised as a major cultural event.

Andrea Rinaldo
President of the Istituto Veneto di Scienze, Lettere ed Arti

It is now more than thirty-five years since Venice had an exhibition on facial deformities and caricature in the modern age. Yet, since the major exhibition of 1987, Effetto Arcimboldo: trasformazioni del volto nel sedicesimo e nel ventesimo secolo, *there have been some important monograph exhibitions devoted to individual masters of caricature, as well as attempts abroad, even in recent years, to present larger surveys. An example was the exhibition* Infinite Jest: Caricature and Satire from Leonardo to Levine, *at the Metropolitan Museum in New York in 2011–12. However, the intention of this exhibition is partly different, while being closely bound up with the city that hosts it: Venice.*

This occasion was desired by Inti Ligabue, president of the Giancarlo Ligabue Foundation, which continues energetically to promote study, research and the dissemination of knowledge of different aspects of art, history and material culture. This work often draws inspiration from works in the Ligabue Collection, such as in this exhibition the well-known Grotesque head of woman *attributed to Leonardo. It also lent itself to stressing a strand of northern Italian continuity in the genre of caricature, or rather in the deformation and transformation of physiognomic traits.*

This strand had already been indicated by some critics at the dawn of modernity, from the author of the handwritten introduction at the beginning of Anton Maria Zanetti's Cini Album and Francesco Albergati Capacelli to Gustavo Frizzoni in illustrating Tiepolo's caricatures. Stemming from Leonardo's visi mostruosi *and the* pitture ridicole *of the Lombards, while including elements of the Carracci's naturalism, this strand flourished in Venice in the first half of the eighteenth century.*

Thanks to the generosity of the Biblioteca-Pinacoteca Ambrosiana in Milan, the Duke of Devonshire Settlement Trust at Chatsworth and the Pinacoteca di Brera, also in Milan, it has proved possible to present a core of seventeen or eighteen of Leonardo's autograph works and mount an exhibition focused on 'grotesque heads' and 'caricature' in northern Italy that includes drawings and paintings by Giovan Paolo Lomazzo, Aurelio Luini, Giovanni Agostino da Lodi, Parmigianino, Annibale and Agostino Carracci, Donato Creti and engravings by Giuseppe Arcimboldo, Battista Franco, Wenceslaus Hollar and others. This entwining of cross-influences and collections is confirmed by the ties between Zanetti and the French collectors of Leonardo's drawings, as well as the presence in his library, as in Tiepolo's, of important texts of the Leonardesque tradition, such as those made by Lomazzo. (Giovanbattista Tiepolo's son Giandomenico in fact owned I grotteschi *of 1587, as can be seen from the sale catalogue of his estate published in Paris in 1845, p. 38, no. 293.) If we compare Lomazzo's painting of the grotesque head of a woman, derived from a drawing by Leonardo at Chatsworth, with the heads in Francis Bacon's* Triptych *at the Sainsbury Centre in Norwich, we realise the persistence of research through the centuries into the human face and its deformities as a reflection of characters, passions, unspeakable animal instincts, inner impulses and perhaps nightmares of the psyche and subconscious, invariably the object of study and attention by artists of the modern and contemporary age.*

Pietro C. Marani
Curator

DE' VISI MOSTRUOSI AND CARICATURES

FROM LEONARDO DA VINCI TO BACON

Front Cover
Leonardo da Vinci, attributed
Grotesque head of woman in profile facing left, c. 1490–1500
Venice, Ligabue Collection
[cat. 4]

Back Cover
Francis Bacon
Three Studies for Portrait of Isabel Rawsthorne, 1965
Norwich, Sainsbury Centre for Visual Arts, University of East Anglia
[cat. 86]

Graphic Design
Federico Dei Rossi

Translations
Richard Sadleir

Editing
Katharine Ridler

© 2023 by Giancarlo Ligabue Foundation, Venice

© 2023 by Marsilio Editori® s.p.a. in Venezia

First edition January 2023

ISBN 979-12-5463-085-3
www.marsilioeditori.it

CONTENTS

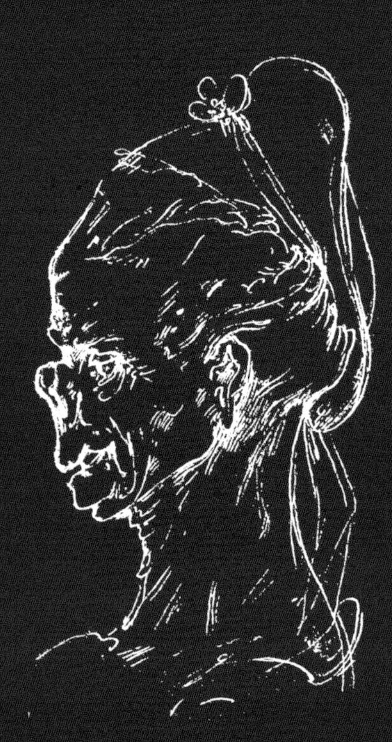

Leonardo and His Followers

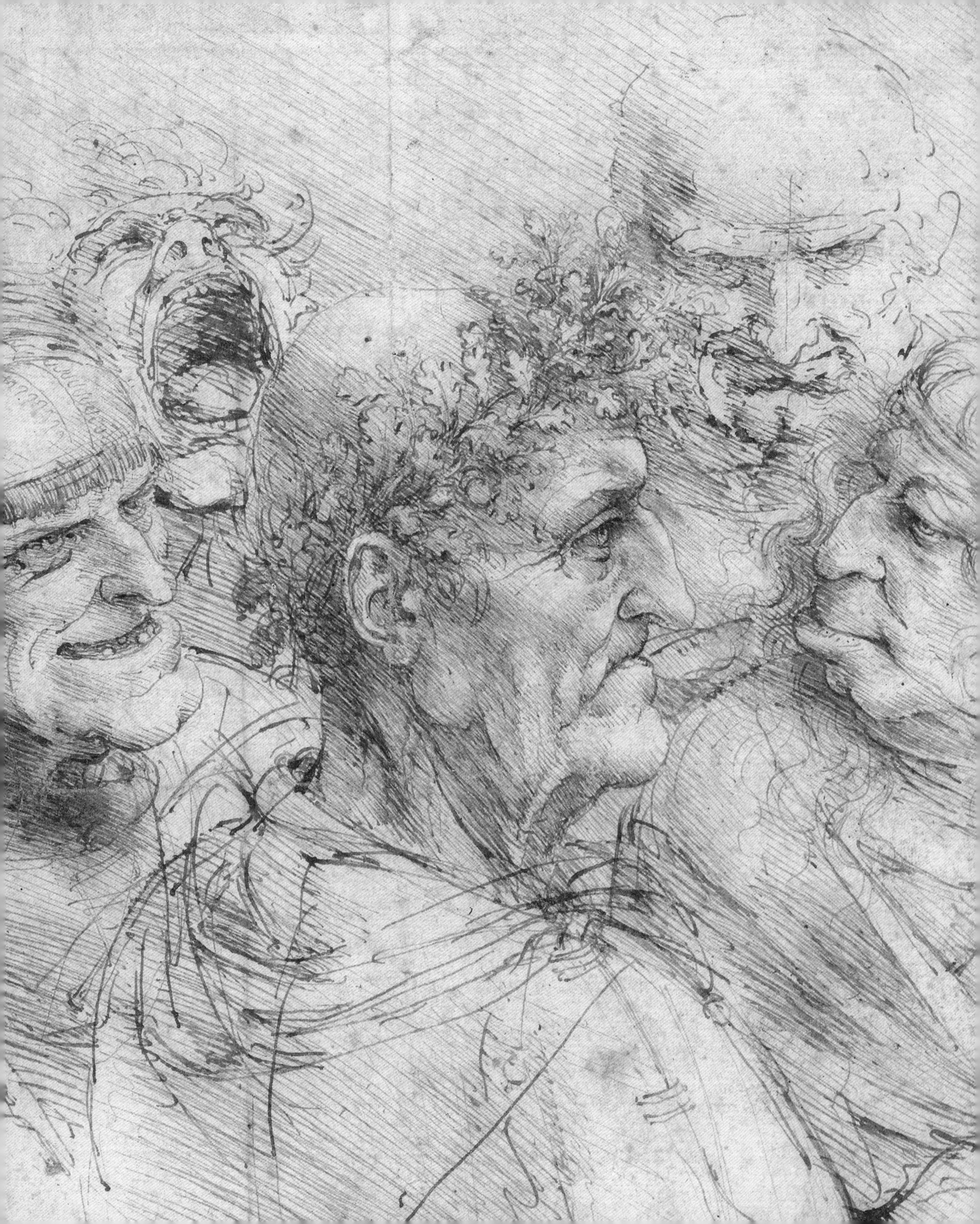

Pietro C. Marani

Monstrous Faces and Caricatures: Leonardo and the Revival of Caricature in Venice by Anton Maria Zanetti

This is not, strictly speaking, an exhibition dealing with Leonardo's 'caricatures', or more precisely 'monstrous faces', although at least seventeen or eighteen of them are presented here. Rather, it seeks to retrace his reception in the north of Italy until his triumphant reappearance in Venice, with Tiepolo and Anton Maria Zanetti, in order to unravel the threads that have become entangled in the attempt to understand who was the inventor of caricature. I seek to clarify whether it was a personal urge on the part of the artists or whether 'caricaturing' – 'exacerbating and increasing the defects of the disproportionately imitated parts' (as Filippo Baldinucci wrote in defining the meaning of *caricare* or 'caricaturing')[1] – may not have been the sign of a crisis in humanism, which appeared at the same time as the emergence of the genre of portraiture and the cult of personality. Less relevant is the question whether caricature first developed in the Bologna of the Carracci, with Annibale in particular, or in Florence before Leonardo,[2] at least a century earlier, since Leonardo's studies of facial deformities seem to belong to his early Milanese period. This would shift the origin of his interests in this field to after about 1482, as many of the drawings present in this exhibition seem to demonstrate, and therefore away from the Florentine context (where caricature was already evident independently of Leonardo) to Lombardy. Although Leonardo's works, except in rare cases, as will appear shortly, cannot be properly termed 'caricatures', some recent discoveries have shown that it is possible to trace an echo of them in Venice and, at least in part, explain the reappearance of interest in this 'genre' in Venice in the work of Anton Maria Zanetti, Rosalba Carriera and Tiepolo; this interest matured partly as a result of their study of the work of the Bolognese artists. The recent new edition of Zanetti's album of caricatures, now in the Fondazione Cini in Venice, and the publication of the inventory of his library, have rekindled interest in this trio and their relations with the Parisian and Milanese circles of Leonardo's collectors and admirers.[3]

Zanetti's sources of inspiration in the Venetian and Bolognese milieus where he developed have been taken for granted, as Pierre-Jean Mariette recorded.[4] These sources had already been

OPPOSITE
Leonardo da Vinci
Five grotesque heads,
c. 1493, detail
Windsor, Royal Library,
inv. RCIN 912490

recalled by earlier critics and briefly evoked by Bettagno and Lucchese, with reference to previous caricatures by Pier Leone Ghezzi, Sebastiano Ricci, Niccolò Bambini, Antonio Balestra, Gaspare Diziani, Francesco Fontebasso and Giovan Battista Tiepolo, who were highly productive in Belluno, Verona and Venice, and even earlier by the Carracci and Donato Creti in Bologna.[5] Scholars have then wondered how Zanetti came to devote himself to caricature and whether this role or some stimulus might have come to him partly through his Parisian acquaintances. They have also explored a Tuscan-Lombard source to clarify a fundamental component of Zanetti's culture that dates back to Leonardo's teste caricate ('grotesque heads') and the theories and treatises inspired by him.

As already noted by the anonymous author of the manuscript sheets placed at the beginning of the Cini Album,

He would take his pencil about with him, and like Leonardo da Vinci, or other painters, at the theatre or elsewhere, he would draw whatever object struck his fervent imagination, and then in the same places he would amuse himself with caricatures . . . In his work we observe an uncommon freedom of drawing and a fervent, capricious imagination, surprisingly high-spirited.[6]

This is an astonishing comment, given its date. And the critics, if I am not mistaken, have so far neglected it, perhaps considering it too obvious. But they have failed to consider that Zanetti's closeness to Leonardo's collectors and admirers, with whom he came into early contact, makes this judgement anything but gratuitous, as has already been explained and as this exhibition seeks to illustrate.

One strand of research leading towards Leonardo is suggested by the fact that the inventory of Zanetti's library included Leonardo's *Treatise on Painting*, as Lucchese recalls.[7] The *Indice de Libri dell'Illustrissimo Sig.re Conte Anton Maria Zanetti*, compiled in 1744 and now transcribed by Bozena Anna Kowalczyk,[8] lists the editio princeps of the *Treatise*, namely that printed in Paris by Raphael Trichet du Fresne in 1651 (on display in this exhibition). Zanetti is likely to have received it through his contacts with French friends or purchased it himself on his trip to Paris. This is notable, since there were editions of Leonardo's *Treatise* even closer to him in date, such as the one printed in Naples in 1733.[9] The *Treatise* contains amusing observations by Leonardo about the teste caricate that might have interested Zanetti, such as paragraph 290's about 'monstrous faces': 'I will not speak of monstrous faces, because one can keep them in mind without any effort.'[10]

In addition to Leonardo's *Treatise*, and the other Leonardesque sources to be mentioned shortly, Zanetti also possessed the 'precious' *Figure diverse*, eighty drawings by Annibale Carracci etched by Simon Guillain II (1618–1654), better known as Le arti di Bologna, published in 1646[11] and present in this exhibition [cat. 42]. This confirms that Milan and Bologna should to be added to the Venetian strand of Zanetti's inspiration for the study of caricatures.

Certainly, Leonardo's studies are not really 'caricatures' in the usual sense, meaning images that elicit a smile or mockery. They are not even, in the strict sense, 'grotesque' heads,[12] in which zoomorphic or phytomorphic elements are often associated with human features, in keeping with the well-known sixteenth-century examples that followed the discovery of the Domus Aurea in Rome, some with symbolic, erotic or pagan implications.[13] Leonardo's are, rather, exaggerated heads exactly in Baldinucci's sense, like the seven in the Codex Trivulzianus, folio 1v. [fig. 1], in which the features are accentuated to bring out the personalities, peculiarities, vices or virtues of each character. In about 1750 this codex came into the hands of Prince Carlo Trivulzio, a distant cousin of Tolemeo Trivulzio who in 1740 had subscribed to *Delle Antiche Statue Greche e Romane* by Anton Maria Zanetti and his cousin Anton Maria Zanetti di Alessandro.[14] As a terminus ante quem, 1750 is too late to argue that the Codex Trivulzianus was known to Zanetti after it came into the hands of Prince Carlo Trivulzio. But Zanetti's relations with the Trivulzio family and (as Lucchese pointed out in 2016[15]) also the relations of the 'Zanetti-Carriera clan' with the Milanese environment and the political sponsors of the Clerici (the patrons of Gian Battista Tiepolo), push his contacts with Milan and some prominent members of the Milanese aristocracy back earlier, to the late 1730s, when Tiepolo frescoed Palazzo Clerici. But even this is too little as a basis for Zanetti's direct knowledge of Leonardo's caricatures, since that dates from even earlier.

In Leonardo's grotesque heads, the accentuation of the features of his subjects serves to symbolise something different, or else to bring out moral qualities or particular virtues in contrast with noble and beautiful faces. As Umberto Eco recalled recently, the identification of the 'beautiful' with the 'good' and the physically ugly with the morally bad stems from Greek culture. Then in the sixteenth and seventeenth centuries came the study of physiognomy, which used analogies

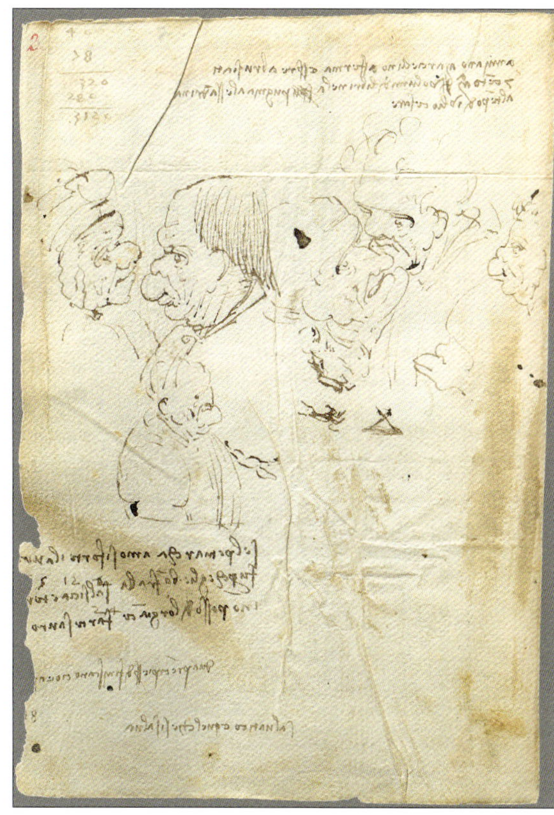

1

1.
Leonardo da Vinci
Seven grotesque heads,
1487–90
Milan, Archivio Storico Civico e Biblioteca Trivulziana, Codex Trivulzianus 2162, fol. 1*v*

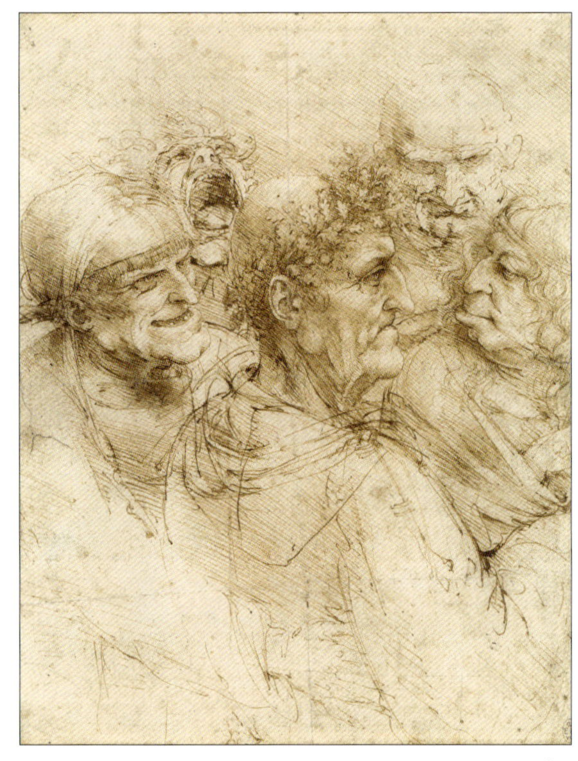
2

2.
Leonardo da Vinci
Five grotesque heads,
c. 1493
Windsor, Royal Library,
inv. RCIN 912490

between human and animal faces to explore the reasons for ugliness.[16] This is the case of the famous allegorical *Five grotesque heads* in the Royal Library in Windsor [fig. 2] (the heads on folio 1v of the Codex Trivulzianus seem to have been a preparatory study for this). They have been interpreted as representing the Four Temperaments, or a satirical composition in which the central figure, dignified and iconographically similar to a Caesar type, is surrounded by four bestial figures alluding to the turmoil and folly of the human race.[17] Wenceslaus Hollar's engraving after this drawing made in 1646 [cat. 44], when it was in the collection of Lord Arundel, was known to Mariette, one of Zanetti's closest friends and correspondents in Paris, mentioned several times in his letters to Francesco Gaburri.[18] Mariette possessed caricatures by Sebastiano Ricci and, as we will see, a whole album now in the Louvre with drawings, supposedly autograph, by Leonardo, in which he mentions Hollar's engraving of Leonardo's Five Heads (fol. 13v).[19] For Mariette, Leonardo introduced the representation of the passions in his caricatures:

Les physionomies singulières étant ce qui contribue le plus à caractériser les passions, Léonard n'étoit pas moins attentif à en faire une exacte recherche. . . . Quelquefois il les chargeoit dans les parties dont le ridicule étoit plus sensible, moins par jeu que pour se les imprimer dans la mémoire avec des caractères inaltérables. Les Carraches, &, depuis eux plusieurs autres peintres, ne se sont guère exercés à faire de ces sortes de charges, que par un simple badinage. Léonard, dont les vues étoient beaucoup plus nobles, avoit pour objet l'étude des passions. Or, il est constant qu'il y a des physionomies qui désignent certains vices. Un homme colère, méprisant, stupide, a presque toujours son caractère peint sur le visage. Léonard, à la faveur de cette étude, étoit devenu grand physionomiste; & il a, dit-on, laissé un traité assez ample sur cette matière.[20]

In 2002 Martin Clayton attributed a completely different significance to this famous drawing. He saw it as an allegory in which the good and honest man, depicted at the centre as the victim of a dishonest action, is contrasted with the evil figures of gypsies seeking to rob him.[21] Kwakkelstein, in 2019,[22] holds that the drawing in Windsor has another meaning: it reflects the artist's generally critical and denigratory view of the Florentine aristocratic classes, with Leonardo's 'caricatures' interpreted as social satire. (Leonardo's monstrous heads seem, in fact, to date from the following Lombard period, and the notion of social satire does not appear to be applicable to this date.) A copy of this drawing has been known since 1671. It was part of the Jabach collection in the mid-seventeenth century and in that year was purchased by the king of France (Louvre, inv. 2516).[23] The link between these Leonardesque precedents and Zanetti appears to be corroborated by the fact that his library contained the edition of the Mariette Album engraved in 1730 by the Comte de Caylus,[24] another acquaintance of Zanetti's, who was informed by his mother in 1728 of his 'operatic caricatures',[25] while the original, as mentioned earlier, is now in the Cabinet des Dessins of the Louvre. Many of these heads owned by Mariette and engraved by Caylus derive from the ones now largely preserved in the collection of the Duke of Devonshire at Chatsworth, of which no fewer than twelve examples are present in this exhibition.

Nevertheless, one is prompted to wonder whether what further stimulated Zanetti's interest in caricature was not in fact the viewing of the Mariette Album in Paris in 1720 (and the ensuing discussions that he must have had with Mariette). I would also like to imagine Mariette showing Zanetti the engraving of Leonardo's *Five Grotesque Heads* by Hollar, which he is known to have possessed, the description of which was later published by Caylus.

Bettagno dated the very earliest caricatures in the album to about 1716 (and Lucchese now dates them to about 1718), while Zanetti 'began very early to make drawings of this sort, immediately after returning from his studies in Bologna, having made his first in Bologna in circles close to the taste of the Carracci and Guercino'.[26] But I wonder whether a comparison between what Bettagno considers his earliest works – consisting of 'small drawings of heads, very incisive and witty, [that] with a few confident lines give a clearly identifiable and personalised character to the caricature'[27] – and the more elaborate ones that present the shoulders and busts of the characters (the full-figure drawings, especially of singers, being even later), does not presuppose a direct knowledge of Mariette's album? In it we see many of Leonardo's subjects presented with head and shoulders or bust, in full or three-quarter profile. It is certain that Mariette acquired the Louvre album with copies of Leonardo's caricatures after 1719, when the album was dispersed after the Van der Schelling sale in Amsterdam.[28]

As is well known, it was the presence of Pierre Crozat in 1716, with whom Zanetti came into fruitful contact,[29] and Mariette's visit to Venice in the winter of 1718–19, that prompted him to travel to Paris in 1720. He was accompanied by Rosalba Carriera and Antonio Pellegrini (the latter also took him to Flanders and London). Zanetti only returned to Venice in the winter of 1721–2. Among much else, he brought back to Venice the complete works of Jacques Callot.

Zanetti may have derived some ideas from Callot's series of hunchbacks [fig. 3], as shown by comparison with one of his drawings in the Cini Album [fig. 4].[30]

So not only should Zanetti's familiarity with the album of Leonardo's caricatures owned by Mariette be considered almost certain, but his knowledge of Leonardo's original drawings owned by Crozat can also be presumed, as well as the brush drawings on linen that later became famous and once belonged to Everhard Jabach (1618–1695). The inventory drawn up in 1695 after Jabach's death describes them as works by Dürer, but Mariette himself had recognised them as autograph works by Leonardo, as can be seen from Mariette's annotations of the catalogue of the Crozat sale in 1741.[31]

It is difficult to believe that Crozat did not show them to Zanetti when he was in Paris. On that occasion the young Zanetti had kept up relations with Jabach's son Gerhard Michael (who died in 1753). It was once again Mariette who recalled how Gerhard Michael 'avait trouvé dans la maison paternelle, en 1721, un reste de dessins qui lui en avait fait prendre le goût . . . Zanetti, qui se trouvait à Paris, lorsque Jabach fit la découverte des dessins qui avaient appartenu au vieux Jabach, ne s'oublia pas et prit pour lui ce qui était de meilleur.'[32] Bernadette Py observed that many drawings that are not found in the catalogue of the posthumous sale of Gerhard Michael's collection in 1753 actually passed into Zanetti's collection, including at least two drawings by Raphael now in Vienna (a third that he owned has not yet been traced), and by Parmigianino,[33] but none by Leonardo.

In a letter of 6 April 1726 to Gaburri, in which he speaks of the sale of the Casnedi drawings to Zaccaria Sagredo (to which I will return shortly), Zanetti recalled his 'friend Jabach' who had purchased 'marvellous and stupendous things' from Lorenzo Cambi of Livorno.[34] Hence it is not unlikely that Zanetti also knew other original sheets of drawings by Leonardo at an early date. Even if it is impossible to reconstruct the previous paths taken by these drawings, which belonged to Giovan Battista Clarici before entering the Ambrosiana,[35] it has been possible to make some comparisons with Zanetti's caricatures in the Cini Album. These include heads with wigs and deformed faces with exaggerated noses, chins, lips and breasts, whose prototypes by Leonardo (scattered between the Ambrosiana, the Royal Library in Windsor and at Chatsworth) were taken up and varied in drawings by the circle of Leonardo, by Melzi and then Aurelio Luini, Lomazzo and Figino, all the way to Lasinio.[36] A typical example is the drawing of a head pasted to folio 50 of the Zanetti Album [fig. 5]: the Abbot Motta, which Lucchese appropriately describes as 'a profile almost like a grotesque mask'.[37] It has a long prehistory: it derives from a drawing by Leonardo in the Royal Library at Windsor (inv. RCIN 912462r[38] [fig. 6]), also replicated on a sheet now in the Louvre (inv. no. 2571br[39] [fig. 7]), or those of a female head with an exaggerated conical hairstyle gathered into a bun or braid in the album on page 30.[40] This was the subject of many variants by Zanetti, which go back to anonymous works

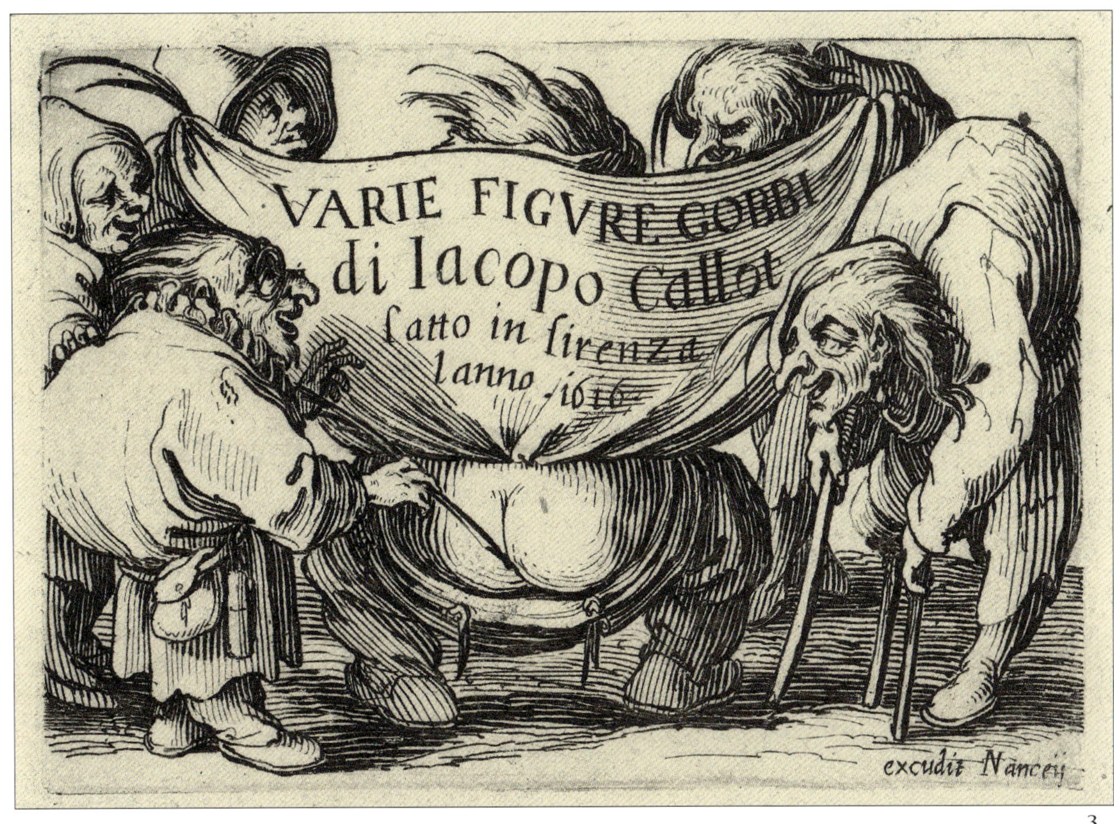

3

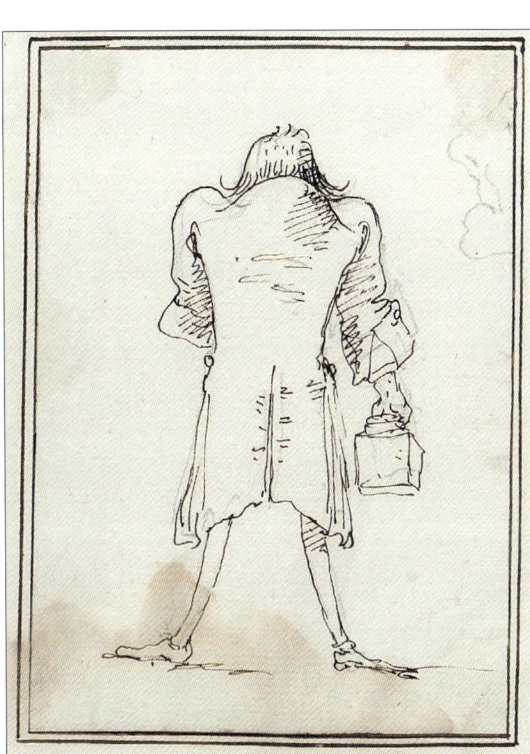

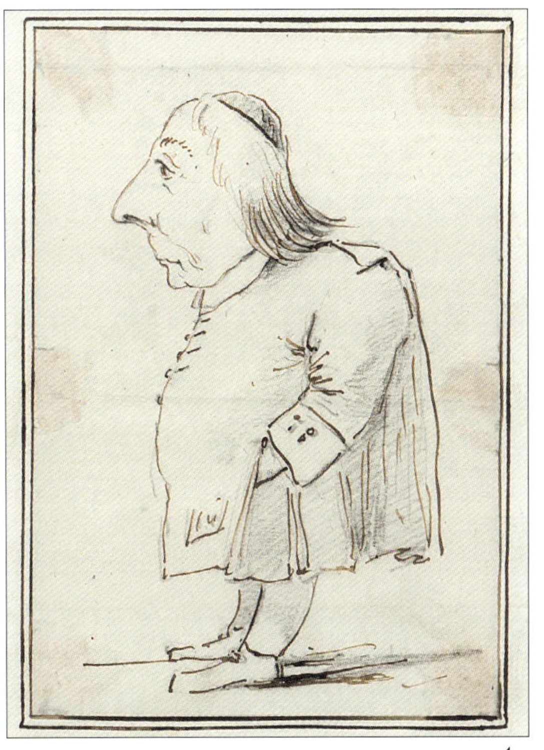

4

3.
Jacques Callot
Various figures of hunchbacks,
Florence, 1616
Frankfurt, Städel Museum

4.
Anton Maria Zanetti
Caricature of a hunchbacked man from behind,
sixth decade of the eighteenth century (?)
and
Caricature of a hunchbacked priest, in profile facing left,
fifth decade of the eighteenth century
Zanetti Album, p. 62
Venice, Fondazione Giorgio Cini, Gabinetto dei Disegni e delle Stampe,
invv. 36694, 36695

5.
Anton Maria Zanetti
Abbot Motta, 1727
Zanetti Album, p. 50
Venice, Fondazione Giorgio Cini, Gabinetto dei Disegni e delle Stampe, inv. 36656

6.
Leonardo da Vinci
A man with a sugar-loaf hat in profile, c. 1485
Windsor, Royal Library, inv. RCIN 912462

7.
School of Leonardo da Vinci, *Four caricatural profiles*, no date
Paris, Musée du Louvre, Département des Arts Graphiques, inv. 2571br

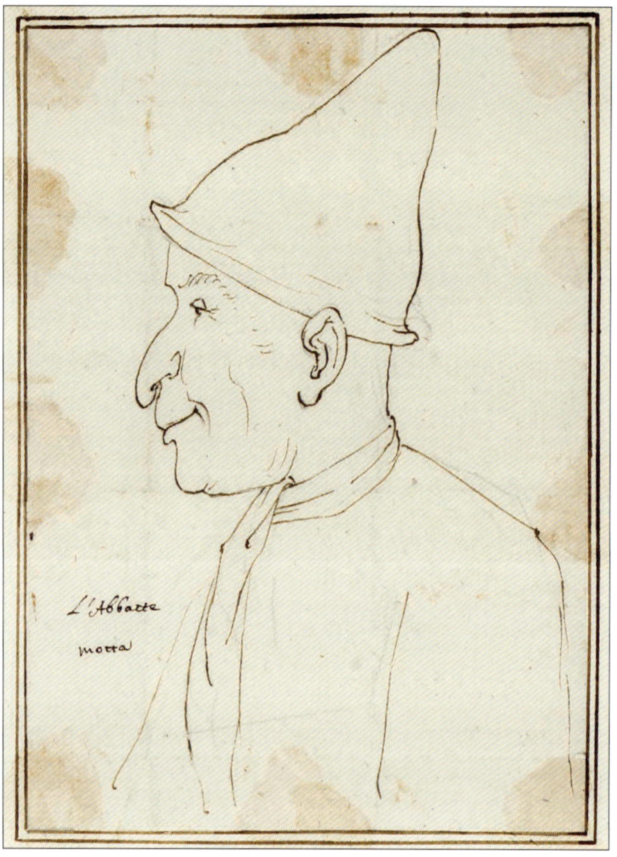

5

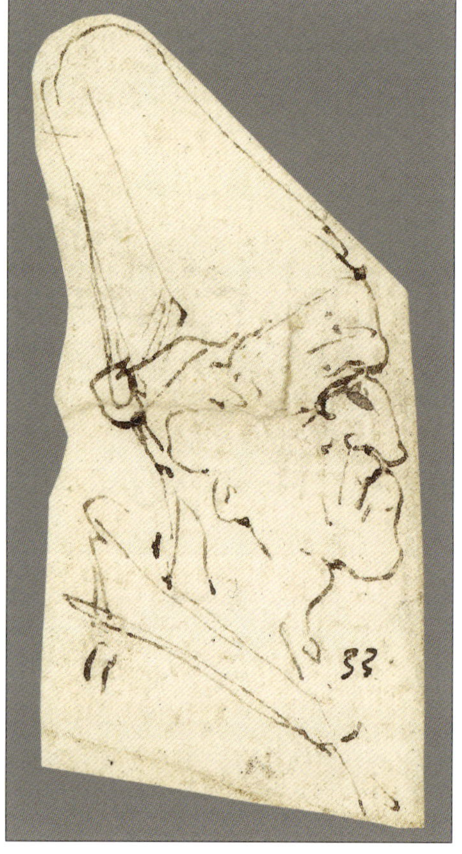

6

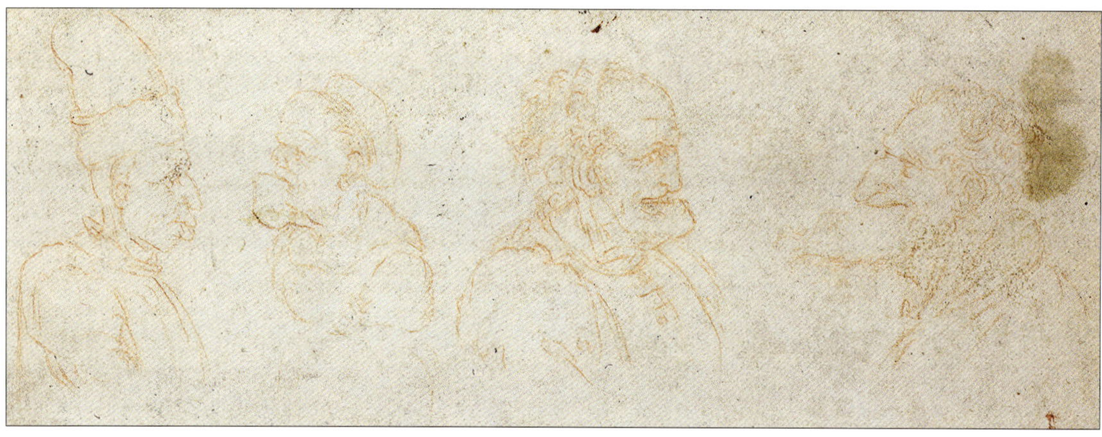

7

in the Ambrosiana (for example, cod. F 274 inf. 54[41]), to reappear in Carlo Lasinio's woodcuts [cats 83–5] after Leonardo's drawings.[42] Other derivations can be suggested in the caricature of the man with a conical hat that goes back to the drawings in the circle of Lomazzo in the Accademia della Val di Blenio, as in the sheet in the Ambrosiana (cod. F 274 inf. 26) depicting Compa' Vanetto [cat. 25][43]. The members of the academy, Lomazzo, Aurelio Luini and associates, disguised themselves as Bacchic characters and spoke facchinesco (porter's slang), like Compa' Zavargna or the *Homo ridiculo* depicted on a sheet of paper in the Accademia Carrara in Bergamo, present in this exhibition, and the work perhaps of Lomazzo or Giovan Ambrogio Figino (see the entry here for R. Antonelli, cat. 28).[44] They parallel works by Brambilla,[45] Girolamo Figino[46] or Arcimboldo,[47] some of them present in this exhibition.

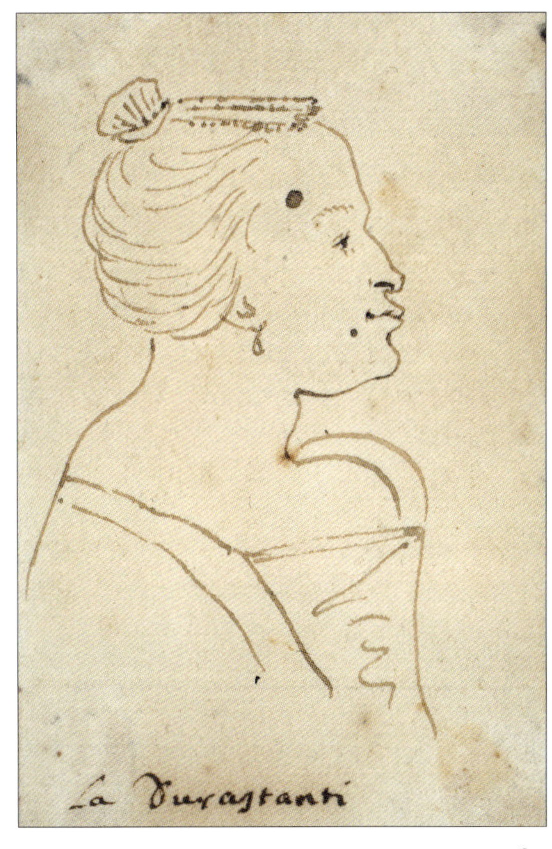

8

8.
Anton Maria Zanetti
Margherita Durastanti,
c. 1721
plate VIII (fol. 14)
Venice, Fondazione Giorgio Cini, Gabinetto dei Disegni e delle Stampe, inv. 36443

One is therefore prompted to wonder whether Zanetti's literary sources should not now be viewed in a different light. In his *Idea del Tempio della pittura* of 1590,[48] Giovan Paolo Lomazzo stated that Leonardo 'drew monstrous faces, such that no one has ever been able to match him, though many have been excellent in this. But of all these things, none have been printed; there exist only the works he drew with his own hand.'[49] The books owned by Zanetti according to the Index of 1744[50] included not only Lomazzo's *Idea del tempio* but also his *Trattato dell'arte della pittura*, printed in Milan in 1584. Lomazzo's observation about the lack of prints of Leonardo's caricatures may have prompted Zanetti to look for the originals, or have copies made, or perhaps to buy Caylus's album after 1730. The 1744 Index has no reference, however, to *De Humana Physiognomia* by Giovan Battista Della Porta, published for the first time in 1599, which transmits an echo of the theories of Leonardo and Lomazzo.[51] After all, we do not own all the books we read, or read all those we own.

Zanetti was certainly aware, nevertheless, of those original drawings by Leonardo that were added in 1726 to Zaccaria Sagredo's collection in Venice, coming from the Casnedi family in Milan, who had purchased them from the Arconati family in Castellazzo. Leonardo's cartoons for Saint Anne and Leda were in this collection, as well as the purported original cartoons for the heads of the Apostles in the *Last Supper* now in the Musée des Beaux-Arts in Strasbourg.[52] Zanetti sent news of the purchase in his letter to Gaburri of 6 April 1726, mentioned earlier: he referred to Sagredo's 'great acquisition of the drawings of the Marquis Casnedo'.[53] This makes it likely that Zanetti had gained first-hand knowledge of Leonardo's originals (or those purportedly such), as well as of his art and art theories, to the point where Zanetti also sought some models or examples of caricature to study. All this evidence points to an early date for the accentuation of a Leonardesque vein in Zanetti's work, from the year of Crozat's presence in Venice in 1716 to the meeting with Mariette in 1718–19, the trip to Paris in 1720, the meeting with Jabach's son in 1721 and the arrival of Leonardo's cartoons in Venice in 1726. Set out together in this way, this train of evidence, considered as a whole for the first time by the present writer,[54] together with the presence in Zanetti's library of a fair number of texts on Leonardo (or in the Leonardesque tradition), sheds a very different light on Zanetti's caricatures and his interest in drawing, on the teste caricate and Leonardo's theories in relation to the points considered so far. In addition to the publication of the Mariette Album by Caylus in 1730, we also need to bear in mind the possibility that Zanetti was fully informed of the sale of Crozat's collection in Paris in 1741, in which at least nine drawings (originally fourteen) on linen formerly in Everhard Jabach's collection and known from an inventory of 1695 (as mentioned earlier) were presented as by Leonardo.[55] While

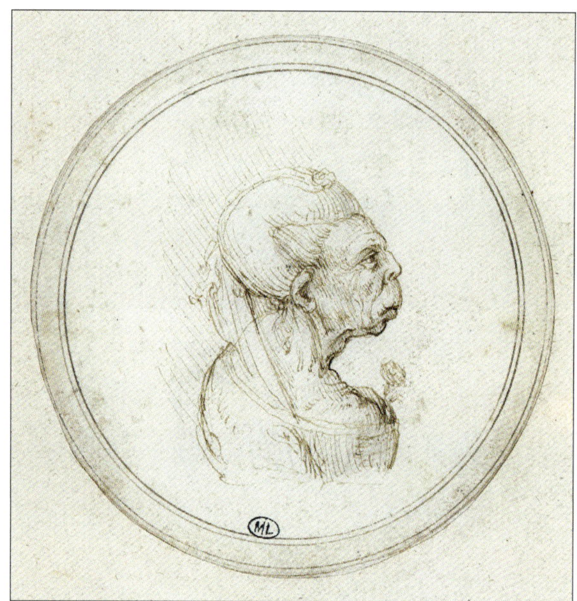

9

9.
Copy after Leonardo da Vinci, *Bust of an old woman in profile, with a carnation in her breast*, no date
Paris, Musée du Louvre, Département des Arts Graphiques, inv. RF 28731r

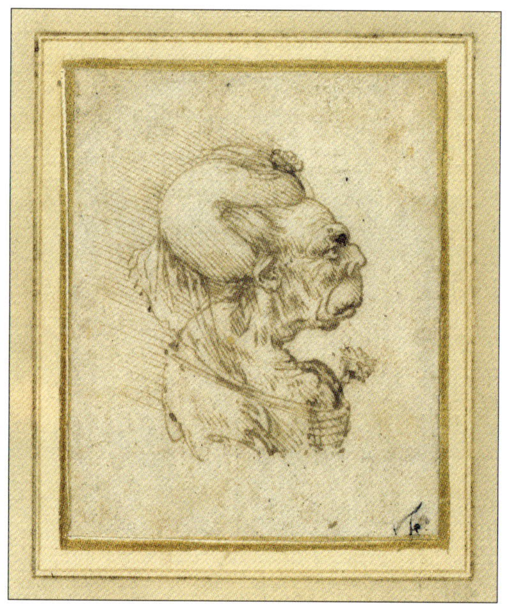

10

10.
Leonardo da Vinci
Grotesque head of an old woman, 1489–90
Washington, National Gallery of Art, Gift of Dian Woodner, inv. 2022.84.1

many of these works were highly refined drawings, and in the case of Sagredo's cartoons almost monochrome paintings, it is nevertheless certain that, given his friendship with Mariette and Crozat, Zanetti would have been aware of Leonardo's ability to delineate rapidly the caricatures in the album owned by Mariette, which the latter must almost certainly have shown him. There seems to be an affinity between Zanetti's terseness, his rapid and economical impromptu sketching, and what can perhaps be considered the only true existing caricature by Leonardo: that of a cleric now in the Biblioteca Ambrosiana (cod. F 274 inf. 25)[56] and present in this exhibition [cat. 18]. By its perspective and humour it anticipates certain Zanetti half-length caricatures.[57] Further evidence of visual contact with Leonardo's cartoons in Paris via Mariette in 1720 seems to be provided by Zanetti's cartoon of the singer Durastanti [fig. 8] from the summer of 1721. It reflects the anatomical exaggerations in the bursting breasts visible in the caricature of an old lady in the Mariette Album [fig. 9], derived from a drawing by Leonardo formerly in the collection of the Duke of Devonshire and now in Washington DC [fig. 10].[58] In the summer of 1721 Zanetti was in London, a guest of the singer whose caricature he drew. And here according to Crozat (in a letter to Rosalba Carriera of 19 July 1721), he had to calm the inner turmoil that seized him on seeing and admiring 'des magniffiques desseins' which he found in great quantity 'chez gens qui ne sont pas autrement grands connaisseurs'.[59] That these may have included Leonardo's drawings of *visi mostruosi* is a fascinating conjecture. Since Zanetti had passed through Flanders, one cannot fail to link this memory and journey to the fact that the *visi mostruosi* (which later entered the collection of William Cavendish, second Duke of Devonshire, and are now mainly at Chatsworth) were in Rotterdam until 1723 (probably after having been in the Earl of Arundel's collection) in the possession of Nicholaes Anthoni Flinck, who had also owned the Mariette Album. Flinck's collection of drawings was sold the following year in Rotterdam.[60] Could these 'magniffiques desseins', seen by Mariette before he went to London in 1721, have included the grotesque heads by Leonardo now at Chatsworth?

[1] F. Baldinucci, *Notizie de' professori del disegno da Cimabue in qua* (Florence: Per Santi Franchi, 1681–1728), vol. V, ed. 1974, pp. 32–3.

[2] The debate on the origins of caricature was critically established and recapitulated by F. Tempesti, 'Introduzione', in *Maestri della caricatura: Leonardo, Aspertini, Michelangelo, Parmigianino, Passarotti, Zuccari, Carracci, Guercino, Callot, Bernini, Bocchi, Crespi, Ferretti, Ghezzi, Zanetti, Tiepolo etc.*, ed. L. Corti (Florence: Istituto Alinari, 1979), pp. 5–17. Until then it had been assumed, following Ernst Krist (1967) and Enrico Castelnuovo (1973), that caricature, partly on the basis of Baldinucci's statements, derived from the Bolognese school and therefore Annibale Carracci. The debate has continued in more recent years through contributions that have appeared in exhibitions devoted to caricatures, such as that held at the Metropolitan Museum in New York in 2011–12: *Infinite Jest: Caricature and Satire from Leonardo to Levine*, ed. C. C. McPhee and N. M. Orenstein, exh. cat. (New York and New Haven and London: The Metropolitan Museum of Art and Yale University Press, 2011); or those on the Carracci and Leonardo, e.g. M. Clayton, *Leonardo da Vinci: The Divine and the Grotesque* (London: Thames & Hudson, 2002); M. W. Kwakkelstein and M. Plomp, *Leonardo da Vinci: The Language of Faces* (Haarlem: Thoth, 2018); and on Tiepolo and Zanetti. For more on these studies see elsewhere in this catalogue.

[3] See E. Lucchese, *L'Album di caricature di Anton Maria Zanetti alla Fondazione Cini* (Venice: Lineadacqua, 2015). Zanetti's caricatures were previously studied by Alessandro Bettagno: *Caricature di Anton Maria Zanetti* (Cataloghi di mostre, 29), ed. A. Bettagno, exh. cat. (Fondazione Giorgio Cini, Venice: Neri Pozza, 1969); Bettagno, ed., *Caricature di Anton Maria Zanetti: disegni della Fondazione Giorgio Cini* (Milan: Pirelli; Venice: Fondazione Giorgio Cini, 1970). On Zanetti's library see B. A. Kowalczyk, 'Il "prezioso" manoscritto della collezione Bettagno: l'Indice della Biblioteca di Anton Maria Zanetti', in *Venezia Settecento: studi in memoria di Alessandro Bettagno*, ed. B. A. Kowalczyk (Cinisello Balsamo: Silvana Editoriale, 2015), pp. 31–6. On the basis of these new studies I have tried to bring out Zanetti's debt to the Leonardescque tradition: see P. C. Marani, 'Suggestioni leonardesche nella cultura e nelle caricature di Anton Maria Zanetti dell'Album Cini', *Arte Veneta*, 73 (2016 [2017]), pp. 187–96, some of which I reproduce here. While the connections between Zanetti and Parisian and English circles are well known, as is the work he performed as artistic consultant for the Prince of Lichtenstein in Vienna, to date less is known about his close ties to the court of Saxony, on which see M. Magrini, 'Anton Maria Zanetti e Dresda', in *Venezia Settecento*, pp. 229–37.

[4] Lucchese, *L'Album di caricature*, p. 5 quoting Pierre-Jean Mariette, who relates that Zanetti in his youth had contemplated 'les ouvrages inimitables des Carraches' in Bologna.

[5] Donato Creti's drawings of caricatures in the Uffizi and Fondazione Cini should be borne in mind, for which see M. Riccòmini, *Donato Creti: le opere su carta. Catalogo ragionato* (Turin: Umberto Allemandi & Co., 2012), pp. 50, 76, nos 37.40, 90.27, drawings dated 1685 and 1688 respectively.

[6] Transcribed by Bettagno, *Caricature di Zanetti*, p. 97.

[7] Lucchese, *L'Album di caricature*, p. 13.

[8] Kowalczyk, 'Il "prezioso" manoscritto', pp. 31–6.

[9] For this and the *editio princeps* of 1651 see *Leonardo: dagli studi di proporzioni al Trattato della Pittura*, ed. P. C. Marani and M. T. Fiorio, exh. cat. (sala delle Asse, Castello Sforzesco, Milan, 7 December 2007–2 March 2008; Milan: Electa, 2007), pp. 140–52.

[10] *Leonardo da Vinci: Libro di Pittura, Codice Urbinate lat. 1270 nella Biblioteca Apostolica Vaticana*, ed. C. Pedretti, transcript. C. Vecce, 2 vols (Florence: Giunti, 1995), vol. II, pp. 261–2. The original (c. 1490–92) is in Paris, Institut de France, Ms. A, fol. 106*v*.

[11] Kowalczyk, 'Il "prezioso" manoscritto', 2015, p. 33.

[12] On Leonardo's *teste caricate* see the fundamental essay by E. Gombrich, 'Leonardo's Grotesque Heads: Prolegomena to their Study', in *Leonardo: saggi e ricerche*, ed. Comitato per le Onoranze a Leonardo nel Quinto Centenario della Nascita (Rome: Poligrafico dello Stato, 1954), pp. 197–219. See also Gombrich, 'Leonardo da Vinci's Method of Analysis and Permutation: The Grotesque Heads', in *The Heritage of Apelles: Studies in the Art of the Renaissance* (London: Phaidon Press, 1976), pp. 57–75.

[13] See P. Morel, *Les grotesques: les figures de l'imaginaire dans la peinture italienne de la fin de la Renaissance* (Paris: Flammarion, 1997); see also more recently A. Zamperini, *Le grottesche: il sogno della pittura nella decorazione parietale* (San Giovanni Lupatoto, Verona: Arsenale, 2007).

[14] Carlo Trivulzio (Milan, 1715–1789), an abbot, childless, was the son of Giorgio Teodoro Trivulzio, Marquis of Sesto Ulteriano. Antonio Tolomeo Gallio Trivulzio (Milan, 1692–1767) was the son of Antonio Gaetano Gallio Trivulzio, the son of Tolomeo II Gallio, Duke of Alvito, and of Ottavia Trivulzio, a branch of the family. There was a sixth or seventh degree of cousinhood between them. I thank Marino Viganò for clarifying these points. On the Codex Trivulzianus see *Il Codice di*

Leonardo da Vinci nel Castello Sforzesco, ed. P. C. Marani and G. Piazza, exh. cat. (Sala delle Asse, Castello Sforzesco, Milan, 24 March–21 May 2006; Milan: Electa, 2006).

[15] E. Lucchese, 'Attorno alla Gallerie di Palazzo Clerici', in *Tiepolo a Milano: la decorazione dei Palazzi Archinto, Casati e Clerici*, ed. L. Finocchi Ghersi (Rome: Artemide, 2016), pp. 69–91, esp. 73–5.

[16] U. Eco, 'La bruttezza' (2017), in U. Eco, *Sulle spalle dei giganti* (Milan: La Nave di Teseo, 2021), pp. 13, 17.

[17] On this famous drawing see K. Clark with C. Pedretti, *The Drawings of Leonardo da Vinci in the Collection of Her Majesty the Queen at Windsor Castle*, 2nd ed. rev., 2 vols (London: Phaidon, 1968–9), vol. I, pp. 84–5.

[18] For the ties between Zanetti and Mariette see Bettagno, *Caricature di Zanetti*, passim; Lucchese, *L'Album di caricature*, p. 5. See also M. G. Bottari and S. Ticozzi, *Raccolta di lettere sulla pittura, scultura e architettura*, 8 vols (Milan: Giovanni Silvestri, 1822), vol. II, e.g. Lettera LXVIII, p. 167.

[19] On the album of caricatures by Leonardo owned by Mariette see *Dessins et manuscrits de Léonard de Vinci*, ed. F. Viatte and V. Forcione, exh. cat. (Musée du Louvre, Paris, 5 May–14 July 2003; Paris: Réunion des Musées Nationaux, 2003), pp. 217–27. On Mariette as collector and scholar see *Le cabinet d'un grand amateur. P.-J. Mariette 1694–1774*, ed. R. Bacou, exh. cat. (Musée du Louvre, Paris, 1967; Paris: Réunion des Musées Nationaux, 1967). The engraving of Leonardo's *Five Grotesque Heads* is therefore also cited by the Comte de Caylus, *Recueil de testes de caractère et de charges, dessinées par Leonard de Vinci Florentin, et gravées par M. le C.te de C.* (Paris: Mariette, 1730), p. 24 (in 'Catalogue des pièces qui on été gravées d'après les tableaux, ou desseins de Leonard de Vinci').

[20] P.-J. Mariette quoted in Caylus, *Recueil de testes*, pp. 12–13.

[21] M. Clayton, 'Leonardo's "Gypsies" and the "Wolf with the Eagle"', *Apollo*, 155, August 2002, pp. 27–33; Clayton, ed., *Leonardo da Vinci: The Divine and the Grotesque*, exh. cat. (Queen's Gallery, London, 30 November 2002–30 March 2003; London: Thames & Hudson, 2002), pp. 96–9. See also P. C. Marani in *Leonardo da Vinci 1452–1519: il disegno del mondo*, ed. P. C. Marani and M. T. Fiorio, exh. cat. (Palazzo Reale, Milan, 15 April–19 July 2015; Milan and Geneva: Skira, 2015), p. 556, cat. V.16.

[22] See Kwakkelstein, in *Leonardo da Vinci: The Language*, and Kwakkelstein, in *Leonardo da Vinci: l'uomo modello del mondo*, ed. A. Perissa Torrini, exh. cat. (Gallerie dell'Accademia, Venice, 17 April–14 July 2019; Cinisello Balsamo: Silvana Editoriale, 2019), pp. 43–52, in particular pp. 47–8.

[23] See Forcione in *Dessins et manuscrits*, p. 205.

[24] Kowalczyk, 'Il "prezioso" manoscritto', p. 36.

[25] Lucchese, *L'Album di caricature*, p. 5.

[26] Bettagno, *Caricature di Zanetti*, pp. 10–11.

[27] Ibid., p. 11. Bettagno mentions in particular the small heads 'abbreviated' in fols 15 (by Noris), 30 (by Salicola), 16 (by Pellegrini) and 17 (by Marco Ricci).

[28] See Forcione, in *Dessins et manuscrits* , p. 214. A possible alternative is that Zanetti may have seen the Louvre album with copies of the caricatures not in Paris in 1720 but in Amsterdam (after the Van der Schelling sale in 1719) during the same trip.

[29] Bettagno, *Caricature di Zanetti*, p. 8.

[30] Compare the hunchbacks depicted on the title page of Callot's work with that pasted in the Cini Album, fol. 62; see Lucchese, *L'Album di caricature*, p. 310, no. 56.Iii.

[31] See B. Py, *Everhard Jabach collectionneur (1618–1695): les dessins de l'Inventaire de 1695* (Paris: Réunion des Musées Nationaux, 2001), pp. 270–74; see also Py, *L'Honneur de la curiosité: de Dürer à Poussin. Les dessins de la seconde collection Jabach*, exh. cat. (Musée du Louvre, Paris, 17 January–15 April 2002; Paris, 2002), which displays a Leonardo drawing in Rennes, inv. 794.1.2506, that had belonged to Jabach and was then in Crozat's collection. On Jabach see also the fundamental A. Schnapper, *Curieux du Grand Siècle: collections et collectionneurs dans la France du XVIIe siècle*, ed. M. Szanto and S. Mouquin, 2nd rev. ed. (Paris: Flammarion, 2005), esp. pp. 267–82. Jabach also had the drawings by the finest masters in his collection copied, often passing them off as originals, and had the newly sketched ones completed and 'embellished'; for this see P. C. Marani, 'Collezionismo e filologia: a proposito dei disegni di Boltraffio, Solario e Luini dalla collezione Jabach al Louvre', *Artibus et Historiae: An Art Anthology*, 61 (XXXI), 2010, pp. 133–48, with bibliography.

[32] Mariette quoted in Py, *Everhard Jabach* , p. 19. This circumstance seems to have escaped the attention of both Bettagno and Lucchese.

[33] Ibid., pp. 19, 31, 32, nos 5 and 6.

[34] Zanetti to Francesco Gaburri, 6 April 1726, in Bottari and Ticozzi, *Raccolta di lettere sulla pittura*, Lettera LXIX, pp. 169–71, esp. p. 171.

[35] See, however, S. Mara, 'Il *Libro di disegni* della Biblioteca Ambrosiana', *Arte lombarda*, CLVIII–CLIX (1–2), 2010, pp. 4–118, which illustrates a collection of Leonardo's drawings, subsequently dismembered.

[36] I tried to compare some of Zanetti's caricatures with these

prototypes and Leonardesque derivations in Marani, 'Suggestioni leonardesche'.

[37] Lucchese, *L'Album di caricature*, p. 286, no. 45.II.

[38] See Clark, *Drawings of Leonardo*, vol. I, p. 76.

[39] See P. C. Marani, ed., *I disegni di Leonardo da Vinci e della sua cerchia nelle collezioni pubblici in Francia*, Edizione Nazionale dei Manoscritti e dei Disegni di Leonardo da Vinci, V (Florence: Giunti, 2008), p. 156, no. 103.

[40] Lucchese, *L'Album di caricature*, pp. 193–4, no. 28.VI.

[41] L. Cogliati Arano, in *Leonardo all'Ambrosiana: il Codice Atlantico. I disegni di Leonardo e della sua cerchia*, ed. A. Marinoni and L. Cogliati Arano, exh. cat. (Biblioteca Ambrosiana, Milan, 1982; Milan: Electa, 1982), p. 120, no. 29d.

[42] See E. Villata, ed., *Intorno a Leonardo: rarità dell'Ente Raccolta Vinciana*, exh. cat. (Castello Sforzesco, Milan, 9 November 2013–2 February 2014; Milan: Ente Raccolta Vinciana, 2013), p. 21.

[43] Cogliati Arano, *in Leonardo all'Ambrosiana*, p. 154, no. 61. On the Accademia della Val di Blenio see *Rabisch: il grottesco nell'arte del Cinquecento. L'Accademia della Val di Blenio, Lomazzo e l'ambiente milanese*, ed. G. Bora, M. Khan Rossi and F. Porzio, exh. cat. (Museo Cantonale d'Arte, Lugano, 28 March–21 June 1998; Milan: Skira, 1998). On the role of Lomazzo see R. P. Ciardi, 'Lomazzo, Giovan Paolo', in *Dizionario biografico degli italiani* (Rome: Istituto della Enciclopedia Italiana, 2005), vol. LXV, pp. 460–67; D. Isella, ed., *Rabisch: Giovanni Paolo Lomazzo e i Facchini della Val di Blenio* (Turin: Einaudi, 1993).

[44] On the drawing in Bergamo see P. C. Marani, *Leonardo e i leonardeschi a Brera* (Florence: Cantini, 1987), p. 244, fig. 165.

[45] On Brambilla see F. Paliaga, 'Giovanni Antonio Brambilla, le "teste di carattere" di Leonardo e la commedia dell'arte', *Raccolta Vinciana*, XXVI, 1995, pp. 219–54 (p. 237 for the Accademia Carrara drawing with the doubtful attribution to Lomazzo).

[46] M. Pavesi, 'Giovan Paolo Lomazzo pittore milanese 1538–1592', PhD thesis, Università Cattolica del Sacro Cuore di Milano, 2009, p. 294, attributes the *Homo ridiculo* in the Accademia Carrara to Girolamo Figino. This attribution had already been doubtfully advanced in 1998 by Giacomo Berra in *Rabisch: il grottesco*, p. 148, no. 18.

[47] On the paintings and the phytomorphic or zoomorphic heads by Arcimboldo and their possible Leonardesque sources see G. Berra, 'L'Arcimboldo "C'huom forma d'ogni cosa": capricci pittorici, elogi letterari e scherzi poetici nella Milano di fine Cinquecento', in *Arcimboldo: artista milanese tra Leonardo e Caravaggio*, ed. S. Ferino Pagden, exh. cat. (Palazzo Reale, Milan, 10 February–22 May 2011; Milan: Skira, 2011), pp. 327ff. For the components of Arcimboldo's scientific-naturalistic culture see P. C. Marani, 'Maniera Milan: 1513–1564 circa', in *Prima di Carlo Borromeo: lettere e arti a Milano nel primo Cinquecento*, ed. E. Bellini and A. Rovetta, conference proceedings (Biblioteca Ambrosiana, Milan), *Studia Borromaica*, 27, 2013, esp. pp. 41ff.

[48] See G. P. Lomazzo, *Idea del tempio della pittura* (Milan: Gottardo Pontio, 1590), in R. P. Ciardi, ed., *Giovan Paolo Lomazzo: scritti sulle arti*, 2 vols (Florence: Centro Di, 1973–5), vol. II.

[49] Lomazzo, *Idea del tempio*, in ibid., vol. I, p. 259.

[50] Kowalczyck, 'Il "prezioso" manoscritto', p. 34.

[51] *Intorno a Leonardo*, pp. 54–5, no. 14.

[52] On the Strasbourg cartoons see A. Ballarin, 'I cartoni con le teste di Cristo e degli Apostoli dal Cenacolo di Leonardo: la serie del Musée des Beaux-Arts di Strasburgo e quella già del Museo Granducale di Weimar (1996–1999)', in *Leonardo a Milano: problemi di leonardismo milanese tra Quattrocento e Cinquecento. Giovanni Antonio Boltraffio prima della Pala Casio*, 4 vols (Verona: Grafiche Aurora, 2010 [2011], vol. II, pp. 734–852; P. C. Marani, *'Bella quanto l'originale istesso': la copia del Cenacolo della Royal Academy di Londra. Vicende, fortuna, attribuzione* (Vicchio [Florence]: LoGisma, 2016), passim.

[53] Zanetti to Gaburri, 6 April 1726, in Bottari and Ticozzi, *Lettere artistiche*, Lettera LXIX, pp. 169–71.

[54] Marani, 'Suggestioni leonardesche'.

[55] F. Viatte, in *Dessins et manuscrits* , pp. 60–70, nos 6, 8, 9.

[56] See Cogliati Arano, in *Leonardo all'Ambrosiana*, p. 107, no. 13.

[57] Marani, 'Suggestioni leonardesche', p. 195, figs 15 and 16 (from the Cini Album, fol. 40).

[58] Mariette Album, fol. 7*v* (Louvre, Département des Arts Graphiques, RF 28731); see Forcione, in *Dessins et manuscrits*, pp. 218, 223, n. 73. It was derived from the head formerly at Chatsworth and now National Gallery of Art, Washington DC. The caricature of the old woman with a flower between her breasts was then engraved in Caylus's book, on display in this exhibition. On Leonardo's drawing, see P. C. Marani, in *The Touch of the Artist: Master Drawings from the Woodner Collections*, ed. M. Morgan Grasselli, exh. cat. (National Gallery of Art, Washington DC, 1 October 1995–28 January 1996; New York: Harry N. Abrams, 1995), pp. 80–83; see fig. 2 for the corresponding engraving in the Caylus Album.

[59] See Bettagno, *Caricature di Zanetti*, p. 101; Lucchese, *L'Album di caricature*, no. 13.IV, p. 136, with full reference to Crozat's letter to Rosalba Carriera and bibliography.

[60] See Forcione, in *Dessins et manuscrits*, p. 206. William Cavendish, second Duke of Devonshire (1665–1729) bought 125 drawings at the Flinck sale in 1724. The stamp of Nicholaes Anthoni Flinck ('F') is found on some of the grotesque heads in the Devonshire Collection, 17 of which are copied in the Mariette Album now in the Louvre. Jonathan Richardson mentioned in 1728 that the whole collection 'du grand Connoisseur Mr. Flinck de Rotterdam' was entirely 'ajoutée' to the Duke of Devonshire; see Forcione, in *Dessins et manuscrits*, p. 210, n. 55.

1.

Leonardo da Vinci (1452–1519)
Grotesque head and bust of a man in profile facing left, c. 1490
Metalpoint, pen and sepia ink on paper, glued to backing paper, 153 × 112 mm
Milan, Veneranda Biblioteca Ambrosiana, Pinacoteca, cod. F 274 inf. 53

The sheet comes from the *Libro di disegni* compiled and owned by the architect and engineer Giovan Battista Clarici (1542–1602) of Urbino. For many centuries it has been kept in the Biblioteca Ambrosiana in Milan (Mara 2020, p. 218) and is among the most famous of Leonardo's 'caricatures' there. Engraved in 1784 by Gerli as plate XXIII, it has been repeatedly exhibited (Lucerne 1946; Paris-Tours 1956; Milan 1982; Venice 1992; Milan 1998) and published as one of Leonardo's heads that are closest to caricature; indeed it has been described as 'one of the most ruthless caricatures' by Leonardo, in which a human being is depicted in deepest degradation (Cogliati Arano, 1992, p. 10). In reality we may observe the typical exaggeration of features – the flattened snub nose, the marked prognathism, the receding, almost non-existent chin compared to the triple folds beneath it – of a character probably taken from everyday life. This is also shown by the hint of the torso and his garment, the large cap squashed on his forehead, the left arm raised to the chest and holding what looks like a saddlebag on his back (evident in the engraving by Gerli). Hence it would be more correct to speak of this as a 'grotesque' head, with the quality and refinement of the handling creating an astonishing contrast, as if Leonardo was not depicting a repulsive face but one with the graceful features of ideal beauty. The fine hatching in front of the face and on the neck and cap, with dense parallel lines spreading out to define the shoulder and left arm, may also help in dating the work. In contrast with the earlier dates previously proposed, relating it to the years 1485–90, these features now seem to suggest a date closer to 1490, in keeping with the heads in the Codex Trivulzianus in the Biblioteca Trivulziana, Castello Sforzesco in Milan (folio 1*v* has a sketch of the head with a hat that appears to be a draft for this drawing), and with the use of metalpoint. A connection with the small heads in the collection of the Duke of Devonshire at Chatsworth [cats 5–16] is often invoked for the style of this drawing but this is much finer and lighter: in the Chatsworth heads (sometimes dated much later, between 1495 and 1506–8: Forcione, in Paris 2003, p. 196) a more decisive inking is prevalent, with heavier lines, but characterised by shaded parallel hatching that indicates a date before 1500. The less marked atmospheric effect here might also be attributed to a slight fading of the sheet due to its probable exposure to light in the Ambrosiana. It comes from an album (Mara 2010), compiled perhaps in Milan between 1584 and 1594, whose sheets were unbound and exhibited for a long time in the gallery from the mid-nineteenth century on. The drawing has satirical or moralising overtones. Leonardo's motto 'Acquire something in your youth that will repair the ravages of old age' (Rossi 1998) has been applied to this head. The type of this sickly face with its vacant and disillusioned, 'almost animal' expression (Rossi, in Milan 1998, p. 88), was sometimes replicated by Leonardo, with slight variations. Two similar heads, one with similar headgear and both with a flattened nose and almost no chin, appear on two sheets at Chatsworth (Forcione, in Paris 2003, nos 66 A, 67 B, pp. 198–9; Bambach 2003, n. 73). These are also interesting for their stylistic difference from the Ambrosiana head. An echo of the second is found in two drawings by an anonymous Lombard artist in the Louvre's Département des Arts Graphiques, inv. 2296, 2297 (Forcione, in Paris 2003, pp. 202–4, nos 70, 71). The drawing seems to anticipate by a century the 'portraits' of artisans and workers by Annibale Carracci, engraved in a sequence of eighty variations in 1646 (present in this exhibition, cat. 42), as well as Annibale's naturalistic outlook in portraying the features of characters taken from everyday life, as we see in the drawing in the Louvre exhibited here [cat. 40]. This almost suggests the possibility that Leonardo was also collecting types and typologies of portraits of monstrous characters ('I do not speak of monstrous faces, because they can easily be kept in mind'), drawn from common life with a view to the composition of one of his many 'treatises', in this case the treatise on physiognomy. Finally, the posture of the figure, with his left arm folded over his torso, recalls that of contemporary court portraits, for example the *Lady with an Ermine*, constituting a grotesque counterpart to it.

PCM

Bibliography

Gerli 1794, plate XXIII; Beltrami and Fumagalli 1904, no. XVIII; Bodmer 1931, p. 390; Lucerna 1946, no. 134; Tours-Paris1956, no. 34; Gombrich [1976] 1986, pp. 93–4, fig. 171; Cogliati Arano 1980b, p. 124; Cogliati Arano, in Milan 1982, p. 98; Marani 1990, p. 60; Caroli 1991, p. 149; Cogliati Arano 1992, p. 10, fig. 12; Cogliati Arano, in *Venezia* 1992, p. 315; Kwakkelstein 1994, pp. 107–8; Rossi, in Milan 1998, p. 88; Cogliati Arano 2005, pp. 288–9, fig. 4; Cogliati Arano, in *Antichi disegni dalla Collezione Ligabue* 2005, p. 28, fig. on p. 29; Mara 2010, pp. 104, 107, fig. 11.

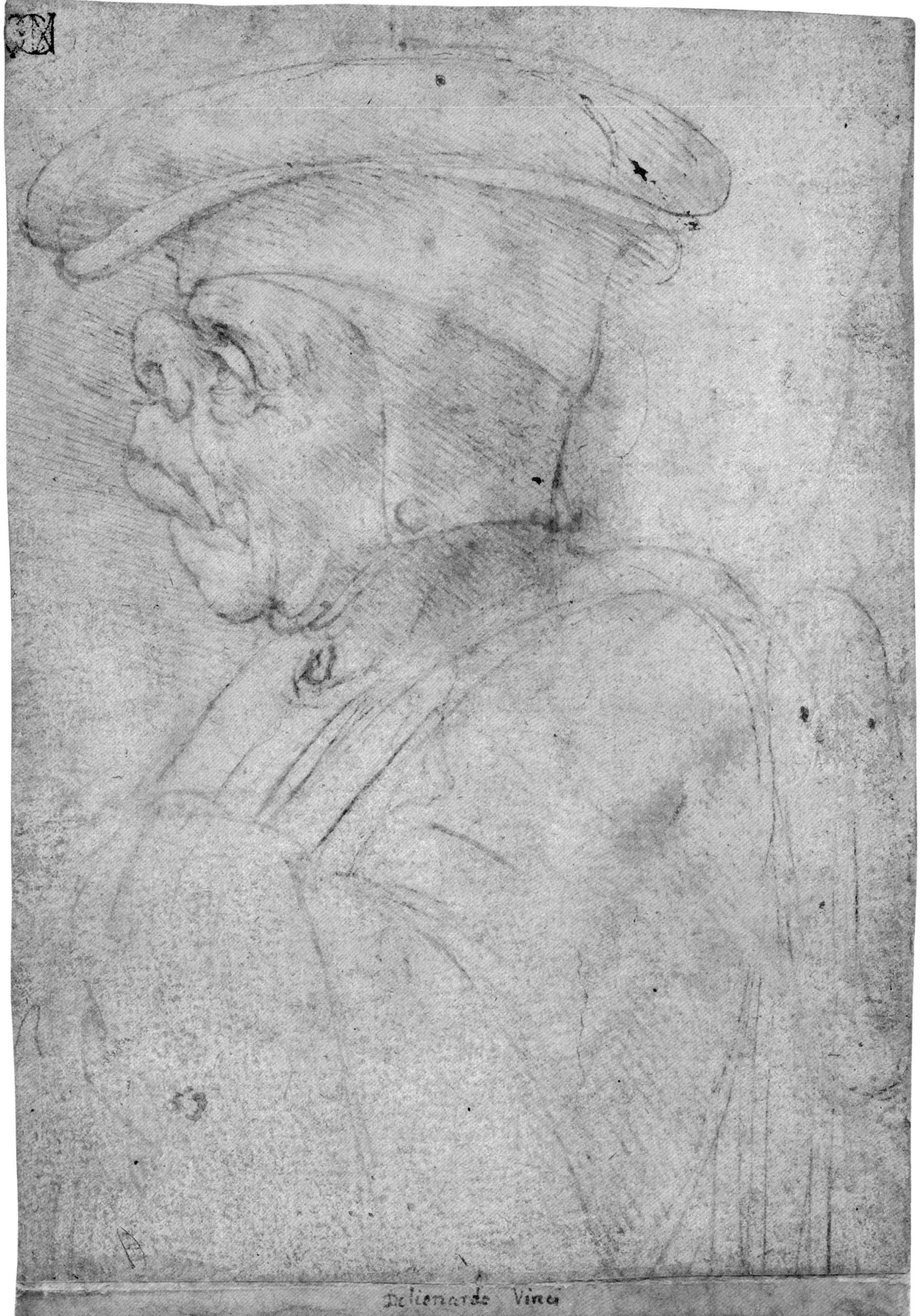

1.

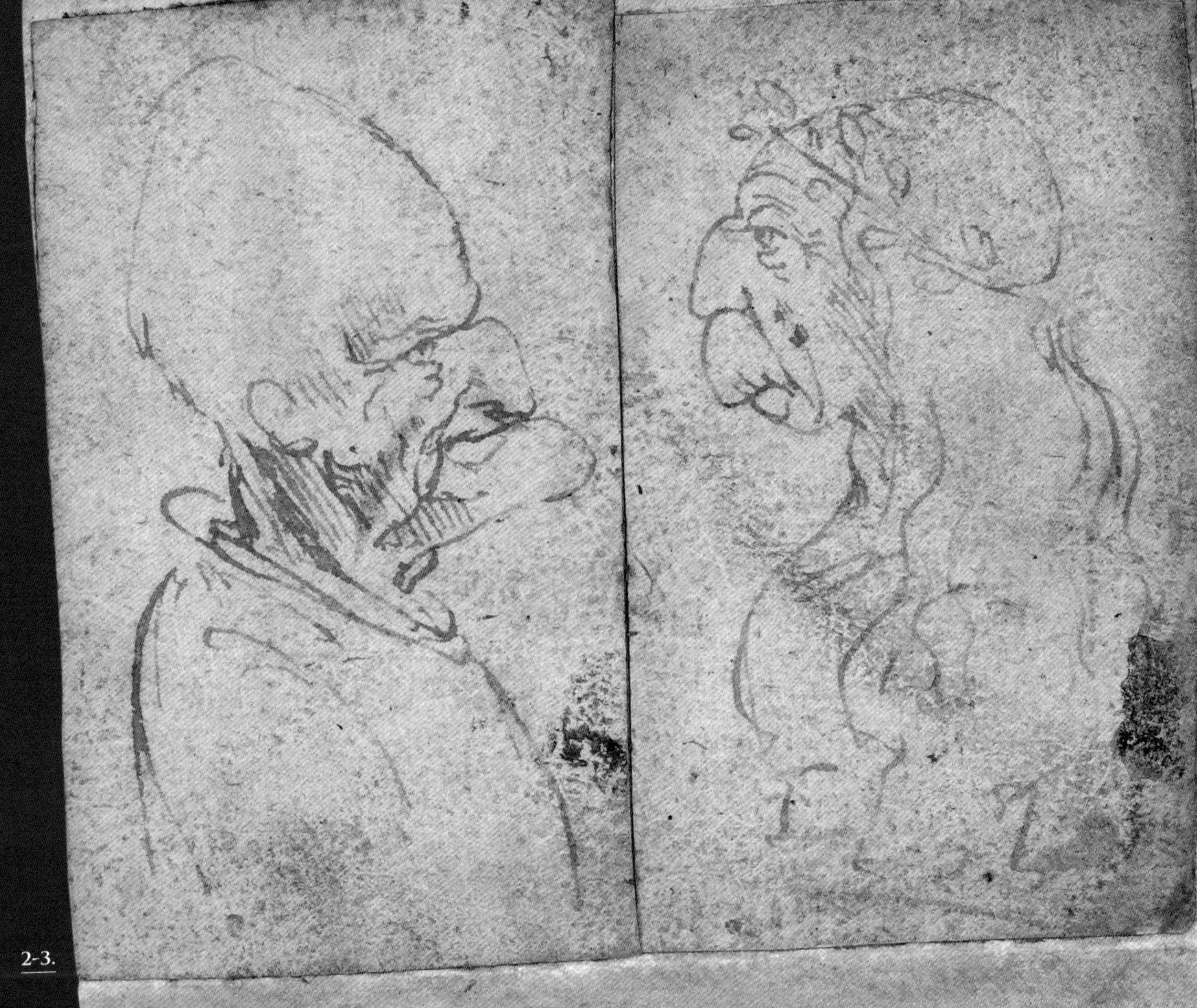

2-3.

2.
Leonardo da Vinci (1452–1519)
Caricature of the bust of a man, c. 1500
Pen, sepia ink, glued to paper
with the following sheet, 77 × 47 mm
Milan, Veneranda Biblioteca
Ambrosiana, Pinacoteca,
cod. F 274 inf. 27a

3.
Leonardo da Vinci (1452–1519)
Caricature of the bust of a woman with a crown of leaves, c. 1490
Pen, light sepia ink, glued to paper
with the previous sheet, 76 × 47 mm
Milan, Veneranda Biblioteca
Ambrosiana, Pinacoteca,
cod. F 274 inf. 27b

These also come from the *Libro di disegni* compiled by Giovan Battista Clarici (Mara 2010), long present in the Biblioteca Ambrosiana (perhaps as early as 1618 and certainly before 1661). It was dismembered in the modern period (around 1840–43, perhaps by Giuseppe Vallardi). These are two separate sheets of paper that had already been placed side by side in Clarici's book of drawings and pasted onto the same backing paper. Gerli also seems to show that they were from two distinct phases or independent drawings unconnected with each other, since he etched and published them separately in his 1784 volume. Considered autograph works by Bodmer and Venturi, Cogliati Arano judged the female bust 'by the hand of an imitator'. Her opinion was contradicted by Marani, who noted the left-handed hatching typical of the master on the woman's face, an observation accepted by Marco Rossi, who more recently considered them both autograph. The hatching and the more marked handling in the bust of the man suggest, rather, drawings from different periods, the female one being youthful and from his Sforza period, and the male one slightly later, with the ink beginning to stain. Compare this with the profile of the man with the protruding chin also in the Biblioteca Ambrosiana (cod. F 271 inf. 17; Cogliati Arano, in Milan 1982, cat. 19, p. 113), thought to be very late. The strong contrast between the extreme ugliness and repulsiveness of the woman's face (with hooked nose and strongly protruding upper lip) and the refinement of her clothing and attributes (dressed like a young maiden with flowing hair and crowned with a chaplet of leaves) seem to anticipate the famous drawing now in the National Gallery of Art, Washington DC, Woodner Collection (formerly at Chatsworth). This depicts an old woman with a carnation set in the bodice between her breasts (Marani, in Washington 1995, pp. 80–83, no. 11), as if saying 'though I am so ugly, I am kind in heart and soul'. The reverse image is also presented in the caricature of an old woman with a flower in her bodice in Chatsworth, in the Spencer copy and in that in the Gallerie dell'Accademia in Venice (in this exhibition, cat. 20, bottom left). Engraved by Hollar, then reproduced in the Mariette Album and also engraved by Caylus, this 'grotesque' proved popular. Yet the concept expressed there certainly derives from this half-bust figure in the Ambrosiana, which inexplicably has not found the same favour. From one of these versions also derives the painting by Lomazzo exhibited here [cat. 36], although the flower no longer appears between the woman's breasts. The leaves of the wreath in their rapid, flickering depiction recall the curls in the hair of the 'grotesque' in the Ligabue Collection [cat. 4]. Leonardo's process of increasing the man's grotesque physiognomy can be traced by observing in sequence the other drawings in the Ambrosiana, such as cod. F 263 inf. 92, where the male profile is still within the bounds of normality despite the slightly protruding chin; cod. F 274 inf. 30, in which the same profile is presented with the chin more marked, and on through the two now deformed heads on cod. F 274 inf. 34a, all the way to the present head that, although reversed, finally exaggerates this feature in an unnatural and grotesque way. Marco Rossi stresses the satirical connotations of the two drawings, calling them grotesque 'types' that would be widely imitated in sixteenth-century Lombardy and, largely for their comic and satirical overtones, in the Accademia della Val di Blenio, where Giovan Paolo Lomazzo and Aurelio Luini would repeat this playful, extroverted attitude, as shown by their drawings in this exhibition [cats 25 and 36, Lomazzo; cats 27 and 29, Luini].

PCM

Bibliography
Gerli 1784a, plates XXII, XXVII; Bodmer 1931, pp. 167, 390; Venturi, 1939, V, p. 214, nos 6, 7; Lucerne 1946, no. 133; Cogliati Arano 1980b, p. 124: Cogliati Arano, in Milan 1982, p. 117; Marani 1990, p. 57; Rossi, in Milan 1998, p. 90, no. 28; Mara 2010, p. 106; Mara 2019, pp. 369–71.

4.
Leonardo da Vinci (1452–1519), attributed
Grotesque head of woman in profile facing left, c. 1490–1500
Pen and clear sepia ink with stylus
or silverpoint, 117–18 × 63–6 mm
Stamp at the bottom right (star) of the Nicholas Lanière collection (1588–1666) (Lugt) and mark RH (Richard Houlditch, d. 1736). On the pasteboard mount (conjecturally by Jonathan Richardson Jr, 1694–1771) appear the inscriptions 'Leonard da Venci', 'Lodovico Carracci' and on the front of the passepartout, beneath the drawing, in pen 'Leonardo'
Venice, Ligabue Collection

The drawing was purchased in the Venice antiques market (Piero Scarpa) by Giancarlo Ligabue in the 1970s. It was initially attributed to an artist in the circle of Leonardo by Cogliati Arano (2005) and then, following laboratory analyses by Paolo Spezzani (Cogliati Arano, Spezzani 2007), assigned to Leonardo himself with additions 'in a later period'. Digital infrared analyses have shown that the brown ink lines disappear completely, while 'the fine lines that remain visible are, in all probability, silverpoint or possibly very thin leadpoint'. The monstrous face of the toothless old woman depicted here – with her flattened snub nose, drooping lips, double or triple wrinkled chin, hair pulled back and gathered in a veil fastened by a slender coronal with a large flower – has no exact equivalent in the series of grotesque heads drawn by Leonardo, seeming truly surprising and unique. The various features of the head, however, are all Leonardesque in origin, including the suggestion of a flower that

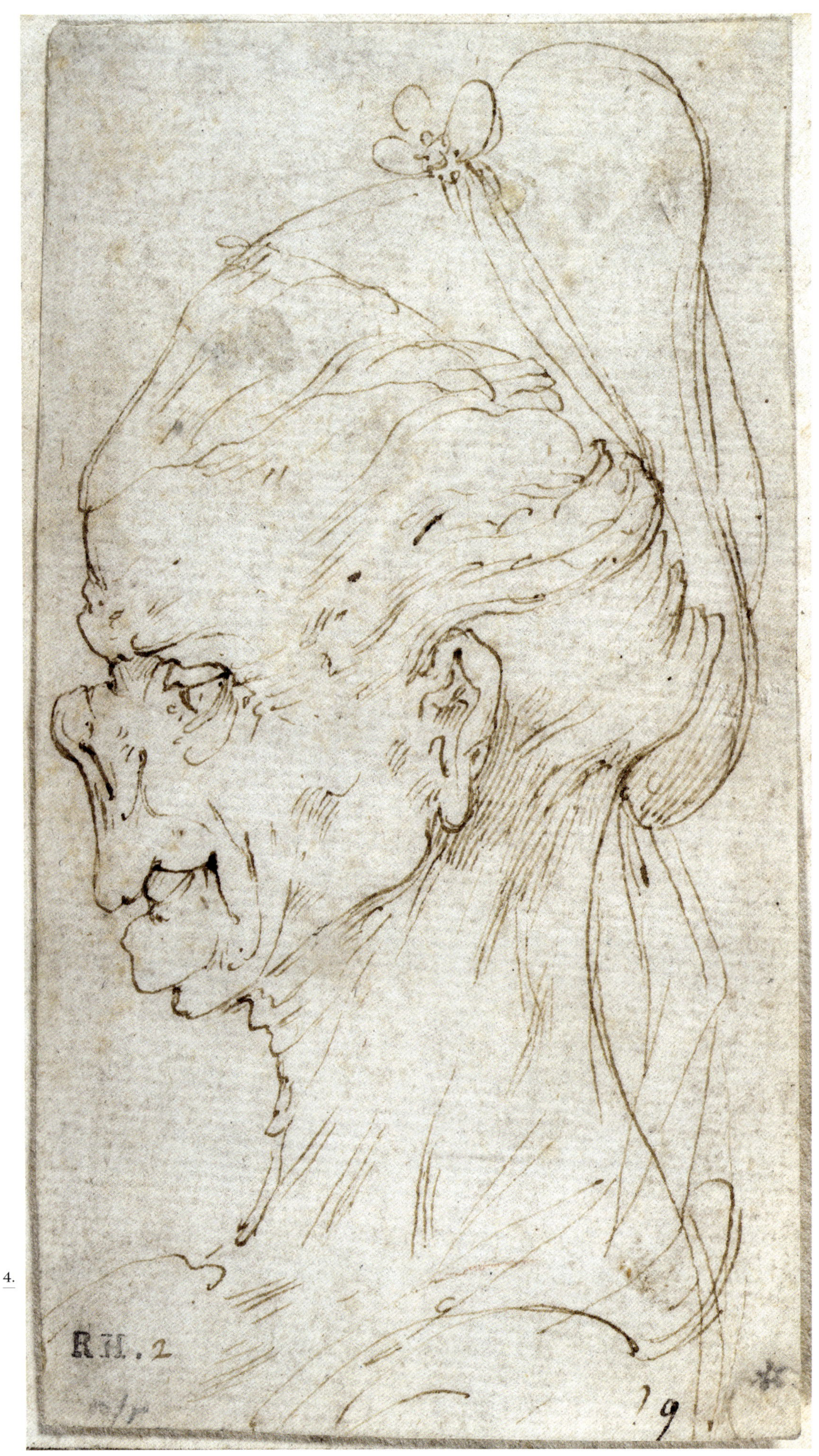

4.

seems to have been sketched quickly in front of the neck, the flattened nose, reminiscent of that of the head in the Ambrosiana cod. F 274 inf. 53 [cat. 1], the conical hairstyle (as in a caricature at Chatsworth) and the flower in the coronal. This is one of the most felicitous, animated and sparkling parts of the drawing, similar to the chaplet of leaves in the caricature in the Ambrosiana (cod. F 274 inf. 27b; [cat. 3]). Although the hatching does not appear unequivocally to be left-handed, the drawing, in the light of the analyses, seems to have been first traced in metalpoint (a normal practice for Leonardo before 1490), before being inked with light and sensitive touches of the pen (as in the upper part of the head) and then reinforced in the profile. This leads Cogliati Arano to speak of probably eighteenth-century retouching 'evident in the shading on the neck, in the ear and in the small outlines made with the right hand both on the cheeks and around the eye and mouth'. Cogliati Arano (Cogliati Arano and Spezzani 2007, p. 199, fig. 2) published a drawing of the head of an old man in profile facing right that appeared in the antique market in London (Christie's, 4 July 1995), from the milieu of Leonardo, in which 'the forehead, the recess between the forehead and the nose, and the nose itself with the typical nostrils, are very similar' to the drawing in the Ligabue Collection. That drawing, its location now unknown, came from the collection of Lord Arundel and bore the stamp of J. Richardson, a collecting history that it probably shares with the Ligabue drawing. The attribution to Ludovico Carracci on the supporting pasteboard, although imprecise, is indicative of the fact that sixteenth-century north Italian drawings of this type, depicting deformed and almost hideous heads and features, drawn with a continuous and nervous line, may have reached the Carracci in Bologna, partly through the Lombard Mannerists in the second half of the century, such as Giovan Paolo Lomazzo and Aurelio Luini (see the drawing by Luini from the Louvre in this exhibition [cat. 28]).

PCM

Bibliography
Cogliati Arano 2005; Cogliati Arano, in *Antichi disegni dalla Collezione Ligabue*, 2005, pp. 25–31; Cogliati Arano and Spezzani 2007.

5-8.

Leonardo da Vinci (1452–1519)
and workshop
Four grotesque heads, c. 1495–1505
Pen and ink, A 47 × 37 mm;
B 45 × 34 mm; C 49 × 37 mm;
D 48 × 37 mm
Chatsworth, The Devonshire
Collections, OMD 821 A, B, C, D

The sheets in the collection of the Duke of Devonshire probably derive from the collection of Sir Thomas Howard, second Earl of Arundel, together with the few dispersed at the Christie's sale in 1984 [cat. 22–5]. These last passed to the J. Paul Getty Museum in Los Angeles, then to Ian Woodner and were finally placed on deposit at the National Gallery of Art, Washington DC, as well as in private collections in New York (for all four sheets sold in 1984 see Bambach 2003, pp. 451–8, nos 69–72). From Sir Thomas Howard, second Earl of Arundel, they passed into the collection of Nicholaes Anthoni Flinck. From the sale of his collection in Amsterdam in 1723 they reached William Cavendish, second Duke of Devonshire (where they received their current mounting with the drawings pasted to cardstock and with gilt fillets). According to Varena Forcione (in Paris 2003), at least twenty-five of the Chatsworth heads seem to be originals by Leonardo, even taking into account the slight disparities in their quality and preservation – impoverished and flattened in the handling after being subjected to repeated remounting. Initially rejected by Kenneth Clark (1935) and A. E. Popham (1946), who both later accepted them, they were excluded by Berenson (1938), while Adolfo Venturi published them complete in the fifth issue of the drawings by the Reale Commissione Vinciana (1939). Considered original also by Gombrich (1954), the Chatsworth group, compared with that of the grotesque heads at Windsor, appears to reveal different elements and intentions on Leonardo's part. They are definitely not caricatures intended to elicit laughter, but rather infinite variations on the theme of physiognomy, or 'doodles', sketches made almost abstractedly, but for this reason indicative of the artist's psychology and perhaps his subconscious. In contrast with this interpretation, however, in the second edition of Leonardo's drawings at Windsor (Clark and Pedretti 1968–9, vol. I, p. XLIV), Clark accepted the group as autograph. After their interpretation by Gombrich, the theme of the *teste caricate*, often focused on the Chatsworth group, has been explored more recently by Michael Kwakkelstein, Sara Taglialagamba, Domenico Laurenza and Varena Forcione. Fundamental to the reception of this 'genre', the heads at Chatsworth have recently been interpreted as a satirical series, representing madness and the malevolence and meanness of humanity (Kwakkelstein, in Perissa Torrini 2019a). Kwakkelstein also suggested, given that the busts are shown clothed in expensive Florentine garments and headdresses, that these characters should be identified 'as high-ranking Florentine citizens', targeting these elites with moral criticism for their ignorance, vices and vanity. But the success of these depictions among the very social classes that Leonardo claimed to criticise (apart from the fact that the origin of the series in Chatsworth is most likely Lombard and not Florentine) prompts reservations about this interpretation. In fact, Leonardo's grotesque heads and 'monstrous faces' were immediately replicated in the fresco decorations in the church of Santa Maria Immacolata at Rivolta d'Adda in Cremona, dated 1506, commissioned by the members of the confraternity of the same name from Martino Piazza and Giovan Pietro Carioni (as established by Mario Marubbi), and other echoes are found in Villa Medici at Frascarolo, Varese (Porzio, in Lugano 1998, p. 30). Many were then copied by Francesco Melzi, a cultured Milanese noble (as in the Pembroke series at Wilton House, attributed to Melzi by Pedretti in 1973, followed by Trutty-Coohil and Pedretti 1993 and Kwakkelstein 1994), and then

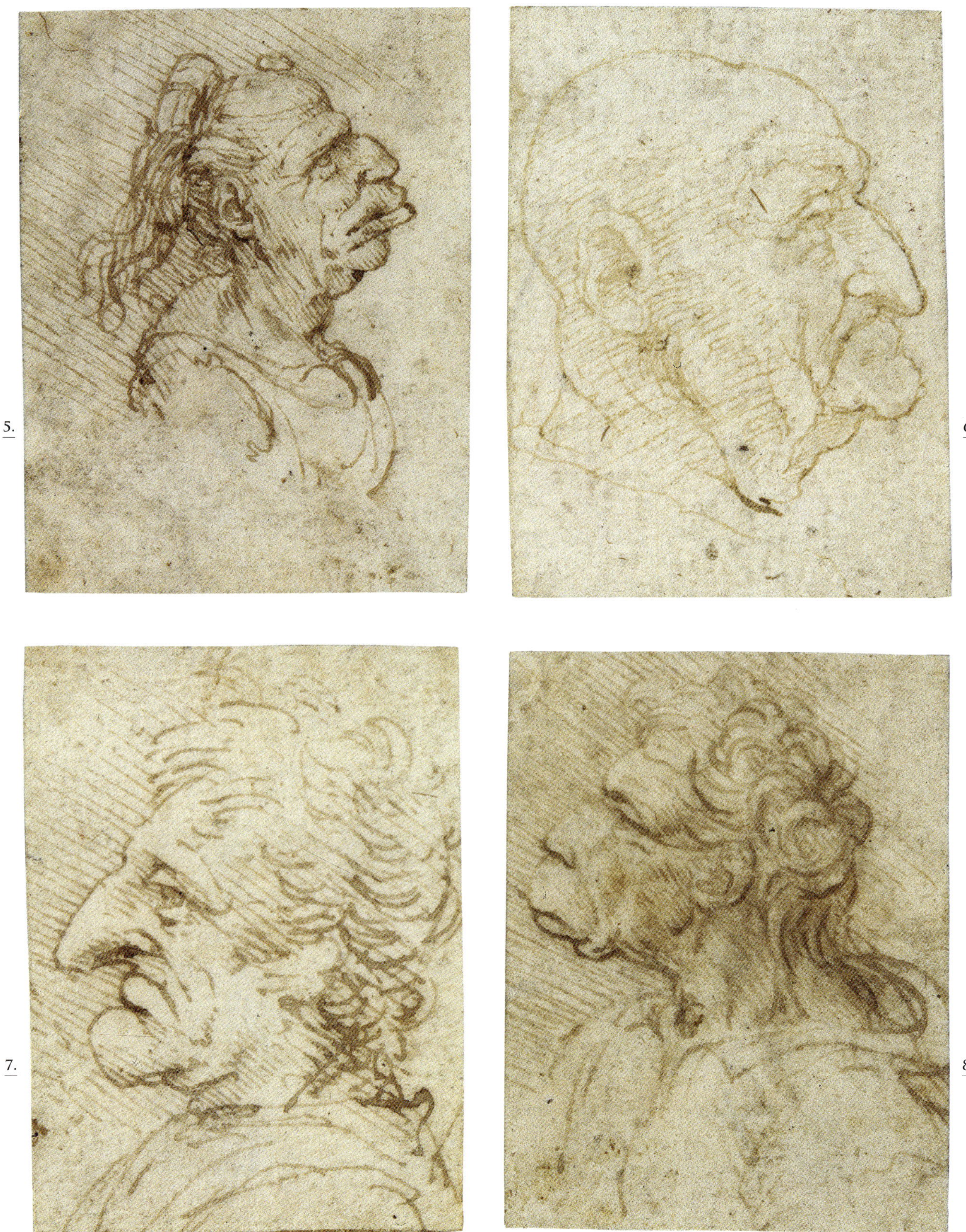

5.

6.

7.

8.

repeated in the Mariette Album in the Louvre, engraved by the Count of Caylus in 1730 (Forcione, in Paris 2003, pp. 206–37). They were then copied by a Lombard artist around 1590–1600 (in the Spencer grotesques: Trutty-Coohill and Pedretti 1993, for example no. 55) and again engraved by Wenceslaus Hollar in the mid-seventeenth century.
Among the four at Chatsworth (inv. OMD 821), which have not been much studied in the bibliography, the boldest are certainly heads A and D. The first depicts a woman with large protruding lips and chin, the second a man with marked prognathism and an ape-like face. The busts and heads are both drawn with a rapid, confident line and the handling has created stains and rapid, darting hatching. Noteworthy is the treatment of the curls on the head on sheet D, whose face has been compared to that of a goat but whose locks also recall the movement of waves and air. Sheet C is weaker, with the head of a man with a big nose and protruding chin, missing the chiaroscuro effect achieved in the two previous heads; but it should still be considered autograph or a replica by the workshop. Sheet B appears to be the least successful of the four and an outlier in the series in scale, type and size. It is not a head set on its bust, like the others in the Chatsworth series, but a simple profile of a man's head facing right, devoid of three-dimensional effects and executed with right-handed hatching. In fact, it appears to be a reduced copy of Leonardo's much more vigorous drawing in the Biblioteca Ambrosiana, cod. F 263 inf. 94 (for example, Rossi, in Milan 1998, p. 83, no. 22), faithful to the point of repeating the double line of the nose visible in the original but reversing the hatching. While A and D were repeatedly copied and engraved (A in Mariette Album, RF 28760; Caylus 35; Hollar P. 1565; D in Mariette Album, RF 28761; Caylus 36; *Characaturas*), all the way to Hollar and the volume of the *Characatures* (as Forcione identified in detail), B and C were not copied or engraved, an indication of the lower value assigned to them by subsequent collectors and copyists.

PCM

Bibliography

Strong 1905, p. 114; Venturi 1939, vol. V, p. 212, no. 15; Caroli 1991, pp. 160–62; Forcione, in Paris 2003, pp. 220, 225, 230, 234 (821 A), 220, 225, 230, 234 (821 D); Kwakkelstein, in Perissa Torrini 2019a, pp. 47–8, fig. 6 (821 D).

9-12.

Leonardo da Vinci (1452–1519)
Four grotesque heads, c. 1495–1505
Pen and ink, A 51 × 37 mm;
B 52 × 37 mm; C 50 × 43 mm;
D 52 × 45 mm
Chatsworth, The Devonshire Collections, inv. OMD 823 A, B, C, D

The four small sheets were exhibited in New York and Paris in 2003. The first head of the old man with the snub nose and hat (A) recalls the drawing in the Ambrosiana cod. F 274 inf. 53 [cat. 1] and also the head of the old woman in the Ligabue Collection [cat. 4]. It seems to have been inspired by a dog's head (Kwakkelstein, in Perissa Torrini 2019a). The second head of a woman with the large hat and protruding chin (B) was more widely known. It was copied, together with the head of an old man with big ears, onto a sheet in the Metropolitan Museum in New York (inv. 1975.96) from the Pembroke collection at Wilton House. Pedretti attributed it to Francesco Melzi, followed by all subsequent scholars (Bean, Trutty-Coohill, Kwakkelstein and Forcione, in Paris 2003, p. 201, no. 69). The head of a woman (B), was copied in the Mariette Album (RF 28749) in the Louvre and in the 1730 volume by Caylus (24), as well as in the group of the so-called 'Spencer grotesques' (New York, Public Library), in turn brought together in the two-volume edition of Rabelais's works published in 1659 or 1669 (see Bambach 2003, p. 460, fig. 175). Head D, open-mouthed and toothless, was copied in the Mariette Album (RF 28734) and in the Caylus (9), while C, of an old man with a sharp chin and wearing a hat, appears alien to the group, being of a more generic type, variously treated in Leonardo's sketches, and out of place in the Chatsworth series. (It looks like a fragment cut from a larger sheet, rather than a 'cameo' constructed and centred on the sheet like the others.) Despite this, it should be considered an autograph work.

PCM

Bibliography

Strong 1905, p. 114; Venturi, 1939, vol. V, p. 212, no. 16; Clark and Pedretti 1968–9, vol. I, p. 59 (below at no. 12398); Bean 1982, p. 136, no. 129; Caroli 1991, pp. 154, 156, nos 5–7, p. 157, no. 9; Trutty-Coohill and Pedretti 1993, pp. 70–71; Jaffé 1994, p. 171, no. 886; Kwakkelstein 1994, pp. 107–12, plates 49b, 49f; Bambach 2003, pp. 459–61, no. 73; Forcione, in Paris 2003, pp. 198–9, no. 66; p. 201, no. 69, 218, 219, 223, 224, 229, 233; Taglialagamba 2007, p. 179, fig. 14 (823 D); Kwakkelstein, in Perissa Torrini 2019a, pp. 47–8, fig. 5 (823 A).

13-16.

Leonardo da Vinci (1452–1519)
and workshop (?)
Four grotesque heads, c. 1495–1505
Pen and ink, A 60 × 47 mm;
B 64 × 47 mm; C 55 × 45 mm;
D 56 × 45 mm
Chatsworth, The Devonshire Collections, inv. OMD 824 A, B, C, D

These are among the most fascinating and famous *têtes grotesques en bustes* of the Chatsworth series, exhibited repeatedly (Pittsburgh, Cleveland, Fort Worth, Los Angeles, Miami in 1987–8 and again in Paris in 2003), and well known for some centuries. That of the head of an old woman with a high conical hairstyle (A) was reproduced in the Mariette Album (RF 28751) and then engraved by Caylus (26); there is a copy in the Biblioteca Ambrosiana (cod. F 274 inf. 54d [cat. 19]) by an imitator of Leonardo and one in the Gallerie dell'Accademia in Venice (inv. 229), in a sheet by the school of Leonardo that includes other heads formerly in Chatsworth (such as that of the young man laughing, which passed in 1984 to the J. Paul Getty Museum). Carlo Lasinio used it to make his colour print today in the

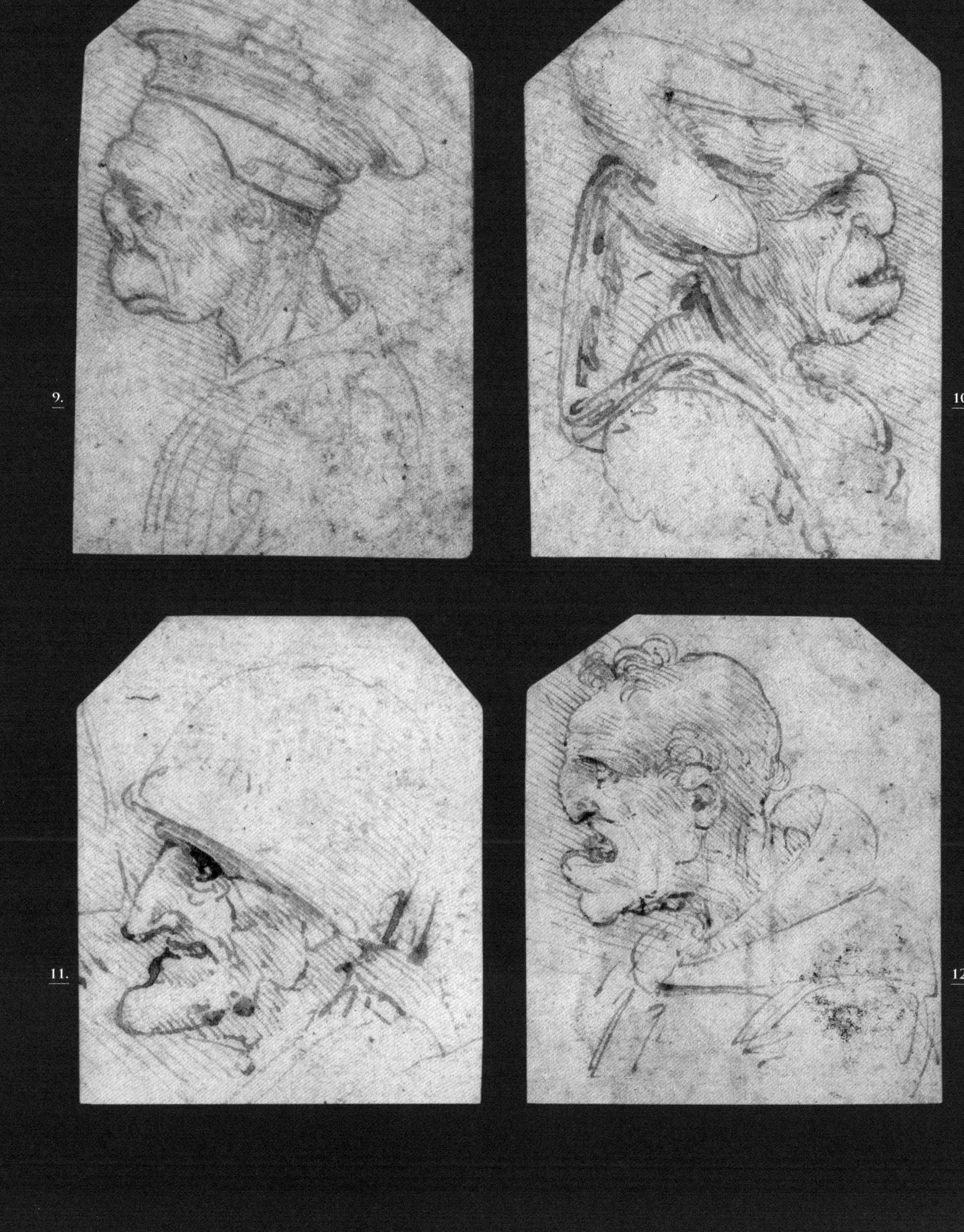
9.
10.
11.
12.

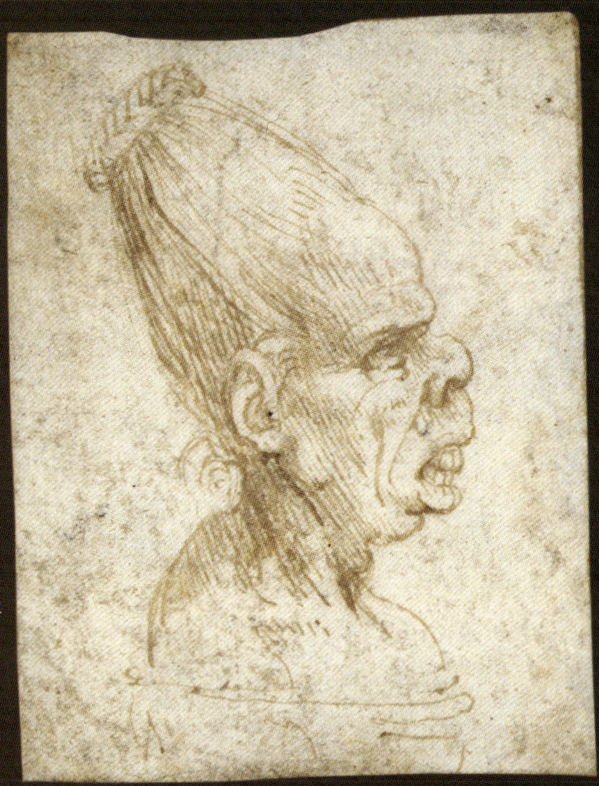

13.

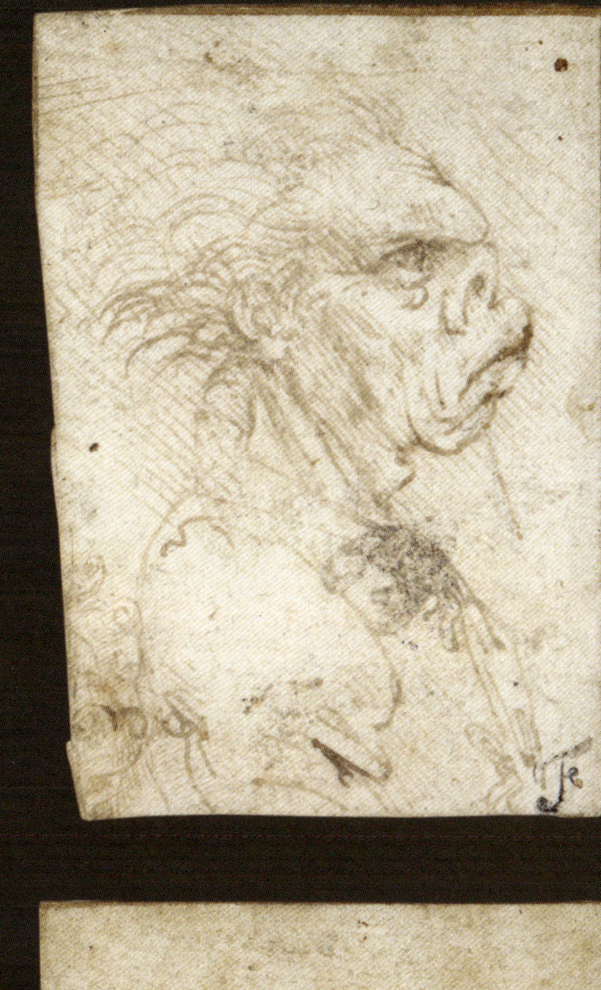

14.

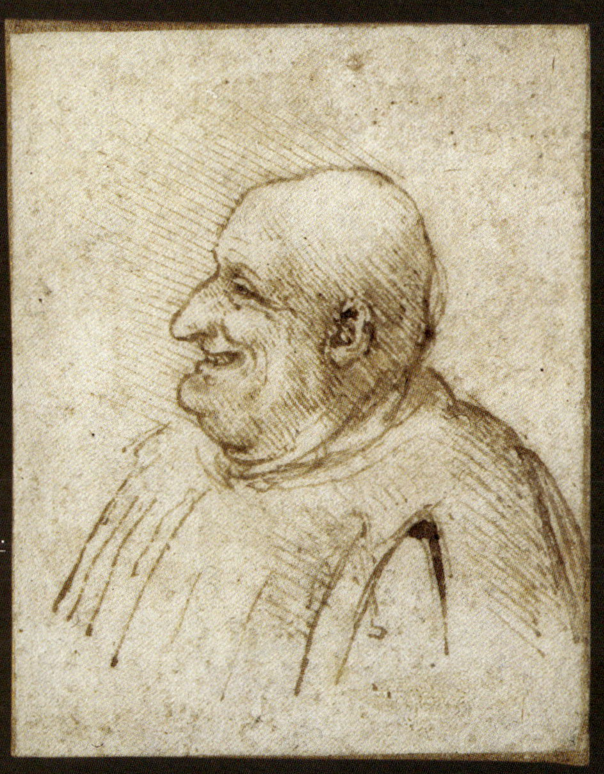

15.

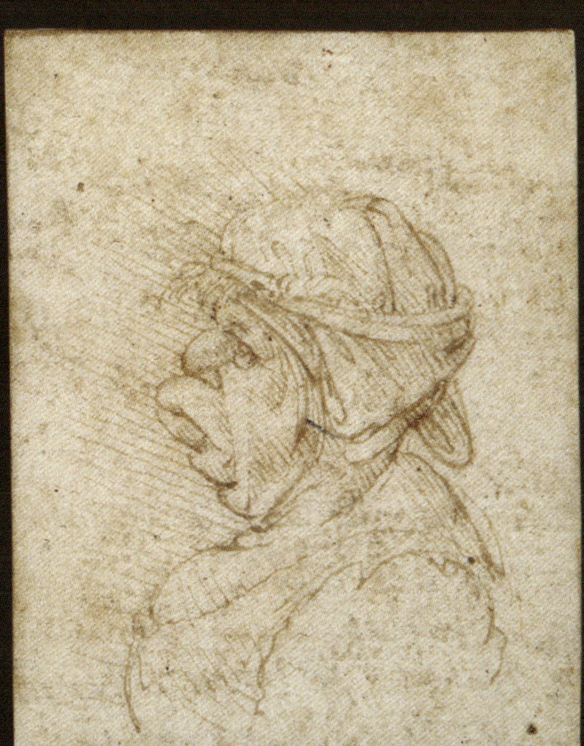

16.

Raccolta Vinciana in Milan (on which see Marani 2017, p. 193, fig. 12; for other prints by Lasinio see cats 83–5), while the animal face with its snub nose on sheet B, remarkable for its rapacious gaze and fierce appearance, returns in the Mariette Album (RF 28754), and consequently the volume of Caylus's engravings (29). The corpulent male figure bust in C is linked to a type drawn several times by Leonardo, of which there is a copy in the Ambrosiana (cod. F 263 inf. 98; Cogliati Arano, in Milan 1982, p. 118, no. 27), and a later version in the same Library (cod. F 274 inf. 45), inscribed 'Merlino Cocalio', perhaps by one of the artists in the Accademia della Val di Blenio that orbited around Lomazzo (Cogliati Arano 1980b, p. 122, no. XIVb, engraved by Gerli in 1784, plate XIV). Neither C nor D, with the head of a woman with protruding lips wearing a kind of turban, alluding to a bird's head according to Kwakkelstein (but this does not seem to be the case), appear to have been copied into the Mariette Album. This may have been because they were considered of poorer quality, although it is still necessary to confirm their authenticity (they might actually be workshop copies).

PCM

Bibliography

Strong 1905, p. 114; Venturi, 1939, vol. V, p. 24, plate CCXXI, nos 1–4; Caroli 1991, p. 154, no. 1, p. 155, nos 2–4; Trutty-Coohill and Pedretti 1993, p. 67, no. 30; Kwakkelstein 1994, pp. 107–12, plates 49h, k, l; Jaffé 1994, p. 171, no. 887; Trutty-Coohill 1998, p. 191, n. 39; Forcione, in Paris 2003, pp. 198–9, no. 67 (the image on p. 199, no. 67A, mistakenly repeats the drawing at Chatsworth inv. 822 A, already reproduced by Forcione, in Paris 2003, p. 197, no. 65A), pp. 224, 225, 230, 234; Taglialagamba 2007, pp. 179ff., fig. 11 (824 A), fig. 12 (824 C); Kwakkelstein, in Perissa Torrini 2019a, pp. 47–8, fig. 4 (824 D).

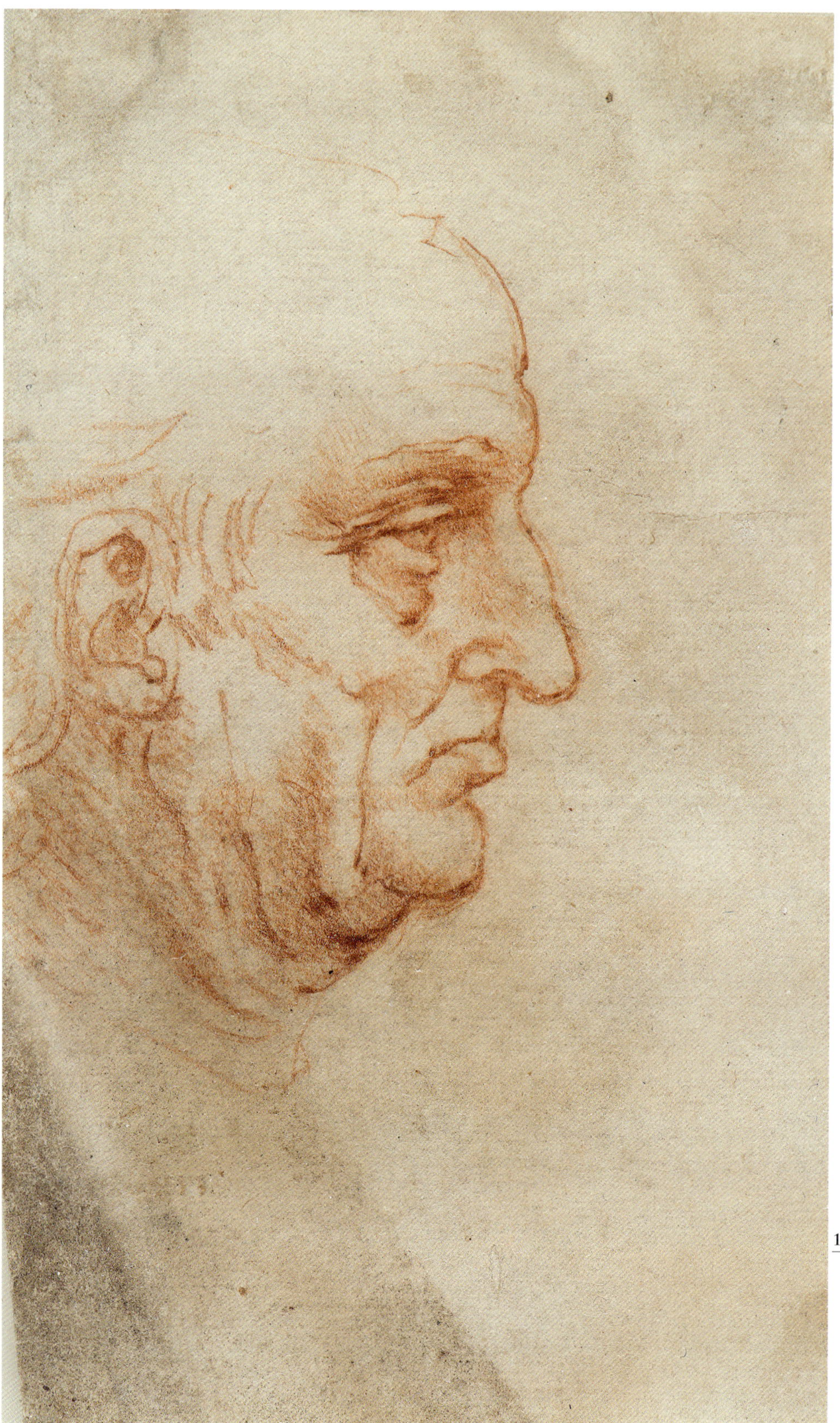

17*r*.

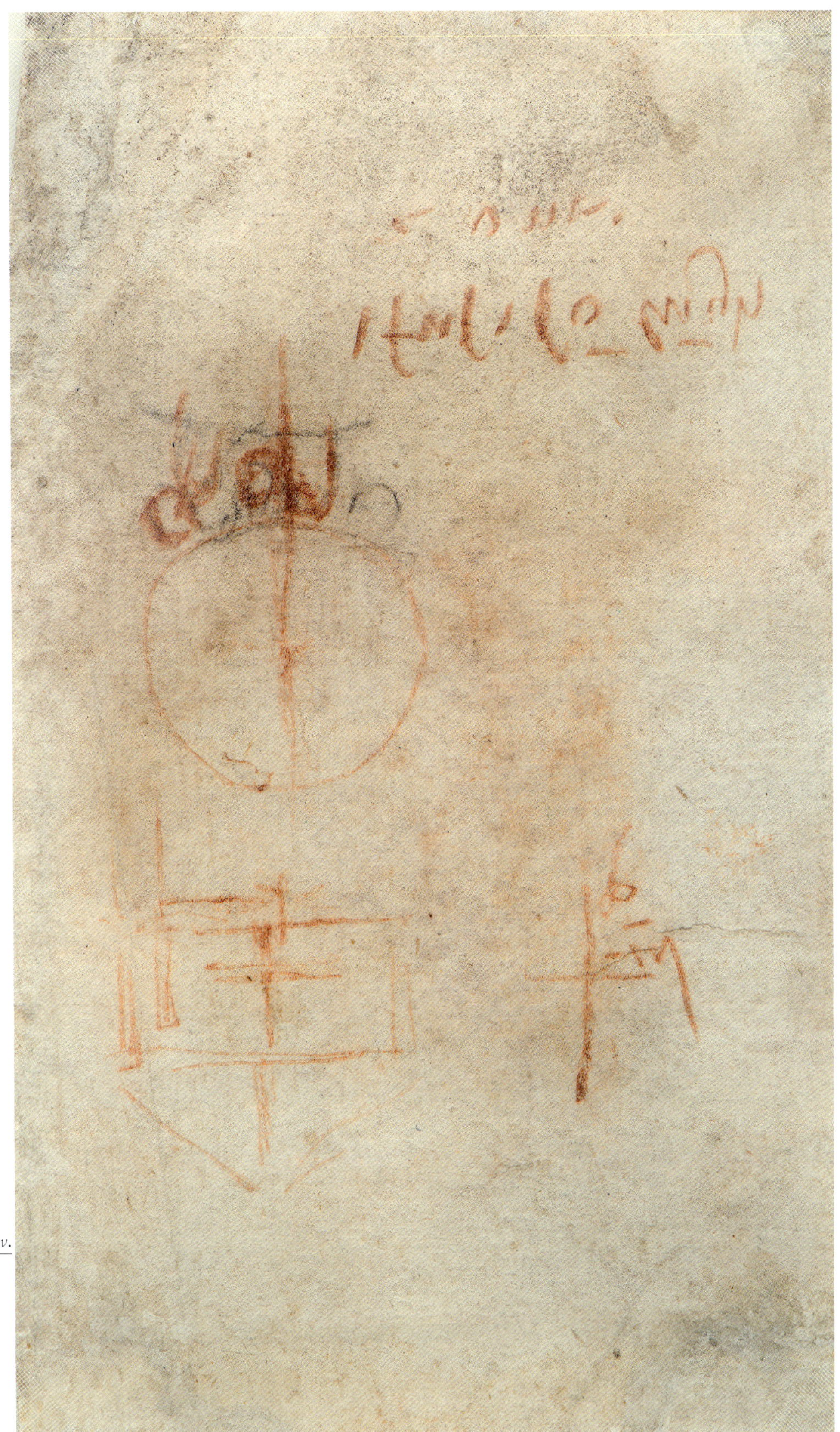

17*v*.

17.
Leonardo da Vinci (1452–1519)
Head of an old man in profile facing right, c. 1508–10
(on the verso, drawings of gears and the words 'braccia 1' and 'i fusi son lunghi 5 [?] once')
Red pencil on yellowed white paper, 129 × 78 mm
Milan, Pinacoteca di Brera, Gabinetto dei disegni, inv. Chron. Reg. 7415

This sheet reached the Pinacoteca di Brera with the bequest of Lamberto Vitali (Milan, 1896–1992), a famous collector and historian of photography as well as a friend of Giorgio Morandi, whose general catalogue he edited. The bequest included various archaeological relics and works, paintings and drawings of ancient and modern art. Vitali had purchased Leonardo's drawing at a Finarte auction on 3 December 1975 (no. 217), where it appeared as 'Leonardo da Vinci (School): Head of a man in profile, 130 × 78 mm. Sanguine on yellowish paper; on the back it has notes in sanguine.' The low auction price (less than 300 dollars) caused a stir, since the drawing was attributed to the school of Leonardo, despite the clearly autograph annotations on the back. In 1976 it was confirmed as an original Leonardo by Konrad Oberhuber, at the time curator of drawings at the Fogg Art Museum in Cambridge, Massachusetts, in a letter to its owner (although 'somebody may have reinforced it later on a little bit'; see Marani 2001, p. 98, for references to the correspondence now in the Archive of Lamberto Vitali's heirs). The sheet was also considered autograph by Federico Zeri and Carlo Pedretti. The latter repeatedly published it (1979, 1980, 1985), dating it to about 1510–11 and identifying the sketches and notes on the verso as connected with the drawing for a water meter designed by Leonardo for Bernardo Rucellai when he was 'in Franza' (that is, during his stay in Milan, then occupied by the French) and recorded in early sources (Benvenuto di Lorenzo della Golpaja).
The profile of a bald man, with heavy eyelids, double chin and drooping cheeks, protruding lower lip and gaze lost in the void, seems less a caricature

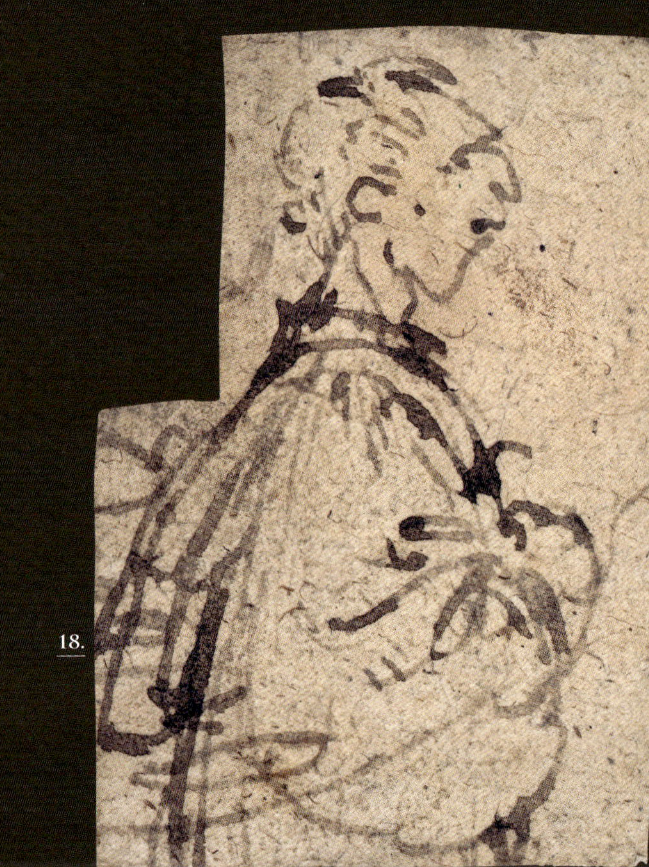

18.

than a sympathetic depiction of old age, whose effects the artist seems to share emotionally. While the fine hatching on the lower part of the face is undeniably performed with the left hand, it remains to be ascertained whether what seem to be lines retracing the profile and the forehead are not rather *pentimenti* and reinforcements made by Leonardo himself, who customarily surrounded his heads with two or three outlines until he attained the volume and three-dimensional effect he sought (as in the profile of the girl in the Ambrosiana, cod. F 274 inf. 14). Here we seem to see a pacific Leonardo, who portrays old age for what it represents (physical decay, fatigue, lack of ideals and perspectives), far from the nightmarish and misshapen forms with which he had distorted the heads of old men and women in previous years, making this phase of life appear grotesque and almost caricatural. Pedretti compared this noble head with a profile drawn on a sheet in the Royal Library at Windsor (inv. CIN 912599), which also contains a sketch of the whole water meter pavilion, but the man looks much younger and does not match the type presented here. A general resemblance appears, however, in the head drawn in two replicas by Melzi depicting a draped figure: one in Turin's Biblioteca Reale (no. 15584), the other at Windsor (inv. CIN 912584), both also in red pencil, which Pedretti believes recall anatomical models that can be assigned to c. 1510 (Pedretti 1975, p. 33, no. 16; Clark and Pedretti 1968, vol. I, p. 115). So an earlier dating to about 1508–10 appears possible for this head of a melancholy old man.

PCM

Bibliography

Pedretti 1979; Pedretti 1980, vol. II, p. 860, figs 115*r*, 116*v*; Pedretti 1985, vol. III, p. 863, figs 115*r*, 116*v*; Contardi, in Rome-Milan-Florence 1998, p. 9; Marani 2001, pp. 98–9, no. 63.

18.

Leonardo da Vinci (1452–1519)
Caricature of a cleric (?), c. 1510–16
Pen and sepia ink on paper, glued onto backing paper, 65 × 45 mm
Milan, Veneranda Biblioteca Ambrosiana, Pinacoteca, cod. F 274 inf. 25

Likewise from the *Libro di disegni* compiled by Clarici [cats 1, 2], this small drawing of the head and half-length figure of a man can be seen as one of Leonardo's few original drawings that can really be termed 'caricatures'. This is evident by starting from the figure's head, with hair and tonsure, and then observing the hooked nose, receding chin and half-open mouth, traits that, with a few quick strokes of the pen and ink stains, give the face almost the look of a bird of prey. The pose with the arm raised to the chest also suggests that the figure is holding an aspergillum (since he is not carrying anything on his shoulders). Taken with the tonsure and collar, this has led to the assumption that it is the caricature of a priest or cleric. Leonardo's mocking witticisms and anecdotes about priests are well known. A particularly close match is the jest of the priest who went about blessing houses (Marinoni 1974, pp. 140–41): 'A jest. A priest was making the rounds of his parish on Easter Saturday and sprinkling holy water in the houses, as is customary. He came to a painter's room, where he sprinkled the water on some of his pictures. The painter turned round, rather irately, and asked him why he had sprinkled his paintings. The priest said it was the custom and his duty to do so, and he was doing good. And that he who did good might look for good in return, and, indeed, for better, since God had promised that every good deed that was done on earth should be rewarded a hundred-fold from above [in heaven]. Waiting until the priest left, the painter went to an upper window and flung a large pail of water on the priest saying: 'Here's the reward a hundred-fold from above, which you said would come from the good you did me with your holy water, which spoilt my paintings.'
On the figure's birdlike appearance, we might recall another jest (the jest of the 'archpriest of Santa Maria del Monte in Varese, who was sent a legate to the Duke in exchange for a sparrowhawk', in Marinoni 1974, p. 145, recalls how the jest, found in Madrid, Biblioteca España, Ms. Madrid 8936, fol. 21*v*, c. 1505, may be a variant of the one recounting the erroneous interpretation of an order from the Duke of Ferrara to the Podestà of Carpaneto, who sent the archpriest of Modena to the Duke of Ferrara tied in a sack.) Traditionally assigned to the Sforza years, Carlo Pedretti first proposed dating it to about 1516 (annotation on the old mount of the sheet), while Cogliati Arano favoured a late date, around 1500 and 'perhaps even later', a proposal on which Marani and Rossi agree. But the way the ink has smudged and stained, the rapid handling and the lack of the usual parallel hatching prompts us to consider a much later date, stylistically close to the *Profile of the old man* in the Biblioteca Ambrosiana (cod. F 271 inf. 17; Rossi, in Milan 1998, p. 95), assignable to the last decade of Leonardo's life. It is remarkable how, with just a few terse penstrokes, Leonardo managed to epitomise a human character, in which cunning, wit and conceit are perfectly blended in a way that perhaps he had never attained before. In fact, few comparisons can be suggested and they are all much less incisive than this. See, for example, the rapid sketch of an elderly figure on the fragment in Windsor inv. CIN 912460r, one of the few caricatures completed by the definition of the draped figure (who seems to be holding a child or some animal, Clark thinks a 'lamb'; Clark and Pedretti 1968, p. 76); or also in Windsor inv. CIN 912464, fragments that both come from a sheet of the Codex Atlanticus, 878*v* (formerly 320*v*-a), at any rate very old, perhaps connected with the *Adoration of the Magi* in the Uffizi (Pedretti 1978–9, vol. II, p. 159). Leonardo's terse and fierce vision anticipates by two centuries Anton Maria Zanetti's rapid and mocking caricatures, which abound in the *Libro di disegni* now in the Fondazione Cini, partly because of that abbreviated conical shape of the figure [cat. 53] found in a caricature by Zanetti like the one on folio 40 of the Cini Album.

PCM

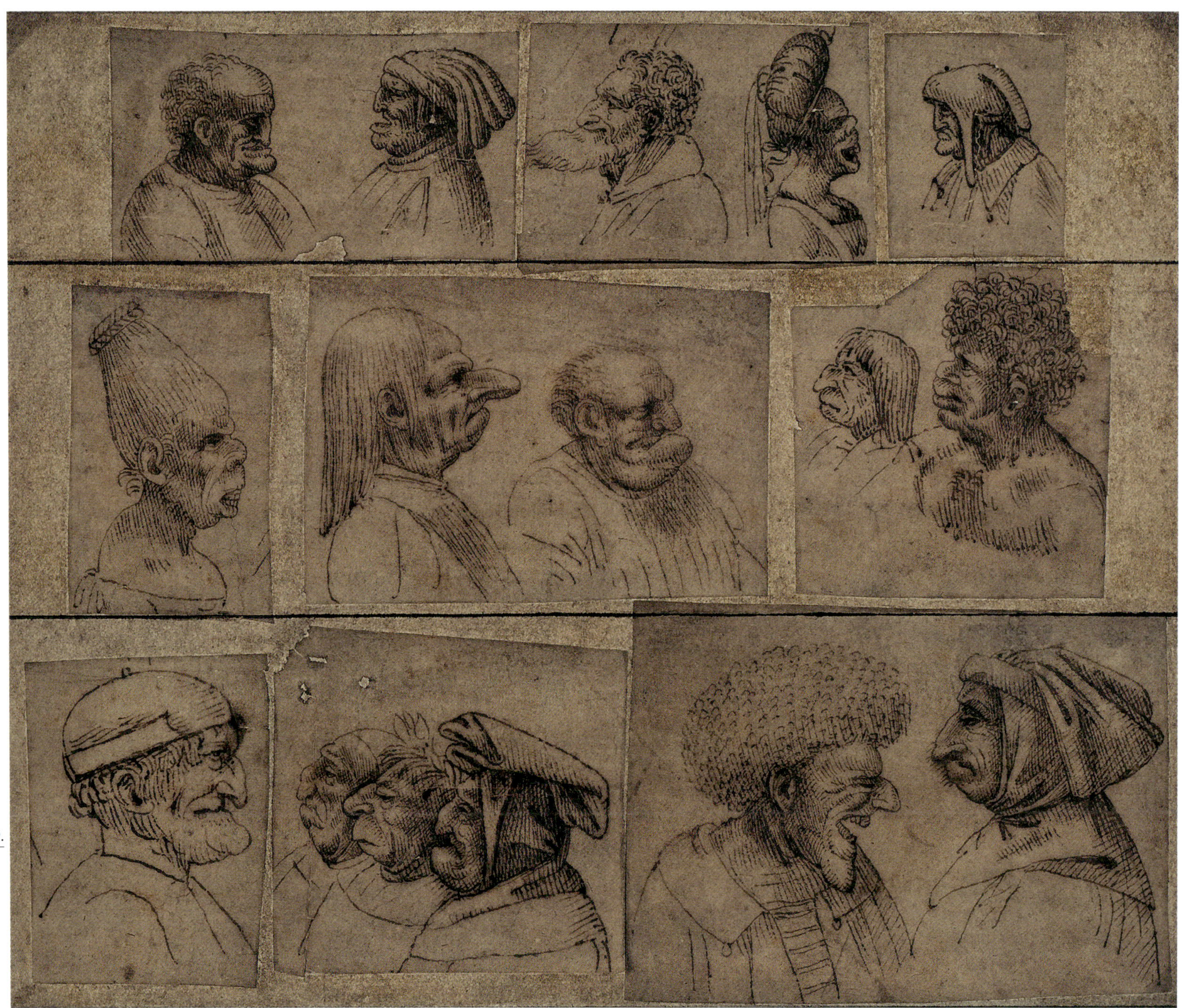

19.

Bibliography
Gerli 1974, plate XXV; Venturi, 1939, vol. V, no. 213/8; Cogliati Arano 1980b, p. 124; Cogliati Arano, in Milan 1982, p. 107, no. 13; Coleman 1984, p. 50; Marani 1990, p. 56; Caroli 1991, p. 151; Cogliati Arano, in Venice 1992, p. 308; Mara 2010, pp. 84, 104; Marani [2016] 2017, p. 193, p. 195 fig. 15; Mara 2019, pp. 369–71.

19.

Imitators of Leonardo
Nine fragments with sixteen studies of grotesque heads, 16th century (?)
Pen and brown ink on paper, pasted onto backing paper, 177 × 215 mm
Milan, Veneranda Biblioteca Ambrosiana, Pinacoteca, cod. F 274 inf. 54

54A.
Two male grotesque heads facing each other
40 × 74 mm

The corpulent male subject, with face in profile to the right, is characterised by a high rounded forehead and pronounced chin and is reproduced in Gerli, plate XXV. The figure wearing a hat has a conspicuously protruding lower lip and is also present in the same Gerli plate; the same subject is also represented in plate XXVI and has similarities with cod. F 274 inf. 50.

54B.
Man with horizontal beard and woman with tall headdress
42 × 65 mm

The head characterised by a thick beard projecting forward almost parallel to the ground reappears with some small variations on the sheet attributed to Francesco Melzi in the Gallerie dell'Accademia in Venice (inv. 229, in Cogliati Arano 1980a, no. 24), and in Gerli, plate XXIV. The head of the old woman is less detailed in Gerli, plate XXII. Mariette, in 1730, reproduced a similar female figure in fig. 22.

54C.
Male head with hat
40 × 33 mm

The male head is characterized by a flat nose and frowning expression. It is present in Gerli, plate XXVI (Cogliati Arano, in Milan 1982, indicates it as unpublished).

54D.
Grotesque head of an old woman with a tall coiffure
59 × 37 mm

The female head is a copy of a drawing by Leonardo (824 A) in the Chatsworth collection (Cogliati Arano, in Milan 1982; Jaffé 1987–93, no. 43A). We find the same subject in a drawing at the Gallerie dell'Accademia in Venice (inv. 229, in Cogliati Arano 1980a, no. 24) and in another drawing, attributed to Francesco Melzi (Pedretti 1973, no. 2), now in Los Angeles at the Elmer Belt Library of Vinciana, University of California, Los Angeles. Gerli reproduces it as plate XXV, facing left.

54E.
Two male heads with contrasting features
60 × 85 mm

The first subject, thin, with a strongly pronounced nose, receding chin, high, rounded forehead and long straight hair, is related to that in the *Libro di disegni* cod. F 274 inf. n. 45e, which belonged to Federico Borromeo (Mara 2010). It is also present in a sheet attributed to Francesco Melzi in the Royal Collection Trust (RCIN 912491). The corpulent subject, with receding hairline, neckless and with a toothless mouth, together with those on fragment 54f, is depicted in drawing 142022 at the Morgan Library & Museum, New York, attributed to Francesco Melzi. Both subjects on the fragment are present in Gerli, plate XXIV, the first in two variants with slight differences.

54F.
Two male figures representing thin and fat types
60 × 58 mm

The first subject is thin, has straight hair, a fringe, a large hooked nose and frowning mouth; the second has thick curly hair and displays a bare, muscular, hirsute chest. Both subjects are reproduced in Gerli, plate XXIV and, together with the fat subject in fragment 54e, are depicted in drawing 142022 at New York's Morgan Library & Museum, attributed to Francesco Melzi.

54G.
Head of an old man wearing a soft bonnet
60 × 44 mm

Man in profile, facing right, characterised by a bonnet, large hooked nose, toothless mouth and prominent chin. Gerli reproduces it as plate XXV.

54H.
Grotesque heads of Dante, Petrarch and Boccaccio
61 × 65 mm

The three subjects were identified as Dante, Petrarch and Boccaccio on the basis of a suggestion made by the linguist Gianfranco Folena to Augusto Marinoni (Cogliati Arano, in Milan 1982, p. 121). The clue leading to the identification were the bonnets in the figures of Dante and Boccaccio and Petrarch's laurel wreath. The facial features reflect stereotypical male caricatures. Leonardo had already drawn other forms of the caricature of Dante, with the same hooked nose and cross-bite, but with longer limbs (see Chatsworth, Devonshire Collection, inv. OMD 818 A).
The three subjects are reproduced in Gerli, plate XXIV, and are also related to a drawing in the Gallerie dell'Accademia in Venice, inv. 229 (Cogliati Arano 1980a, n. 24). Mariette presents an image similar to figure 19 in his album. The three heads are also found in a drawing (Pedretti, 1973, no. 2) attributed to Francesco Melzi, currently at the Elmer Belt Library of Vinciana, University of California, Los Angeles.

54I.
Laughing man and serious man facing each other
70 × 10 mm

The first subject is characterised by thick curly shock of hair and features convulsed by laughter. It derives from a subject by Leonardo in the Chatsworth collection (Commissione Vinciana V, 212, 6). The head is reproduced inby Gerli, plate XXIV. Mariette's figure 25 derives from a drawing similar to that depicting the head wearing a bonnet (54a).

RC

Bibliography
Gerli 1784a, plates XXII, XXIV, XXV, XXVI; Cogliati Arano 1980b, p. 124; Cogliati Arano, in Milano 1982, p. 120, no. 29, ill.; Jaffé 1987–93, no. 43; Bora 1991, p. 213, fig. 13 [cod. F 274 inf. 54a–i]; Milan 1998, p. 88, no. 27, ill.; Venice 1999, p. 100; Bambach 2003, no. 137, pp. 695–6, ill. pp. 686–7; Mara 2010, p. 100, n. 198, fig. 7.

20.

Francesco Melzi (1491–1570), attributed
Five grotesque heads, c. 1550
Pen and brown ink on paper without visible watermark, 183 × 125 mm
Venice, Gallerie dell'Accademia, inv. 229

The sheet presents five grotesque faces, four men and a woman, not in dialogue with each other. They are by the same hand, which is also found in another drawing in the same collection, inv. 229 (Cogliati Arano 1980a, no. 24).
The caricatures depicted here were widely circulated. In 1966 Cogliati Arano noticed the presence of the image of the caricature with bust cut off high, depicted at the bottom of the sheet, in Gerli, plate XXIV, also reproduced in one of the fragments (54e [cat. 19]) on the sheet with grotesque heads by imitators of Leonardo. It is also comparable with cod. F 274 inf. 50 in the Ambrosiana.
The sheet was attributed to Leonardo by Selvatico (1854); then Loeser (1903) attributed it to a copyist and Cogliati Arano attributed it to the author of the drawing in the British Museum no. 1886-6-9-40, which presents the same technique and measurements (in Popham and Pouncey 1950, fig. CX, no. 119). The attribution to Melzi was put forward, at first doubtfully, by Berenson (1961), who observed a certain affinity with Melzi's cod. F 274 inf. 8 in the Ambrosiana.
Of the five figures, the accentuations of the features typical of caricature are evident in the female and male subjects represented in the last line. The others are studies of faces where the deterioration of the features is due to old age. The female figure, an old woman with hair gathered in a thin braid, with withered neck and eyes and nose sunk into her face, with prominent forehead and teeth, also inspired Giovan Paolo Lomazzo's painting in a private collection [cat. 36]. It is a variant on the study of vanity, unable to cope with old age. In this case, the subject is made pathetic not only by her facial features but also by the bodice that supports a shrivelled breast and reveals a hump on her shoulders.

RC

Bibliography
Gerli 1784a, plate XXIV; Selvatico 1854, cornice V, no. 10; Uzielli 1884, no. 26; Loeser 1903; Heydenreich 1949, plate XXXVI; Popham and Pouncey 1950, fig. CX; Gombrich 1954, p. 208; Berenson 1961 (1st ed. 1938), no. 263, p. 274; Cogliati Arano 1966; Cogliati Arano 1980a, p. 18; Nepi Scirè 1982.

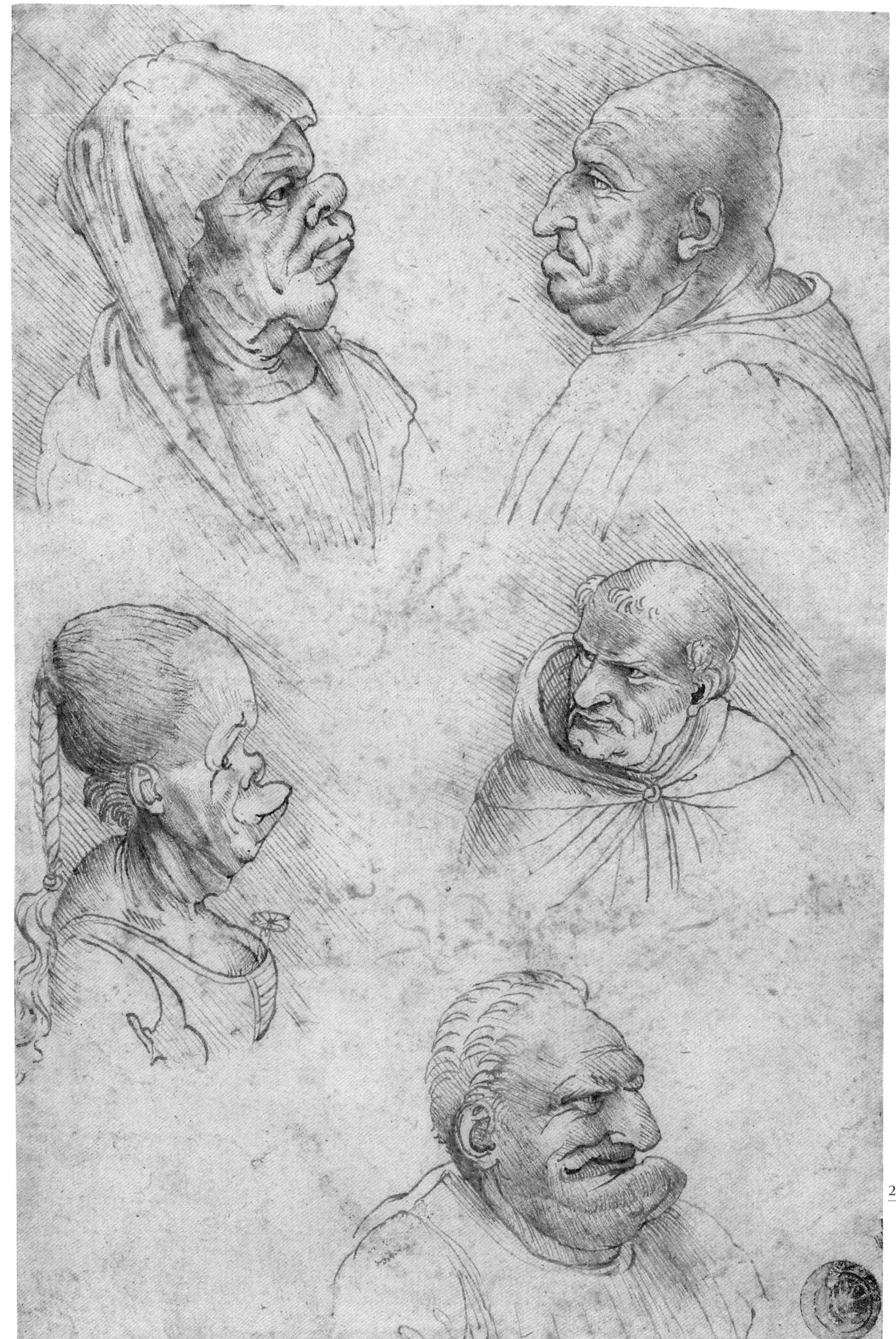

20.

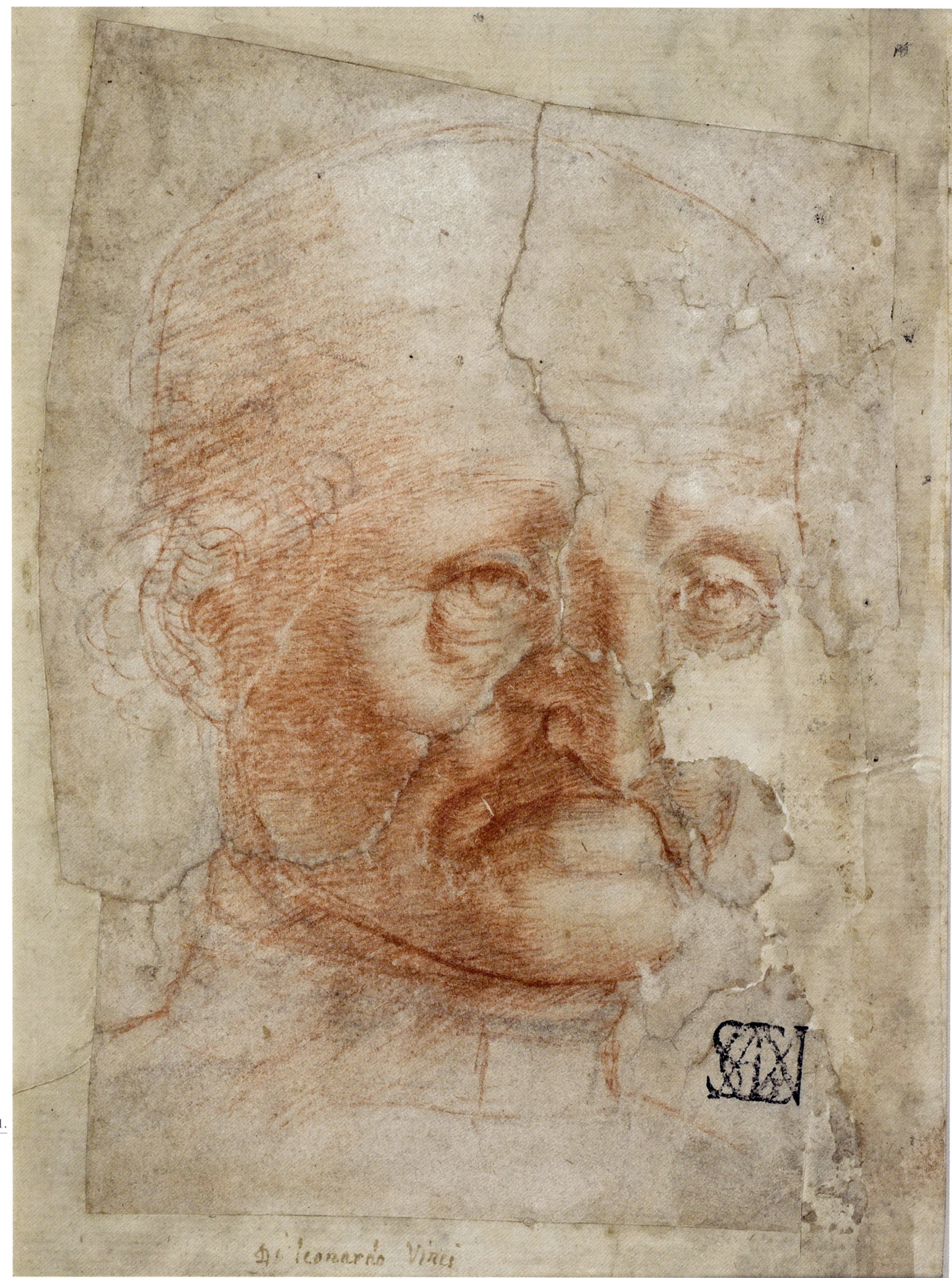

21.

21.

Francesco Melzi (1491–1570), attributed
Head of an old man, c. 1515–19
Red pencil over black pencil on backing paper, 142 × 107 mm
(backing 204 × 126 mm)
Milan, Veneranda Biblioteca Ambrosiana, Pinacoteca, cod. F 263 inf. 35*r*

The head drawn on this sheet, turned three-quarters to the right, has elements of detail in the face and less defined outlines in the rest. The drawing was mentioned by Jonathan Richardson in 1722 as a portrait of Artus in the *Libro di disegni*. Mara (2019, p. 96) acknowledges its origin in the *Libro di disegni* in the Biblioteca Ambrosiana by Giovan Battista Clarici and also specifies the page number, 31. It also retains its original backing in the *Libro di disegni*, as shown by the watercolour border on the lower margin, like the other sheets in that volume.
For a long time this face was interpreted as a portrait of Artus Gouffier de Boisy (1475–1519), being regarded as a replica of the physiognomy of the *condottiere* in the *Libro* cod. F 274 inf. 11 today attributed to Bramantino. Bossi, who was the first to propose the attribution to Francesco Melzi, still described it as 'Artus in red pencil and portrayed full face' (BAMi, Bossi, Ms. S.P. 6/13 sec. B. fols 156–157 in Mara 2010, p. 118). Gerli reproduces the head, plate XII. The attribution to Melzi was confirmed by Cogliati Arano (in Milan 1982, p. 137, no. 43) and Marani (1987, p. 95, no. 38; 1998, p. 377).
The face has features marked by old age, from heavy bags under the eyes to downturned corners of the toothless mouth, the whole marked by deep wrinkles. The type is part of the case studies of facial changes in old age, often associated with caricatures expressing mockery, with the morphological variations of the features being even more strongly marked.

RC

Bibliography
Richardson 1722, p. 24; Gerli 1784a, plate XII; Müntz 1899, p. 516; Beltrami and Fumagalli 1904, p. 12, no. VII, plate VII; Suida 1953, p. 60, plate LVIII, fig. 84; Cogliati Arano 1980b, p. 120, no. XIIb; Cogliati Arano, in Milan 1982, p. 137, no. 43, ill.; Pedretti and Dalli Regoli 1985, pp. 74–5, 95, no. 38; Marani 1987a; Ricardi 1991, p. 141, fig. 9; Kwakkelstein 1997, pp. 197–8; Marani 1998; Mara 2010, pp. 95 n. 151, 96 n. 156, 97 fig. 6; Bambach 2019, vol. III, p. 523, plate 13.33; Mara 2019, p. 361, fig. 7.

22.

Giovanni Agostino da Lodi (1495–1520)
Head of a bearded man, c. 1500–05
Grey pencil on paper, 165 × 131 mm
Milan, Gabinetto dei Disegni, Castello Sforzesco, inv. Sc. B 36

Coming from the Fondo di Santa Maria dei Miracoli at San Celso in Milan, the drawing entered the Castello Sforzesco in 1924. First published by Bora (1992, pp. 122 ill., 125, 134 n. 53,) as by Giovanni Agostino da Lodi, this black pencil study is notable for its caricatural physiognomy achieved by severely contracting the eyebrows with deep-set eyes and by deforming the gaunt facial features surrounded by a long, thick beard. Some expressive qualities of this study reappear in two male profiles in red pencil, one in the British Museum (inv. 1859.0806.76), the other in the Getty Museum, Los Angeles (inv. 90.GB.116), engraved by Gerli in 1784 (plate VI*) and traced by Bora (1991, p. 212, n. 27, figs 13, 14). Moreover, in the drawing in Milan its graphic value is apparent, with some influence from north European prints (Marani 2008, pp. 103–4, no. 55). Annalisa Perissa Torrini, developing an idea of Bora (1992, p. 125–7), suggests a possible similarity between the subject of the drawing and the head of Holofernes in Giorgione's *Judith* of about 1504, bringing out the influences between the Venetian painter and the followers of Leonardo (Perissa Torrini 2019b, pp. 62, 63, fig. 15). Then, the verisimilitude of the features and the psychological characters of the subject follow the models of Leonardo's *Last Supper*, so suggesting a date between about 1500 and 1505 for this drawing. Restored in 2012 by Letizia Montalbano at the Opificio delle Pietre Dure, the head was subsequently exhibited at the Castello Sforzesco, in 2012–13 at the Peterzano exhibition (Rossi 2012, p. 86 ill.) and in 2019–20 at *Intorno a Leonardo* (Milan, Castello Sforzesco, 10 September 2019–1 January 2020, curated by G. Mori and A. Alberti).

RA

Bibliography
Bora 1992, pp. 125–7, 134 n. 53, ill. p. 122; Bora, in Venice 1992, p. 372, no. 79; Marani 2003, p. 173; Rossi 2012, pp. 86–7, no. 5; Perissa Torrini 2019b, pp. 63, 62 ill.

23.

Giovanni Agostino da Lodi (1495–1520)
Head of a man, c. 1500–05
Red pencil on paper, 162 × 108 mm
Dresden, Staatliche Kunstsammlungen Kupferstichkabinett, inv. C 1923-14

This drawing in red pencil, a graphic medium widely used by the artist, should be seen as a possible study from life, given the extraordinary rendering of the physiognomic details. Coming from the London collection of William Mayor (Lugt 2799) with an attribution to Leonardo, the drawing was ascribed to Cesare da Sesto (Parker 1926, p. 36, plate 40) and tentatively to the Pseudo Boccaccino or to Giovanni Agostino da Lodi with an annotation by Poncey on the frame; finally it was attributed by Bora to the artist from Lodi (Bora 1987, p. 145, n. 7; Bora, in Milan 1987, p. 85, no. 30). Bora then confirmed this attribution elsewhere (Bora, in Venice 1992, pp. 372–3, no. 79; Bora 2003, p. 372, n. 96). The naturalism of the drawing reflects the influence of Leonardo's studies of states of mind in the drawings of the heads for the *Last Supper* (Bora, in Venice 1992, p. 372). An example is the *Study for James the Great* (Royal Collection/ HM King Charles III,

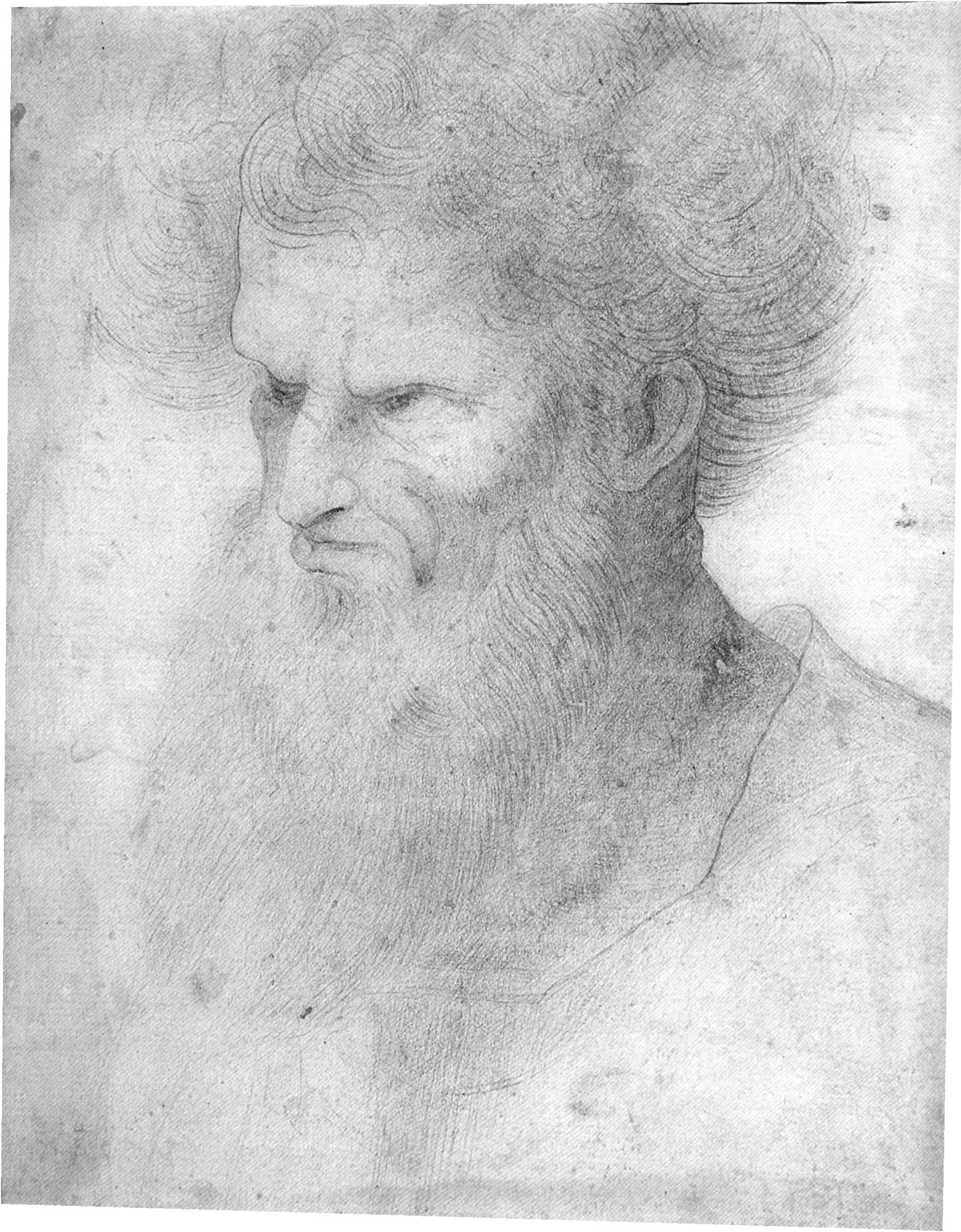

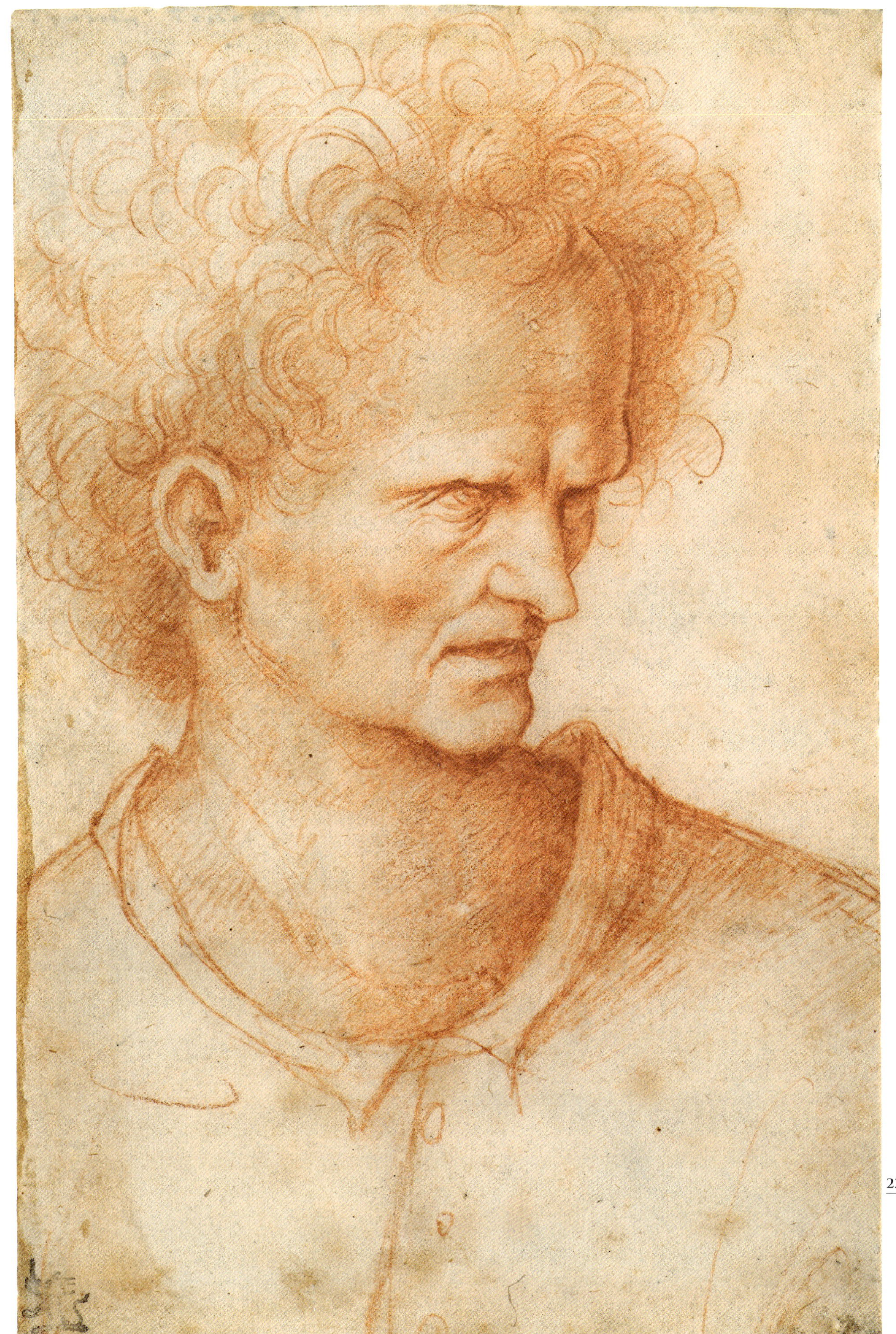

23.

inv. 912552), which closely matches the frowning gaze of wonder as well as the backward contraction of the bust. The drawing reveals Lodi's research during his work in Venice (Humfrey 1992, p. 43) between 1500 and 1505, when experimentation with red pencil, as a medium borrowed from Leonardo, was the basis of his studies of heads as examples of humanity, starting from the *Washing of the Feet* dated 1500 (Melli 2006, pp. 78–80, cat. 13). The modulation of the handling creates vibrant chiaroscuro passages that heighten certain details typically favoured by the artist: the great shock of hair, evident for example in the drawing in the Gallerie dell'Accademia in Venice (no. 262), or the angular, gaunt features of the face, similar to the male head in the Biblioteca Ambrosiana (cod. F 274 inf. 6), which seems to represent the same subject but viewed in profile.

RA

Bibliography

Parker 1926, pp. 36–7, plate 40 (Cesare da Sesto); Bora, in Milan 1987, p. 85, no. 30; Bora 1987, p. 145 n. 7; Bora, in Venice 1992, pp. 372–3, no. 79; Perissa Torrini, in Venice 1999, p. 104, no. 33; Bora 2003, p. 327 n. 96; Marani 2003, p. 175; Melli 2006, pp. 78–80, no. 13.

24.

Circle of Francesco Mazzola, called Parmigianino (1503–1540)
Head of a man in profile with chaplet of leaves, 1524-1526 (?)
Pen and brown ink on paper, 135 × 110 mm
Milan, Castello Sforzesco, Gabinetto dei Disegni, Au. A 50

The drawing represents a male head crowned by a leafy chaplet and with strongly marked features, in a profile that accentuates the long arched nose and gives prominence to the tiny ear.
There are no precise matches for the subject in Parmigianino's paintings or graphic works, but the attribution to the circle of the master is perfectly coherent. This appears in both the rapid pen and ink technique as well as the possible comparison with a large group of drawings with studies of heads, some of them with markedly caricatural features that Achim Gnann ascribed to the Roman period 1524–6 (Gnann 2007, nos 258–77), and in particular with the *Man in profile with a feathered hat* and with a long pointed nose (Chatsworth, Devonshire Collection, inv. OMD 774; Gnann 2007, I, p. 392, n. 277, II, p. 249). In the version etched by Lucas Vorsterman the Younger (c. 1624–1668) it bears the title *L'Archi Buffon di Parma* (Parma 2003, p. 141, no. 258).
From its heightened grotesque character, the head bore an original attribution in the typewritten inventory of the cabinet of drawings (also known as the Nicodemi Inventory) to the Milanese artist Giuseppe Arcimboldo (1527–1593), later doubted (by adding a pencilled '?' to the entry). The attribution to the circle of Parmigianino is recent, having been formulated for the exhibition *Simone Peterzano* at the Castello Sforzesco in Milan (Rossi 2012), as a result of a first examination of the core collection of its provenance.
The drawing's original location was the same as the large body of drawings attributable to the workshop of the master of Caravaggio, namely the vestry of Santa Maria presso San Celso in Milan, from which the Municipality of Milan in 1924 purchased two large volumes (with 2611 drawings) associated with the activities of the Accademia di San Luca. Once in the civic collections, they were detached from the pages where they had previously been kept, and were arranged by author and school on the principles of the nascent collection of drawings.

AA

Bibliography

Rossi 2012, pp. 82, 85 fig. 4.

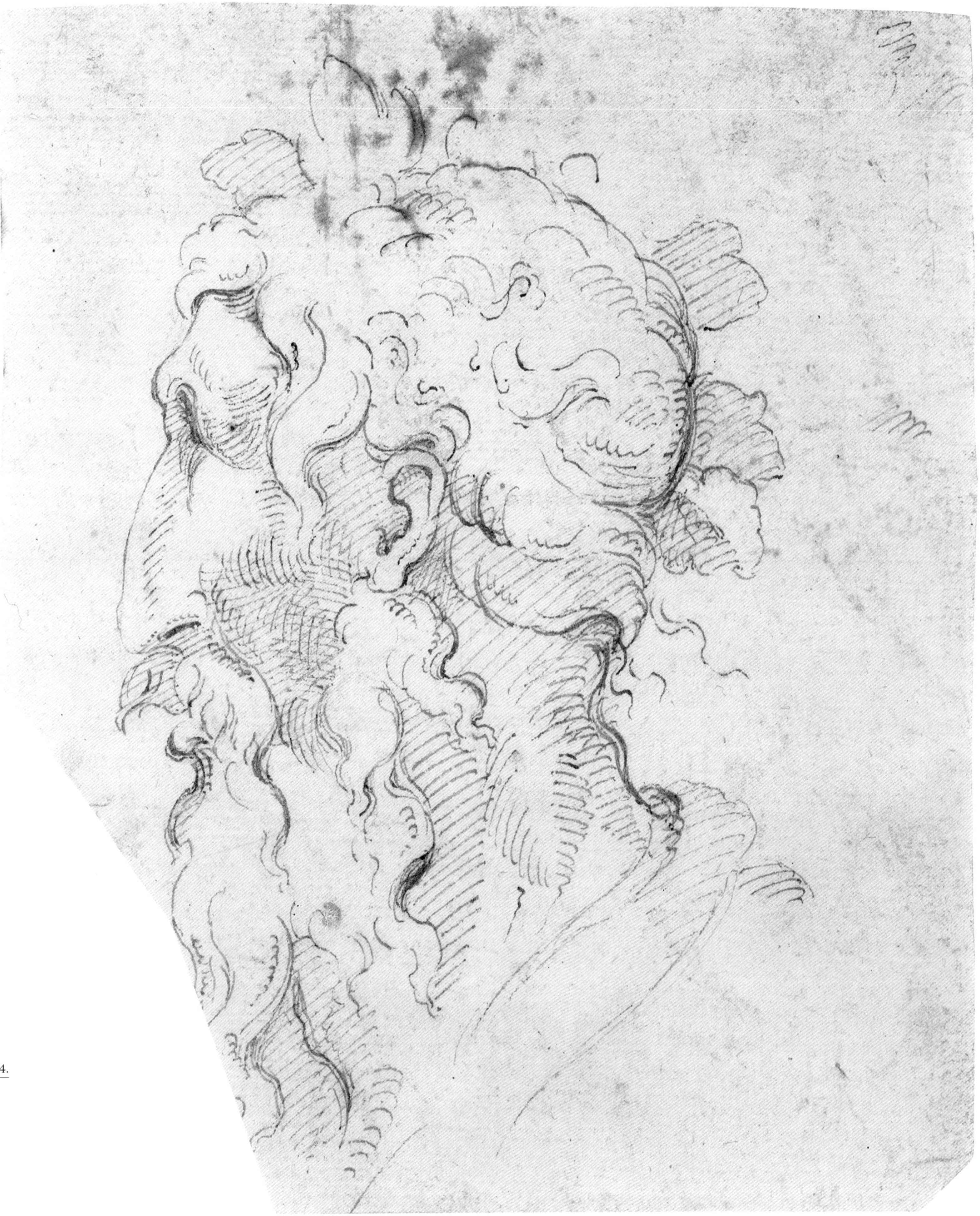

24.

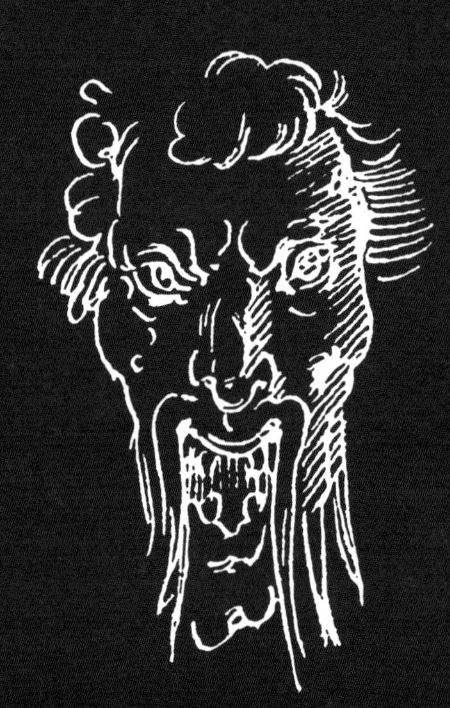

Ridiculous and Grotesque Heads in Northern Italy

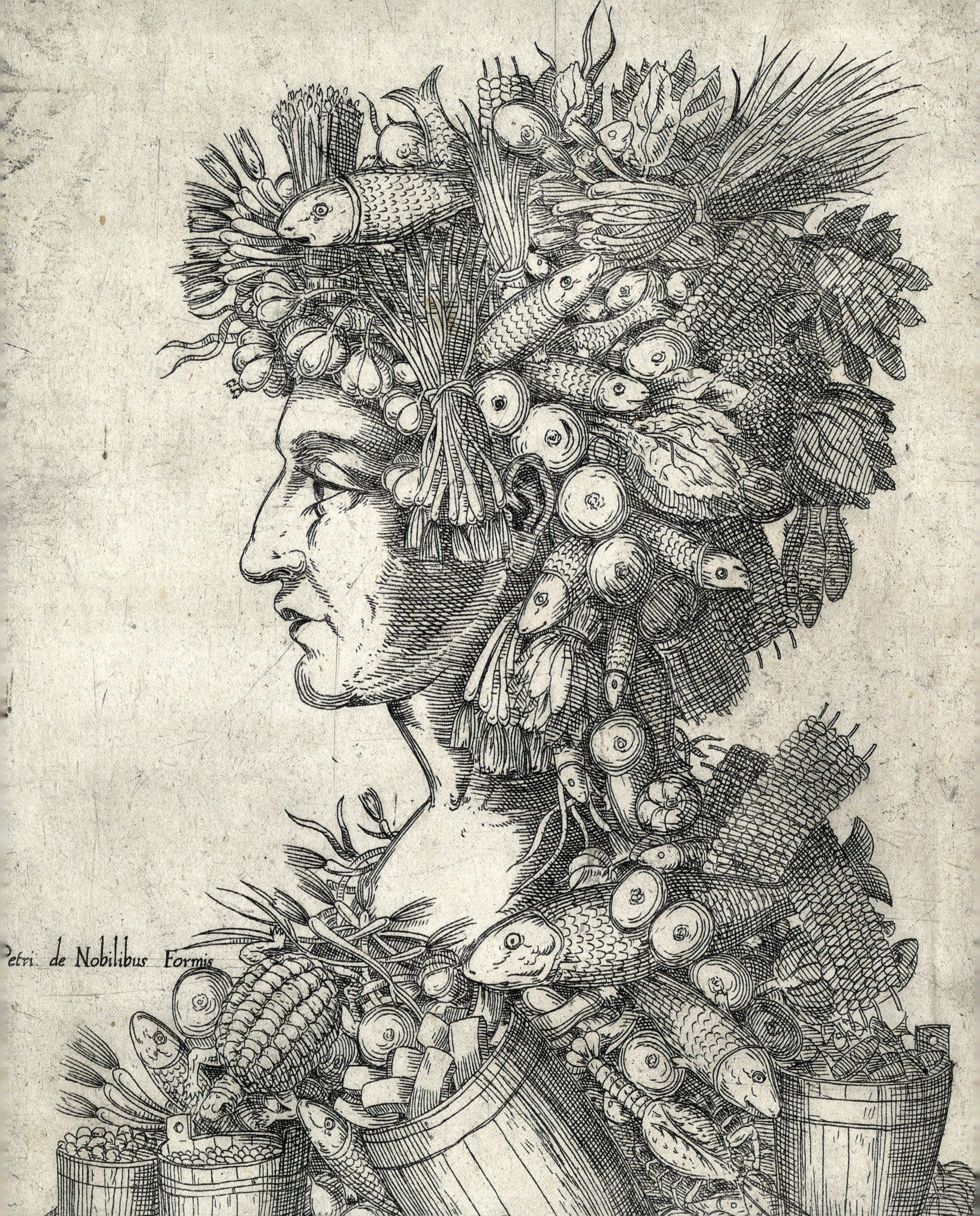
Petri de Nobilibus Formis

Laura Corti

From Paintings of the Ridiculous to the Naturalism of Annibale Carracci

OPPOSITE
Giovanni Antonio Brambilla, *Lent*, 1575–85, detail
Paris, Bibliothèque Nationale de France

The time and places of representations of the ridiculous in drawing, verse and music are clearly defined: the last decades of the sixteenth century and the early seventeenth century, in the area extending from Bologna to cover the middle section of the Po Valley. Those who made this flowering possible were not a large group, while their followers who spread it in reproducible ways to more extensive places and times were far more numerous. We should not, however, overlook the influence of Leonardo da Vinci in the genesis and dissemination of this genre, clearly expressed in other parts of this catalogue.

The artists who devoted themselves to these figurative jests, as Fernando Tempesti defined them in his book on caricature in the Alinari series[1] edited by Antonio Boschetto,[2] were divided into two classes: one was 'mannerist' – focused on the grotesque, analogies and visual metaphors[3] – and the other naturalist, in the wake of the Carracci's reinvention of the genre. But I believe that the dividing line is much narrower and the analogies far more explicit. And so attention turns to Bologna with its 'natural, expressive, "popular" component', as Francesco Arcangeli put it in 1970,[4] 'where difference is configured in expressive ways. Something extroverted and ardent, imaginative and abnormal, sensuous and pathetic, pervades the most typical and profound works . . . compared to the more incurably popular, introverted and melancholy restraint of Lombard art'.[5] Hence the geographical limitation is justified in this differently popular strand of artistic expression, even with their common 'Lombard' matrix, which had characterised it since the Middle Ages.

Giovan Paolo Lomazzo (Milan, 1538–1592) was active in Milan [fig. 1], as was the circle that gathered round him in the Accademia della Val di Blenio (*Vall d'Bregn*).[6] As a painter, Lomazzo travelled widely in Italy and Northern Europe and as a collector he was well placed among Milanese artists. In the Counter-Reformation climate of Carlo Borromeo's Milan, afflicted by the plague in 1577–8, he appears a somewhat eccentric figure, but this did not affect his work as an artist and thinker.

The Accademia della Val di Blenio (peripheral in name rather than substance) was founded in 1560 with the patronage of Count Pirro Visconti Borromeo of Brebbia, *Compa'* ('friend') *Cont*. From

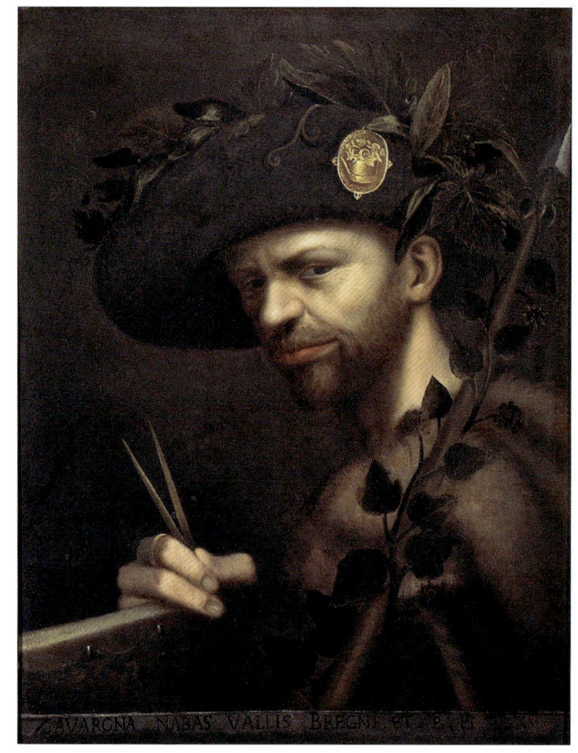

1.
Giovan Paolo Lomazzo
Self-Portrait, c. 1568
Milan, Pinacoteca di Brera

1568 for many years it was presided over by Lomazzo himself, *Compa' Zavargna*; because of the blindness that afflicted him in the early months of 1572, he became above all a writer and theorist of art [cats 37, 38]. The academy was 'poetic in nature', albeit anti-literary and irregular in a way that has been compared to that of actors. It brought together leading figures in the Lombard arts, ranging from the military engineer Giacomo Soldati[7] to the most varied creators of the sumptuary arts: embroiderers such as Scipione Delfinone, medallists such as Annibale Fontana, engravers, bronze workers such as Cesare Brambilla, as well as musicians such as Giuseppe Caimo[8] and famous theatrical figures such as Isabella Andreini.[9] Purportedly the academy was dedicated to porters, an occupation associated with men from the Alpine valleys. This association was also made in Tommaso Garzoni's treatise of 1585 on the art of memory, *La piazza universale di tutte le professioni del mondo e nobili et ignobili*,[10] which described them as individuals with a 'rascally' manner, 'coarse' attitude, 'clumsy' gait, 'ignorant' action and 'foolish' outlook. In addition, the language of porters had been used since the mid-fifteenth century in counter-cultural poetry, theatre and music to represent coarse mountaineers.[11] Their language was the unifying thread running through a *divertissement* that included the figurative arts. Lomazzo as a painter was the principal representative of this, obviously only until 1572. The mocking and libertarian spirit characteristic of the academy was not viewed kindly in the high Counter-Reformation, especially in Milan with Carlo Borromeo as its pastor. Living proof of this was one member, *Compa' Lovign*, who was banned from painting by a commission with a religious character. This was Aurelio Luini (Milan, 1530–1593), son of the well-known Bernardino Luini and Margherita Lomazzo. He produced the double drawing now in the Louvre, on the verso identified as *Compa' Braghetogn*, depicted with his teeth clenching a stick on which a bird is perched.

If the derivation is Leonardesque in its exaggerated lines, the inspiration, popular, playful and 'porterly', is characterised by that melancholy and introverted aspect of Lombard art that prompts thoughts of the atmosphere on the evening after any village fair. On the recto of the sheet appears

Compa' Digliagor [cat. 29] in a cap like a street artist (presumably he was not one), with crooked and coarse features, a sort of mask, less composed than the peasant in the Biblioteca Ambrosiana sketched by Luini with his hat jammed onto his lank hair but with a shrewd gaze [cat. 27]. Equally lively, although with a profile corresponding to his temperament, is *L'ostinat* ('obstinate') *Giambogn* [fig. 2], by an unknown hand, but certainly a member of the academy.

These mocking drawings in the dismembered notebook in the Ambrosiana belonged to its founder, Cardinal Federico Borromeo, a passionate connoisseur and collector with an interest in artistic expression quite different from that of his rigid cousin Carlo Borromeo's collection[12] forms a record of the likenesses of the members of the Accademia della Val di Blenio. They included *Sor* ('Sir') *Caputagn Nasotrà* (Francesco Giussano) [fig. 3] drawn by a hand still unidentified. It is not clear whether it is meant to depict him as frowning or 'asinine', but he was a skilled swordsman and appointed captain of the academy for this very reason.[13] Then there is the lesser known *Compa' Vanetto* of Lomazzo, shown wearing a tall hat that rivals his big nose [cat. 25].

The great chancellor of the academy was *Compa' Borgnin*, better known to posterity as Giovanni Ambrogio Brambilla (Milan?, recorded from 1560 to 1591). He won the greatest fame of them

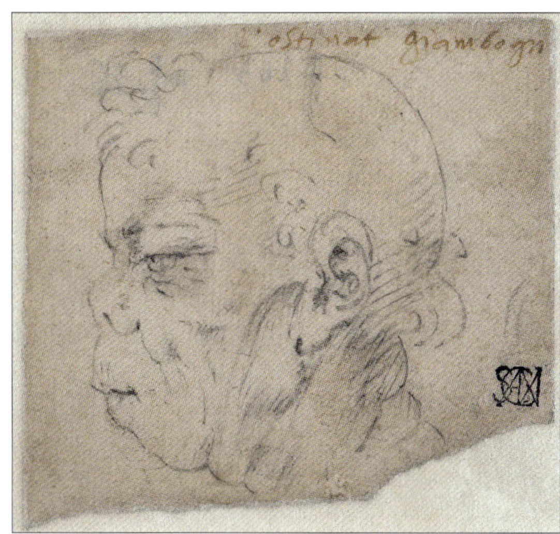

2

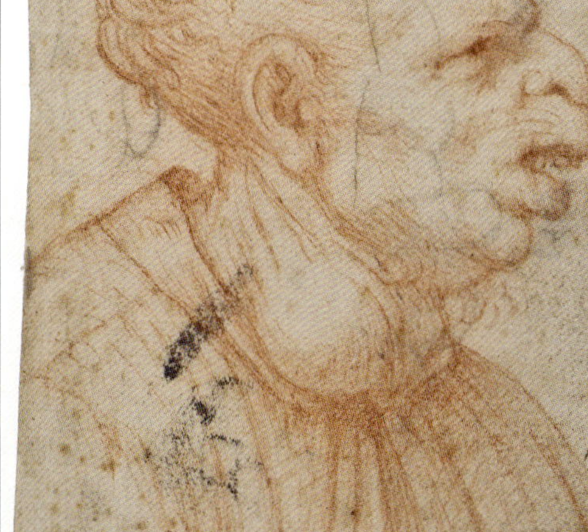

3

2.
Unknown artist
L'ostinat Giambogn,
last quarter of the sixteenth century
Milan, Veneranda Biblioteca Ambrosiana, Pinacoteca, cod. F 263 inf. 26

3.
Unknown artist
Portrait of Sor Caputagn Nasotrà, last quarter of the sixteenth century
Milan, Veneranda Biblioteca Ambrosiana, Pinacoteca, cod. F 274 inf. 23*r*

all for the medium in which he worked, the graphic arts of reproduction, engraving and etching, largely in Rome from 1575 to 1599. In his youthful years he was also a poet with fourteen of his associates, as Lomazzo records, in the *Rabisch dra Academiglia dor Compa' Zavargna, nabad dra Vall d'Bregn, ed tucch i su fidigl soghit, con ra ricenciglia dra Valada* ('Arabesques of the Academy of Compare Zavargna, Abbot of the Valley of Blenio, and of all his faithful subjects, with permission of the inhabitants of the Valley'), published in 1589.[14] In addition to the famous *Caricatures of the Gods of Olympus* (c. 1580), Brambilla depicted humorous subjects closely bound up with the Commedia dell'Arte, such as *Cooking a meal for Zan Trippu when he took a wife* (1583) accompanied by *Zan Trippu's beautiful dance performed at his wedding*, or comic subjects like the scene of the thief who attempts to break into a house but gets doused with water [fig. 4].[15] Like the Carracci, he observed everyday life with close interest and a classifying spirit: *Ritrato de queli che vano vendendo et lavorando per Roma* (portraits of the street vendors and workers in Rome, 1582), which was later widely circulated in the catalogue of the Remondini family of printers.

It is unsurprising that this confraternity, figuratively speaking, included *Merlin Cocalio* [cat. 26], whose real name was Teofilo Folengo (1491–1544). He was a Benedictine who was also the learned and restless author of the *Maccheronee*,[16] poems that adopted local parlance and popular patois to convey the Virgilian model to readers, mediated by the cultivated Quattrocento and Cinquecento literary tradition, both Latin and vernacular. The fundamental expressive impulse of this macaronic language was naturalistic, showing reality as a tangled skein, a mixture of good and evil, high and low, serious and bizarre, reality as determined by instincts and needs, rather than desires or ideals. As a poet, *Merlin Cocalio* drew his light and playful inspiration from wine and large dishes of gnocchi. But the drawing in the Ambrosiana has little in common with the well-known portraits of Folengo, such as the one attributed to Romanino in the Uffizi or the marble bust on his tomb at Campese, except perhaps his protruding chin.

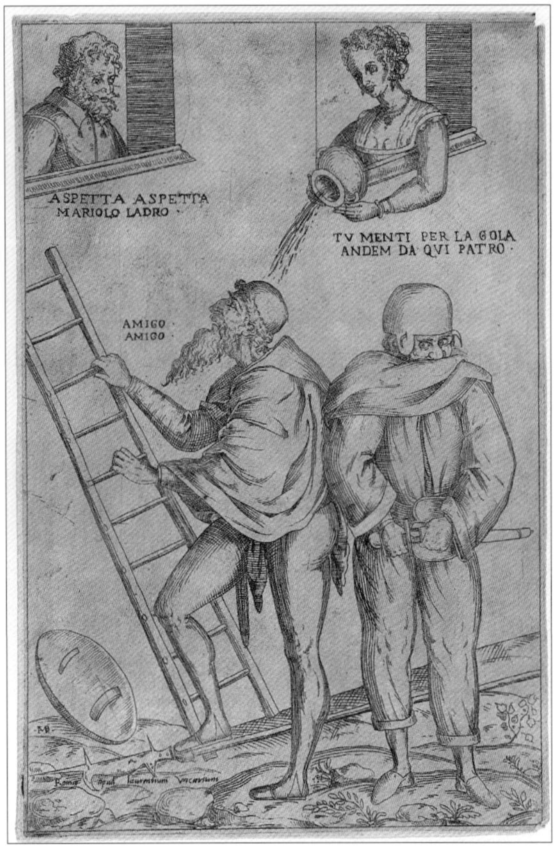

4

4.
Giovanni Ambrogio Brambilla, *Comic scene*, 1575–99
New York, The Metropolitan Museum of Art, inv. 53.686.16, gift of Harry G. Friedman, 1953

Giovanni Ambrogio Figino (1552/3–1608)[17] was not a member of the academy but a pupil of Lomazzo (having entered his workshop when he was eleven[18]). He was as versatile as his master, a gifted painter and prolific draughtsman, a poet appreciated by the men of letters of his time, including Tasso and Marino. Figino was celebrated by Girolamo Borsieri of Como, a collector, musician and adviser to Federico Borromeo, who dedicated madrigals of his own composition to him.[19] Through his relationship with Borsieri, it is clear that his physiognomic studies of highly exaggerated but not totally ridiculous drawings of heads, as in the rich collection in the Gallerie dell'Accademia in Venice [cat. 30], stemmed from his interest in a sort of anti-Renaissance, to use Eugenio Battisti's famous term. Yet they have all the elements of the Renaissance, as is clear in his interweaving of all the arts.

The accepted otherness of the painters of these images is clarified by the presence in the academy of the noble Pirro Visconti Borromeo, a prominent figure in Milan at the time, an art patron and collector, who laid out his *villa di delizia* with a nymphaeum at Lainate, near Milan, between 1585 and 1589. The architect Martino Bassi, the sculptor Francesco Brambilla and the painter Camillo Procaccini contributed to the work, with the support of Lomazzo, by that time blind, who suggested its bizarre decorations. The villa was completed and opened at the same time as the publication of the *Rabisch*, which formed its literary counterpoint and was dedicated to Visconti.

The 'academicians' dressed up as porters and simulated their language, performing rites in the name of Bacchus, protector of the fifty-eight taverns that Milan then boasted, and at the same time enjoying high patronage. And it is thanks to Dante Isella[20] that the porters' patois, which sounds alien, barbaric and droll, has been traced not to artifice but to the true Milanese dialect, with some elements borrowed from the speech of the Valle di Blenio.

The use of local dialects, moreover, the same device used for portraying the stock characters in the Commedia dell'Arte, was a constant feature of the time in music as well. An example is Orazio Vecchi's successful madrigal comedy *L'Amfiparnaso*, in which comic and tragic are united and the characters each speak their own language.[21] Also significant in popular culture and thus for artists were the festivals, such as that of *mosgett* (the little *moggio* or bushel) in Milan, when the offerings of the porters of the Porta Ticinese district were taken to the cathedral in a joyful procession. Another rite was also performed in Piazza Duomo, that of the *cavalasc*, a large wooden horse filled with fancy meats, capons and mortadella, which it then expelled as if defecating amid popular rejoicing. This scurrilous spectacle could hardly have appealed to the future Milanese saint Carlo Borromeo, who kept the offerings and suppressed the bacchanalia.[22]

This opulence of the poor's almost carnivalesque festivities must surely have struck the imagination of Giuseppe Arcimboldo (Milan, 1527–1593), himself the son of a painter, Biagio. His father was employed on the endless construction of the cathedral and Giuseppe grew up in contact with the artists active there from a wide range of backgrounds, mainly from north of the Alps. He left Milan for Vienna in 1562, summoned by the future Habsburg Emperor Maximilian II. Like every court

5.
Giuseppe Arcimboldo
Vertumno / Rudolf II,
1590
Stockholm, Skokloster slott,
inv. SKO 11615

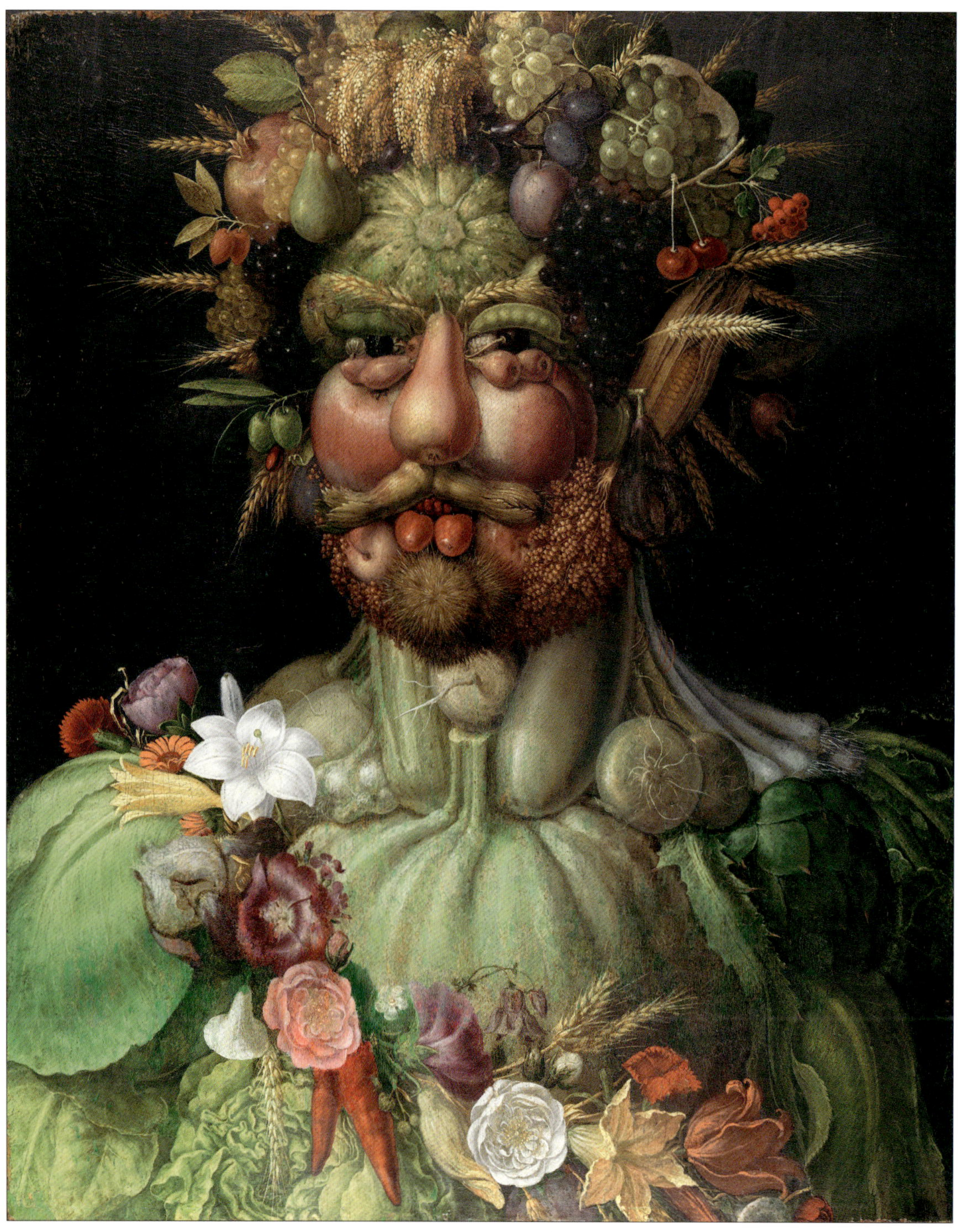

5

artist, he had spent most of his time designing the scenery for festivities and displays and providing drawings for the furnishings necessary for the success of the sovereign's activities. On Maximilian's death (1576) Arcimboldo continued to work for his son and successor Rudolf II, who moved the capital to Prague (1583). There he created a court completely unlike his father's, attracting scientists and scholars as well as charlatans from all over the known world. Here magnificence was reserved for the creation of a *Wunderkammer* and a *Kunstkammer*, of which only a faint trace remains in the Habsburg dynastic collections, after the dispersals due to the Thirty Years' War. How greatly Arcimboldo shared in the lively climate of scientific research at Rudolf's court appears from the animal and plant species that he depicted in his famous 'composite heads' [cats 34, 35], as well as the eighty-one plant varieties displayed in the head of *Spring* (species of European, Asian and American origin) or the sixty-one marine and freshwater organisms in *Water*, the first in the Seasons series and the second in the Elements, both produced for the imperial residence. Arcimboldo had also worked as a draughtsman of the 'things of nature' for the Bolognese scientist Ulisse Aldrovandi.[23] The next phase, taking us back to Milan, was to make his composite heads physiognomically recognisable, as in the case of *Vertumnus* or *Rudolf II* [fig. 5].

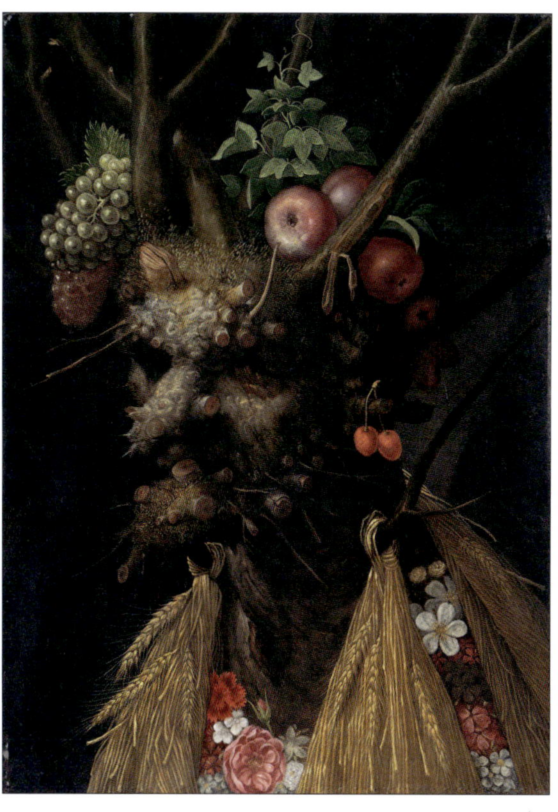

6

6.
Giuseppe Arcimboldo
Four Seasons in one head,
c. 1590
Washington, National
Gallery of Art,
inv. 2010.77.1

To Sylvia Ferino-Pagden we owe the critical rediscovery of Arcimboldo and the curatorship of important exhibitions. She observed in 2011: 'Play, like mirth, wit and jests are essential keys to understanding the Renaissance spirit. However, Arcimboldo's vagaries, jests, capriccios and whims should not be read simply as serious games and imperial allegories.'[24] His originality, I believe, is bound up with his twofold identity as an artist of the city and a court artist. The sources, above all Paolo Morigia, show that his creations were generated in Milan, before he went to Vienna and then Prague.[25] The same insight was earlier expressed in the first modern monograph on him by Benno Geiger (1954).[26] In fact we are indebted to Geiger, as author and collector, for discovering in Arcimboldo the forerunner of Surrealism.[27] The *Four Seasons in one head* [fig. 6], a work signed and given to his friend Gregorio Comanini, who describes it in *Il Figino overo del fine della pittura*, published in 1591,[28] epitomises the far more famous *Seasons*, whose personifications or portraits are a refined assemblage of seasonal produce. Although Arcimboldo was much the best-known, he was not the only Lombard to combine the fruits of the earth to create a physiognomy. Think of *Carnival* and *Lent* by Brambilla, issued as prints by Pietro de' Nobili in Rome [fig. 7].

When Bologna lost its independence, its cosmopolitan culture around its eminent international university began to cede to that of a papal legation, 'of courtly reflection, of hedonistic classicism'.[29] Several artists reacted against this, including Aspertini, the Carracci and Crespi. In various ways they drew their strength from the city's ancient popular roots. Without entering the long-running debate over the 'genre painting' of Annibale Carracci (Bologna, 1560–Rome, 1609), such as his *Bean Eater* or the versions of the *Butcher's Shop*,[30] we can focus on the natural aspects of his and their painting. The portrait in the Galleria Borghese, *Young man laughing* [fig. 8], captures the subject in a moment of joy, whose format and support suggest that it depicts a frequenter of the Accademia dei Desiderosi (1582), later known as the Accademia degli Incamminati, founded by the three Carracci. This portrait reflects the perfect way of grasping the moment, which finds its contrary in Annibale's drawing now at Chatsworth of a sad crippled youth inscribed 'Non so se Dio m'aiuta' ('I don't know if God will help me').[31]

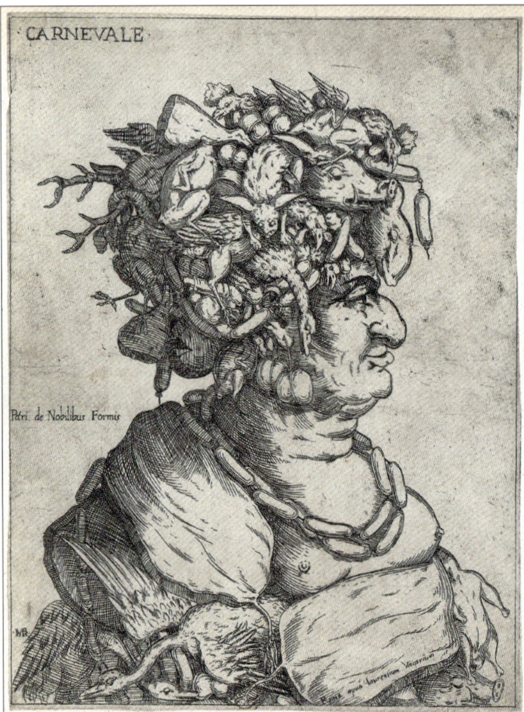

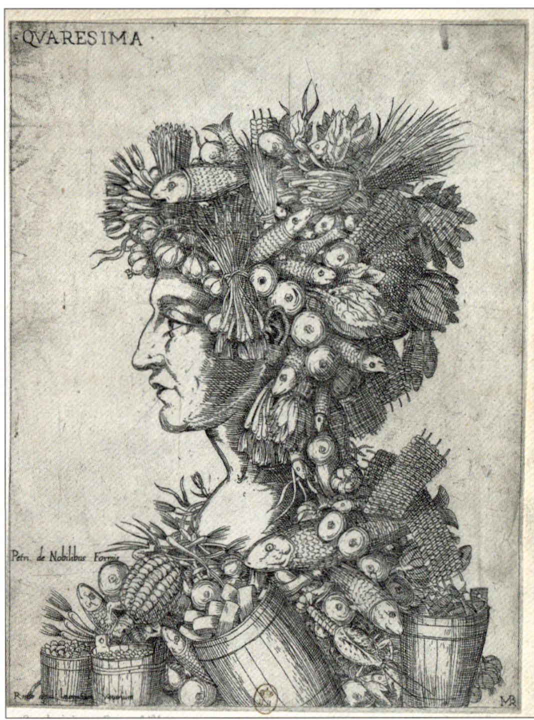

7

7.
Giovanni Antonio Brambilla, *Carnival and Lent*, 1575–85
Paris, Bibliothèque Nationale de France

That the Carracci's caricatures must reflect concrete sights is confirmed by Malvasia, who writes that, after the hours spent 'studying theories, Perspective and Architecture', due to weariness or the lateness of the hour, the Carracci would 'stroll through the town or outside the gates to take the air. And their favoured and fruitful pastime was to take note of especially unusual places, delightful landscapes, or chance encounters with people, making caricatures of the defects they noted in them'.[32]

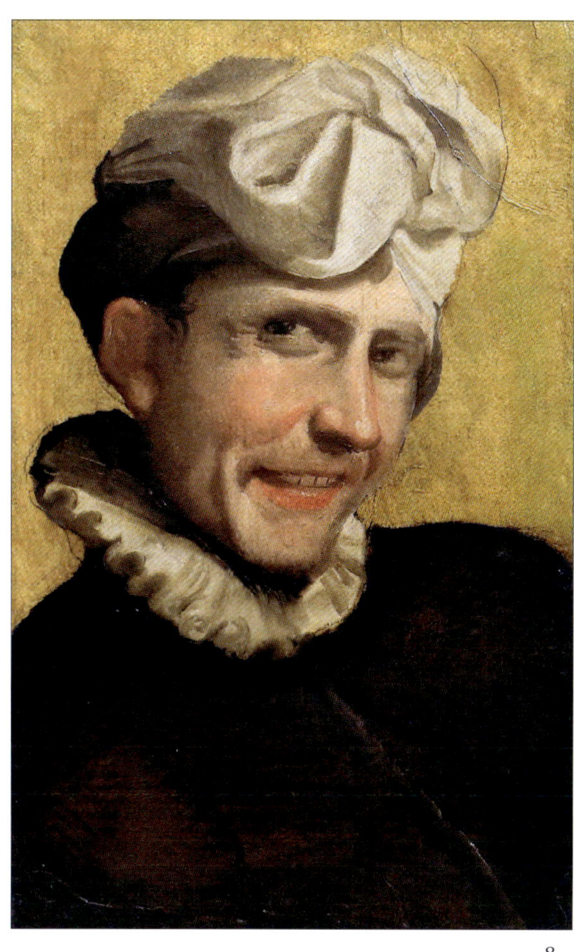

8.
Annibale Carracci
Young man laughing,
c. 1585
Rome, Galleria Borghese

In their walks outside the gates they would have observed that wholly Bolognese quality of civic religious life in the street, where each gate had a chapel attached to it, whose confraternity was required to keep the surrounding urban defences in good repair.[33] So if as the Carracci walked with their sketchbooks and listened to the balladeers, if they were lucky they might hear their friend Giulio Cesare Croce, called Dalla Lira, singing the *Canzonette ridicolose e belle*, which he composed to a violin accompaniment.[34] Their interest in this sound and human landscape is evident in *The Arts of Bologna*, drawn by Annibale Carracci. The series is all lost, except for the *Chimney Sweep* in Edinburgh[35] (like the character sung in the burlesque *villotta* by the Bolognese composer Filippo Azzaiolo[36]), but they are well known from the etchings Simon Guillain made of them.[37] In their daily walks in the city and their drawings from life in their academy, the Carracci set aside the magical, miraculous physiognomy of Cinquecento tradition in favour of experimental research into the natural. A clear example is the series of studies on the verso of the *Return of the prodigal son*, a drawing in Windsor in which academic study shares the space with caricatural sketches.

In this way satire with exaggerated bodily traits entered their vocabulary as 'their favoured and fruitful pastime'[38]. They laughed and made others laugh, even with their increasingly marked differences over the years. Their subjects, especially their 'grotesque portraits', are people and not personages, as in the sheet crowded with sketches of all kinds of faces seen from many different angles, with more or less evident naturalism.[39] Nor can we forget that at the university in Bologna, the scientist Ulisse Aldrovandi (1522–1605) was conducting his studies that culminated in the posthumous publication in 1642 of the *Monstruorum Historia*, and that he was in contact with the Carracci, if one accepts the attribution to Agostino of his portrait at the University Library in Bologna. But the painters certainly preferred to sketch quite naturally whoever observed with them the comedy of life, much more variegated than even the finest performance of their musician friend, the composer Adriano Banchieri, in his musical 'diverting entertainments' conceived at San Michele in Bosco in Bologna.

[1] *Maestri della caricatura: Leonardo, Aspertini, Michelangelo, Parmigianino, Passarotti, Zuccari, Carracci, Guercino, Callot, Bernini, Bocchi, Crespi, Ferretti, Ghezzi, Zanetti, Tiepolo etc.*, ed. L. Corti, intro. F. Tempesti (Florence: Alinari, 1979), p. 7.

[2] Antonio Boschetto (Bologna, 1918–1998) was a student of Roberto Longhi, with whom all his later work was connected as editor, curator and translator, as well as being an art historian. Longhi's executor, he played a significant part alongside Raffaele Mattioli in the creation of the Fondazione di Studi di Storia dell'Arte Roberto Longhi in Florence, acting as a board member and secretary of its first board of trustees.

[3] *Maestri della caricatura*, p. 11.

[4] F. Arcangeli, *Natura ed espressione nell'arte bolognese-emiliana* (Bologna: Alfa, 1970), p. 17.

[5] Ibid., p. 27.

[6] *Rabisch: Il grottesco nell'arte del Cinquecento. L'Accademia della Val di Blenio, Lomazzo e l'ambiente milanese*, ed. G. Bora, M. Kahn Rossi and F. Porzio, exh. cat. (Museo Cantonale d'Arte, Lugano, 28 March–21 June 1998; Milan: Skira, 1998).

[7] Giacomo Soldati was a military engineer (c. 1540–before 1600) active in the service of Filiberto di Savoia, after working on canals in Milan.

[8] Giuseppe Caimo (1545–1584), then a renowned composer mainly active in Milan, was the organist at Sant'Ambrogio and then at Milan's cathedral.

[9] See E. Tamburini, 'I comici gelosi e l'Accademia della Val di Blenio', in *Studi e Testimonianze in Onore di Ferruccio Marotti (III)*, in *Biblioteca teatrale*, 97–8, January–June 2011, pp. 175–95.

[10] T. Garzoni, *La piazza universale di tutte le professioni del mondo* (Venice: Giovan Battista Somasco, 1585; Florence: Olschki, 1996), vol. II, pp. 976–7.

[11] S. Favalier, 'La lingua facchinesca o l'illusione della lingua bergamasca', *Italies*, 24, 2020 (Illusions et Chimères), pp. 105–16.

[12] The book of drawings was reconstructed by S. Mara, 'Il *Libro di disegni* delle Biblioteca Ambrosiana', *Arte Lombarda*, CLVIII–CLIX, 1–2, 2010, pp. 74–118.

[13] E. Pezzini, 'Significato storico e lettura dei "Rabisch" di Giovanni Paolo Lomazzo', *Italique*, 22, 2020, pp. 81–105.

[14] For a recent study with extensive bibliography see E. Pezzini, 'Lomazzo e i "Rabisch": status quaestionis e nuove prospettive', in *Italianistica*, 49, 2020, pp. 177–212.

[15] Another example is in New York, The Metropolitan Museum of Art, inv. 53.686.16 (274 × 183 mm).

[16] [T. Folengo], *Merlini Cocai poëta e Mantuani Liber Macaronices* (Venice: Alexandri Paganini, 1517).

[17] M. Pavesi, *Giovanni Ambrogio Figino pittore* (Santa Palomba, Rome: Aracne, 2018).

[18] M. Pavesi, 'Una "Flagellazione" di Giovanni Antonio Figino al Museo del Prado', *Nuovi studi: rivista di arte antica e moderna*, 15, 2009 [2010], pp. 189–213.

[19] See https://www.italianisti.it/pubblicazioni/atti-di-congresso/la-letteratura-italiana-e-le-arti/Rosa%20Giulio%20

-%20Testo%20letterario%20e%20specifico%20filmico%20i%20livelli%20estetici%20della%20transcodifica%20(1)(1).pdf (accessed 30 September 2022).

[20] D. Isella, *Lombardia stravagante: testi e studi dal Quattrocento al Seicento tra lettere e arti* (Turin: Einaudi, 2005).

[21] The famous *L'Amfiparnaso* by Orazio Vecchi (1550–1605) was published in Venice in 1597 but written and performed in Modena in 1594. It is still performed occasionally. The characters are taken from the Commedia dell'Arte and the composition brings together all the musical forms then in vogue. See N. Pirrotta, '"Commedia dell'Arte" e opera', *Musical Quarterly*, XLI, 3, 1955, pp. 305–24.

[22] L. Bertolini, 'L'estetica del grottesco nelle *Rime* di Giovan Paolo Lomazzo', in *Fillide. Il sublime rovesciato: comico, umorismo e affini*, 24, 2022, pp. 1–15.

[23] G. Olmi and L. Tongiorgi Tomasi, 'Giuseppe Arcimboldo tra natura, arte e artificio', in *Arcimboldo*, ed. S. Ferino-Pagden, exh. cat. (Gallerie Nazionali di Arte Antica, Palazzo Barberini, Rome, 20 October 2017–11 February 2018; Milan: Skira, 2017), p. 85.

[24] S. Ferino-Pagden, 'I mestieri e gli esordi della caricatura', in *Arcimboldo: artista milanese tra Leonardo e Caravaggio*, cur. S. Ferino-Pagden, exh. cat. (Palazzo Reale, Milan, 10 February–22 May 2011; Milan: Skira, 2011), p. 157.

[25] G. Berra, 'L'Arcimboldo "c'huom forma d'ogni cosa": capricci pittorici, elogi letterari e scherzi poetici nella Milano di fine Cinquecento', in ibid., pp. 283–313.

[26] For a detailed examination of Benno Geiger's 1954 study see F. Porzio, 'Arcimboldo: le Stagioni "milanesi" e l'origine dell'invenzione', in ibid., pp. 221–53.

[27] B. Geiger, *I dipinti ghiribizzosi di Giuseppe Arcimboldo: pittore illusionista del Cinquecento (1527–1593)*, with note on Arcimboldo as musician by L. Levi and epilogue by O. Kokoschka (Florence: Vallecchi, 1954); followed by F.-C. Legrand and F. Sluys, *Arcimboldo et les arcimboldesques* (Paris: Editions d'Art André de Rache, 1955). See also the recent *Face à Arcimboldo*, cur. C. Parisi and A. Horvath, exh. cat. (Centre Pompidou-Metz, 29 May–22 November 2021; Paris: Éditions du Centre Pompidou-Metz, 2021).

[28] Washington DC, National Gallery of Art, 2010.77.1. First shown in *Arcimboldo 1526–1593*, cur. S. Ferino-Pagden, exh. cat. (Musée du Luxembourg, Paris, 15 September 2007–13 January 2008; Kunstistorisches Museum, Vienna, 12 February–1 June 2008; Milan: Skira, 2007), fig. 5.

[29] Arcangeli, *Natura ed espressione*, p. 32.

[30] S. Ebert-Schifferer, 'Quando mangiare fagioli fa una rivoluzione: considerazioni su realismo e "genere"', in *Nuova luce su Annibale Carracci*, ed. S. Ebert-Schifferer and S. Ginzburg (Rome: De Luca, 2011), pp. 21–39.

[31] Chatsworth, Duke of Devonshire Collection, *A hunchback boy*, red chalk with red wash on paper, 264 × 225 mm; C. Robertson, 'Annibale Carracci and Invenzione: Medium and Functions in Early Drawings', *Master Drawings*, 35 (1), 1997, pp. 3–42, fig. 19.

[32] C. C. Malvasia, *Felsina Pittrice: vite de' pittori bolognesi*, 2 vols (1678; Bologna: Guidi all'Ancora, 1841), vol. I, pp. 306–11.

[33] M. Fanti, 'Le chiese sulle mura', in *Le mura perdute: storia e immagini dell'ultima cerchia fortificata di Bologna*, ed. G. Roversi (Casalecchio di Reno, Bologna: Grafis, 1985), pp. 97–124.

[34] Giulio Cesare Croce (Bologna 1550–1609), a prolific author, best known for *Bertoldo e Bertoldino*, was portrayed by Agostino Carracci on the title page of its 1608 edition: see M. Pigozzi, 'Annibale Carracci, Giulio Cesare Croce e Agostino Carracci', in *Le arti e il cibo: modalità ed esempi di un rapporto*, ed. S. Davidson and F. Lollini, conference proceedings (Università di Bologna, 15–16 October 2012; Bologna: Bononia University Press, 2014), pp. 231–43. For a list of the works by Croce intended to stir laughter see L. Strappini, 'Croce', in *Dizionario Biografico degli Italiani*, vol. XXXI (Rome: Istituto della Enciclopedia Italiana, 1985).

[35] Edinburgh, Scottish National Gallery of Modern Art (Modern Two), Print Room, D 4984.

[36] *Dal Primo libro de Villotte alla Padoana* (Venice: Antonio Gardano, 1557); R. Nielsen, 'Azzaiolo, Filippo', in *Dizionario Biografico degli Italiani*, vol. IV (Rome: Istituto della Enciclopedia Italiana, 1962).

[37] G. Sapori, 'Risfogliando le "Arti di Bologna": Carracci, Agostini, Massani, Algardi, Guillain', in Ebert-Schifferer and Ginzburg, ed., *Nuova luce su Annibale Carracci*, p. 130.

[38] Malvasia, *Felsina Pittrice*, pp. 306–11.

[39] London, British Museum, cat. Pp, 3.17; D. Benati, in *Annibale Carracci*, ed. D. Benati and E. Riccòmini, exh. cat. (Museo Civico Archeologico, Bologna, 22 September 2006–7 January 2007; Chiostro del Bramante, Rome, 25 January–6 May 2007; Milan: Mondadori Electa, 2006), no. VIII.11.

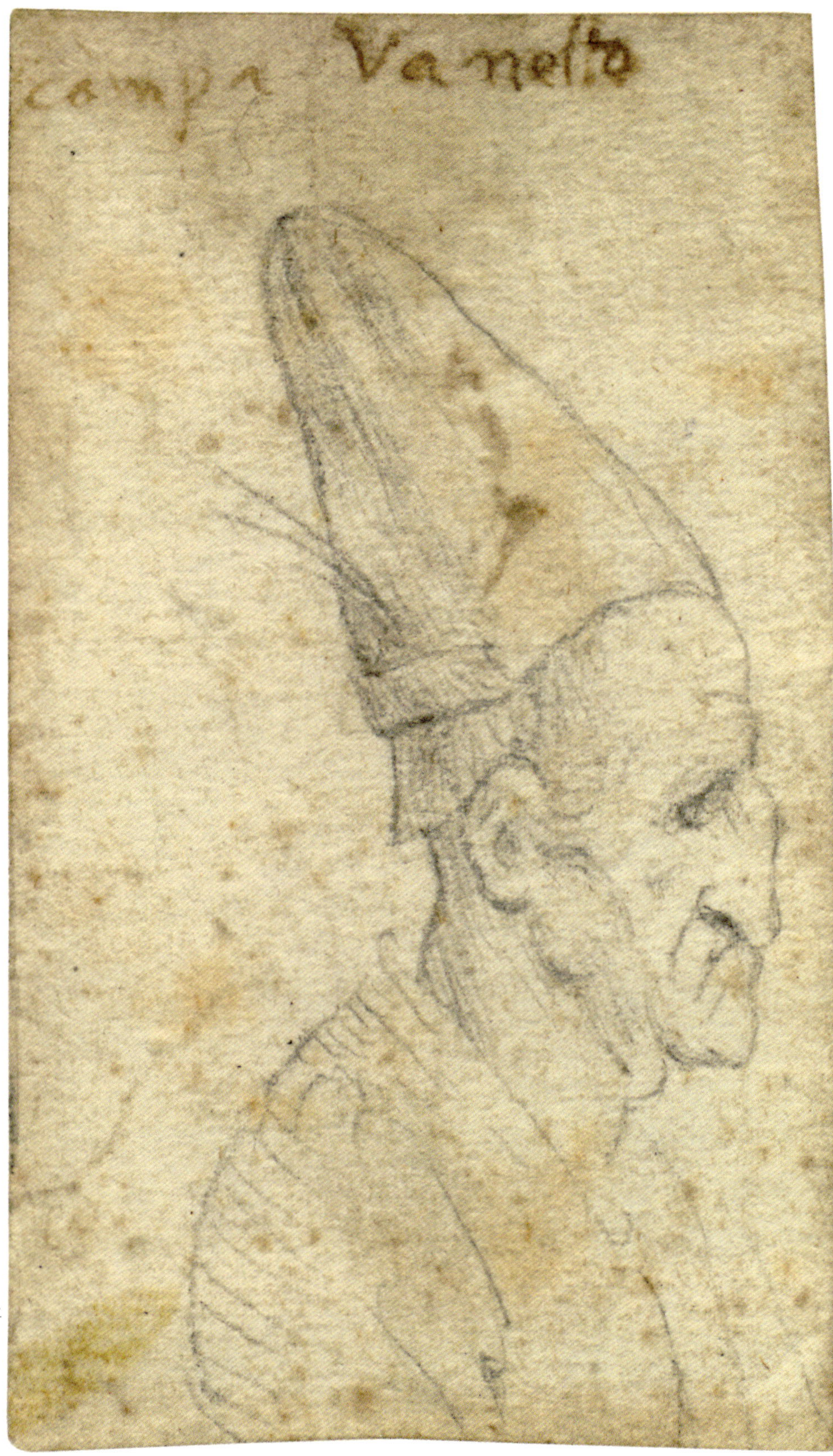

25.

25.
Giovan Paolo Lomazzo (1538–1600)
Compa' Vanetto, c. 1560–70
Black pencil on paper, 76 × 46 mm
Milan, Veneranda Biblioteca Ambrosiana, Pinacoteca, cod. F 274 inf. 26b

On the same sheeet:
Anonymous, *Male head*, no date
Black pencil on paper
Milan, Veneranda Biblioteca Ambrosiana, Pinacoteca, cod. F 274 inf. 26a

Included in Gerli's collection in 1784 (plate XXIV) and published in 1939 by the Commissione Vinciana (Venturi 1939, V, plate CCXIV, fig. 5), this grotesque profile in black pencil with curious conical headgear is accompanied by the inscription 'Compa' Vanetto', revealing that it is connected with the Accademia della Val di Blenio. As recently shown, the drawing was part of a sheet in the *Libro di disegni* by Giovan Battista Clarici (1542–1602) (Mara 2010, p. 106, n. 231; Mara 2019, p. 364), together with two grotesque heads by Leonardo, one male, the other female (Milan, Biblioteca Ambrosiana, cod. F. 274 inf. 27a-b) facing each other (M. Rossi, in Milan 1998, p. 90, no. 28), and another small male face likewise caricatured (Milan, Biblioteca Ambrosiana, cod. F 274 inf. 26a; Cogliati Arano 1982, p. 149, no. 55). Assigned to an imitator of Leonardo by Cogliati Arano (1982, p. 154, no. 61), and as a weak imitation of a study by Leonardo (Clayton 2002, p. 84, no. 34, n. 2), the drawing repeats the study by Leonardo drawn in black pencil in the Morgan Library and Museum, New York (inv. 1993.418), while recalling the profile with a conical hat in the Spencer collection, Inv. II 31 (Trutty-Coohill 1993, p. 50, fig. 13; Paliaga 1995a, p. 152, n. 40, fig. 22;), and that on sheet inv. 2571br in the Louvre (Marani 2008, p. 156, cat. 103). The identity of the figure depicted is evoked in the writing in porter's dialect present in other grotesque portraits in the Ambrosiana associated with the Accademia della Val di Blenio, with Lomazzo's hand identified in the inscriptions (Mara 2019, p. 364). The attribution of the drawing, already limited to Lomazzo's circle (Paliaga 1995a,

p. 152, n. 41), largely matches his manner between the 1560s and 70s. This appears in the grotesque style also apparent in the set of grotesque male faces in seveeral pictorial works by Lomazzo himself (Pavesi 2013, pp. 158–9, 160, figs 1, 3).

RA

Bibliography
Gerli 1784a, plate XXIV; Venturi 1939, V, plate CCXIV, fig. 5; Cogliati Arano 1981, pp. 6–7, ill.; Cogliati Arano 1982, p. 154, no. 61, fig. 61; Paliaga 1995a, p. 152, fig. 22; Perissa Torrini, in Venezia 1999, p. 100, no. 31; Mara 2010, p. 106; Marani 2017, p. 192, fig. 13.

26.

Giovan Paolo Lomazzo (1538–1600)
Cocal, c. 1560–70
Red pencil on paper, 105 × 86 mm
Written at the top: 'Sig. Cocal'
Milan, Veneranda Biblioteca
Ambrosiana, Pinacoteca,
cod. F 274 inf. 45c

On the same sheet:
Leonardesque artist
Head of a bald man in profile facing right, c. 1560–70
Red pencil, 93 × 84 mm
Milan, Veneranda Biblioteca
Ambrosiana, Pinacoteca,
cod. F 274 inf. 45a

Giovan Paolo Lomazzo (attributed)
Merlin Cocalio, c. 1560–70
Black pencil, 85 × 75 mm
Milan, Veneranda Biblioteca
Ambrosiana, Pinacoteca,
cod. F 274 inf. 45b

Leonardesque artist
Caricatural male and female profiles facing each other, late sixteenth century
Pen and brown ink, 93 × 127 mm
Milan, Veneranda Biblioteca
Ambrosiana, Pinacoteca
cod. F 274 inf. 45d

Leonardesque artist
Two grotesque heads in profile,
late sixteenth century
Pen and brown ink, 80 × 124 mm
Milan, Veneranda Biblioteca
Ambrosiana, Pinacoteca,
cod. F 274 inf. 45e

This grotesque male profile with a voluminous conical hat with upturned brim is glued, with four other studies of grotesque heads (Rossi, in Milan 1998, p. 88, no. 27, ill.), to paper backing that coincides with the verso of page 57 of the *Libro di disegni* by Giovan Battista Clarici (Mara 2010, p. 100, fig. 7; Mara 2019, pp. 345–81). It was engraved by Gerli (plate XIVb) and faces a second caricature (cod. F 274 inf. 40*r*) not present on the sheet in Clarici's *Libro*. The writing in pen, which it has been suggested reads 'Sig. Cocal' (Mara 2010, p. 100), shows that the profile comes out of the Accademia of the Val di Blenio (Porzio, in Ferino Pagden 2011a, pp. 246 ill., 373 no. 262), a possible grotesque portrait of one of its members, and close to Lomazzo's compositional and stylistic techniques between about 1560 and 1570. The deformity of the physical features, entrusted to red pencil, such as the long nose flattened towards the upper lip and the severe fixity of the frowning gaze, can be compared with the profile of the *Sor Caputagn Nasotra* in the Ambrosiana (cod. F 274 inf. 23*r*), from Clarici's *Libro*. Here the inscription written in pen in porter's dialect has been attributed to Lomazzo (Mara 2019, pp. 364–6, fig. 10c).
This drawing might also reflect a hypothetical knowledge of Leonardo's drawings in the possession of Francesco Melzi, as suggested by the *Merlino Cocalio* on the Clarici sheet, to the left of ours (Mara 2010, fig. 7), derived from Leonardo's drawing in the collection of the Duke of Devonshire at Chatsworth, inv. OMD 824 C (Paliaga 1995a, p. 151, figs 16, 17). And it might be connected with the contents of Leonardo's 'libricciulo' with fifty drawings in 'red pencil' of 'old people and peasant women, and deformed peasant women', owned by Aurelio Luini, which was an indispensable model for the artists of the Val di Blenio in the years when Lomazzo was its 'abbot' (Mara 2020, pp. 223–4).

RA

Bibliography
Rossi, in Milan 1998, p. 88, no. 27; Porzio, in Ferino-Pagden 2011a, p. 246 ill., no. 262, p. 247, no. 301; Mara 2010, p. 100, fig. 7.

27.

Aurelio Luini (1530–1593)
Grotesque head with hat, 1560s
Pen and ink on paper, 104 × 82 mm
Milan, Veneranda Biblioteca
Ambrosiana, Pinacoteca,
cod. F 263 inf. 31

Caricatured with conspicuously irreverent and deformed features, this head in profile with a hat is by an artist of the Accademia della Val di Blenio, clearly identified by its stylistic qualities as Aurelio Luini (Bora 1989, p. 101, fig. 17), present in Lomazzo's 'tables of names' (Agosti, Agosti 1997, p. 20 n. 50, p. 54 n. 308, p. 66 n. 366). As in the series recently analysed by Tantardini and ascribed to Aurelio Luini, datable to between 1560 and 1570 in the Val di Blenio (Tantardini 2016, pp. 215–17, figs 1–5), this male face also attains an impressive level of physiognomic exaggeration by the freely drawn lines. The Leonardesque deformities of the profile seem to recall that booklet containing 'old people and peasant women, and deformed peasant women laughing heartily' for a total of fifty drawings in 'red pencil' by Leonardo, recorded as in the possession of Aurelio Luini da Lomazzo in both the *Trattato* and the *Idea del tempio della pittura* (Lomazzo 1973-1975, vol. I, p. 290, n. 2; vol. II, p. 315 n. 3). Without rejecting the theory of the booklet and its contents, not necessarily autograph (Bora 1989, p. 90), the reference to the 'Monstrous faces by Leonardo in the keeping of Aurelio Lovino', reported by Lomazzo, gives a significant value to the free and confident handling (Bora, in Lugano 1998, p. 182, nos 34, 35; Rossetti 2021, pp. 371–2, n. 77). The drawing could depict the head of a countryman or peasant, in keeping with the type repeated in the other drawings. Examples are *Compa' Bragheton*, the profile of a man in a hat, with a stick clenched between his teeth on which a bird is perched; the verso

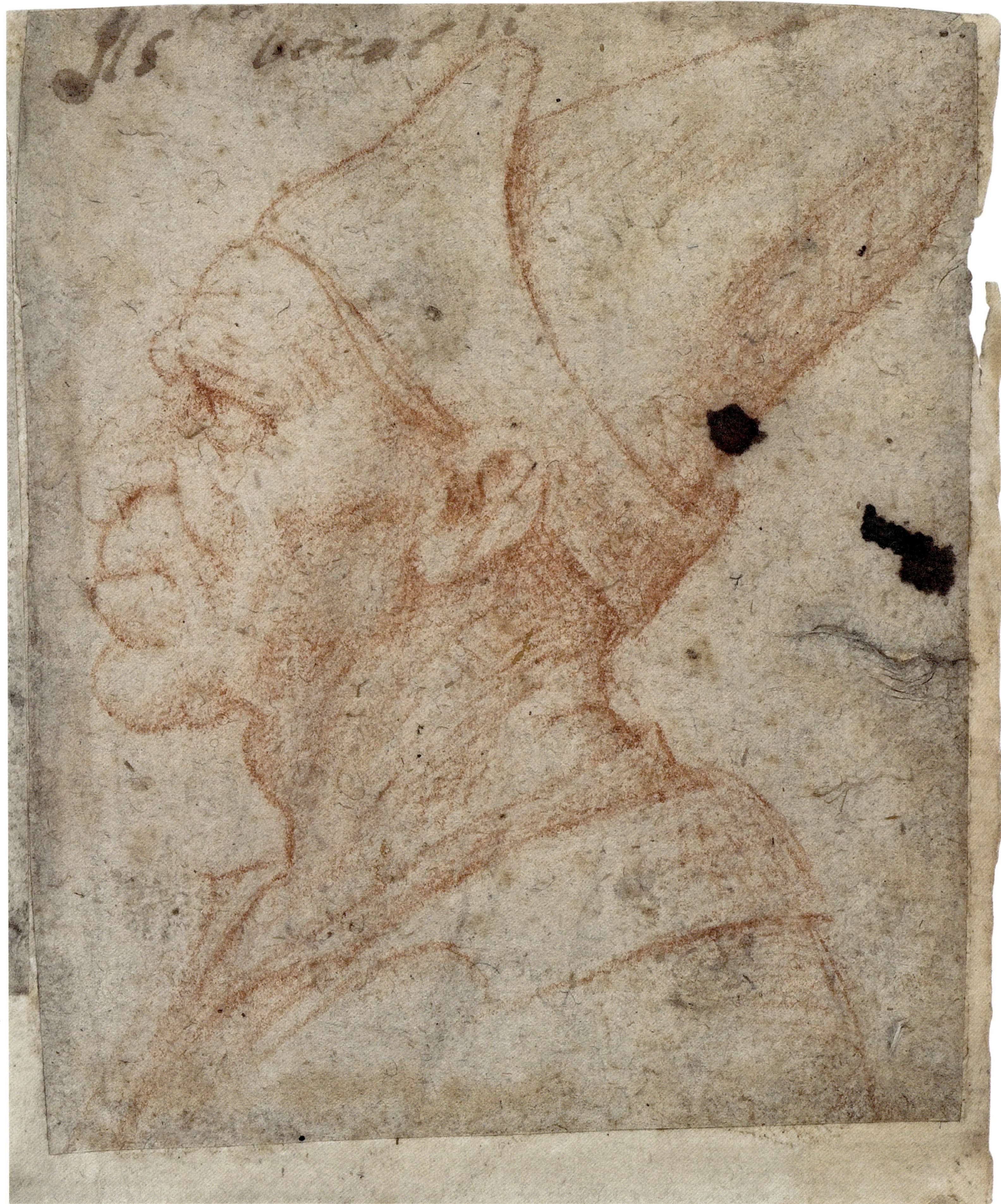

26.

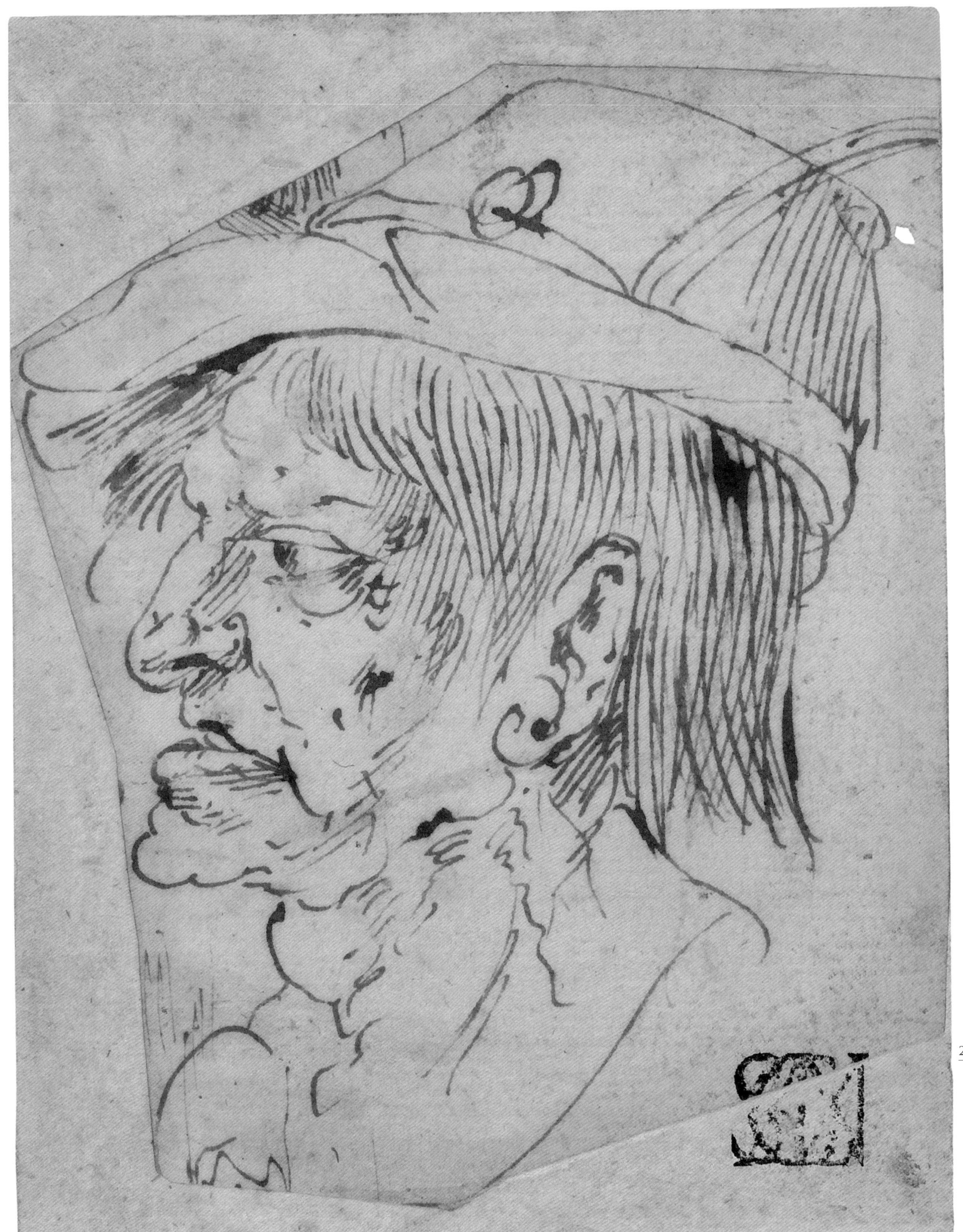

27.

of *Compa' Digliagor* in the Louvre (inv. 2652), a figure with whom he seems to share the porterly type; and the *Head of a Peasant*, in the Musei Civici, Pavia (Malaspina Collection, no. 68), assigned to Luini by Bora (1998, p. 51, fig. 21).

RA

Bibliography

Bora 1989, p. 101, fig. 17; Lomazzo 1993, p. XIV, n. 9, fig. 6; Bora 1998b, p. 51, fig. 20; Bora, in Lugano 1998, p. 182, nos 34-35; Porzio 2011, p. 242; Porzio, in Ferino-Pagden 2011a, p. 373, no. 257; Tantardini 2016, p. 218, fig. 2.

28.

Giovanni Ambrogio Figino
(1552/1553–1608), attributed
Homo ridiculo, c. 1565–70
Black pencil on paper, 178 × 128 mm
Bergamo, Fondazione Accademia Carrara, inv. 478

The title of this drawing derives from the inscription at the top right, 'Menari/ homo ridiculo'. It shows the bust of a male figure viewed from the front, wearing a robe and hat of the Quattrocento. The character of the face, without stressing any particular physical defects, is brought out by a mocking smile and a sleepy expression framed by a thick, long beard. Made known by Fiorio as a Lombard drawing datable to the 1520s (Fiorio, in Rossi 1982, p. 15), it has been compared by Marani to the drawing technique of Giovanni Ambrogio Figino (Marani 1987a, p. 242, no. 48, fig. 165), and hesitantly to that of Lomazzo (Marani 2017, pp. 192, 194 ill.). Berra compared it to Girolamo Figino with a dating to the 1560s (Berra, in Lugano 1998, pp. 148, no. 18, 158 ill.). Paliaga identified the hand in the inscription with that used by Lomazzo and his circle in other character heads in the Biblioteca Ambrosiana (Paliaga 1995b, pp. 235–7). As already assumed by Marani (in Rossi 1996, p. 24), it is proposed to credit the drawing to the youthful output of Giovanni Ambrogio Figino at the time when he was a pupil of Lomazzo, when 'he had at his disposal the rich collection of Leonardesque drawings' by this artist (Ciardi 1968, pp. 35–6) and could copy works by the followers of Leonardo and anatomical studies (Marani, in Pescarmona 1986, pp. 60–62, no. 14; Pavesi, in Perissa Torrini 2019a, pp. 144–5, no. 16). In this drawing, Figino seems to be inspired by 'Leonardesque inflections uttered by Lombards' (Ciardi 1968, p. 37), depicting his subject in the ways described by Lomazzo in the *Trattato*, where he refers to 'certain bonnets in old-fashioned style, with the rest of the garments in the form that were then worn by countrypeople, and still in our times are worn by some, but not so ridiculous' (Book VI, Chapter XXXII, fols 359–360).

RA

Bibliography

Fiorio, in Rossi 1982, p. 15; Marani 1987a, p. 242, no. 48, fig. 165; Paliaga 1995b, pp. 235–7, 237 ill.; Rossi 1996, pp. 24–5; Berra, in Lugano 1998, p. 148, no. 18, p. 138 ill.; Marani 2017, p. 192, fig. 14.

29.

Aurelio Luini (1530–1593)
Or Compa' Digliagor, 1570s
Pen and ink on paper, 123 × 86 mm
Paris, Musée du Louvre, Département des Arts Graphiques, Cabinet des dessins, inv. 2652

From the album of Giuseppe Vallardi, the drawing is the recto of a sheet whose verso shows another caricatured profile of a man, clenching a stick between his teeth on which a bird is perched (Berra 2009, p. 77, fig. 6). The drawing here has been described as a 'head in caricature of a man, viewed from the front, bearing these strange words written by the artist on his bonnet: "Or Compa' Dignagora"' (Vallardi 1855, p. 54, no. 238). The image might have come from Giovan Battista Clarici's *Libro di disegni* (Mara 2019, p. 366), which contains various drawings by the artists in the Accademia della Val di Blenio (Mara 2010, p. 85). It has been attributed to Aurelio Luini da Bora and is held to be a study within the sphere of the academy (Bora 1989, p. 88), of which the artist was a member with the name *Compa' Lovign* (Isella 2005b, p. 81). The depiction of this figure as nearly monstrous has been interpreted because of its inscription as *compare diavolo* ('friend devil'), a subject not present in Lomazzo's *Rabisch*, but related to that cultural context as is the profile on the verso (Bora, in Lugano 1998, p. 182, nos 34, 35). It is possible, in fact, that the figures on this sheet in the Louvre are the figurative expression of two caricatural portraits of members of the academy (Porzio 2010, pp. 200, 201 ill.) produced in about the 1560s. The features, though treated experimentally, are a graphic rendering of the artist's reflection on the feelings expressed in Leonardo's grotesque heads (Tantardini 2016, pp. 221–4). The dilated and deformed features, in Aurelio Luini's distinctively easy and confident handling, seem to combine Leonardo's models with the grotesque motifs of Lombard ornaments from the later Cinquecento, such as those found in Cremona (Bora, in Lugano 1998, p. 182, nos 34, 35).

RA

Bibliography

Vallardi 1855, p. 54, no. 238; Bora 1989, p. 88, fig. 8; Lomazzo 1993, p. XIV, n. 9, fig. 6; Paliaga 1995a, p. 150, fig. 13; Bora, in Lugano 1998, pp. 171 ill., 182, nos 34, 35; Porzio 2010, pp. 200, 201 ill.; Porzio 2011, p. 244 ill.; Porzio, in Ferino-Pagden 2011a, p. 373, no. 258; Mara 2019, p. 366, fig. 10c.; Bodart 2022, pp. 162-163, tav. XXVIII.

30.

Giovanni Ambrogio Figino
(1552/1553–1608)
Grotesque head of a man, c. 1570
Charcoal and white chalk on blue paper, 268 × 205 mm
Venice, Gallerie dell'Accademia, inv. 1108r

The drawing is on a sheet that represents two images: on the recto this head of a man with clearly senile features and, on the verso that of a young bearded man, rediscovered only after restoration in 1986, with the removal of the backing paper.

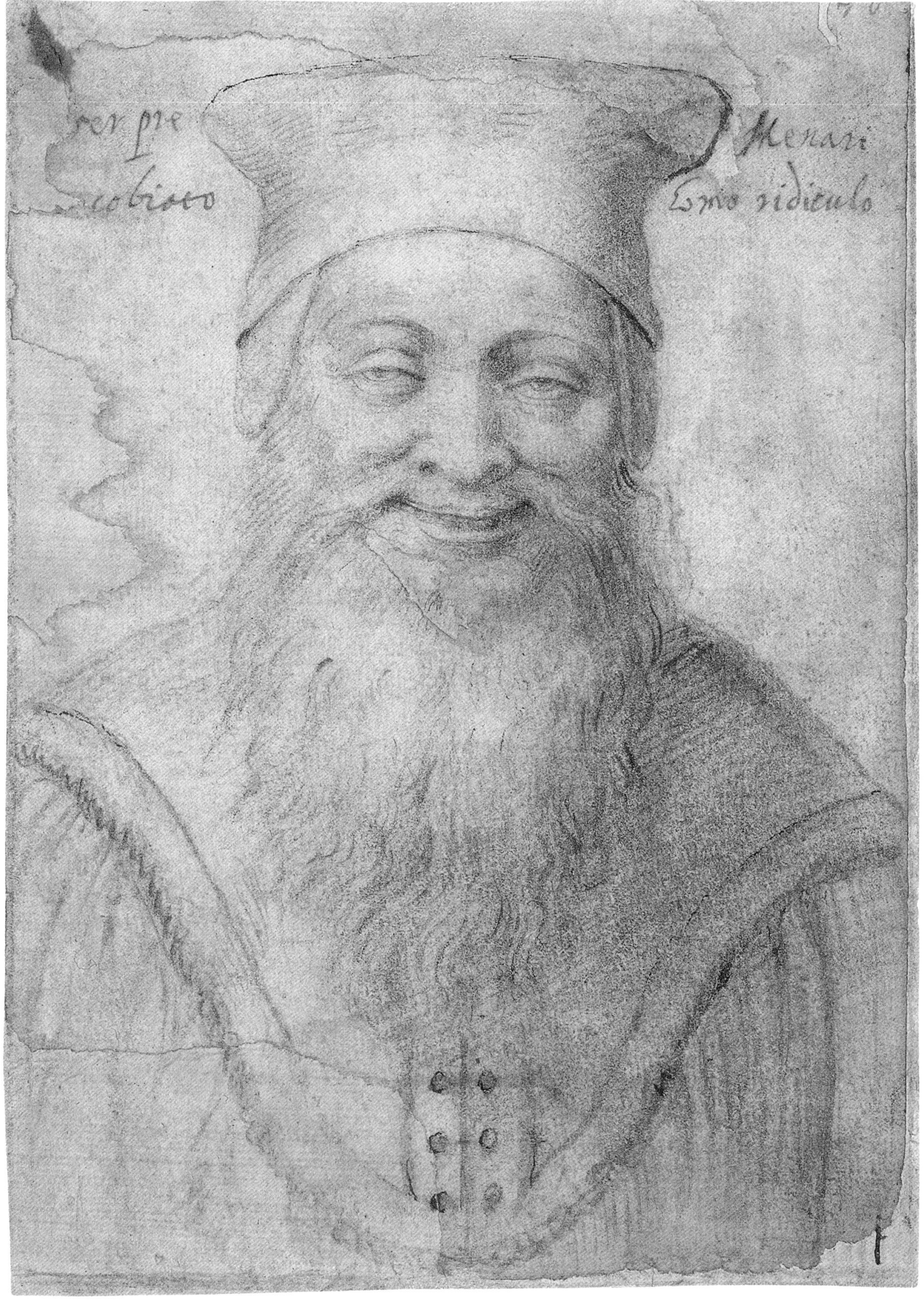

28.

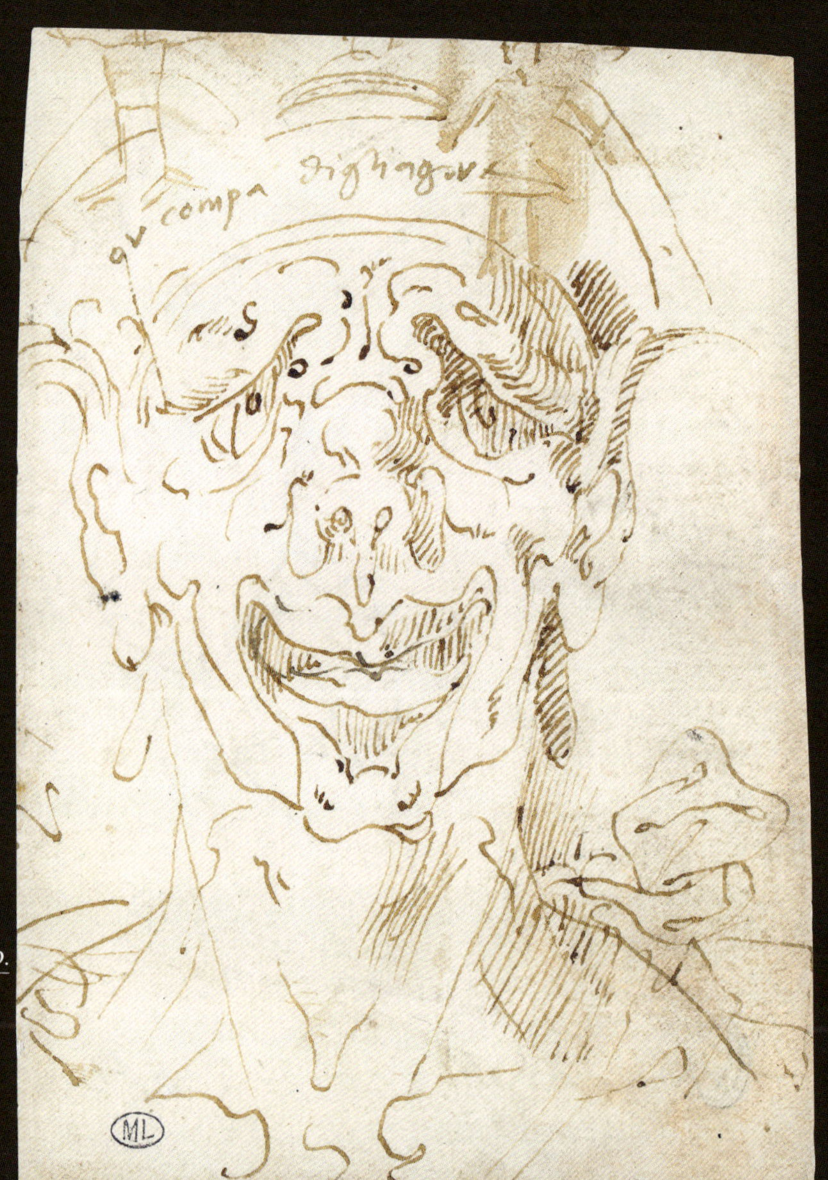

29.

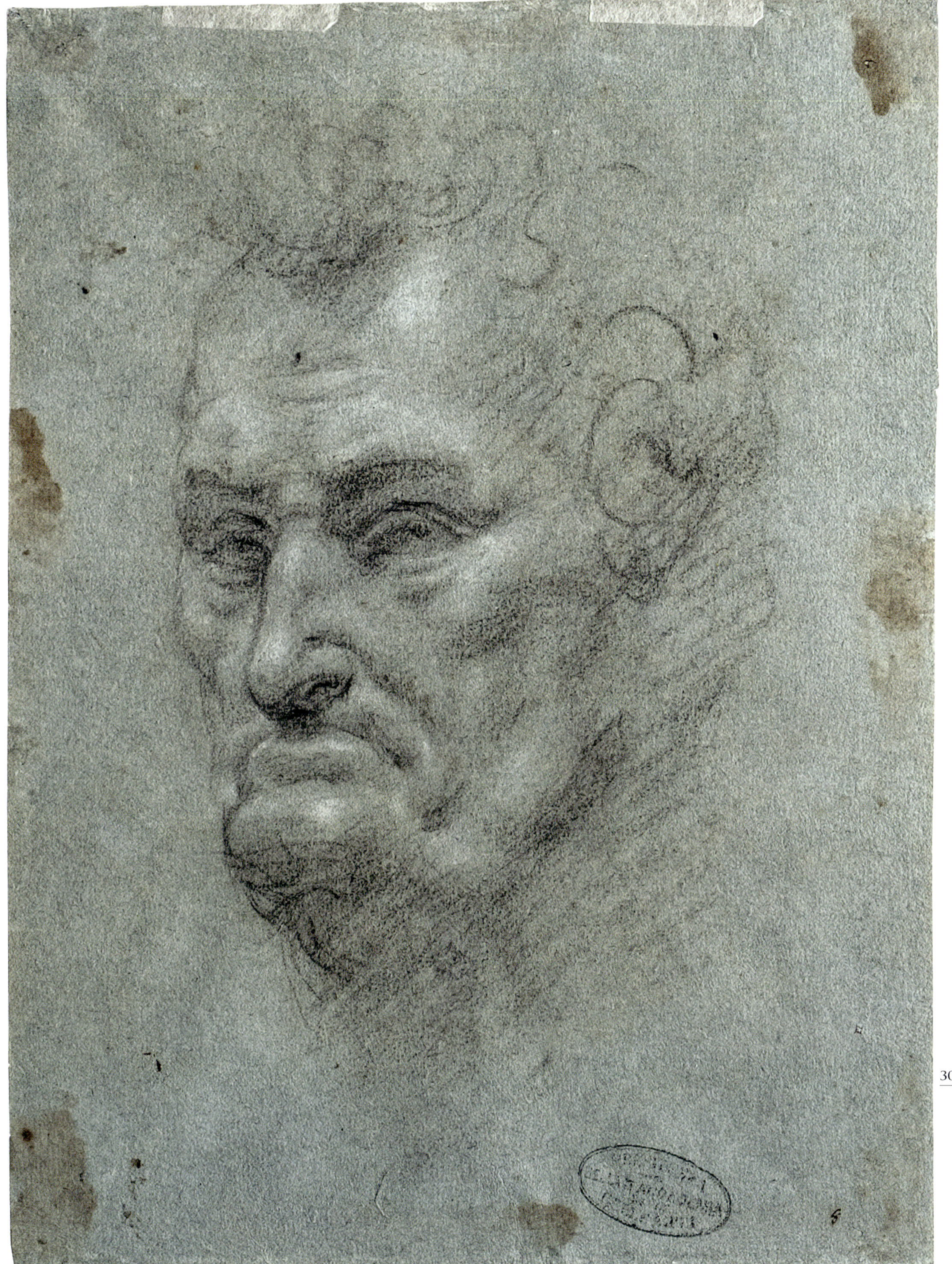

30.

The attribution to Figino had already appeared in the 1832 manuscript inventory (Venice, Archivio Soprintendenza Beni artistici e storici, *Elenco Generale dei Disegni della Raccolta del Cav. Bossi*, 1832), and has been regularly confirmed since then. Ciardi (1968, p. 156) stressed its marked derivation from Leonardo updated with a Mannerist vocabulary; in particular he recalled the analogy with Leonardo's faces of old men and women, like the drawing at Windsor RCIN 912474 or that in the Royal Library of Turin inv. 15575. Perissa Torrini (1987, p. 41) notes the very fine quality of the drawing, attributable to Figino's early output, when he took a particularly close interest in Leonardo's work through the teachings of Paolo Lomazzo and, probably, direct study of a collection of Leonardo's drawings (Laurenza 2006). The association of senile faces with the production of caricatures was developed fairly systematically by Leonardo. Yet his studies of such faces often tended less towards the purposes of caricature than representing the dignity of the figures, despite, or even enhanced by, the signs of age. In this drawing by Figino, the face, although marked by time's relentless passing, expresses pride in the gaze and dignity, and in this way it belongs to the Leonardesque tradition just described. The drawing reveals Figino's particular aptitude for portraiture, with which he has always traditionally been credited (Bora 1971, p. 54), and his care to reproduce such characteristic features, even those not reflecting canonically aesthetic perfection; this arises from his need to represent a true image, which in all his characters is also a reflection of vice or virtue. His portrait of St Charles Borromeo (Ambrosiana, Milan) with emaciated features and a large nose is perhaps the most significant example of this.

RC

Bibliography

Moschini 1931; Ciardi 1968, p. 156; Nepi Scirè 1982; Perissa Torrini 1987, p. 41; Nepi Scirè, Perissa Torrini, in Venice 1999.

31.

Battista Franco (c. 1510–1561), attributed
Two grotesque heads, c. 1550–60
Etching, 120 × 152 mm
Florence, Gabinetto dei Disegni e delle Stampe delle Gallerie degli Uffizi, inv. 2636 st. sc.

The etchings come from a series of six plates in the Gabinetto dei Disegni e delle Stampe of the Uffizi (inv. 2632–2636), to which should be added at least two others at the Rijksmuseum in Amsterdam (inv. RP-P-1999-111; fig. 1 on p. 80; Zelen 2015, pp. 41–2, fols 88, 89).
Anna Omodeo (1965) correctly related the series to the Venetian context (with an unconvincing attribution to Giacomo Franco). But the typically Leonardesque matrix of what appears to be an exercise in representing different physiognomic types with exaggerated features, combined with their distinctive arrangement in pairs, has more recently suggested a comparison with the work of the Milanese Giovanni Ambrogio Brambilla, an artist close to Lomazzo and a founding member of the Accademia della Val di Blenio (Paliaga 1995b; Paliaga, in Lugano 1998).
However, this attribution is untenable after comparison with the technique and style of the engraver, whose career has now been fully revealed (Alberti 2020). The examples in Amsterdam, exceptionally still mounted (when they are not directly printed on the pages of an album of prints composed in Venice around 1568), confirms their assignment to the Venetian environment, as the work of an engraver close to the graphic style of Battista Franco (Zelen 2015, p. 18; three of the plates in Amsterdam, inv. RP-P-1999-108 and RP-P-1999-111) match the specimens in the Uffizi inv. 2636, 2633, 2637, while two have not previously been published).
In the scene shown here, the reference to the Leonardesque matrix is less generic than elsewhere, since the figure on the right precisely matches the likeness of an autograph male face in red pencil in the Louvre (inv. 2249; Viatte, in Paris 2003, no. 57). This raises the question of the circulation of this and the other models in this series as drawn copies in Venice.

AA

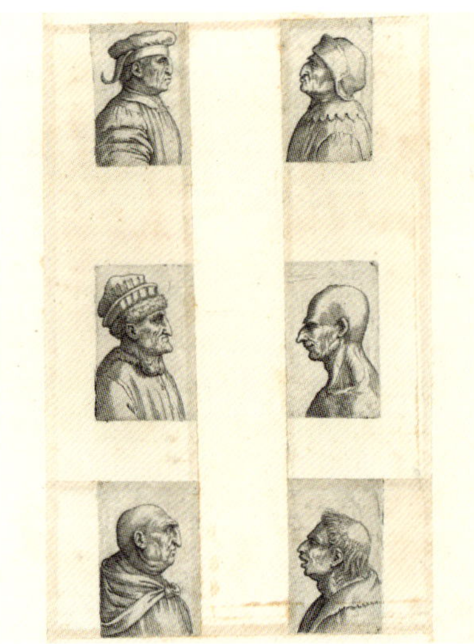

1. Battista Franco attributed, *Six grotesque heads*, c. 1550–60. Amsterdam, Rijksmuseum, inv. RP-P-1999-111

Bibliography

Omodeo 1965, p. 26, no. 19.5; Paliaga 1995b, pp. 219–25; Paliaga, in Lugano 1998, p. 175 fig., pp. 182–3, no. 37; Mara 2010, p. 94 n. 140; Ferino-Pagden 2011a, pp. 231 fig. 373, no. 252; Zelen 2015, pp. 18, 19 fig. 14, p. 41, fol. 88; Alberti 2020, p. 65, n. 30.

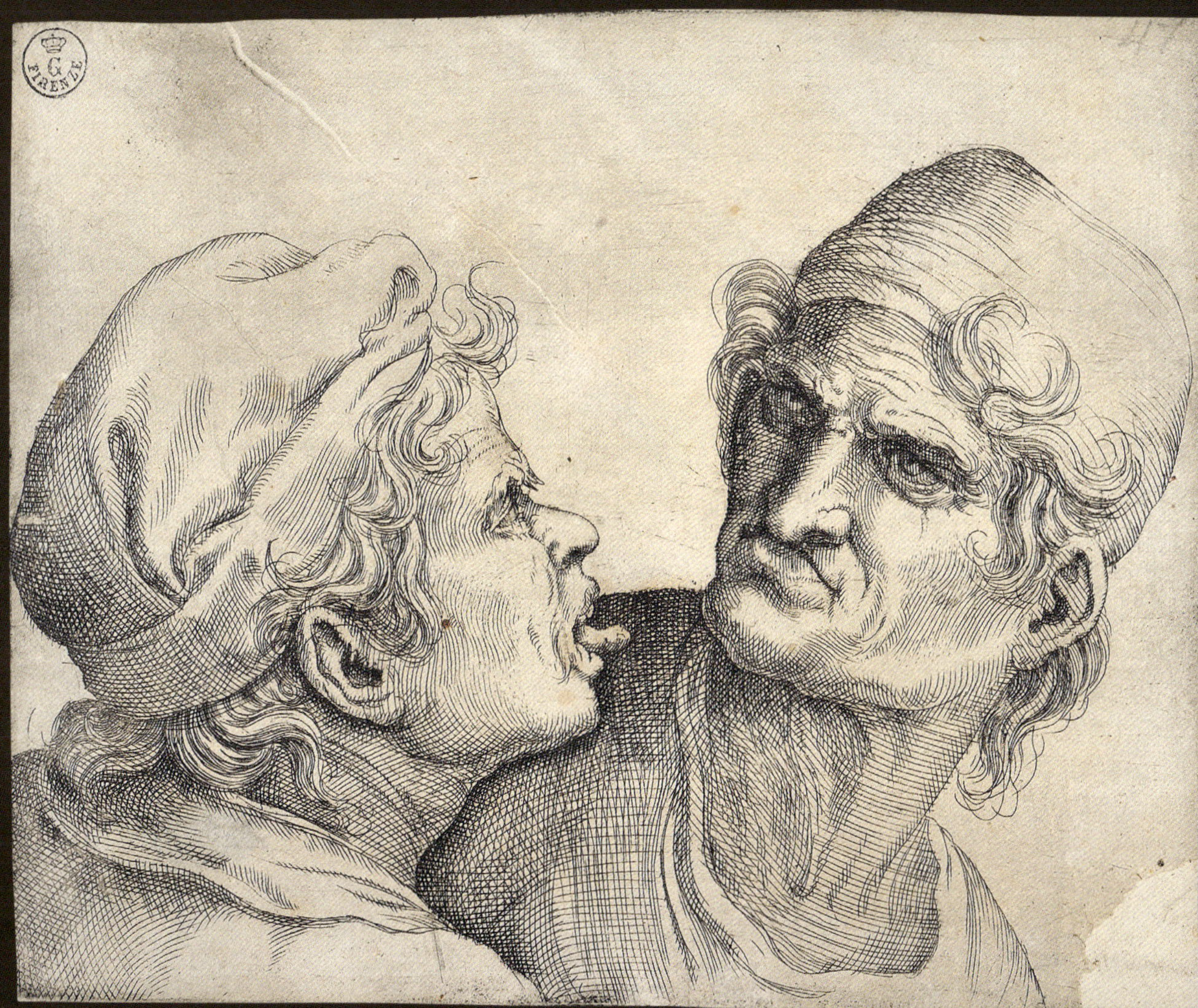

31.

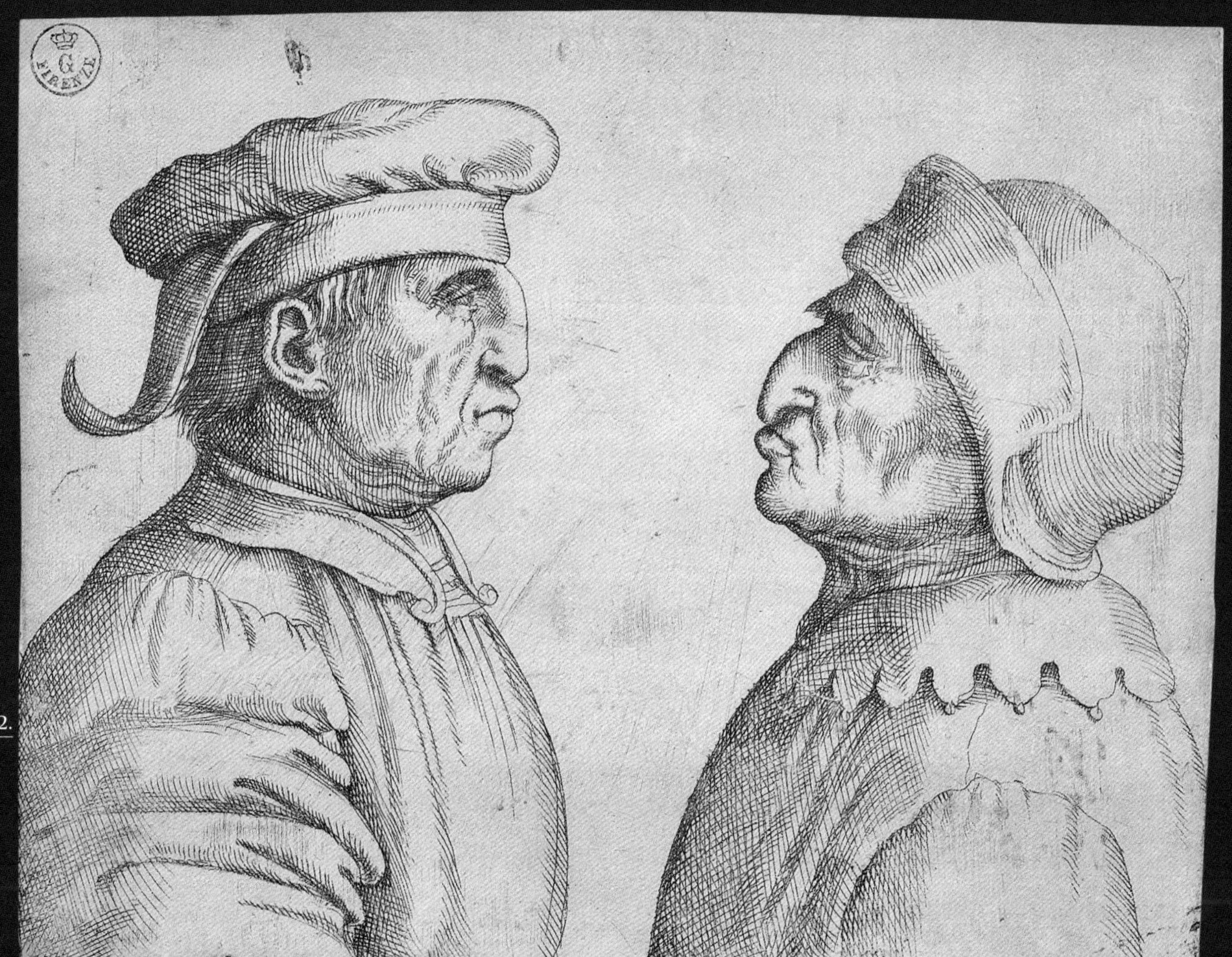

32.

32.

Battista Franco (c. 1510–1561), attributed
Two grotesque heads in profile, c. 1550–60
Etching, 113 × 145 mm
Florence, Gabinetto dei Disegni e delle Stampe delle Gallerie degli Uffizi, inv. 2637 st. sc.

Belonging to the same series as cat. 31 (which see for a conjectural reconstruction and discussion of attribution), this plate presents a schematic composition, with the two figures facing each other in profile derived from Leonardo's widely imitated prototype, which received its finest known interpretation in the series by Wenceslaus Hollar dating from about 1645 (see Perissa Torrini 2018).
The two figures have in common a distinctive hooked nose and the form of their garments which, as Anna Omodeo (1965) observed in her fundamental contribution on Venetian popular prints, seem to draw on previous models, from the late fifteenth or early sixteenth century.
The difficulty in precisely establishing the chronology of the series, most likely from the mid-sixteenth century or the sixth decade at the latest, at present prevents a fuller discussion of the relationships or any reciprocal influences with contemporary engravings inspired by Leonardo. This is particularly true of the four pairs engraved by Hans Liefrinck also dating from 1550 to 1560 (Luyckx and Leeflang 2021, pp. 133-135, nn. 202-205), as well as a Venetian series of three woodcuts in which we can make out the faces of the same figures as in Battista Franco's etchings (London, British Museum, inv. 1854.1113.169, inv. 1854.1113.170, inv. 1854.1113.171; Urbini 2019). Limiting ourselves to a comparison of their forms, the male figure on the right here reappears, with variations in the clothes and hat, in the British Museum woodcuts bearing at the top the words 'tiffanio di paltanai/ da comachio./ ivris consvlto' (inv. 1854.1113.169) and in that with 'fiapolin dei smagrii bob è antigo nicoloto' (inv. 1854.1113.171). It corresponds, reversed, to the Amsterdam drawing (inv. RP-P-1999-111-d), while 'abain di frac[...] da poveia iuris consvlto' (British Museum, inv. 1854.1113.170) repeats the profile of the man on the left here.
Another example of the rare etching exhibited here, formerly cut into two parts that were then mounted to distance the likenesses from each other, is preserved in the Rijksmuseum, Amsterdam, in a Venetian album of prints from 1568 (inv. RP-P-1999-111; see fig. 1 on p. 80).

AA

Bibliography
Omodeo 1965, p. 27, no. 19.6; Paliaga 1995b, pp. 219–25; Paliaga, in Lugano 1998, pp. 175 fig., 182–3, no. 37; Mara 2010, p. 94 n. 140; Zelen 2015, p. 42, fol. 89; Alberti 2020, p. 65 n. 30.

33.

Francesco Urbini (active 1530–1540), attributed
Dish on low foot with composite head of penises
Polychrome maiolica, ø 23.3 cm
Oxford, Ashmolean Museum, University of Oxford, inv. WA2003.136
On the scroll: IZAC. ED. ATESTA. ANU. ESSOF. EMOC. ADRAUG. EM. OMOH. INGO
'Ogni homo me guarda come fosse una testa de cazi'
On verso: '1536 El breve de[n]tro voi legerite Come giudei se i[n]te[n]der el vorite' and the mark 'FR'
Specimen on display: porcelain copy by Limoges, 2005. Private collection, Milan

This dish was sold on the antiques market in 1855, then remained in a private collection until 2003, when it was purchased by the Ashmolean Museum.
The writing on the back and the style have made it possible to ascribe it to Umbrian ceramic work from the 1530s. Wilson (2005) ascribes the letters 'FR' on the reverse to the ceramist Francesco Urbini. He is not mentioned in sources in the archives, but is believed to have been active in the workshop of the master potter Giorgio Andreoli, and he has been credited with a group of historiated maiolica wares made between 1531 and 1536.
At first glance indecipherable, the inscription on the scroll (IZAC. ED. ATESTA. ANU. ESSOF. EMOC. ADRAUG. EM. OMOH. INGO) actually reads in translation: 'Every man looks at me as if I were a head of dicks'. It becomes intelligible when read from right to left, as in the Semitic languages, as recommended on the reverse: '1536 El breve de[n]tro voi legerite Come giudei se i[n]te[n]der el vorite' ('If you wish to understand the meaning, then read the text as Jews do'). Made up of penises and testicles, the head painted on this cup is an original parody of the Renaissance iconography found on plates painted with profiles of 'bella donna', also evoked by the coral earring, the phalluses arranged to emulate a coiffure gathered with a ribbon and the scroll bearing the inscription. Other examples of 'bella donna' reinterpreted in an erotic key were

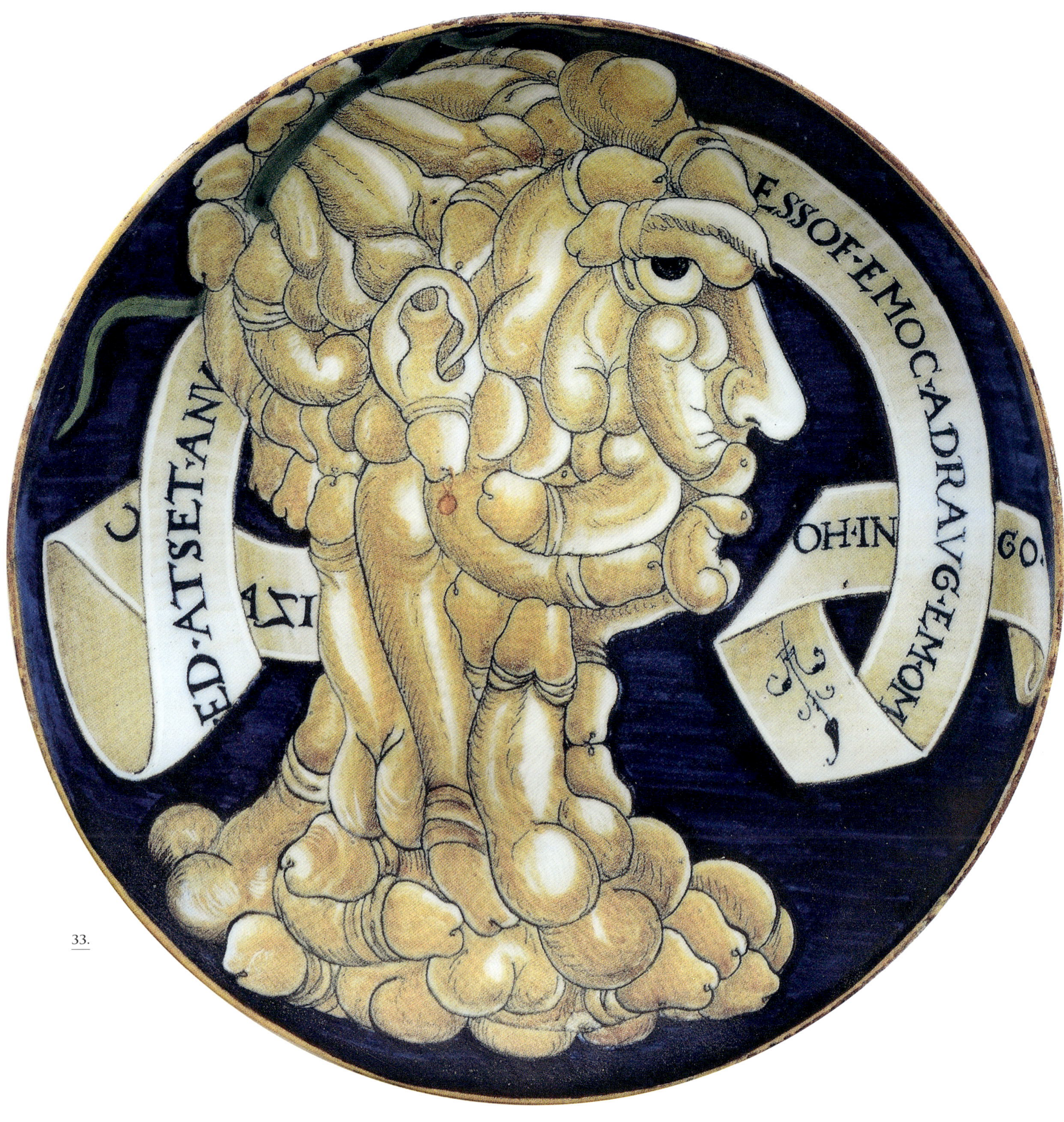

33.

produced by the Casteldurante workshops, but none as monumental as this. A similar iconography appears on some medals struck between 1535 and 1540 (for example, the medal of Pietro Aretino or the one with the alleged head of the humanist Paolo Giovio) with 'phallic' portraits. This is evidence of a Cinquecento cultural climate in which it was not unusual to use images from the erotic and sexual repertoire for satirical purposes.
In the context of this exhibition, we recall a passage from Giovan Paolo Lomazzo's *Trattato della pittura* (1584) that refers to Leonardo's lost drawings with erotic subjects: 'one of which was of a handsome youth, with the member in his forehead and without a nose, and with another face behind the head, with the virile member under the chin, and the ears attached to the testicles, which two heads had the ears of a faun; and the other monster had the member on the tip of its nose'.
Moreover, it is possible that the Umbrian ceramist may have seen Leonardo's grotesque heads, which enjoyed extraordinary favour in the Accademia della Val di Blenio. They were the precedent to which Giuseppe Arcimboldo (1527–1593) also looked for his 'composite heads'. The right-to-left inscription, again, points to a milieu close to Leonardo.
The closest reference to the Ashmolean dish can be identified in a pen drawing (formerly belonging to the painter Sir Thomas Lawrence, 1769–1830) – formerly ascribed to Leonardo and then Giulio Romano, before being more recently attributed by Wilson (2005) to Francesco Salviati. Wilson has conjectured that print might have been made from this drawing and that Francesco Urbini perhaps took inspiration from one of them.
Parronchi (1991) tried to relate the drawing, medals and maiolica to each other but without reaching any conclusion. More recently, Wied (2008) has suggested that the subject may testify to a culture that was more common and widely shared than the few surviving specimens suggest.

PC

Bibliography
Parronchi 1991, pp. 52–6; Wilson 2005, pp. 10–44 (with previous bibliography); Biscarini and Nardelli 2005, pp. 48–50; Wied 2008, pp. 60–61; Porzio 2011, p. 237; Boutin Vitela 2014, pp. 172–3.

34.

Anonymous (after Giuseppe Arcimboldo, 1527–1593)
Humani Victus Instrumenta: Ars Coquinaria, 1569
Engraving, 232 × 184 mm
Copenhagen, Designmuseum Danmark 106/367

35.

Anonymous (after Giuseppe Arcimboldo, 1527–1593)
Humani Victus Instrumenta: Agricoltura, 1567
Engraving, 238 × 177 mm
Copenhagen, Designmuseum Danmark inv. 104/367

Originally distributed by the publisher Giovan Francesco Camocio, active in Venice between 1552 and 1574–5 (a second edition was made by Angelo Salvadori), the two engravings here have been traced back to the painter Giuseppe Arcimboldo and the context of the Habsburg court in Vienna.
The first reference to the subjects appeared in the *Trattato della pittura* by Giovan Paolo Lomazzo (1584). It refers to the 'capriccioso pittore' as having produced an *Agriculture* consisting of 'all the implements belonging to this art'. The excursus then refers to a work representing *Cooking* composed in a similar way by the painter Carlo da Crema (Carlo Urbino). The same association was made by Lanzi (1795), who recalled the popularity of composite heads of this type at the Habsburg courts in Vienna and then Prague. In the light of Carlo Urbino's work as a copyist, it is possible that he was able to represent the idea of another artist, so that both engravings would derive from compositions by Arcimboldo. Lomazzo himself (1590) seems to point in this direction when he recalls that the Milanese artist 'has also represented cooking in the form of a female with her implements and utensils', though the description of the subject does not correspond to the gender of the figure in the engraving, which has male rather than female features.
Regardless of the genesis of these engravings – which Romberg (2007) considers were commissioned by Arcimboldo himself, perhaps to perpetuate the memory of lost originals – they constitute significant testimony to his work, his training and the Milanese culture in which he developed in contact with the Accademia della Val di Blenio. Porzio (2011) represents his work in terms of a popular-comic context, connecting Arcimboldo's working method with carnival imagery and certain humorous rituals in which tools and implements were removed from their original setting with burlesque intentions. Hence in the engravings here, pans and utensils compose the image of *Cooking*, while sickles and other tools are associated with *Agriculture*.
These seem essentially to provide original evidence of that process of theoretical and social ennobling of popular influences that proved successful at the court of Maximilian II and found effective (and spectacular) expression in collecting in the *Wunderkammern*, which brought together *naturalia*, *artificialia* and *mirabilia*. Likewise, with a classificatory approach that we could define as proto-scientific, Arcimboldo took objects from the real world and assembled them into deliberately ambiguous or at least estranging portraits, stripped of any naturalistic reference to human anatomy, so moving towards an effective synthesis of popular with 'aristocratic' culture.

PC

Bibliography
Lomazzo 1584, p. 349–50; Lomazzo 1590, p. 154; Lanzi 1795–6, p. 427; Alfons 1957, pp. 90–91; Geiger 1960 p. 54; Hulten 1987, pp. 114–15; Maiorino 1991, p. 54; Romberg 2007, pp. 183–4; Porzio 2011, pp. 232–3.

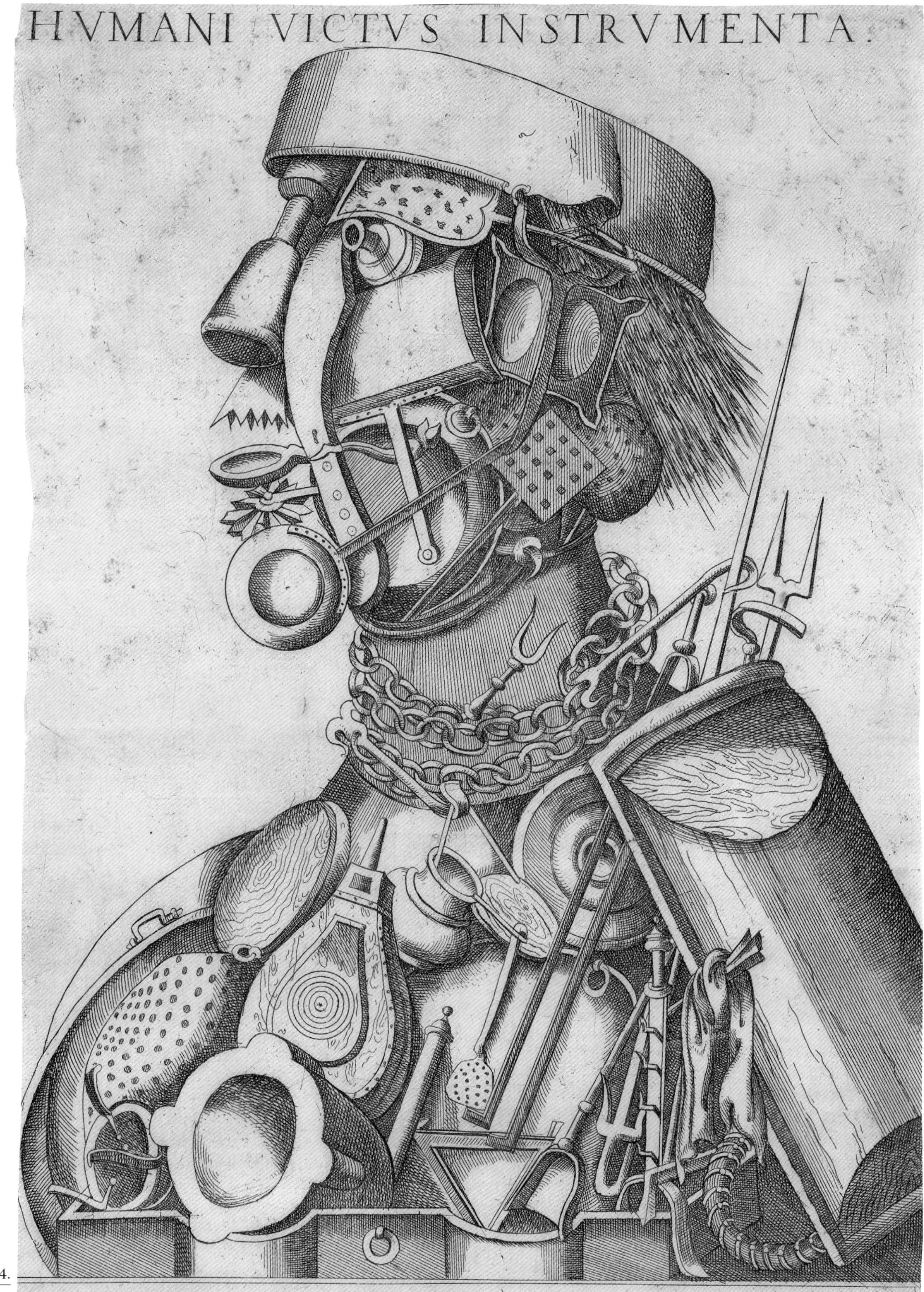

34.

Che miri ò sciocho questa mia pittura
Di tanti al viuer nostro atti stromenti,
E fai nel tuo pensier uari argomenti,
Imagine non è, non è figura.
Egli è di condir cibi alma fattura,
Che à Prencipi, e gran Regi, in Oro, e Argenti
Commune serue, e a tutte l'altre genti
Tolti a le giande; e a la uil lor pastura.

Perciò è ben degna ch'in metalli, e'n marmi
Non che in carta si stampi, e che si dica
Questo per human uso è fatto essempio.
Quindi Natura a l'Arte adombrar parmi,
Che per bisogno si fe à l'arte amica,
Lungi dal suo costume antico, et empio.

Con Priuilegio.

In Venetia.

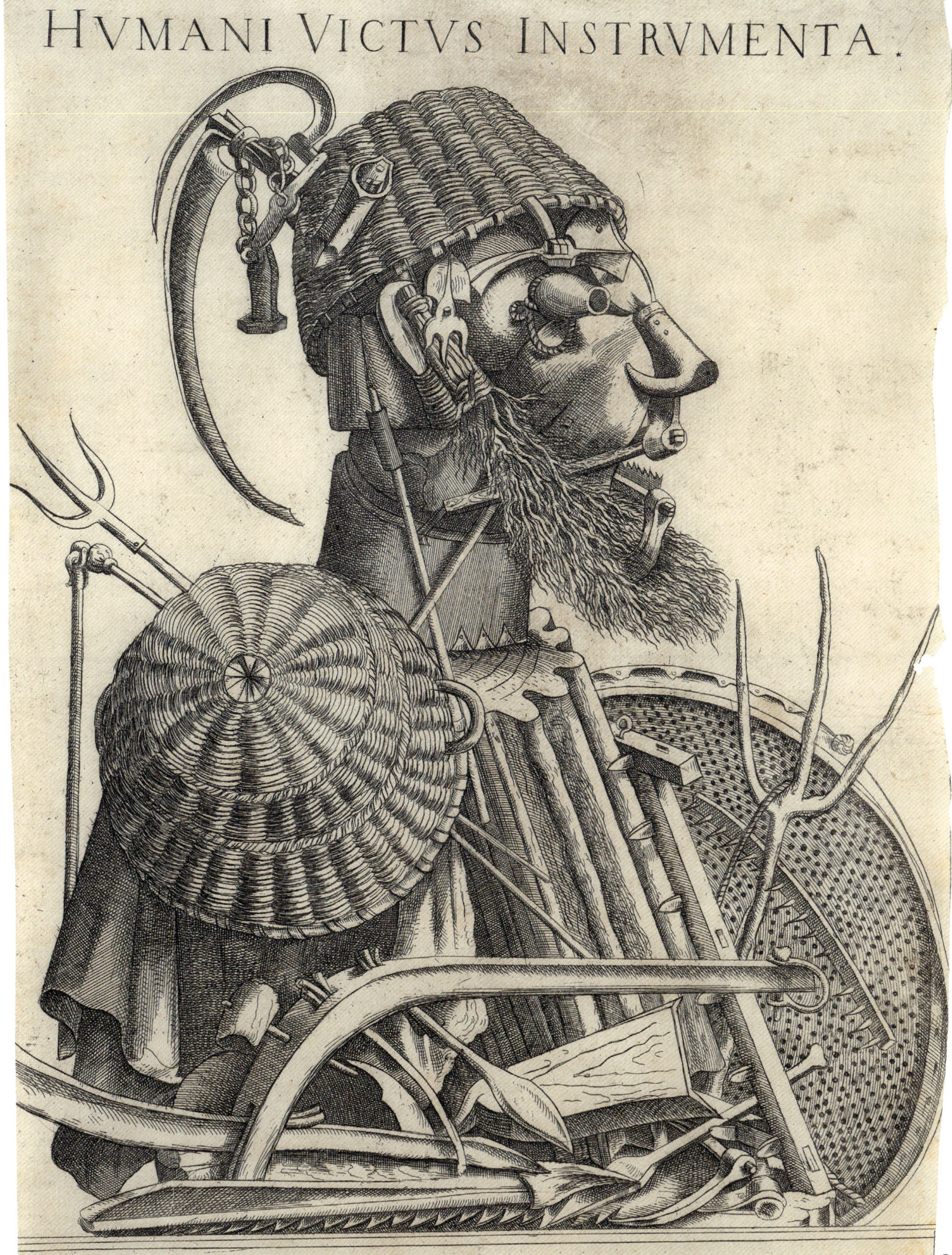
HVMANI VICTVS INSTRVMENTA.
No ue ſmarauegie, s'a ſto me cao,
Ghe ſe attaccò agno cao de maſſaria,
Che ſai pur, che al mondo el no ghe cao,
Che no habbi dentro la ſò fantaſia;
Per queſto el Mondo è bello, inchina in cao,
Agnon tegna la ſoa, queſta è la mia;
Mi no uuò andar'in preſtio da negun,
Ch'hag'ho con mi quel che gha inſiembre agnun.
Zappe, Vanghe, bail, forche, e roſtieggi,
Menare, menaruotti, e menaritti,
Tinazzi, uetolar, botte, e maſtieggi,
Seſole, falce, ſcuelle, e boccalitti,
Verſuri, roppegar, chiudi, e martieggi,
Tanaggie, ſubbie, ſeghe, e ceſtilitti,
Ste coſe, e de le altre uu haueri,
S'allegramente uu me compreri.
In Venetia Giacomo Dini.

35.

36.

Giovan Paolo Lomazzo (1538–1592)
Grotesque head of a woman facing right,
c. 1560
Oil and tempera on panel, 26 × 18 cm
On the verso, illegible inscription
in pencil
Milan, private collection

The painting was attributed to Giovan Paolo Lomazzo by Roberto Longhi when it was in a private collection in Paris. One of Longhi's two letters, dated 8 February 1958 and addressed to the owner with the proposed attribution to Lomazzo, observed that 'à Milan, pendant tout le siècle, on eut l'habitude de s'inspirer des dessins de Léonard, surtout dans le cièrcle de maniéristes comme Lomazzo et Figino.' Published for the first time by Dante Isella (1993, fig. 11), the attribution to Lomazzo was accepted by Francesco Porzio as 'an instructive conjecture and for the present acceptable, if we observe the manner of shading and the way the pigment is applied'. He noted, however, that 'the morphological evidence necessary for a reliable conclusion' was lacking, though Lomazzo himself claimed to have painted 'pictures, bizarreries, stories, friezes, grotesques' (Lomazzo 1587, p. 529). It was recorded in the catalogue of Leonardo's *Dessins et manuscrits* held at the Musée du Louvre as a 'copie peinte attribuée à Lomazzo' by Varena Forcione (Forcione, in Paris 2003). It has been observed that the handling of this intriguing painting is 'too summary, especially in the forehead and breast of the deformed lady, shaded with full-bodied brown and reddish brushstrokes, to stand comparison with certain works by Lomazzo, with their carefully studied chiaroscuro transitions, rendered with subtle and almost miniaturist touches of color and very carefully judged balance between light and shade' (Pavesi 2009, pp. 308–9). My own feeling is that, apart from Pavesi noting how 'certain details (such as the glowing reflections on the hair) contain pictorial passages that are very far from contemptible', the chiaroscuro and the rendering of the face with reddish shadows are in close keeping with Lomazzo's so-called *Self-Portrait* in the Pinacoteca di Brera. This also appears in the rendering of the ear and especially the eye, which seems even more alive and animalistic thanks to two touches of white applied with the tip of the brush. Further passages of miniaturist skill may have been reduced by early restoration.
This painting derives from a drawing by Leonardo in the collection of the Duke of Devonshire at Chatsworth, inv. OMD 822 A (Forcione, in Paris 2003, pp. 197–8, no. 65 A). This was copied on a sheet in the Accademia in Venice [cat. 20], formerly in Giuseppe Bossi's collection, with five caricatured heads attributed to an imitator of Leonardo, perhaps Francesco Melzi, then in the Mariette Album now in the Louvre (Forcione, in Paris 2003, pp. 220, 225, no. 73), then in a drawing now in the Spencer collection (I, 26; Trutty-Coohill 1993, p. 93, no. 26), and in two copies now in Berlin, in the Album of engravings of the Comte de Caylus of 1730, no. 34 (Forcione, in Paris 2003, pp. 230, 234, no. 74, exhibited here, cat. 50), a copy of which appeared in the library of Anton Maria Zanetti and, finally, in the book of *Characaturas* engraved by Wenceslaus Hollar and republished in 1786 [cat. 79]. The reception of this head was enshrined in the important essay by Ernst Gombrich on *Leonardo's Grotesque Heads* (1954), which reproduced the copy in Venice among the small number of grotesques by Leonardo selected (Gombrich 1954, plate CXII/14). Compared to Leonardo's original and all these derivations, the painting has some variants: the flower in the woman's bodice is absent, the head is stockier, the lips more elongated and the breasts far more prominent. Marani (1995, p. 83, figs 4, 5) has published two other paintings attributable to Lomazzo from the later seventeenth century (sold on the antiquarian market in Milan and then in a private collection in Lugano) that reproduce Leonardo's grotesque heads. This shows that the circulation of copies of Leonardo's originals went beyond drawings and engravings to include painted versions, and continued in the following centuries, combining the genre of 'comic' and pauperist paintings. The effects of the physiognomic deformity in this painting, perhaps more evident than in Leonardo's original, enable us to go even further. In keeping with Gombrich's interpretation (1954) of Leonardo's grotesque heads, which considered them as a form of unconscious and autobiographical representation, we can interpret a painting of this kind, so animalistic and obtuse, as foreshadowing the psychoanalytical and visionary themes explored by Francis Bacon in his portraits. One of those in the *Triptych* in the Israel Museum in Jerusalem offers a rare head in profile, as in the present painting.

PCM

Bibliography
Isella 1993, p. XIV, fig. 11; Porzio, in Lugano 1998, cat. 30, p. 181; Forcione, in Paris 2003, p. 220, under fol. 21*v*; Pavesi 2009, pp. 308–9.

37.

Giovan Paolo Lomazzo (1538–1592)
Trattato dell'arte della pittura, scultura, et architettura di Gio. Paolo Lomazzo Milanese Pittore, diviso in sette libri
Milan, Paolo Gottardo Pontio, 1584
Paper volume, fols [20], 700 pp., fol. [1], 219 × 151 mm
Milan, Castello Sforzesco, Ente Raccolta Vinciana, inv. RV E III. 37

The *Trattato dell'arte della pittura*, printed for the first time in Milan in 1584, is divided into seven parts or books and closes with a 'Table of the names of the most illustrious artificers both ancient and modern'. They include 'Agostino di Bramantino, Milanese painter, a follower of Bramantino' (Lomazzo, *Trattato*, fol. 681), identified with Giovanni Agostino da Lodi (Moro 1989, pp. 40–41; Agosti, Agosti 1997, p. 15), 'Aurelio Lovino, Milanese, a very proficient painter' (Isella, in Lomazzo 1993, pp. 360–62; Agosti, Agosti 1997, p. 20, n. 50) and 'Girolamo Figino, a Milanese painter and illuminator, a follower of Melzo' (Agosti, Agosti 1997, p. 31, n. 135). These artists played a significant part in developing the theme of grotesque and ridiculous heads in the earlier and later Cinquecento. After presenting the variety of states of mind in his second book (fols 106–107), Lomazzo praises the example of

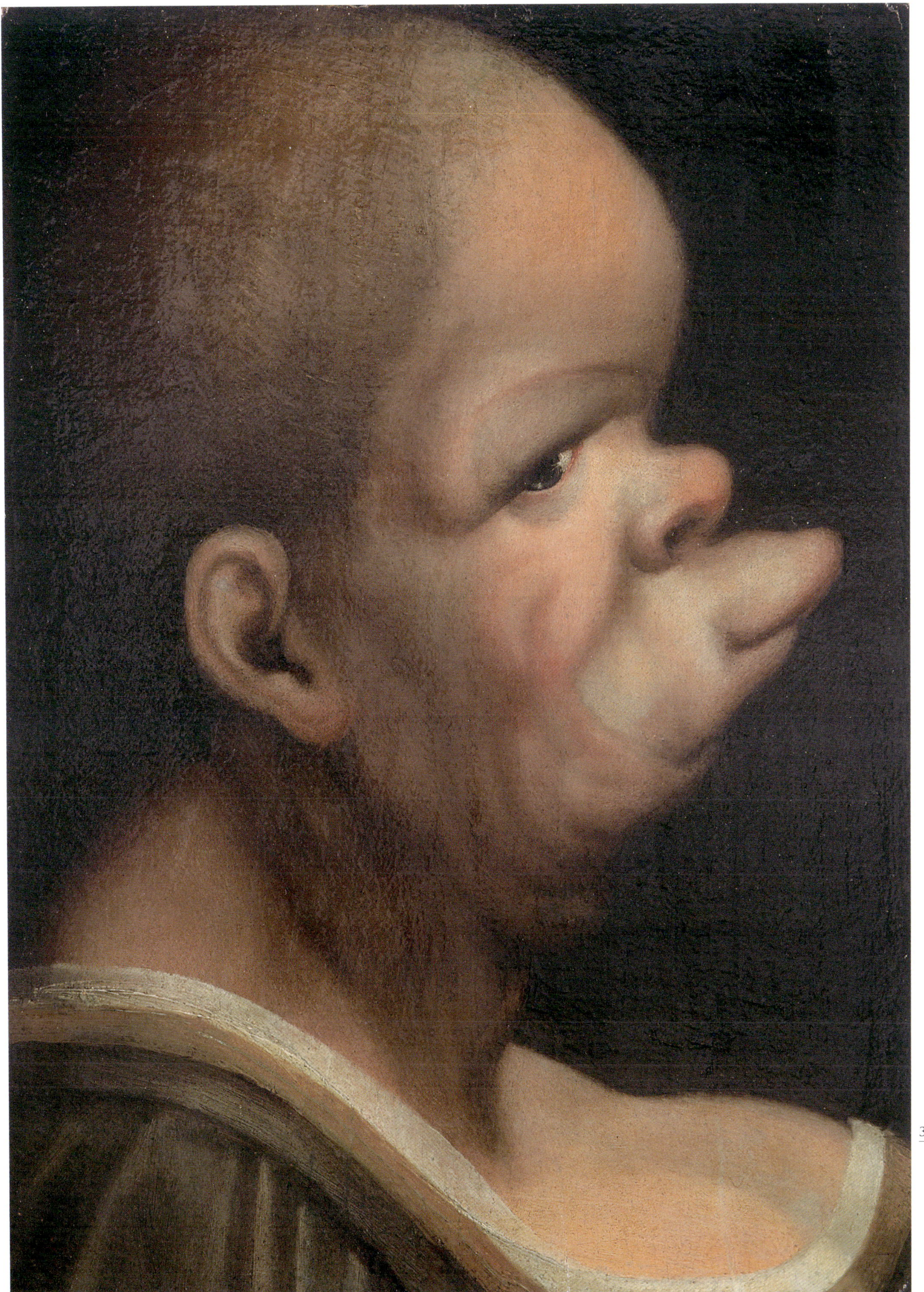

36.

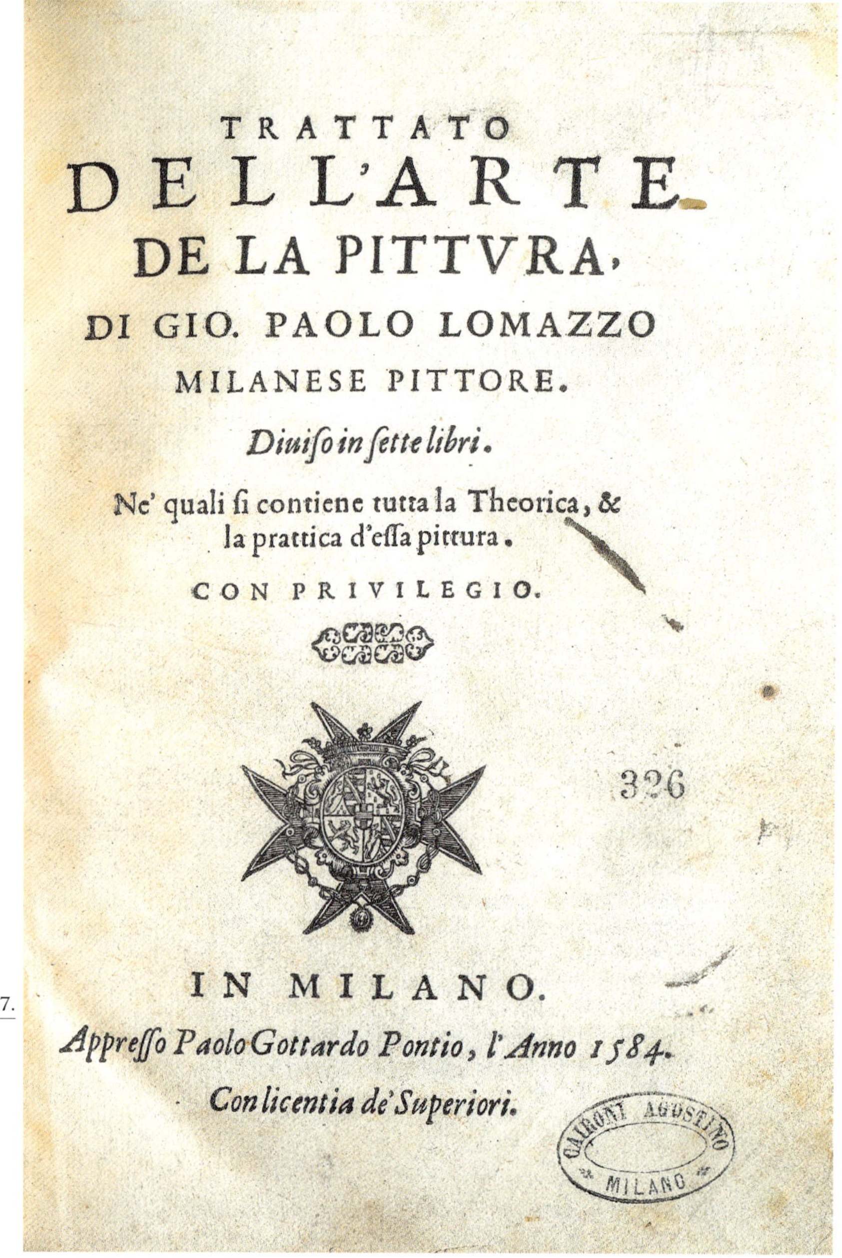
TRATTATO
DELL'ARTE
DE LA PITTVRA,
DI GIO. PAOLO LOMAZZO
MILANESE PITTORE.
Diuiſo in ſette libri.
Ne' quali ſi contiene tutta la Theorica, & la prattica d'eſſa pittura.
CON PRIVILEGIO.
IN MILANO.
Appreſſo Paolo Gottardo Pontio, l'Anno 1584.
Con licentia de' Superiori.
326
CAIRONI AGOSTINO MILANO

37.

Leonardo, resting on the observation of nature, 'From which, by diligently observing all their gestures with those ridiculous sayings . . . he thus drew them in such a way that they also moved the viewers to laughter' (ch. I, fol. 107). Then in Book VI he enumerates the characters of the compositions, for example 'of mirth and laughter' (ch. XXXII), indicating subjects that elicit laughter at first sight, like those by Leonardo, who 'greatly delighted in drawing old people with deformities and countrymen and women laughing, which are still seen in various places, such as some fifty drawn by his hand that Aurelio Lovino keeps in a book' (*Trattato*, fols 359–360). In Book VII he devotes the chapter on the form of 'monstrous' men ('Della forma de l'homini monstroosi') to cases where nature observes no rules but produces abnormal bodies and unsightly faces, such as those seen among Leonardo's papers (cha. XXVI, fols 636–639).

RA

Bibliography
Lomazzo 1973–1975, vol. I, pp. I–CXII; Agosti, Agosti 1997, pp. 5–43; Castellani, in Lugano 1998, pp. 308 ill., 316–17, no. 127; Guffanti, in Milan 2007, pp. 80–81, no. 17; Villata 2013, pp. 48–9, no. 11.

38.

Giovan Paolo Lomazzo (1538–1592)
Idea del tempio della pittura
di Gio. Paolo Lomazzo pittore
Milan, Paolo Gottardo Pontio, 1590
Paper volume, fols [16], pp. 168,
210 × 141 mm
Milan, Castello Sforzesco, Ente
Raccolta Vinciana, inv. RV A. II. 5

Published six years after the *Trattato*, the *Idea del tempio della pittura* appears closely related to the earlier work. This makes it difficult to decide the 'logical and chronological priority of the composition of one over the other', as Ciardi put it: their origins should be sought in the youthful *Libro dei sogni* of 1563 (Lomazzo 1973–1975, vol. I, pp. LIV–LX). Retracing the *Trattato*, the Milanese author set his portrait in the medallion on the title page below the dedication (the same portrait appears in his other works and is reproduced in a medal by Annibale Fontana). The characterisation of the face is in keeping with the anatomical study of the bust exhibited as the 'abbot' of the Accademia della Val di Blenio (founded in 1560), a position Lomazzo held from August 1568 on. The text, consisting of thirty-eight chapters devoted to the 'most noble art of painting and the shaping of it as a temple in which all the parts of it will be seen distinctly and arranged in order' (c. 1), is introduced by a series of 'tables', the first relating to the chapters, the second presenting 'the notable things contained in the present work' and the last the names 'of the most illustrious artificers, ancient and modern' (unnumbered folios). In the sequence of chapters the author recalls the 'ugly monstrous figures, with a beautiful and different grace' depicted by Leonardo and owned in part by Aurelio Luini (ch. 16, fols 54–55). In the closing chapter, dealing with painting and the honours of the greatest painters, the author includes

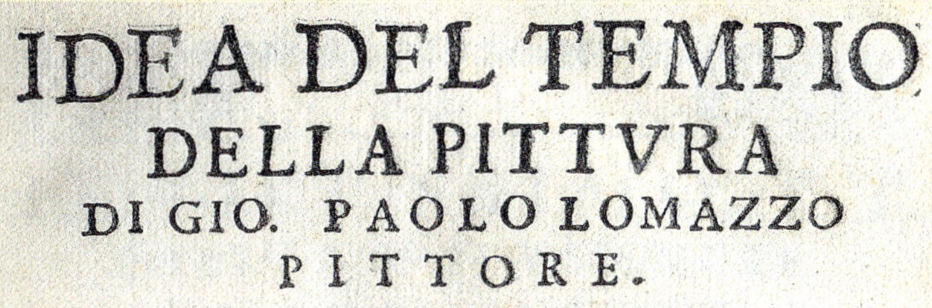

IDEA DEL TEMPIO
DELLA PITTVRA
DI GIO. PAOLO LOMAZZO
PITTORE.
NELLA QVALE EGLI DISCORRE
dell'origine, & fondamento delle cose contenute nel
suo trattato dell'arte della pittura.
All'Inuittiß. et Potentiß. Signore il Rè Don Filippo d'Austria &c.
CON PRIVILEGIO.

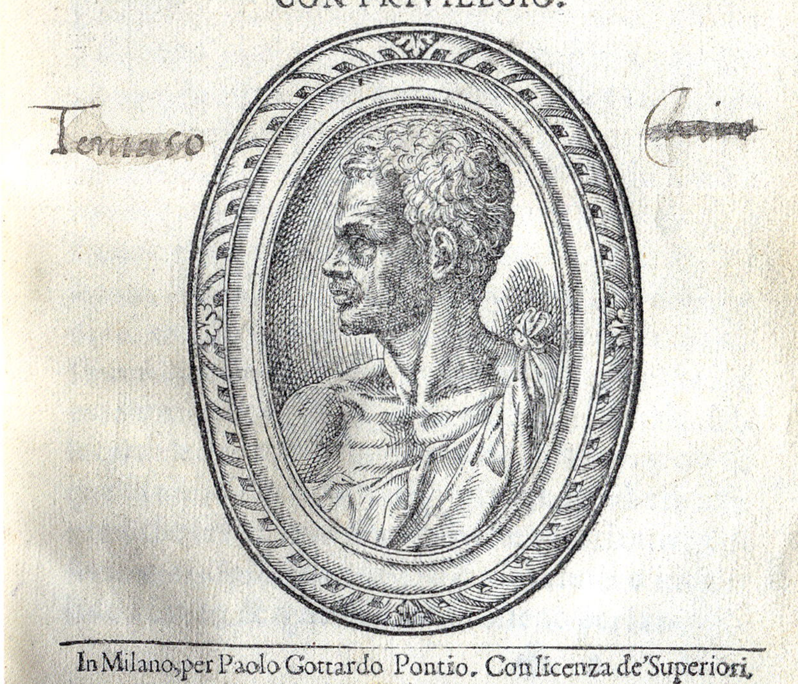

In Milano, per Paolo Gottardo Pontio. Con licenza de' Superiori.

LIBRO PRIMO
DE LA
PROPORTIONE
NATVRALE, ET
ARTIFICIALE
DE LE COSE.
DI GIO. PAOLO LOMAZZO,
MILANESE PITTORE.

38.

2. Giovan Paolo Lomazzo, *Idea del tempio della pittura*, 1590, inv. RV A II.5

the works of Giuseppe Arcimboldo, who illustrated ingenious 'inventions and capricci' (ch. 38, fol. 154), and again Aurelio Luini, also of the Val di Blenio (Agosti, Agosti 1997, p. 66), skilled in painting 'a large number of figures by means of that art, with which he seems to have been born, as well as anatomy, of which he possesses the foundations', and in this way capable of representing a rich range of grotesque figures (ch. 38, fol. 163).

RA

Bibliography

Lomazzo 1973–1975, vol. I, pp. 241–373; Castellani, in Lugano 1998, pp. 309 ill., 317, no. 130; Milan 2007, p. 82 ill.; Villata 2013, pp. 50–51, no. 12.

39.

Camillo Procaccini (1561–1629)
Two female heads, c. 1590
Graphite and sanguine on white paper, 199 × 178 mm
Venice, Gallerie dell'Accademia, inv. 335

The drawing, attributed to Giulio Cesare Procaccini by Selvatico (1854) and in the early inventories of the Accademia, was correctly reattributed to Camillo Procaccini by Neilson (1979). The sheet depicts an old woman with a goitre wearing a bonnet and a young woman viewed from behind, with her face in three-quarter profile facing left, with elaborately coiffed hair falling over the nape of her neck. The elderly subject has in some cases been interpreted as a man (Bora 1998a, p. 204) given the lack of any clear gender markers.

Camillo Procaccini's studies contain further examples of subjects with elegant traits paired with others more caricatural in appearance, as in the four heads erroneously catalogued as female figures (inv. 338). Hence there are studies of heads that have affinities even in the details with those on this sheet, like the head of a young woman and another drawing of two female heads (inv. 386).

The substantial corpus of drawings by Camillo reveals a specific interest in representing grotesque heads in his early works (Cassinelli and Vanoli, in Rancate 2007). This continued during his stay in Milan, where it matched the local taste favouring this genre. In this way Procaccini's drawing brings out the ties between the language of the features caricatured in the Lombard tradition united with a Bolognese matrix in the spirit of Bartolomeo Passarotti.

This subject might be one of those that presented a comparison between figures embodying old age and youth, alluding directly to time and the vanity of beauty (for example in Leonardo, Florence, Gabinetto dei Disegni e delle Stampe delle Gallerie degli Uffizi, inv. 423 E). A variation on the theme is the series of 'ill-assorted couples', such as the pair by Wenceslaus Hollar inspired by Leonardo in the Royal Collection at Windsor RCIN 803715. Another variation on this theme depicts morphological oppositions in paired figures. The drawing in Venice certainly belongs to this strand, as a chiasmic representation: youth and old age, the harmony of the forms of the young woman and the disharmony heightened in the features of the old woman.

RC

Bibliography
Selvatico 1854; Ruggeri 1977, p. 21, plate 2; Neilson 1979, p. 167, and plate 365; Nepi Scirè 1982; Di Giampaolo 1993; Bora 1998a, p. 204; Cassinelli and Vanoli, in Rancate 2007, pp. 43–90.

40.

Annibale Carracci (1560–1609)
Bearded head of a man in profile facing left, 1602 *ante quem*
Brown ink in pen glued to early backing, 89 × 78 mm
Paris, Musée du Louvre, Département des Arts Graphiques, Cabinet des dessins, inv. 7393

This drawing belonged to the collection of Comte Charles Paul de Saint-Morys, which entered the Louvre between 1796 and 1797 (Arquié-Bruley, Labbé and Bicart-Sée 1987, p. 166). The subject was probably inspired by a real face, since it turns up again in the fresco by Domenichino in Grottaferrata, *La costruzione dell'abbazia* (Mignosi Tantillo 1996, p. 2014, fig. 29), and other drawings, some in different poses, as in the bocce player in the drawing at Windsor (inv. RCIN 901928) and the face portrayed frontally in the sheet of the *Adoration of the Shepherds* in the J. Paul Getty Museum in Los Angeles (inv. 86.GA.726-1).

The attribution to Agostino derives from Wittkower (1952, p. 121) on the drawing at Windsor (inv. RCIN 901928). He also directed attention to all the similar subjects in different collections: studies of heads in Darmstadt (inv. AE 1348), *The Adoration of the Shepherds* in the Getty Museum, the caricatures in the Oppé collection, the similar ones in Turin (Cart. 21-16066), the drawing in the British Museum of a putto defecating (inv. Pp, 3.12) and the group of figures in the museums of Cleveland (inv. 41603) and Stockholm (inv. NM 937/1863). The attribution of the drawings to the corpus of Annibale's work was advanced by Loisel Legrand (1999, p. 258 and; 2004, p. 257) in the case of the drawing at Windsor, because of the presence of a head matching that of St Gregory for the lost altarpiece *St Gregory praying for Souls in Purgatory*, in the Salviati chapel at San Gregorio Magno in Rome (Posner 1971, no. 130).

Apart from the matter of attribution, the drawing reveals the significance of caricature in Annibale Carracci's work. As Loisel (1999, p. 258) observes, Bellori relates that Annibale enjoyed transforming human faces into animals. In the study of our subject, he performed this

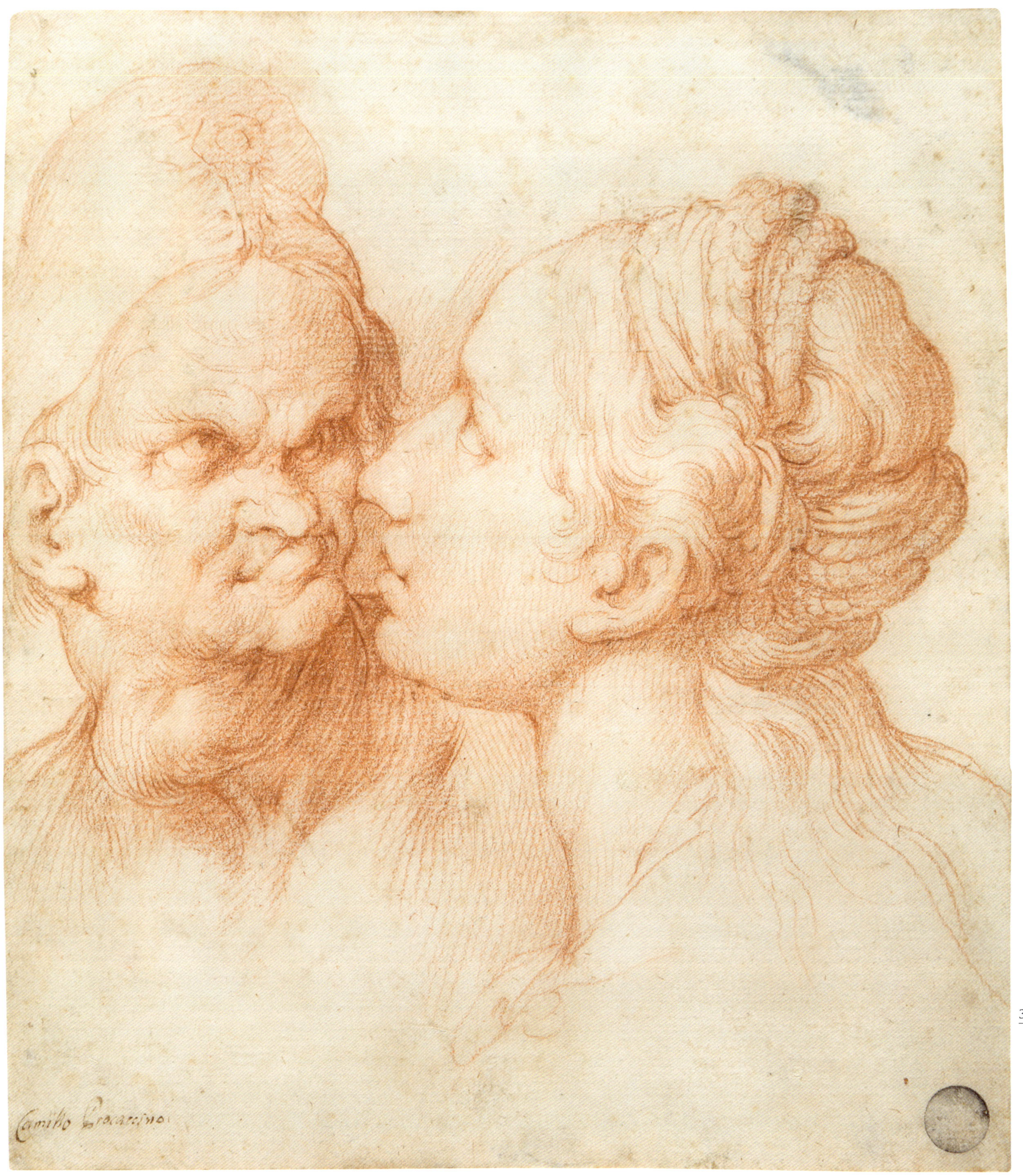

39.

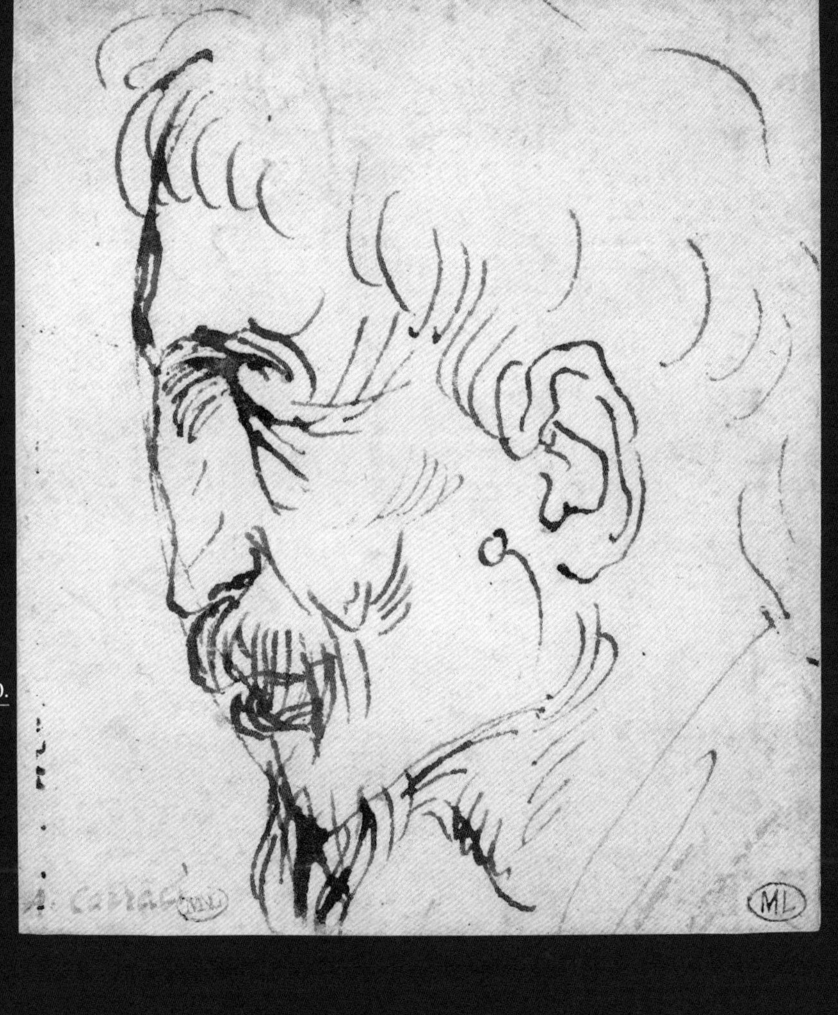

40.

mutation in the drawing in the British Museum (inv. Pp, 3.12). On the right it depicts the profile of the man's head and on the left a study of the head of a satyr that combines the traits of our subject with those of a goat.

RC

Bibliography
Bacou 1961, no. 19; Posner 1971, vol. I, p. 66, fig. 60, p. 163 n. 71; Arquié-Bruley, Labbé and Biscart-Sée 1987, p. 166; Loisel Legrand, 1999, p. 258, no. 82; Loisel 2004, p. 257, no. 549.

41.

Agostino Carracci (1557–1602)
Grotesque mask, c. 1593
Pen and black ink on white paper, upper corners cropped in bevelled form, 86 × 53 mm
Chatsworth, The Devonshire Collection, vol. 5, fol. 46

This fragment passed from the collection of John Talman to that of Richard Boyle, third Earl of Burlington, into that of William, fourth Duke of Devonshire, and so to the Duke of Devonshire's collection at Chatsworth. It is the only drawing by Agostino Carracci from the Burlington legacy. Its fragmentary condition has been altered by bevelling the upper corners and inserting it in a gilded frame made when it was part of John Talman's collection.
It bears no traditional attribution and its ascription to Agostino Carracci derives from comparison with another fragment, probably from the same sheet, in the Uffizi and with a historical attribution to 'Agostino Caracci' (Jaffé 1994, p. 62).
The subject represented is a male head with an extremely elongated face, particularly grotesque in the coarse grinning mouth from which sprout four large square teeth. The mouth is framed by long, thick compact whiskers that might equally be interpreted as skin growths, since they recur at the base of the left cheek. The face is a mixture of the human and the animal, probably constituting a model for a decorative

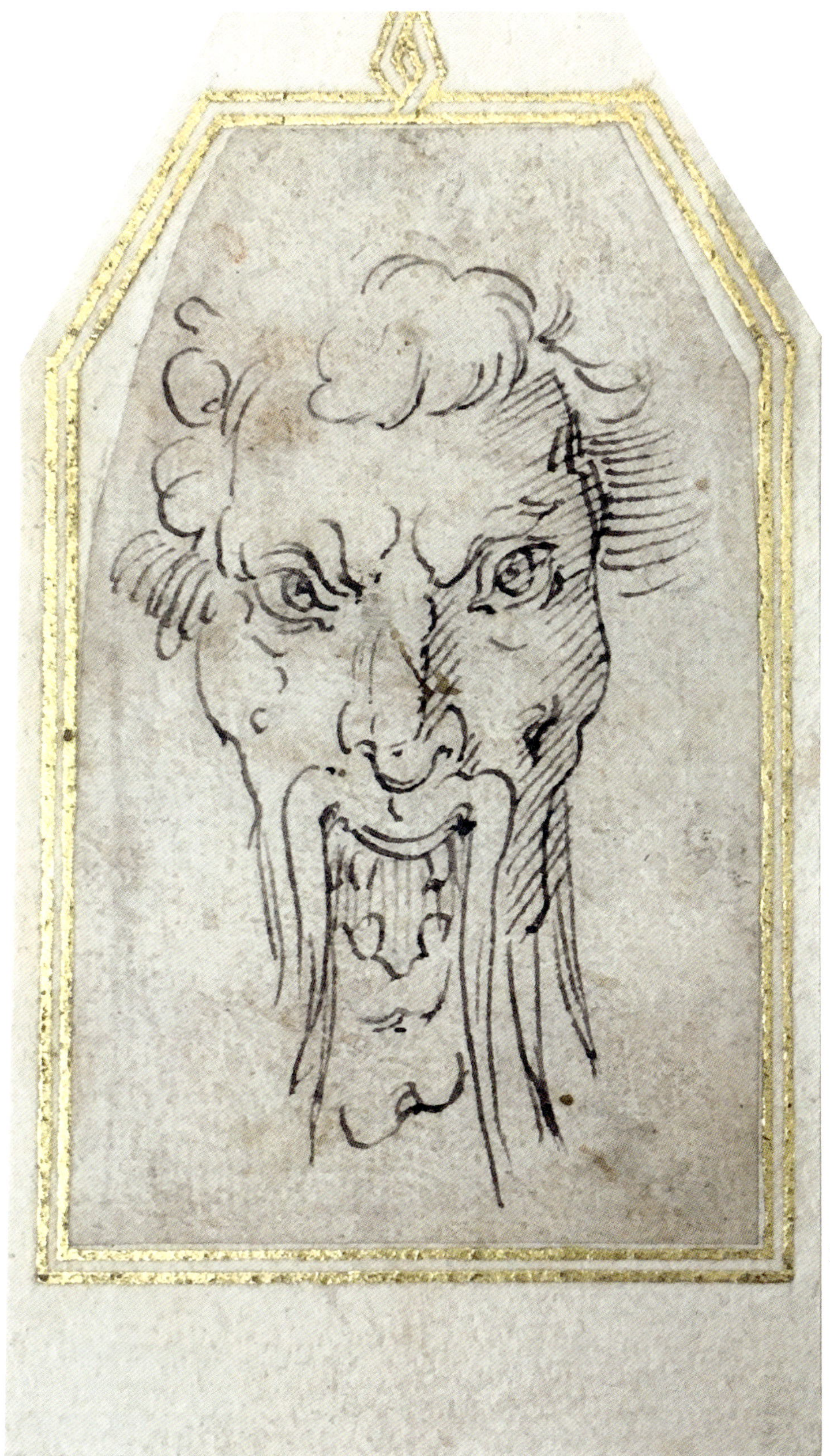

41.

feature that Jaffé relates to an etching in the Getty collection (inv. B.XVIII, Jaffé 1994, p. 156, no. 273), on which a seventeenth-century hand has written in ink: 'Agostino Caracci engraved, for the doors of the Galleria Sampieri, in Bologna.'
The theme of grotesque ornaments was highly developed in the figurative repertoire of both Agostino and Annibale, especially in the framing elements and embellishments of their youthful decorative works in Bologna, for example in Palazzo Fava.
In the Chatsworth fragment the presence of the mole on the cheek and the elongated nose also evoke Annibale's caricatural face of a man in profile (Louvre), present in the exhibition [cat. 40].

RC

Bibliography:
Jaffé 1994, p. 62, no. 462 (vol. V, fol. 46).

42.

After Annibale Carracci (1560–1609)
Diverse figure al numero di ottanta, disegnate di penna nell'hore di ricreatione da Annibale Carracci intagliate in rame e cavate dagli originali da Simone Guilino Parigino dedicate a tutti i virtuosi et intendenti della professione della pittura e del disegno, Rome, printed by Lodovico Grignani, 1646
specimen displayed in the exhibition: anastatic copy, Ancona 1993
Milan, private collection

In the 1590s, Annibale Carracci filled a sketchbook with seventy-five drawings, depicting people working at various itinerant trades. The collection remained available to his pupils for some years, then passed through the hands of various collectors until it came to Giovanni Antonio Massani, master of the household of Pope Urban VIII. He published it in 1646 under the pseudonym of Giovanni Atanasio Mosini. The drawings were etched on copper for printing by Simon Guillan II of Paris (1618–1654) under the careful supervision of Alessandro Algardi. Mosini wrote the preface to the publication, recounting the history of the drawings and the technique adopted for the printed edition, then inserted an essay on artistic theory by Gratiadio Machati (the pseudonym of Giovanni Agucchi). Today we have no knowledge of the fate of either the sketchbook with the original drawings or the complete treatise by Machati.
For the history of caricature, it is notable that Mosini in his preface credited Annibale with its invention and used this specific term for the first time (Berra 2009, pp. 80–81). The connection between caricature and the drawings in the collection is described as arising from a pastime Annibale pursued in his hours of 'recreation' and the subjects he chose: common people realistically depicted in their garments and features.
Five plates were added to Annibale's notebook and represent activities not properly related to itinerant trades: '76 a famous spy', '77 an expert bawd' (the two titles are reversed in the index), '78 a girl tending chickens', '79 a boy urinating', '80 the consul from the Levant'.
Study of the various plates reveals the artist's care to represent the subjects in natural poses and with natural features. They are mostly humble figures, yet caricature as stressed by Mosini is not particularly evident. For example, the poses and garments sometimes conceal the faces of the subjects. The vendors of terracotta cooking pots (24) and of ladles and cutting boards (37) have headgear that is firmly lowered over the eyes, concealing their features. But even more often the figures are depicted from behind, as in the case of the seller of rat poison (13) or the baker (27), the house painter (30), the gravedigger (43) or the well cleaner (45). When the physiognomy is clearly recognisable, no exaggerated or extreme features can be seen. The only one who appears with features accentuated is the old woman with a goitre who is arguing with the overseer of the sale of meat (31) and, in the additional plates, the clever bawd, who has a prominent chin (77).

RC

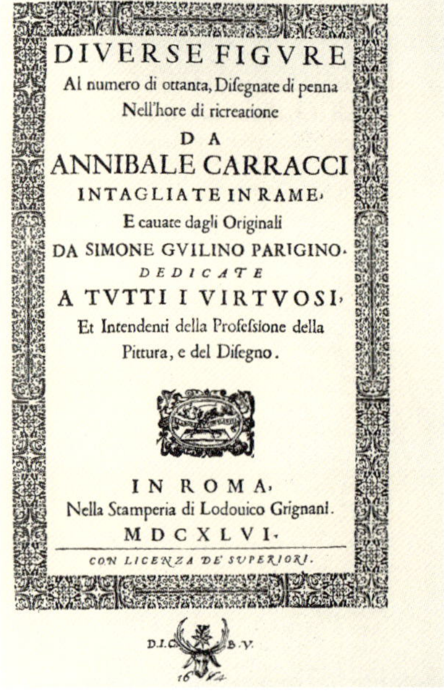
DIVERSE FIGVRE
Al numero di ottanta, Disegnate di penna
Nell'hore di ricreatione
DA
ANNIBALE CARRACCI
INTAGLIATE IN RAME,
E cauate dagli Originali
DA SIMONE GVILINO PARIGINO.
DEDICATE
A TVTTI I VIRTVOSI,
Et Intendenti della Professione della
Pittura, e del Disegno.

IN ROMA,
Nella Stamperia di Lodouico Grignani.
MDCXLVI.
CON LICENZA DE' SVPERIORI.

3. Annibale Carracci, *Diverse figure al numero di ottanta*, 1646, ed. 1993. Milan, private collection

Bibliography
Mahon 1947, pp. 233–75; Marabottini 1966, pp. XIX–XXXII; De Grazia 1984, p. 52; Lévy 2002, pp. 129–57; Berra 2009, pp. 80–81, n. 27.

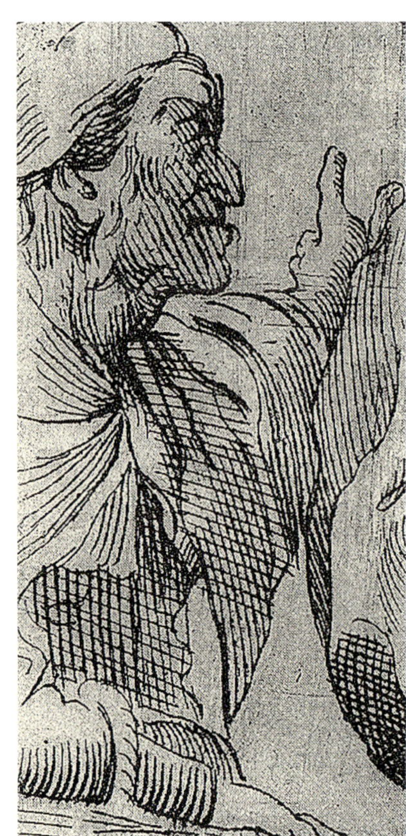

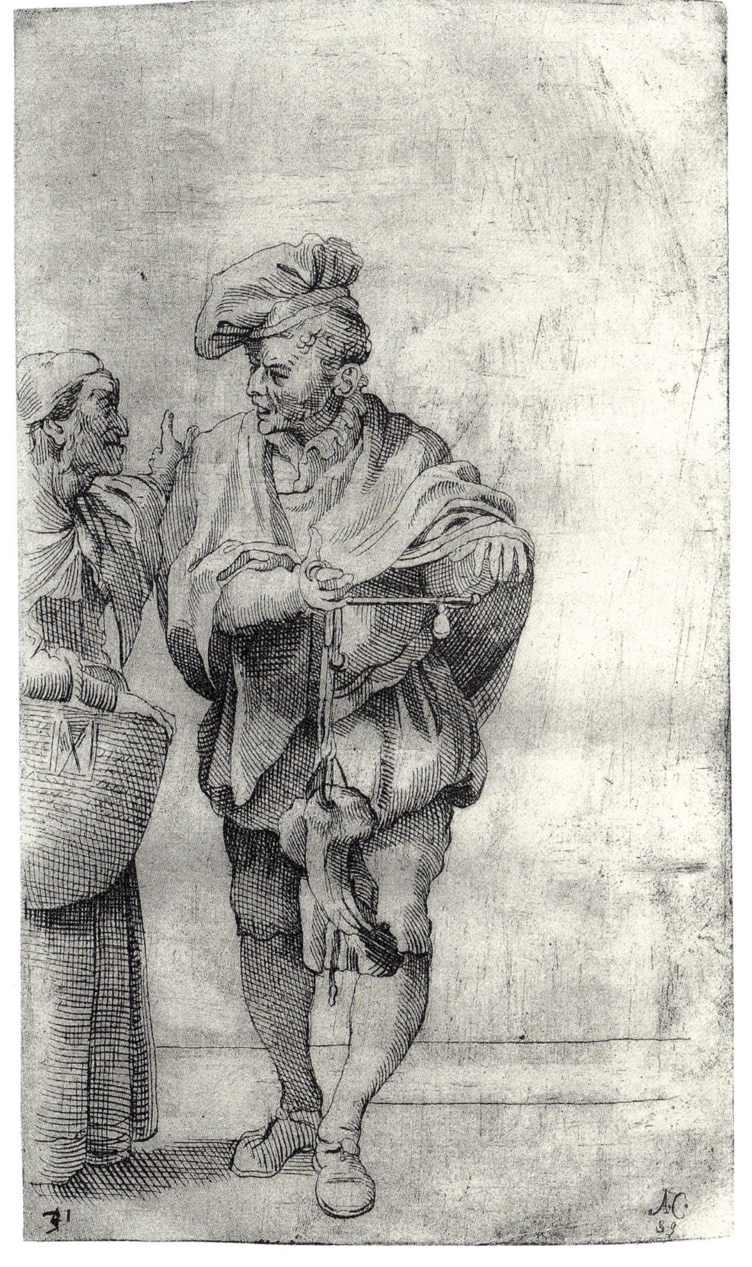

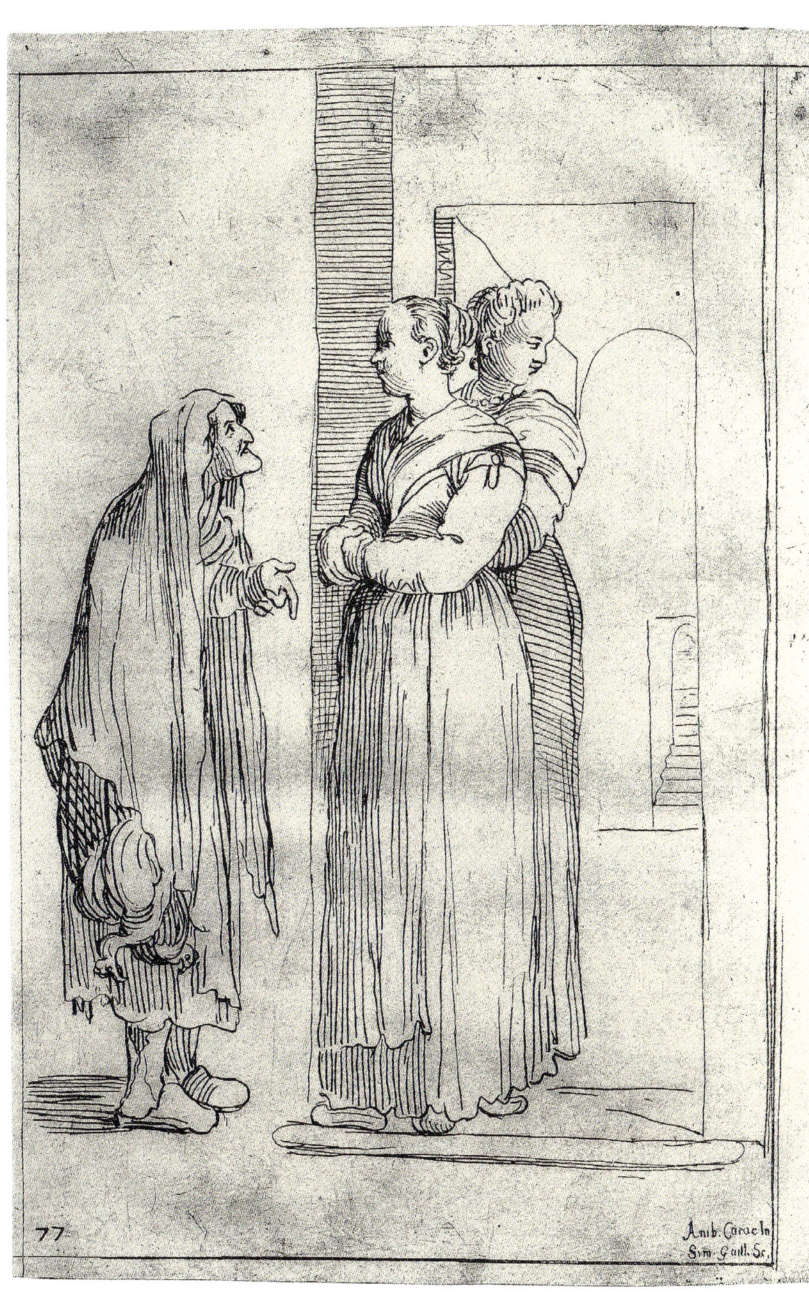

42.

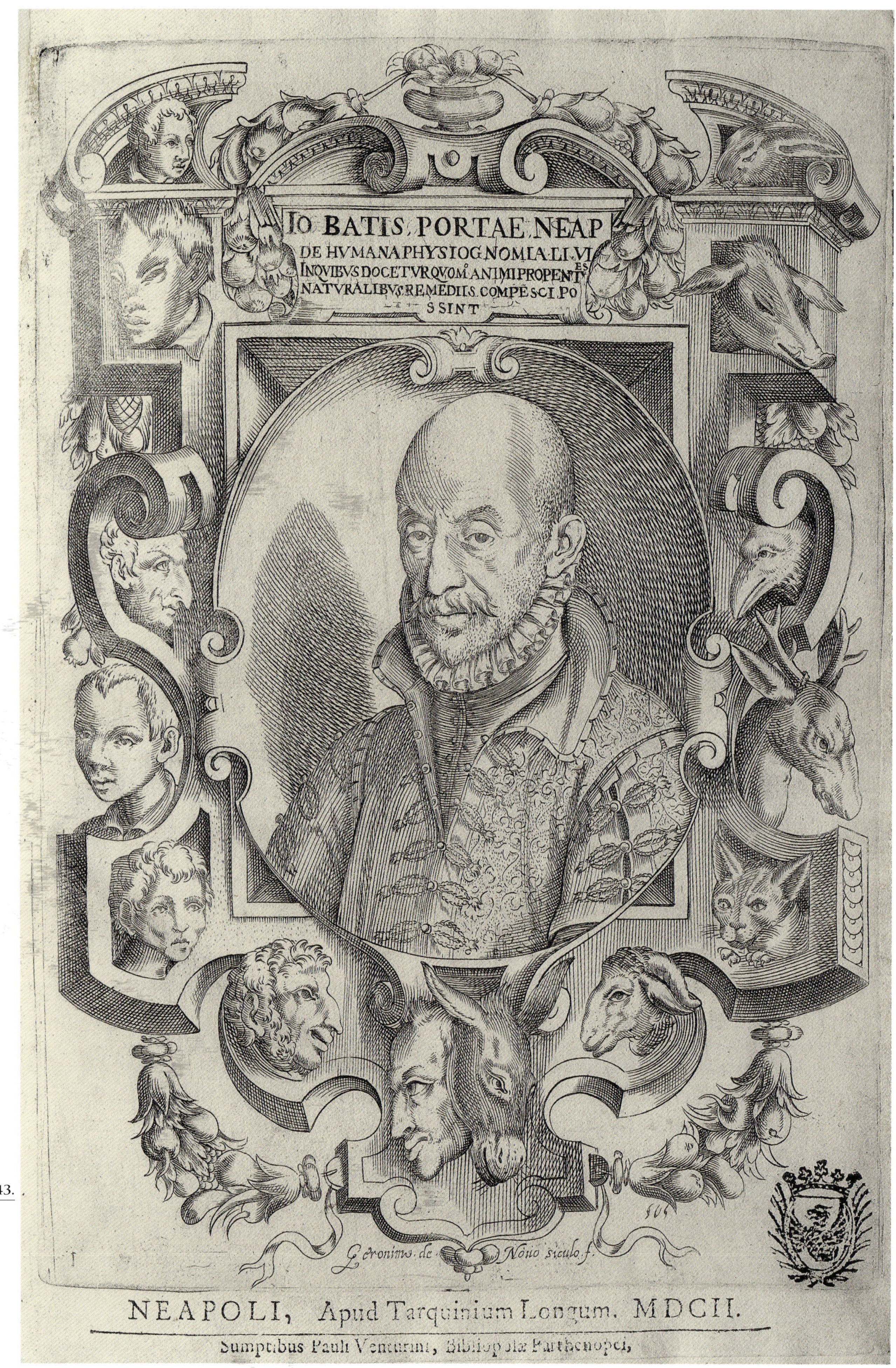
IO. BATIS. PORTAE. NEAP
DE HVMANA PHYSIOGNOMIA. LI. VI
IN QVIBVS DOCETVR QVOMº ANIMI PROPENTES
NATVRALIBVS REMEDIIS. COMPESCI. PO
SSINT

Geronimo de Nolo siculo f.

NEAPOLI, Apud Tarquinium Longum. MDCII.

Sumptibus Pauli Venturini, Bibliopolæ Parthenopei,

43.

43.

Giovan Battista Della Porta
(1535–1616)
De Humana Physiognomia
Giuseppe Cacchi ed., Sorrento, 1586
Printed book illustrated with engravings, 333 × 235 × 27 mm
Milan, Castello Sforzesco, Ente Raccolta Vinciana, inv. ERV G. IV. 3

In the philosopher Giovan Battista della Porta's *De humana Physiognomia*, the subject of the abnormal face goes beyond the boundaries of pure representation or, at most, an enrichment of iconographic technique, to venture into the troubled subject of physiognomic form as the manifestation of human characters and tendencies. Dangerously poised between doctrine, pervaded by magical thinking and a concern not to incur the dangers of censorship, the publication of Della Porta's book met with a number of difficulties. This happened despite the author's assurances that he wished to present a science in which there was no determinism, only the ability to identify *propensiones*, not *actiones*, which are dependent on human freedom.

In essence, Della Porta argued that divine power manifests itself in physical features that recur throughout creation, in animals as well as humans, and these physical analogies have parallels in the manifestations of the character of a person. Such propensities can be identified by comparing human faces, as a whole or in their various parts, to animal traits [fig. 4]. He studied not only the forms of the parts but also the dimensions. Finally, he did not limit his comparisons to faces but included other body parts, such as the chest, hips and buttocks.

The plates accompanying the text were by the Sicilian draughtsman and engraver Geronimo de Novo, who produced the extraordinary title page of the work. The images are highly effective, with close comparisons of the characteristics of animals with human figures. In the descriptions of the features of human faces and more generally heads, the elements of caricature are heightened to reveal similarities. Certainly, these illustrations circulated widely and became a repertoire that inspired the production of caricatures.

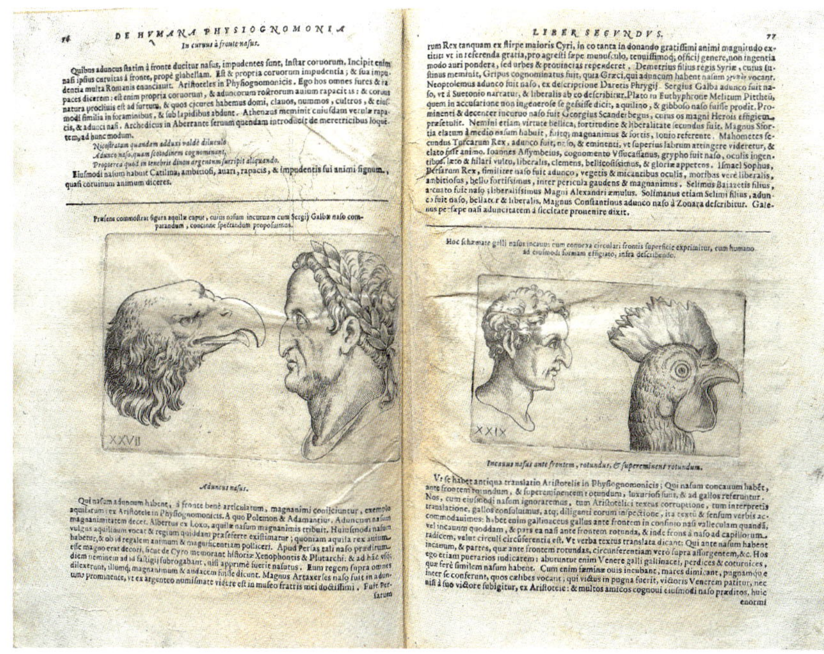
76 DE HVMANA PHYSIOGNOMONIA

In curuus à fronte nasus.

Quibus aduncus statim à fronte ducitur nasus, impudentes sunt, instar coruorum. Incipit enim nasi ipsius caruitas à fronte, propè glabellam. Est & propria coruorum impudentia; & sua impudentia multa Romanis enunciauit. Aristoteles in Physiognomonicis. Ego hos omnes fures & rapaces dicerem: est enim propria coruorum, & aduncorum rostrorum auium rapacitas: & coruus natura procliuis est ad furtum, & quos cicures habemus domi, clauos, nummos, cultros, & eiusmodi similia in foraminibus, & sub lapidibus abdunt. Athenæus meminit cuiusdam vetulæ rapacis, & adunci nasi. Archedicus in Aberrante seruum quendam introducit de meretricibus loquentem, ad hunc modum.

Nicostratam quandam adduxi valdè diluculo
Adunco naso, quam scotodinem cognominant,
Propterea quod in tenebris dinon argentum surripit aliquando.

Eiusmodi nasum habuit Catilina, ambitiosi, auari, rapacis, & impudentis sui animi signum, quasi coruinum animum diceres.

Præsens commostrat figura aquilæ caput, cuius nasum incuruum cum Sergij Galbæ naso comparandum, concinne spectandum proposuimus.

XXVII

Aduncus nasus.

LIBER SECVNDVS. 77

XXIX

Incurus nasus ante frontem, rotundus, & supereminens rotundum.

4. Giovan Battista Della Porta, *De Humana Physiognomia*, 1586, pp. 76–7. Milan, Castello Sforzesco, Ente Raccolta Vinciana

The comparison between animals and humans in caricature immediately found attentive interpreters such as Annibale Carracci, as Massani recalls [cat. 42]: 'Caricatured portraits ... of those persons who have some resemblance to unreasoning animals: since he would only draw a dog, an ox or some other animal, yet it was clearly understood to be the portrait of the person whose behaviour and likeness the artist wished to represent.'

RC

Bibliography

Baltrušaitis 1989; Trabucco 2005, pp. 235–70; Berra 2009, pp. 90–91, fig. 17; New York 2011, pp. 70–71.

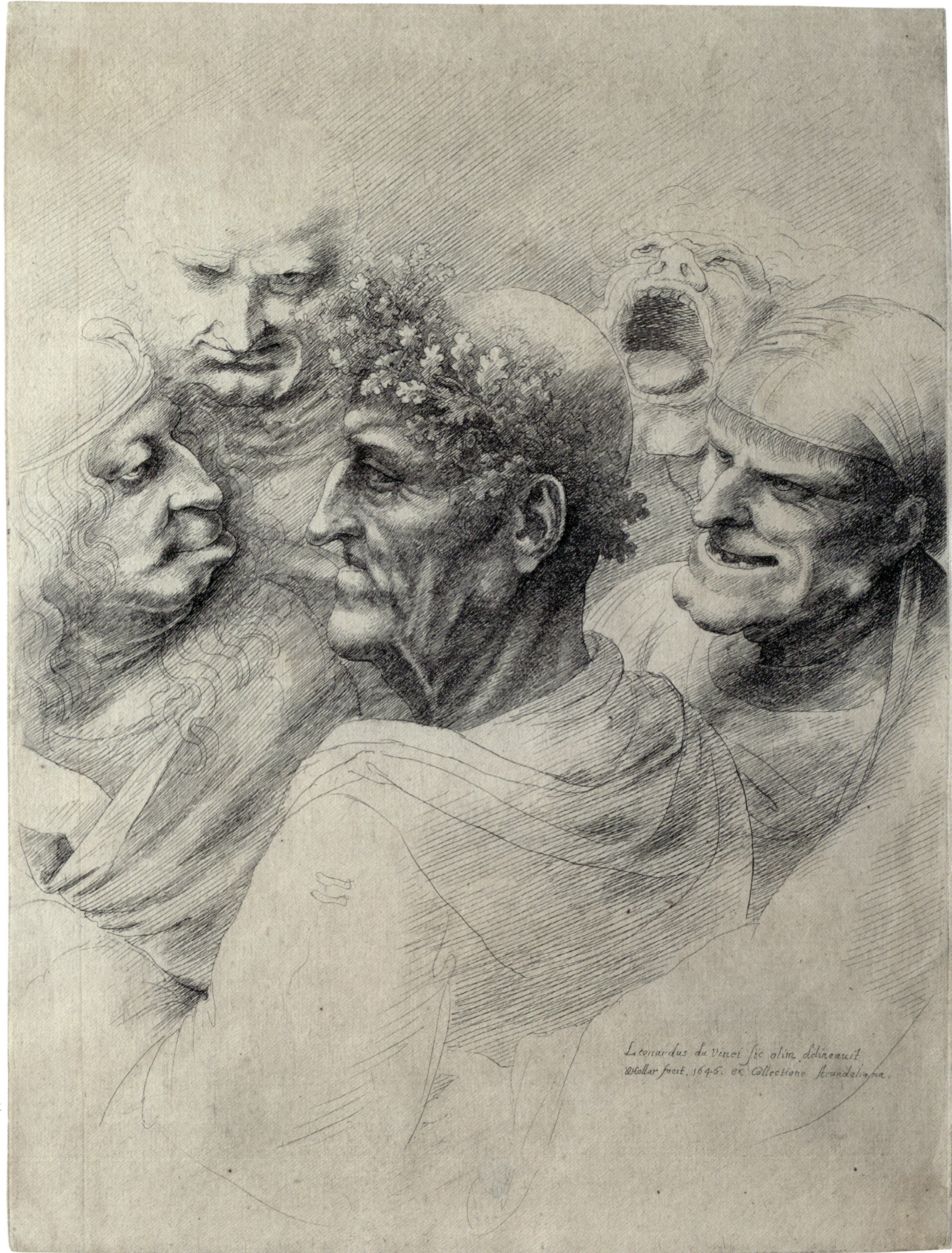
Leonardus da Vinci sic olim delineavit
WHollar fecit, 1646. ex Collectione Arundeliana.

44.

44.

Wenceslaus Hollar (1607–1677)
Five grotesque heads, 1646
Etching, 240 × 185 mm
Lamporecchio, Nuova Fondazione Rossana e Carlo Pedretti, FRCP-S-H.020

This engraving is the largest composition and the most carefully finished in stylistic quality of all the works by Wenceslaus Hollar associated with the commission from Thomas Howard, 21st Earl of Arundel. It is well known that in Antwerp between 1644 and 1652 Hollar made at least three sets of etchings based on Leonardo's drawings, using tracing paper although without seeing the originals. The only such tracing identified so far, taken from drawing inv. RL 12490 at Windsor from the Arundel collection, is preserved at the Tyler Museum in Haarlem (inv. A 5). With remarkable precision, the engraver thus presented Leonardo at the same size, as confirmed by the comparison between the work in question and the *Five grotesque heads* (Windsor, inv. RL 12495, c. 1495). As attested by the inscription 'Leonardus da Vinci sic olim delineavit,/ WHollar fecit, 1646. ex Collectione Arundelliana', the work was etched in 1646, the year of Lord Arundel's death in Padua.

Reproduced reversed, the image is strictly faithful to the original. In this composition Leonardo depicted a group of grotesque heads that relate to each other, as he writes in paragraph 42 of the *Libro di Pittura*: 'bold and quick, with passionate motions, like furies. But the motions should appear a great deal quicker in their arms than their legs.' On the reverse of the autograph drawing in Windsor, Leonardo hastened to jot down a note in which he described evil men, especially those he himself had met.

In addition to the undisputed beauty of the image, this composition was highly successful and replicated in numerous copies (Paris, Musée du Louvre, Département des Arts Graphiques, inv. 2516) [fig. 5], but above all it was revisited in interesting ways in Flemish art. Also belonging to the series of this etching is a counter-proof (New York, The Metropolitan Museum of Art, inv. 1850.0223.298) that shows an identical orientation with respect to Leonardo's original drawing, testifying that tracing paper could be used on the verso as well as the recto.

ST

Bibliography

Pennington 1982, no. P1609; Turner 2009, no. 878; Perissa Torrini 2018, pp. 132–3; Melani 2020, pp. 21–31, esp. pp. 28–9.

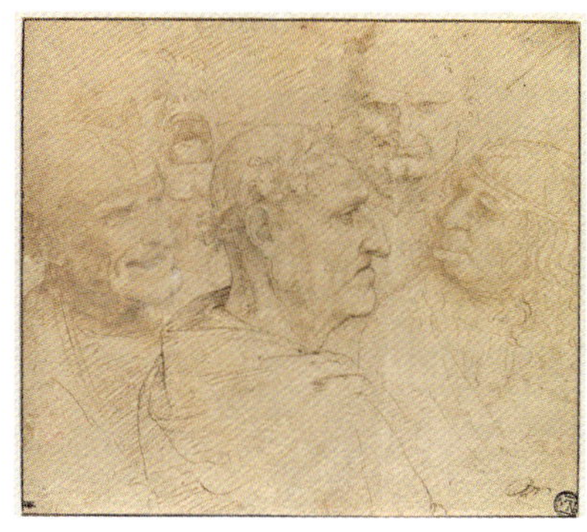

5. Anonymous, after Leonardo da Vinci, *Five grotesque heads*, sixteenth century. Paris, Musée du Louvre, Département des Arts Graphiques, inv. 2516

45.

Wenceslaus Hollar (1607–1677), formerly attributed
Female grotesque head with tall bonnet, c. 1644–52 (?)
Etching, 65 × 42 mm
Lamporecchio, Nuova Fondazione Rossana e Carlo Pedretti, inv. FRCP-S-H.017

This grotesque head is characterised by physiognomic traits so contradictory as to make its features even more repugnant. Its decrepit appearance contrasts with the large eyes with long lashes, while the small nose contrasts with the gaping mouth, whose function is to show the only tooth in the mandible. Both the robe, with a deep neckline and puff sleeves, and the tall headgear, which resembles a French *escoffion* but whose dizzying height makes it a flamboyant hood, seem to identify the subject as a lady with an elegant and carefully groomed appearance despite her grotesque features. This etching, together with a twin reproduction but of lower quality, because it lacks the oblique hatching and shading that distinguish this one (New York, The Metropolitan Museum of Art, inv. Q,5.17), derives from the only work by Hollar considered his autograph by critics. It depicts the same subject but facing in the opposite direction and with the inscription 'Leonardo da/ Vinci inv:/ WHollar fecit/ 1665' (New York, The Metropolitan Museum of Art, inv. 17.50.18-178). It follows that the two prints derived from it are believed to be by another hand according to the most recent critics. Due to the financial pressure on him in Antwerp, Hollar printed numerous copies of works by Leonardo for the market. They were not always documented and ordered, and therefore, we cannot completely exclude the possibility that the copies may be his autograph. There is no doubt that the etching in question derives from the *Pair of aged lovers* (Windsor, inv. RL 12449, c. 1495). In 2014, Carlo Pedretti proposed to read the drawing as a bride escorted by a paranymph, considering it a mother-sheet to the *Five grotesque heads* (Windsor, inv. RL 12495, c. 1495). If so, Hollar would have seen the two parental sheets already divided following the interventions of Pompeo Leoni, and thus etched separately. The allusion to marriage in the two subjects is proven by a drawing by Pieter Paul Rubens after Leonardo (Vienna, Albertina, inv. 17615), which clearly depicts the wedding ring passing from the hands of the paranymph to those of the betrothed. The etching in question also attests to the extraordinary reception of Leonardo in circles in Northern Europe by the affinity with themes in Flemish works depicting marriages of convenience between people of widely different ages. It has been suggested that the so-called *Mock Marriage*, which became famous with Quentin Matsys, and the *Ill-Assorted Couple*, drawn by Jacob Hoefnagel and likewise engraved by Hollar, may have originated from an autograph drawing by Leonardo, now lost.

ST

Bibliography
Pennington 1982, no. 1745, 1745A; Turner 2009, no. 1937; Pedretti 2014, pp. 65–6; Taglialagamba 2014, pp. 120–21; Perissa Torrini 2018, p. 129.

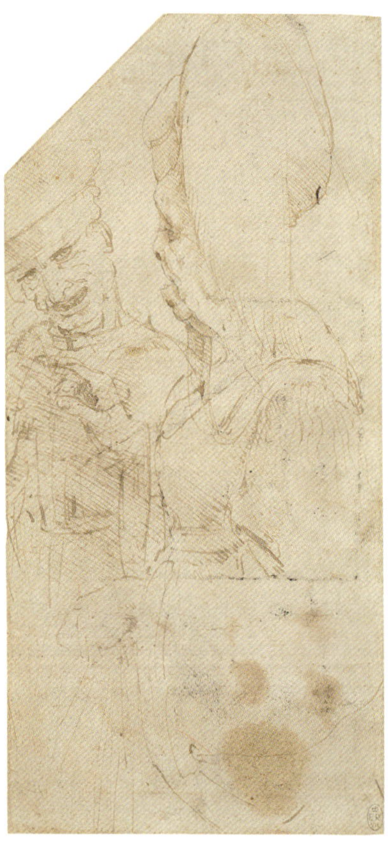

6. Leonardo da Vinci, *Pair of old lovers*, c. 1495. Windsor, Royal Library, inv. RL 12449

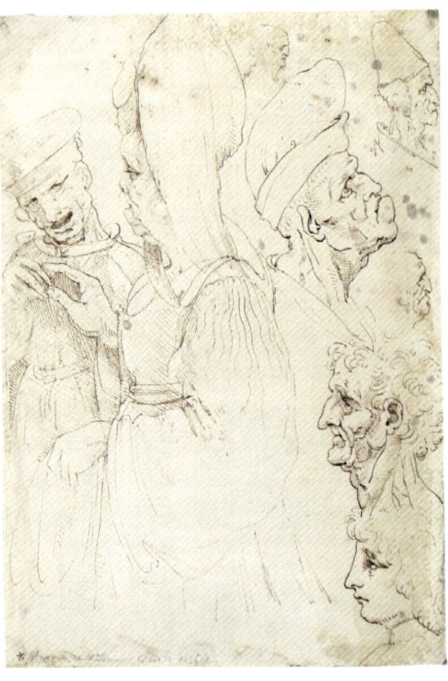

7. Pieter Paul Rubens, after Leonardo da Vinci, *Grotesque heads*, after 1603. Vienna, Albertina, inv. 17615

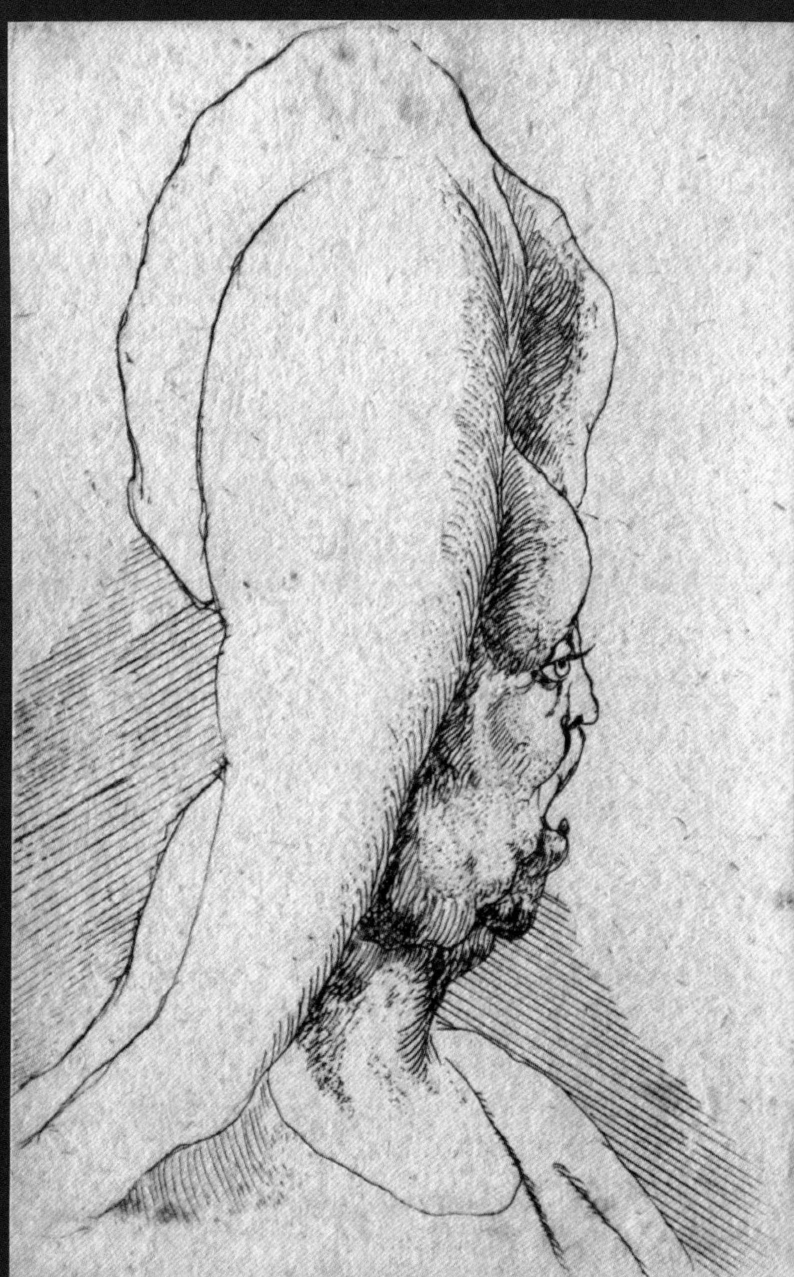

45.

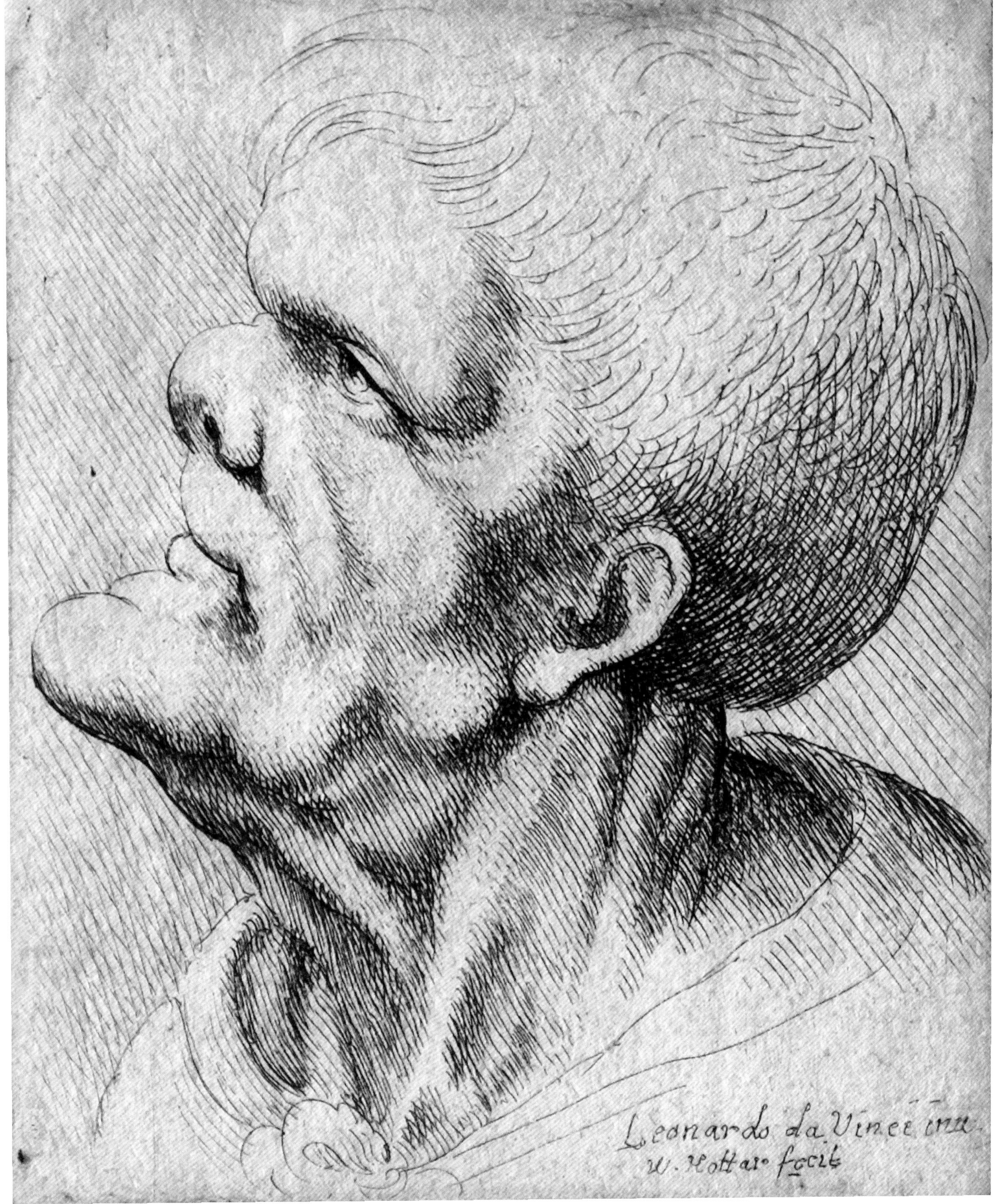
Leonardo da Vinci inu
W. Hollar fecit

46.

Wenceslaus Hollar (1607–1677)
Grotesque male head in profile facing left, c. 1644–52 (?)
Etching, 64 × 52 mm
Lamporecchio, Nuova Fondazione Rossana e Carlo Pedretti, inv. FRCP-S-H.004

This grotesque head, with gaze turned upwards and the torso in three-quarter profile, shows heavily caricatured features – rounded forehead, sunken eyes, snub nose, toothless mouth, prominent chin – contrasting with the anatomical precision of the depiction of the sternocleidomastoid and sternothyroid muscles. Leonardo was interested in the physiological process of physical decay. His studies explore not only the permanent alteration of body parts but also the progressive sclerosis of tissues and muscles that lead to death. In a note on folio 888*r* of the Codex Atlanticus (c. 1480–82), he lists drawings depicting 'many throats of old men', 'many heads of old men', 'the head of an old man with a long chin' and 'the head of a gypsy'. In the *Sesto ragionamento* in the *Libro dei sogni*, Giovan Paolo Lomazzo has Leonardo say: 'I liked above all else to depict old people, only representing them in drawings, all admirable, in pencil and ink'. As attested by the inscription 'Leonardo da Vinci inv:/ W. Hollar fecit', the etching reproduces the sanguine of the *Head of an old man in profile facing right* (Hamburg, Hamburger Kunsthalle, inv. 21482, c. 1490–95), depicting a face in an advanced stage of senility, close to that of a corpse, probably a memory of those bodies on which Leonardo conducted anatomical studies.
In stylistic terms, the lines of the etching are rigid and less clearly defined than Hollar's other copies. The Bohemian engraver failed to repeat some key details, such as the sparse hair and the dull and glassy gaze, though the bust is more firmly drawn and reproduces quite faithfully the robe with a broad neckline closed with a ribbon. The face is turned in the same direction as the original in Hamburg. This is attributable to the use of tracing paper that, given the impossibility of checking the originals, could be transferred to the etching using either the verso or the recto.

ST

Bibliography
Pennington 1982, no. P1575; Turner 2009, no. 1243; Perissa Torrini 2018, p. 131.

47.

Raffaello du Fresne (1611–1661)
Trattato della Pittura di Lionardo da Vinci, novamente dato in luce con la vita dell'istesso autore, s critta da Rafaelle du Fresne
Paris, printed by Giacomo Langlois, 1651
Paper volume, 387 × 261 mm
Milan, Castello Sforzesco, Ente Raccolta Vinciana, inv. RV C. IV. 9

Published in Paris in 1651, with a dedicatory letter from Rafaelle Trichet du Fresne to Queen Christina of Sweden (Brummer 1993, pp. 117–25), the *editio princeps* of the *Trattato della Pittura* was based on the material collected by Cassiano dal Pozzo (1588–1657), in particular an abbreviated version of the *Trattato* with corrections by Pozzo himself (Pavesi, in Milan 2007, pp. 130–33, nos 18–20; Barone 2018, pp. 276–84) and with the figures drawn by Nicolas Poussin (1594–1665) pasted on the manuscript pages (Pavesi, in Milan 2007, pp. 131–2, no. 19; Barone, in Milan 2007, pp. 99–119; Barone 2018, pp. 284–92). The precepts concerning the study of the figures affirm the necessary universality of the painter in the search for variety and disharmony (ch. XXI, p. 5) in human types (chs LXI–LXIV, p. 13), as in the different parts of the face, mouths, noses and eyes (chs CLXXXVII–CLXXXXII, pp. 52–54), brought into harmony with the natural 'accidents of man' (ch. CCXLIV, p. 71) while shunning 'monstrous things' (ch. CLXXII, p. 47). Elements closer to the theme of character heads are made explicit in the characters that make up the 'stories', such as the wrathful who 'with great fierceness move their eyebrows . . . or other expressions, such as laughter, weeping, pain, admiration, fear, and the like' (ch. LXXXXV, p. 25). In the representation 'Of laughing and weeping', finally, more stringent elements appear: the painter must accompany the mood with explicit gestures, concentrating the emotion in the face: 'Those who weep, raise the brows, and bring them close together above the nose, forming many wrinkles on the forehead, and the corners of the mouth are turned downwards. Those who laugh have them turned upwards, and their brows are open and extended' (ch. CCLVII, p. 73). This variety of expression should be recorded in 'a pocket-book, in which you have marked all these variations of features, and after having looked at the face you mean to draw, withdraw a little aside, and note down in your book which of the features are similar to it, to be able to put it all together at home' (ch. CLXXXX, p. 53).

RA

Bibliography
Verga, 1931, vol. I, no. 2, p. 4; Steinitz 1958, pp. 150–52; Sparti 2003, pp. 143–88; Pavesi 2004, p. 129; Guffanti, in Milan 2007, pp. 140–43, no. 28; Guffanti 2009, pp. 569–605; Villata 2013, pp. 56–7, no. 15; Barone, in Milan 2015, pp. 582–3, no. XI.21; Guffanti 2018, pp. 373–411, pp. 547–9.

48.

Donato Creti (1671–1749)
Head of a young woman in profile and caricature of a priest, 1685
Red pencil on paper, 238 × 195 mm
Florence, Gabinetto dei Disegni e delle Stampe delle Gallerie degli Uffizi, inv. 4048 S

At the bottom right there is an inscription by Alessandro Fava in pen, 'Donato Creti f. A.F. 14 luglio 1685 A.F.'. With his son Pietro Ercole, Fava was the patron of the artist, then fourteen years old. A pupil of Lorenzo Pasinelli, he was invited by the Bolognese nobleman 'to come and draw in his house, promising him all the assistance he needed, so that he could study in comfort and without the need to support himself" (Zanotti 1739, vol. II, pp. 102–3). This was confirmed by Creti himself in 1717, recalling that he had 'been raised and protected by the illustrious Signor Conte Alessandro Fava of worthy memory' (Roli 1967, p. 80). Fava put a similar inscription and the

TRATTATO

DELLA PITTVRA

DI LIONARDO

DA VINCI,

Nouamente dato in luce, con la vita dell'iſteſſo autore, ſcritta

DA RAFAELLE DV FRESNE.

Si ſono giunti i tre libri della pittura, & il trattato della ſtatua di Leon Battiſta Alberti, con la vita del medeſimo.

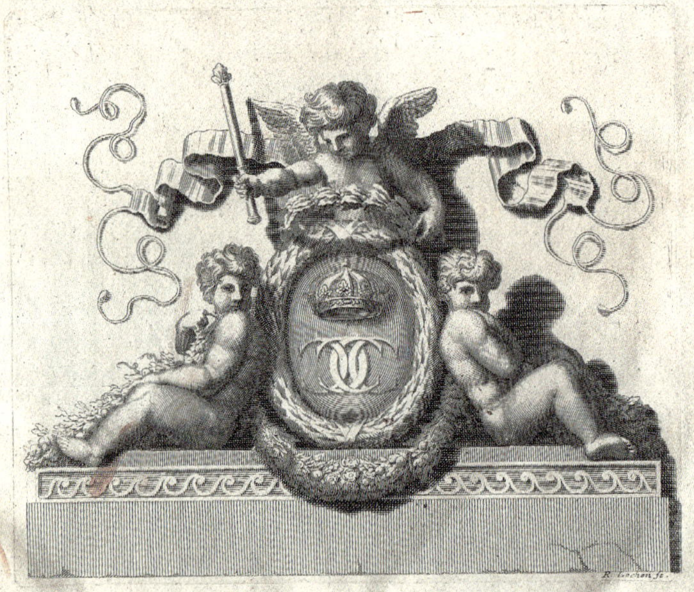

IN PARIGI,

47. Appreſſo Giacomo Langlois, ſtampatore ordinario del rè Chriſtianiſſimo, al monte S. Genoueſa, dirimpetto alla fontana, all'inſegna della Regina di pace.

M. DC. LI.

CON PRIVILEGIO DEL RE.

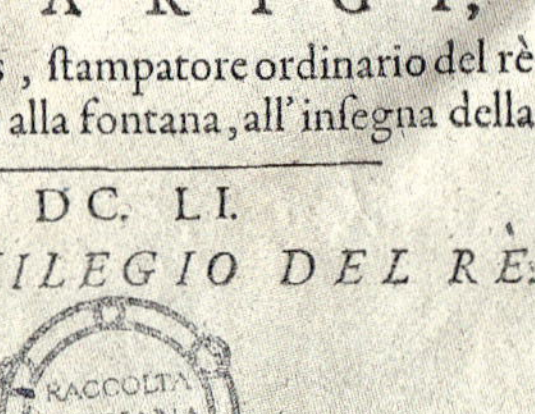

same date on another drawing by Creti in red pencil depicting *Two boys seated on the ground* (Uffizi, inv. 4049 S; Riccomini 2012, p. 50, n. 37.41). In the upper right-hand corner of the sheet there appears an inverted, sketched detail of the profile of the bulging forehead with hooked nose and long chin of the figure on display here, a priest with a skullcap on his head. The repetition, on the same day, of a 'first idea' leading to the image placed as a comic contrast to that of a young woman with her hair gathered behind the nape of her neck, records a precise educational method. First Creti would test his skill by making a rapid copy of a work by his peers and then, in the playful oxymoron created by the female beauty above the 'rather caricatural features' (Mazza 2004a) of the ecclesiastic, Creti would comply with the precepts of the Carracci (see Berra 2009, pp. 80–81) by grasping both the ideal and the caricature by drawing the natural datum.

Fava's comments certified the value of Creti's exercises, revealed in the count's collection by the *Caricature of a cook* (1681) in the spirit of Guercino by Cesare Gennari, now in Princeton (Mazza 2004a, p. 317), and by Giovanni Antonio Burrini's *Studies of heads* of 1679, now at the Los Angeles County Museum of Art, a reinterpretation of the 'Annibale Carracci's character heads, accentuating their caricatural tendencies' (Mazza 2004a, p. 319). Years later, Ercole Graziani and Domenico Maria Fratta, Donato's pupils, vied in drawing caricatures on the floor of the salon of Palazzo Fava (Mazza 2004a, p. 325).

EL

Bibliography

Catalogo della Raccolta 1870, p. 287, no. 27; Alcsuti 1932, p. 26; Roli 1959, p. 329; Roli 1962, pp. 241, 247; Roli 1967, pp. 13–14, 106, no. 27; Roli 1977, p. 252; New York 1989, p. 102; Mazza 1992a, pp. 97, 99, 118, n. 1; Mazza 1992b, pp. 261, 276, n. 187; Mazza 1995, p. 93; Mazza 1997, p. 375; Mazza 1999, p. 183; Mazza, in Bellettini 2001, p. 240; Mazza 2004a, p. 319; Riccòmini 2012, pp. 19, 50, no. 37.40.

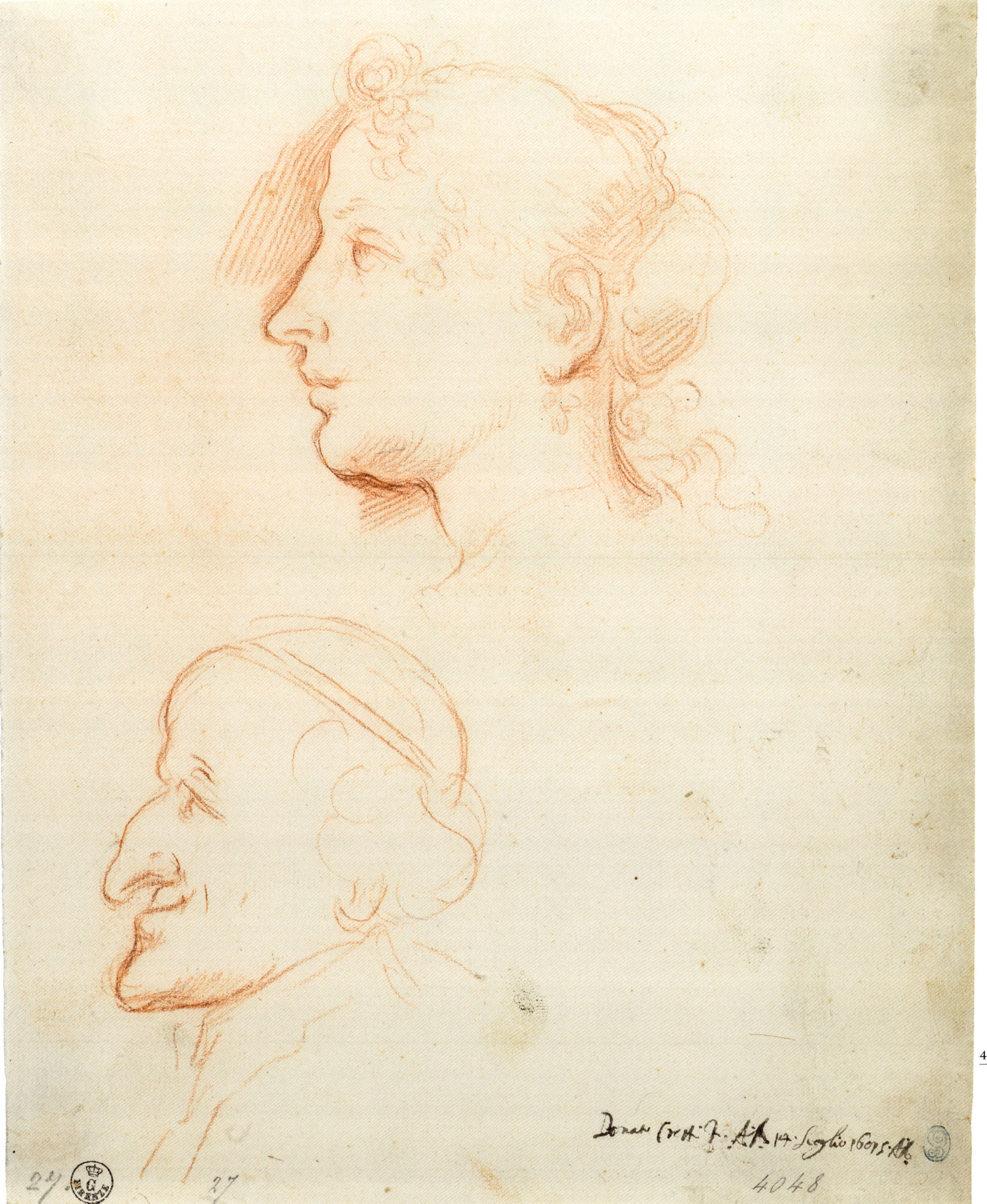

48.

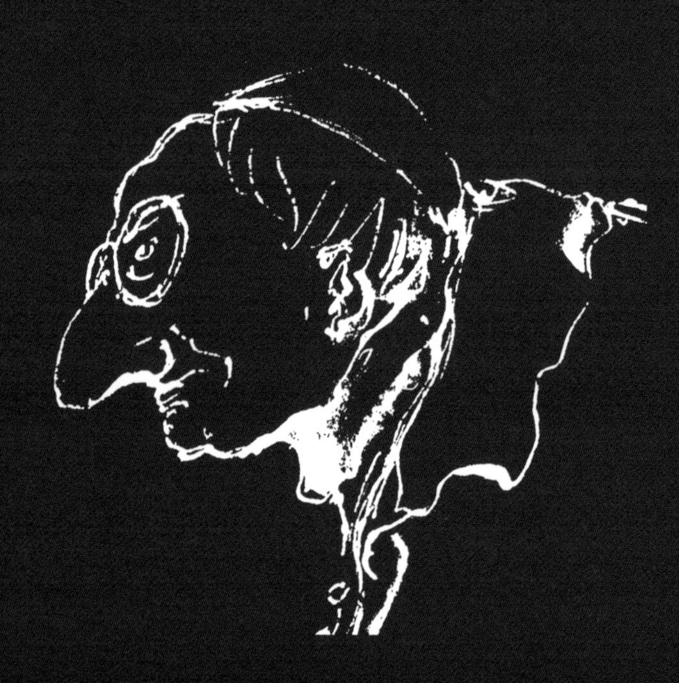

The Circulation of Leonardo's Heads and Caricatures in Eighteenth-Century Venice

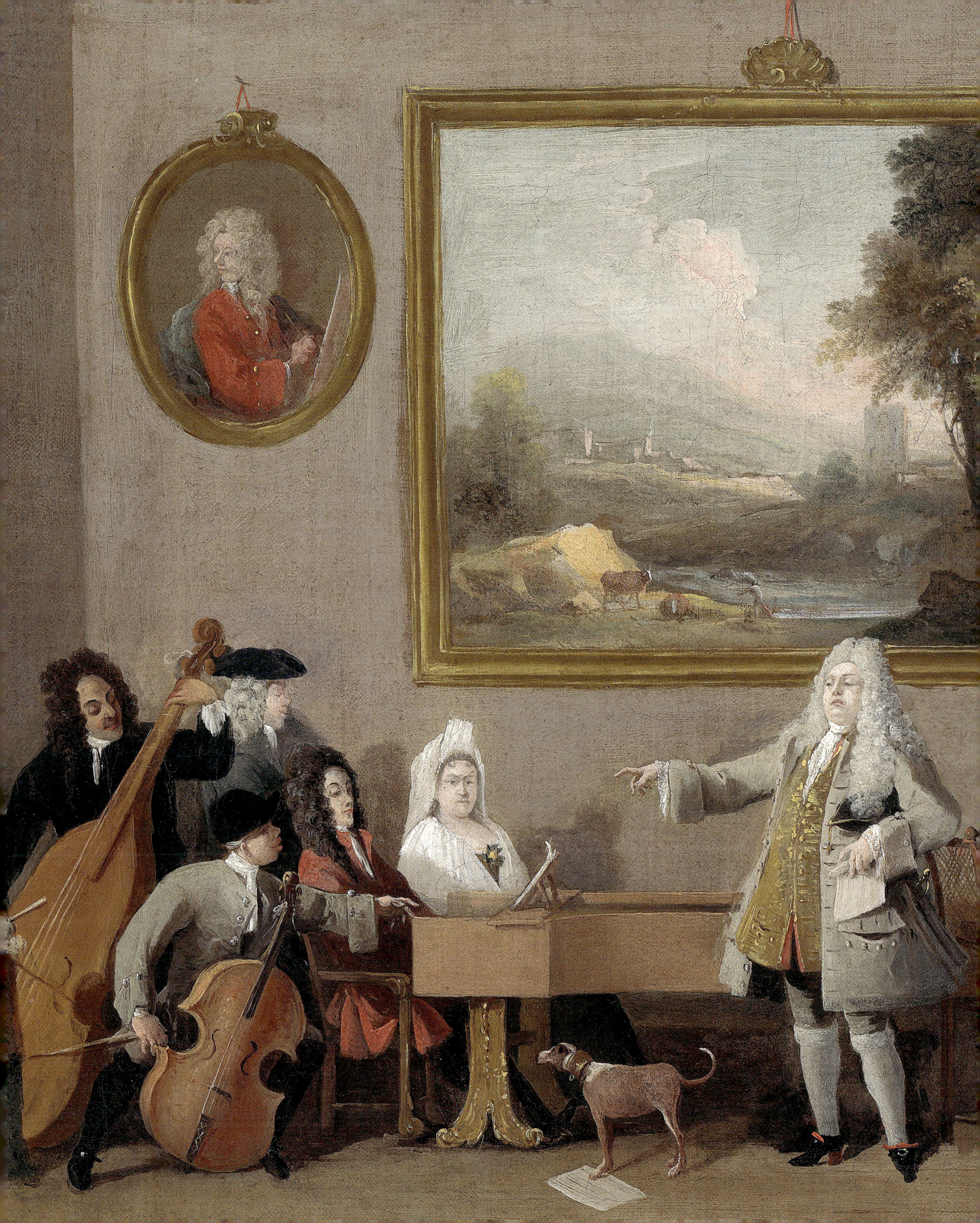

Enrico Lucchese

Caricature and Caricaturists in Eighteenth-Century Venice

The caricatures on the back of Bellini's paintings in the Scuola della Carità[1] and the proliferation in the eighteenth century of droll images by Marco Ricci [fig. 1], Anton Maria Zanetti and Tiepolo, mark the two extremes of the as yet unwritten history of this distinctive genre in Venetian art, which has been less widely explored by scholars than examples in Emilia, Lombardy, Rome or Tuscany.[2] The case of the Tiepolos, given their outstanding stylistic quality, together with the fame of Giambattista and Giandomenico's Pulcinella, has met with the greatest and most constant critical favour, from the article by Max Kozloff to the exhibition in Venice almost twenty years ago.[3] That survey included a section devoted to the Zanetti Album, with the same title as the pamphlet mocking opera by Benedetto Marcello,[4] marking the first step in the practice of caricature before the drawings by the Tiepolos father and son. This interpretation was taken into account in the catalogue of the 350 sheets by Zanetti,[5] which reviewed their connection with the collections that had formerly belonged to Joseph Smith and Francesco Algarotti.[6]

In this century of letter-writing and travelling painters, it is in the correspondence received by Rosalba Carriera that we find the earliest dated example of the custom of making humorous sketches, as a passing comment or postscript, hence a personal expression, an exchange of pleasantries between intimates. An example is the 'companion' drawn by her master Antonio Balestra in his own mocking defence on the verso of a letter of 20 August 1701 [fig. 2].[7] The image is connected not only to his training in Rome, where he had seen caricatures by Maratta and others,[8] but above all his slightly earlier (1700) trip to Lombardy and Emilia and his study of works by the Carracci, including caricatures.[9]

A course of training in Bologna, which the exhibition exemplifies in a youthful drawing by Donato Creti,[10] has also been supposed to have influenced Zanetti's beginnings as a caricaturist.[11] In addition to a period spent in Bologna when he was eighteen, perhaps studying under Giovanni Maria Viani, we know, however, that Zanetti was initiated into drawing by Nicolò Bambini at home. Here his work was supervised by Balestra as well as Sebastiano Ricci,[12] who made a

opposite
Marco Ricci
An opera rehearsal,
c. 1711, detail
Formerly Christie's, London

1.
Marco Ricci
An opera rehearsal, c. 1711
Formerly Christie's, London

2.
Antonio Balestra
Caricature, 1701
Florence, Biblioteca
Medicea Laurenziana,
Ms. Ashb.1781/1, c. 147*v*

3.
Sebastiano Ricci
Caricature of Duke
Ranuccio II Farnese,
before 1694
Darmstadt, Hessisches
Landesmuseum,
inv. AE1965

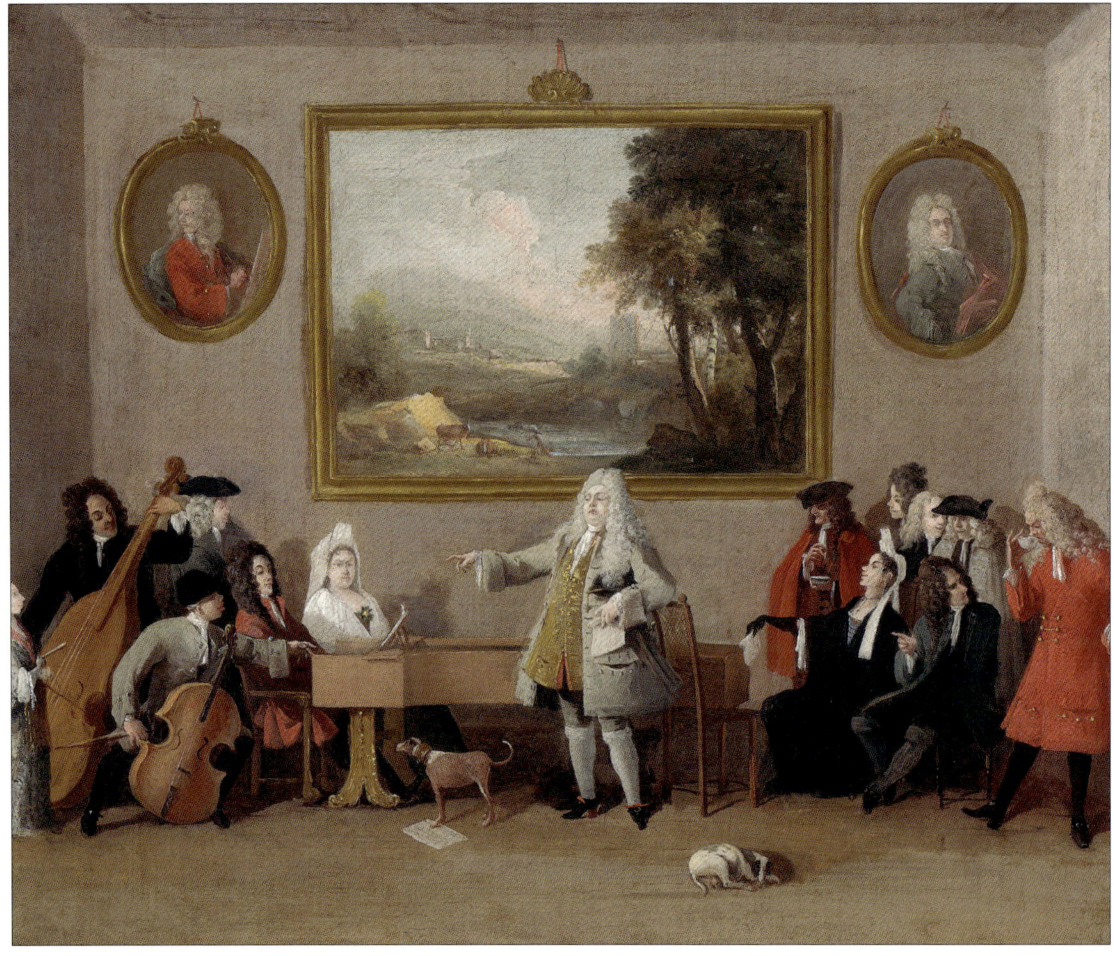

1

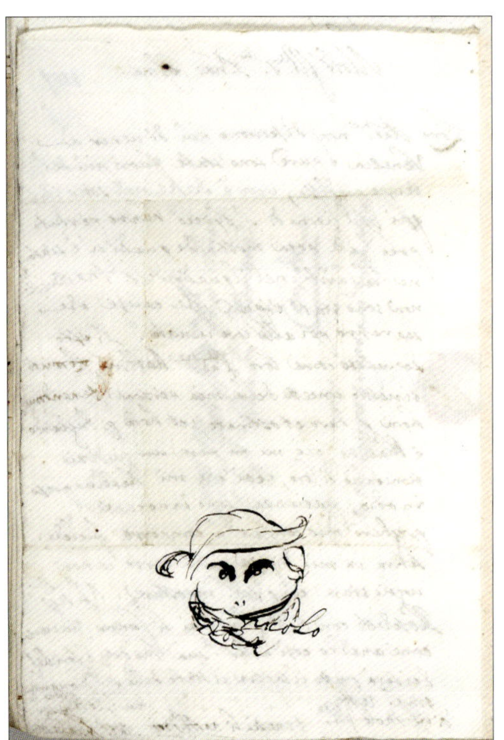

2

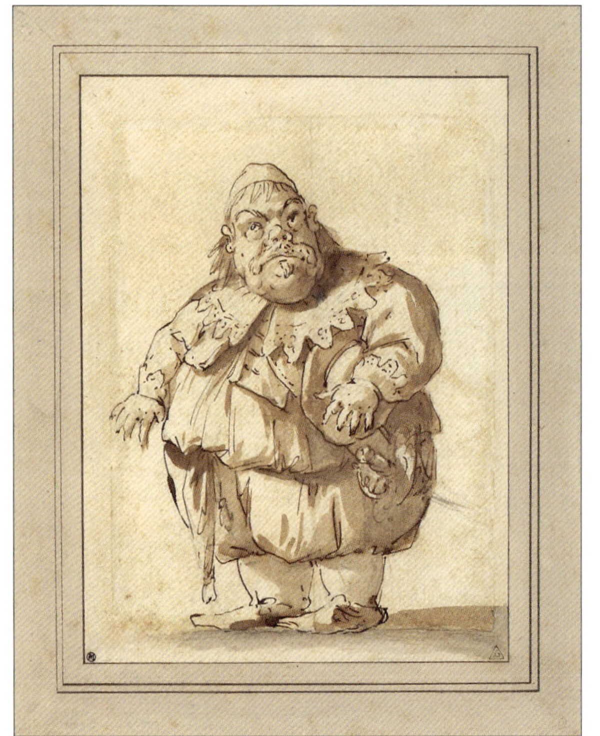

3

Caricature of Duke Ranuccio II Farnese [fig. 3], presumably before his patron's death in 1694. Already in the collection of Pierre-Jean Mariette,[13] one of Zanetti's principal friends and correspondents, the sheet by Marco Ricci, Sebastiano's nephew, seems to be influenced by Guercino's taste for a rich detailing of pictorial effects, lingering on the deformity of the figure. It is rather distant from the terse yet similar self-portrait that Anton Maria made on 22 May 1703, in the corner of a note to Rosalba [fig. 4].[14] The drawing is intentionally free from any attempt at style, in keeping with a childlike visual convention aimed at vivid immediacy.[15] It is the earliest dated example of a series that continued at least until 1750, with the singer Gizziello pasted on the last page of the Zanetti Album.[16]

This strain of humour, explained not only by the experiences just mentioned, originated in and was nurtured by his friendship with Marco Ricci.[17] The Zanetti Album contains the earliest documented caricature by Marco, a set designer as well as a painter of landscapes and capriccios, from November 1703.[18] The drawing seems to anticipate by at least two years the *Rehearsal of an Opera* that Marco painted in Tuscany.[19] This was the first in a series that in his subsequent period in England produced his masterpiece, *An Opera Rehearsal* [see fig. 1] with its vein of humour, a canvas that once belonged to Horace Walpole.[20]

It depicts the divas, musicians and impresarios in a living room rehearsing opera arias under the oval portraits of the two Ricci hanging on the wall. Together with Antonio Pellegrini, who was first Marco's partner and then his rival, they were establishing the new course of monumental pictorial decoration in England. In a peculiar reversal of proportions and again in a cosmopolitan climate, Walpole's *Rehearsal of an Opera* is the Lilliputian founder of eighteenth-century Venetian caricature. The painting fixes themes and formal treatments: the predilection for whole figures, the connection with the opera house, the physiognomies caricatured without exaggeration to unite observation with imagination, which was the secret of the success of Venetian art in Europe, that of the *vedutisti*, who often came from painting scenery for the theatre.[21]

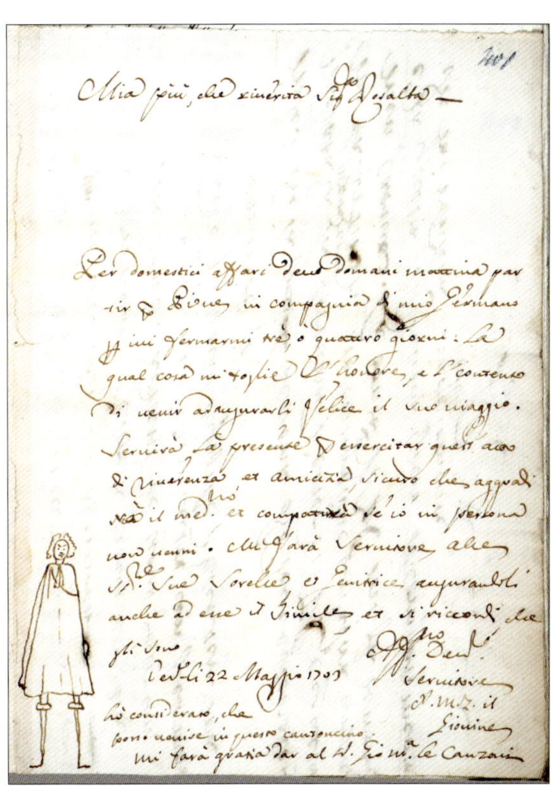
401

Mia più, che riverita Sig.ra Rosalba —

Per domestici affari devo domani mattina partir per Pisa in compagnia di mio Germano
per ivi fermarmi tre, o quattro giorni: La
qual cosa mi toglie l'honore, e il contento
di venir ad augurarli felice il suo viaggio.
Servirà la presente per esercitar quest'atto
di riverenza et amicizia, sicuro che aggradirà il med.mo et compatirà se io in persona
non vengo. Ella farà servitore alle
Sig.re sue Sorelle e Genitrice augurandoli
anche ad esse il simile et si ricordi che
gli sono
Ven.a li 22 Maggio 1703 Aff.mo Devot.o
Servitore
A.M.Z. il
Giovine
hò considerato, che
posso venire in questo cantoncino.
mi farà grazia dar al S. Gio. M.a le Canzoni

4

4.
Anton Maria Zanetti
Caricatured self-portrait,
1703
Florence, Biblioteca Medicea Laurenziana, Ms. Ashb.1781/4, c. 401r

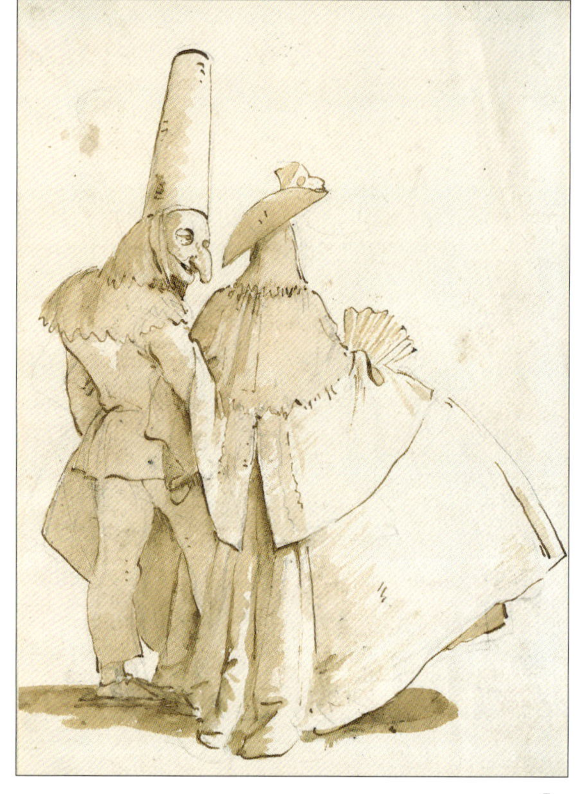
5

5.
Giambattista Tiepolo
A Punchinello and his Lady, fifth decade of eighteenth century
New York, The Morgan Library & Museum, inv. 1996.58, Bequest of Miss Alice Tully

In a note written entirely in rhyme and dating from this time, Rosalba referred to a '*schiribizzo* ['scrawl'] by Marco and Riccio: when I understood it, I laughed heartily'.[22] The term in Venetian could mean a sketch,[23] so Ricci's scrawl may have been at least partly drawn.[24] Rosalba was writing to an artist whom she esteemed, a convinced bachelor and in the company of her brother-in-law Pellegrini and her sister Angela at the time. The artist cannot have been Nicolò Cassana,[25] who had married for the second time in February 1708,[26] but the single Marco. Pellegrini and his wife also wrote letters to Rosalba from England, relating amusing stories with sketches inserted between the lines or along the edges of the sheets. Antonio had been a pupil of the Lombard Paolo Pagani, whose grotesque heads survive,[27] and his drawings are in the vein of 'humorous sketches'[28] rather than caricatures.
In Venice, the association between Marco Ricci and Anton Maria Zanetti – with 'the passion for opera [*musicaria*] that animated the many-sided Venetian all through his life'[29] – formed the basis of a continuous, amusing and unsparing rivalry in caricature between a professional painter, who never departed from a fluent and full-bodied graphic style, and a brilliant amateur, more concerned with comic effect than respect for the canons of verisimilitude or spatial coherence.[30] In the Zanetti and Smith albums, the same figures appear portrayed by one or other of the friends or both, often in the same situation, on a Venetian stage or in the theatre of life. It was a game the pair threw themselves into. And Ricci's drawing in the catalogue,[31] Zanetti's sheets in the Roi bequest in Vicenza[32] and the British Museum,[33] together with later copies by Algarotti for his own collection,[34] testify to the reception of their inventions outside Anton Maria's more intimate circle. Before being mounted in volumes, many caricatures must have circulated independently, presumably in letters, as shown by references in the letters of Abbot Antonio Conti and Zanetti himself, and the folds in the various sheets of drawings.[35]
The vogue for opera produced an increase in caricatures on operatic subjects, for example with Ricci's and Zanetti's drawings of Farinelli, though ridicule was always directed at other figures

in Venice, from commoners to patricians. Goldoni's twin 'books' of 'the *World* and the *Theatre*',[36] were familiar to Anton Maria, whom Goldoni recalled as 'one of the first and strongest supporters of my party, when it came to establishing my credit in the new method of comedies',[37] as well as to Marco, who had probably acted as a puppeteer with his friend and his father Giulio for the young Goldoni.[38]

Apart from appearances in catalogues of drawings by Gaspare Diziani and Francesco Fontebasso,[39] both pupils of Sebastiano Ricci, and some possible caricatures drawn (or collected?) by Louis Dorigny,[40] it is in the relationship between Zanetti and Giambattista Tiepolo, some dozen years after Marco Ricci's death, that we find the hiatus in the history of Venetian caricature.

While the *Capricci* and *Scherzi*, 'Tiepolo's innermost imaginings – his thoughts at their freest and most personal . . . [which] remain forever elusive and tantalising, for all the spell they cast',[41] were combined with the impulse to create heterodox figures such as caricatures,[42] it was significant that the first series of his etchings on record appeared in 1742, added to a printing of Zanetti's *Diversarum Iconum*. The following year Giuliano Giampiccoli's engravings were issued with additions by Tiepolo after works by Marco Ricci, with one of the two title pages dedicated to Zanetti.[43]

Since the previous decade, at least from the time of his studies for the frescoes at Villa Loschi (1734),[44] Tiepolo had drawn Pulcinella [fig. 5], perhaps for little Giandomenico[45] as well as himself. In 'the great theatre of Giambattista', the character became his 'anti-hero', exhibiting, 'in a spectacular dimension, the reality of primary, bodily needs, essentially connected with food: eating, evacuating, sleeping'.[46] Present in two *Scherzi*, Pulcinella was the recognised 'means to reach the world of caricature, an operation of unmasking, in order to make humanity emerge as a body'.[47] Instead of specific individuals with a name and surname, it seems that Giambattista Tiepolo drew the identikits of figures from the Commedia dell'Arte in flesh and blood, accounting for 'some ten per cent of the whole corpus of his drawings in pen and watercolour'.[48] The result is a singular gallery of 'universal types and characters of human fauna: the fat, the lean, the merry friar, the elderly curmudgeon, etc. There is no satirical intent, in the sense of reforming by ridicule. The violence of the deformation exalts the superiority of art over nature also in relation to the hideous. The purpose is to show that there is also "a beauty of deformity"'.[49]

Tiepolo achieved this when his etchings were placed beside Zanetti's chiaroscuro drawings. In this way he came to understand the witty spirit of his fellow citizen, with his well-known collection of drawings, and gained access to his library of illustrated volumes, including his album of caricatures. Compared with those by the amateur, Giambattista's images are works of art rather than humorous sketches, the 'still life of caricature'.[50]

Like Zanetti, Tiepolo also collected his caricatures in volumes. This is shown by the *Tomo terzo de caricature*, from which come four sheets on display here,[51] unbound and dispersed at Christie's auction in London on 9 April 1943.[52] Placed 'in the series of albums produced in Tiepolo's studio before the family left for Madrid in 1762', these sketches are thought to date from between 1754 and 1762.[53] They remained in the family workshop for a long time, reused by Giandomenico in his works. Due to the title, it has been conjectured that the 'production of caricatures by Giambattista, including sheets with Pulcinella', filled 'no fewer than three volumes',[54] based on the record from 1854 in the Corniani Algarotti collection of 'two large books' with a 'copious collection of humorous drawings by Tiepolo', with others 'in portfolios'.[55] These may have been the possible first volumes of the series, or instead the 'Scenes of contemporary life' and 'Diversions for the children'.[56] Regardless of the nineteenth-century records, the writing on the lost binding does not automatically mean there was a 'first volume' and 'second volume' of caricatures: it might refer to the order and not to the contents.

A large number of Tiepolo's caricatures stand out from those in the 'Third volume' by having cropped corners. The reason for this is not clear: perhaps to remove old marks or inscriptions, or as a result of tearing them from other pages,[57] or simply to create an effect of regularity in a mass of materials. As for their provenance, the earliest recorded is the Venetian bequest in 1830 by Teodoro Correr,[58] while it seems that the thirty-two caricatures in the Paul Wallraf collection, formerly owned by the Counts Valmarana,[59] of which a pair of specimens is on display,[60] were part of a group of some 140 sheets owned by the family.[61] It has been assumed that the Valmarana drawings date from the decoration of the villa of that name in Vicenza in 1757,[62] but some of them bear the inscription, not autograph, 'Tiepoletto veneziano 1760'.[63] Above all it has been noted that some drawings in an irregular octagonal format were used by Giandomenico in the 1790s for his *Scenes of life*, probably remaining 'in Tiepolo's studio until his death (in 1804)'.[64] This is the case of the *Caricature of a priest with spectacles*[65] that we find next to another image of an ecclesiastic [fig. 6] derived from an invention of Giambattista's,[66] among the spectators of Giandomenico's *Puppet Theatre*.[67]

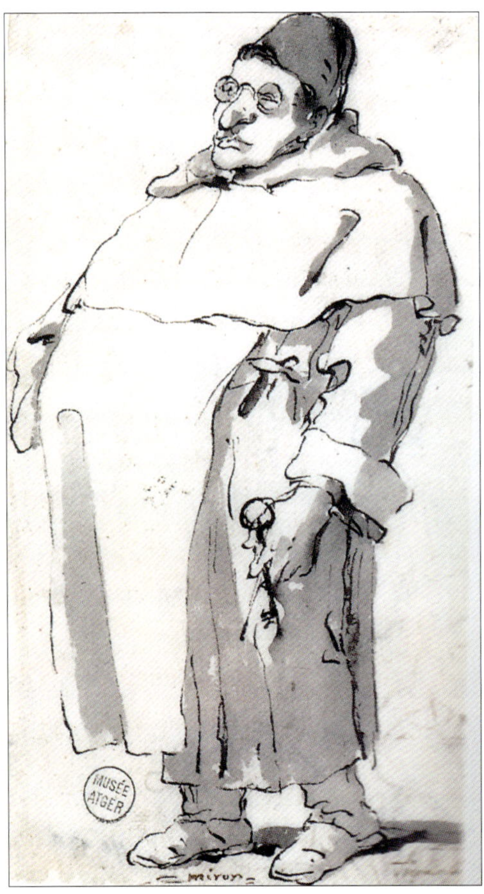

6

6.
Giambattista Tiepolo
Caricature of a fat monk or friar with spectacles and a key in his hand,
sixth decade of eighteenth century
Montpellier, Collection of the Musée Atger, Faculty of Medicine and Surgery of the University of Montpellier, inv. MA 178 r°, gift Xavier Atger 1821

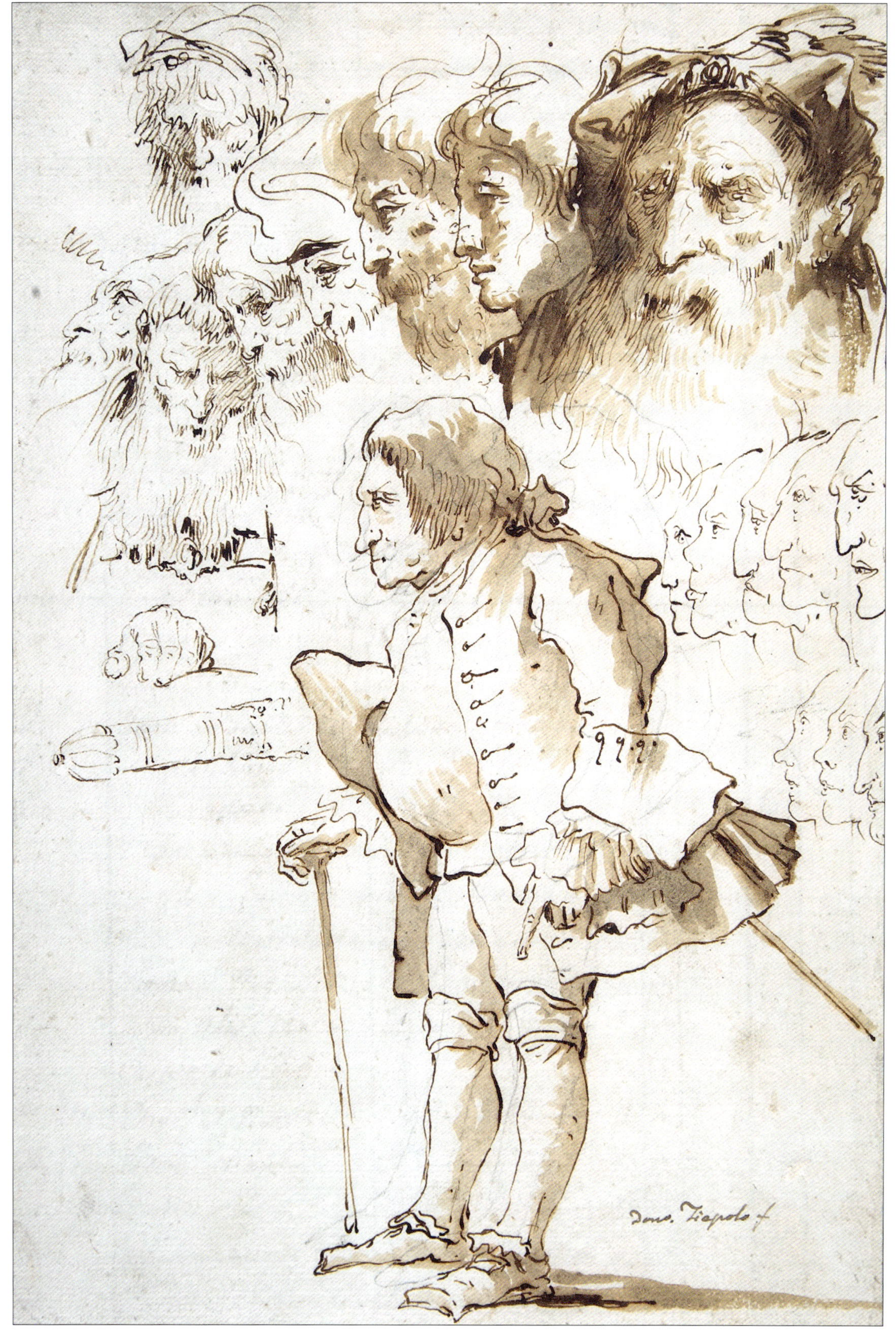

7

7.
Giandomenico Tiepolo
Caricature of a man in profile with a stick and other studies,
first half of the fifth decade of eighteenth century
New York, The Metropolitan Museum of Art,
Rogers Fund, 1937

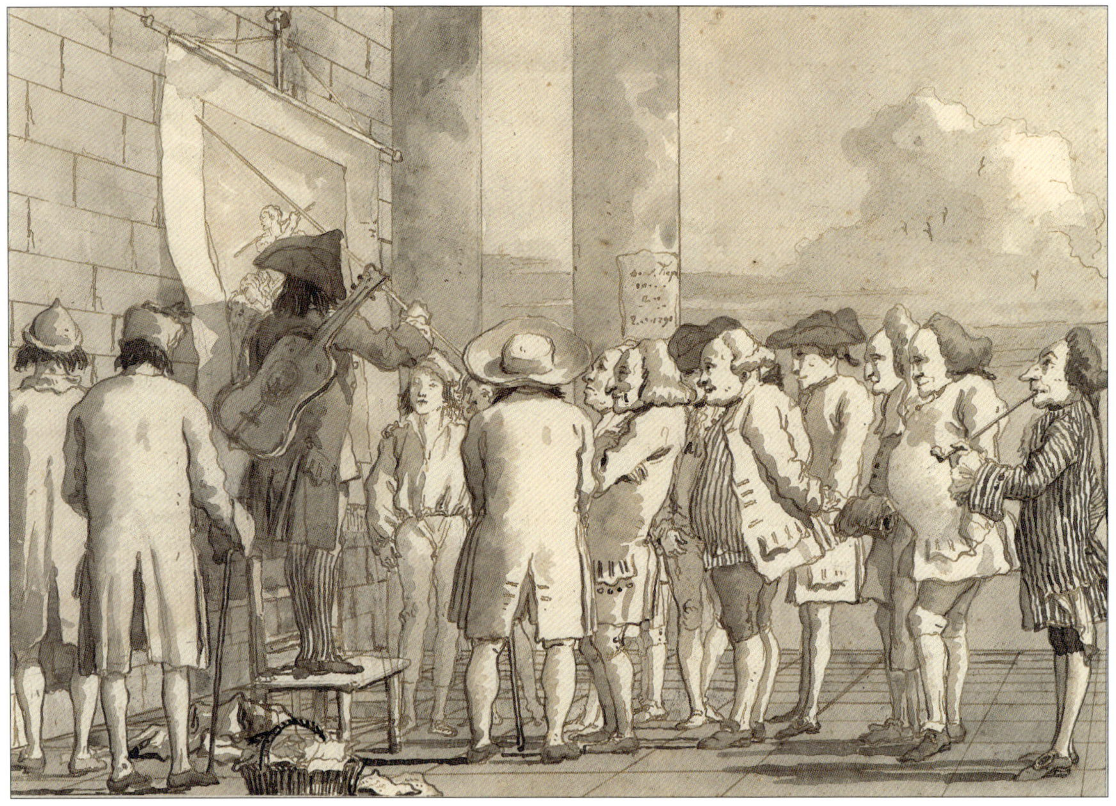

8.
Giandomenico Tiepolo
The Picture Show, 1791
New York, The Morgan Library & Museum, inv. 2017.253, Thaw Collection

8

These reuses reflect the value of the caricatures in the workshop, where they were copied by the pupils, as shown by two sheets compared in this exhibition,[68] or those of the *Elderly couple* in London and New York.[69] The sheet in the Metropolitan Museum in New York [fig. 7] might be 'an old copy by Giandomenico of a pen drawing by his father'.[70] At the bottom it bears the inscription 'Dom. Tiepolo f.' in ink different from that of the sketches on paper, as if attesting, years later, to an earlier formative practice crucial to his training as an artist. In his early work, Giambattista's son had been criticised for his 'carichature'[71] of figures in the Stations of the Cross.

If Giandomenico Tiepolo, a caricaturist, and even more his brother Lorenzo, is concealed amid the sheets today confidently assigned by scholars to his father or held to be by the workshop,[72] it was in the series of *Scenes of life* mentioned earlier that he gave a new significance to Giambattista's creations, transferring images until then isolated on paper, as if under a spotlight, 'into an empirical space: the comic target is not so much degraded nature as decayed society'.[73] In one of those drawings, all bearing the date 1791, a sheet on display, formerly in the *Tomo terzo de caricature*,[74] there appears a figure gazing at *The Picture Show* [fig. 8].[75] Tiepolo's telescope is reversed: 'For the first time the theatre is observed in reverse from behind the scenes rather than from the audience. Domenico, like his uncle [Francesco Guardi], standing outside the theatre and portraying the audience from behind, actually gathers the great theatrical fiction of society into a single stage action.'[76]

Delicate handling sharply accented distinguishes the independent, saturnine work of this last expression of Tiepolo's imagination, giving rise to the extraordinary *Caricature of a man in the form of a bird*.[77] In being disquieting rather than amusing, it is matched by the *Three monkeys* [fig. 9], two of them skeletons,[78] macabre heirs to the *singeries*, one of the themes of Rococo aesthetics.

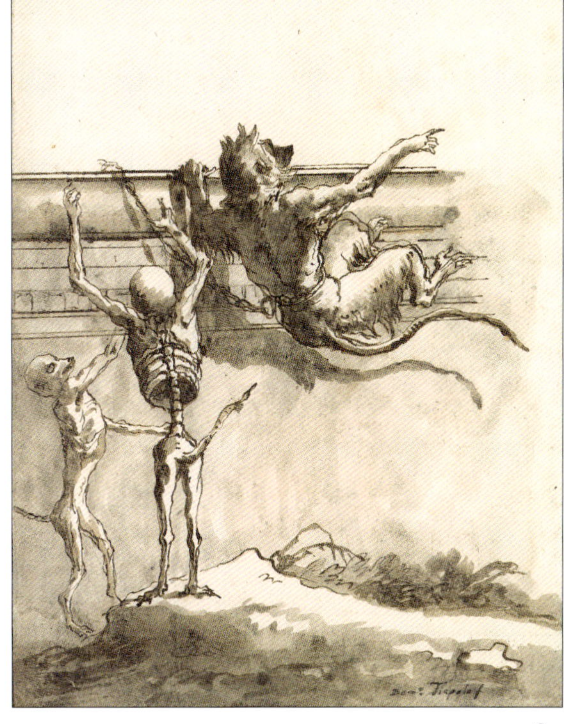

9

9.
Giandomenico Tiepolo
Three Monkeys, c. 1790
New York, The Morgan Library & Museum, inv. 1966.133, Gift of Mrs Rudolf J. Heinemann, in memory of Dr Rudolf J. Heinemann

As he travelled back along his father's path, from caricature Giandomenico came to Pulcinella, the last companion of his earthly and artistic journey. The season for a certain kind of figurative art was coming to an end. In the new neoclassical order, 'simplicity, elegance and correctness excluded excess, caricature', placing such images, at least as Tiepolo still understood them in the fateful year 1797, among 'the ideas that exceed the measure imposed by reason'.[79]

[1] See M. Lucco, in M. Lucco, P. Humfrey and G. C. F. Villa, *Giovanni Bellini: catalogo ragionato*, ed. M. Lucco (Treviso: ZeL Edizioni, 2019), p. 319, no. 18.

[2] See most recently G. Berra, 'Il ritratto "caricato in forma strana, e ridicolosa, e con tanta felicità di somiglianza": la nascita della caricatura e i suoi sviluppi in Italia fino al Settecento', *Mitteilungen des Kunsthistorischen Institutes in Florenz*, 53 (1), 2009, pp. 121–31.

[3] M. Kozloff, 'Caricatures of Giambattista Tiepolo', *Marsyas: Studies in the History of Art*, X, 1960–61 [1961], pp. 13–33; *Tiepolo: ironia e comico* (Cataloghi di mostre, 62), ed. A. Mariuz and G. Pavanello, exh. cat. (Fondazione Giorgio Cini, Venice, 3 September–5 December 2004; Venice: Marsilio, 2004).

[4] W. L. Barcham, 'Il teatro alla moda', in Mariuz and Pavanello, *Tiepolo*, pp. 69–93.

[5] E. Lucchese, *L'album di caricature di Anton Maria Zanetti alla Fondazione Giorgio Cini* (Venice: lineadacqua, 2015).

[6] E. Croft-Murray, 'Venetian Caricatures', in A. Blunt and E. Croft-Murray, *Venetian Drawings of the XVII and XVIII Centuries in the Collection of Her Majesty the Queen at Windsor Castle* (London: Phaidon Press, 1957), pp. 137–83; E. Croft-Murray, *An Album of Eighteenth Century Venetian Operatic Caricatures formerly in the Collection of Count Algarotti*, exh. cat. (Art Gallery of Ontario, Toronto, 20 September–9 November 1980; Toronto: Art Gallery of Ontario, 1980).

[7] E. Lucchese, 'Nel segno della grazia: Antonio Balestra maestro di Anton Maria Zanetti di Girolamo e nella "Scuola del nudo: di Giambattista Tiepolo', *Valori Tattili*, 9, 2017, p. 161.

[8] See Berra, 'Il ritratto "caricato"', pp. 110–14; S. Prosperi Valenti Rodinò, 'La caricatura a Roma nel Settecento', in *Il Settecento e le arti: dall'Arcadia all'Illuminismo. Nuove proposte tra le corti, l'aristocrazia e la borghesia*, conference proceedings (Rome, 23–4 November 2005; Rome: Bardi, 2009), pp. 261–5.

[9] E. Lucchese, 'I pittogrammi nelle lettere', in *Lettere artistiche del Settecento veneziano*, vol. 6: *Anton Maria Zanetti di Girolamo: il carteggio*, Fonti e Documenti per la Storia dell'Arte Veneta', 17, ed. M. Magrini (Verona: Scripta, 2021), p. 168.

[10] Cat. 48.

[11] A. Bettagno, 'Introduzione', in *Caricature di Anton Maria Zanetti* (Cataloghi di mostre, 29), ed. A. Bettagno, exh. cat. (Fondazione Giorgio Cini, Venice, 1969; Vicenza: Neri Pozza, 1969), p. 24.

[12] See E. Lucchese, 'Zanetti, Anton Maria', in *Dizionario biografico degli italiani*, vol. C (Rome: Istituto della Enciclopedia Italiana, 2020), p. 507.

[13] P. Rosenberg, 'Les dessins vénitiens du XVIIIe siècle de la collection de Pierre-Jean Mariette', in *Venezia Settecento: studi in memoria di Alessandro Bettagno*, ed. B. A. Kowalczyk (Milan: Silvana Editoriale, 2015), pp. 124, 126.

[14] *Lettere artistiche*, vol. 6, p. 229, n. 1.

[15] E. Kris, *Ricerche psicoanalitiche sull'arte* (Turin: Einaudi, 1967), p. 188.

[16] Lucchese, *L'album di caricature*, p. 347, no. 76.II.

[17] Ibid., p. 5.

[18] Cat. 54.

[19] A. Scarpa, in Mariuz and Pavanello, *Tiepolo*, pp. 75–7, no. 1.

[20] A. Scarpa Sonino, *Marco Ricci* (Milan: Berenice, 1991), pp. 126–7, n. 53.

[21] See E. Lucchese, 'Il Vedutismo, lo specchio di Venezia', in P. Di Loreto, ed., *Originali, repliche, copie: uno sguardo diverso sui grandi maestri* (Rome: Ugo Bozzi Editore, 2018), pp. 272–3.

[22] B. Sani, *Rosalba Carriera: lettere, diari, frammenti*, Accademia Toscana di Scienze e Lettere 'La Colombaria', Studi, LXXI, 2 vols (Florence: Leo S. Olschki, 1985), vol. I, p. 125, n. 87.

[23] G. Boerio, *Dizionario del dialetto veneziano* (Venice: Andrea Santini e figlio, 1829), p. 554, 'schiribizzi su la carta'.

[24] Lucchese, *L'album di caricature*, p. 5, n. 52.

[25] Scarpa Sonino, *Marco Ricci*, p. 60, suggested hesitantly.

[26] F. Zava Boccazzi, 'Nicolò Cassana a Venezia', *Atti dell'Istituto Veneto di Scienze, Lettere ed Arti*, CXXXVII, 1978–9, p. 616.

[27] See Lucchese, *L'album di caricature*, p. 5.

[28] See Berra, 'Il ritratto "caricato"', p. 73.

[29] G. Stefani, 'La musica e il teatro', in *Lettere artistiche*, vol. 6, p. 187. The neologism '*musicaria*' was coined by Sebastiano Ricci in a letter to Giuseppe Riva on 9 August 1720.

[30] Lucchese, *L'album di caricature*, p. 3.

[31] Cat. 52.

[32] C. Signorini, in *Pinacoteca Civica di Vicenza: lascito Giuseppe Roi*, Catalogo Scientifico delle Collezioni, VI, ed. M. E. Avagnina, G. C. F. Villa (Vicenza: Fondazione Giuseppe Roi – Musei Civici di Vicenza, 2012), pp. 56–60, no. 22.

[33] Lochnan and Croft-Murray, in Croft-Murray, *An Album*, pp. 14, 16–17, nos 4–6.

[34] Croft-Murray, *An Album*.

[35] Lucchese, *L'album di caricature*, p. 12.

[36] G. Ortolani, ed., *Tutte le opere di Carlo Goldoni*, 14 vols (Milan: Arnoldo Mondadori, 1935–56), vol. I, p. 769.

[37] Ibid., vol. VI (1943), p. 864. See Lucchese, *L'album di caricature*, pp. 11–12; Stefani, 'La musica e il teatro', pp. 208–9.

[38] E. Lucchese, 'Carnevale 1750: il cantante Gizziello per i Grimani ai Servi in una tela di Pietro Longhi', *Musica e Figura*, 6, 2019, pp. 112–13.

[39] See Lucchese, *L'album di caricature*, p. 5.

[40] See M. Favilla and R. Rugolo, 'Dorigny e Venezia: da Ca' Tron a Ca' Zenobio e ritorno', in *Louis Dorigny 1654–1742: un pittore della corte francese a Verona*, ed. G. Marini and P. Marini, exh. cat. (Museo di Castelvecchio, Verona, 28 June–2 November 2003; Venice: Marsilio, 2003), p. 59, n. 112.

[41] M. Levey, *Giambattista Tiepolo: la sua vita, la sua arte* (Milan: Arnoldo Mondadori, 1988), p. 217.

[42] Kozloff, 'Caricatures', p. 26.

[43] See Lucchese, 'Zanetti', p. 509.

[44] G. Knox, 'Pulcinella in Arcadia', in Mariuz and Pavanello, *Tiepolo*, p. 97.

[45] A. Mariuz, 'I disegni di Pulcinella di Giandomenico Tiepolo', *Arte Veneta*, XL, 1986, p. 269.

[46] Ibid., p. 270.

[47] G. Pavanello, 'Tutta la vita, dal principio alla fine, è una comica assurdità, ovvero "il segreto di Pulcinella"', in Mariuz and Pavanello, *Tiepolo*, p. 29.

[48] G. Knox, 'Tomo terzo de caricature', in ibid., p. 119.

[49] A. Mariuz, *Giandomenico Tiepolo*, Profili e Saggi di Arte Veneta, IX (Venice: Alfieri, 1971), p. 83.

[50] Kozloff, 'Caricatures', p. 33.

[51] Cats 61, 65–7.

[52] Knox, 'Tomo terzo', p. 119.

[53] Ibid., p. 121.

[54] Pavanello, 'Tutta la vita', p. 26.

[55] M. Levey, 'Two Footnotes to any Tiepolo Monograph', *The Burlington Magazine*, CIV, 708, March 1962, p. 119.

[56] G. Knox, 'Le caricature dei Tiepolo', in *Antichi disegni dalla Collezione Ligabue*, ed. S. Scarpa and P. Scarpa (Milan: Electa, 2005), p. 141.

[57] J. Byam Shaw, 'The Biron Collection of Venetian Eighteenth-Century Drawings in the Metropolitan Museum', *Metropolitan Museum Journal*, 3, 1970, pp. 239, 241, n. 14; Byam Shaw in *Disegni veneti della collezione Lugt*, Cataloghi di mostre, 44, ed. J. Byam Shaw, exh. cat. (Fondazione Giorgio Cini, Venice; Vicenza: Neri Pozza, 1981), p. 74, n. 84.

[58] Knox, 'Tomo terzo', p. 121.

[59] A. Morassi, in *Disegni Veneti del Settecento nella collezione Paul Wallraf*, Cataloghi di mostre, 9, ed. A. Morassi, exh. cat. (Fondazione Giorgio Cini, Venice, 1959; Venice: Neri Pozza, 1959), p. 56, nos 76–87.

[60] Cats 64, 72.

[61] J. Scholz, 'Notes on Old and Modern Drawings. Sei–Settecento Drawings in Venice: Notes on Two Exhibitions and a Publication', *The Art Quarterly*, XIII, 1, 1960, p. 64.

[62] Morassi, in *Disegni Veneti*, p. 59.

[63] For example cat. 64.

[64] Knox, 'Tomo terzo', p. 120.

[65] Cat. 63.

[66] See Knox, in Mariuz and Pavanello, *Tiepolo*, p. 138, no. 71.

[67] See A. M. Gealt and G. Knox, eds, *Giandomenico Tiepolo: scene di vita quotidiana a Venezia e nella terraferma* (Venice: Marsilio, 2005), p. 126, no. 31.

[68] Cats 62, 74.

[69] Knox, in Mariuz and Pavanello, *Tiepolo*, p. 144, n. 90.

[70] Ibid., n. 91.

[71] E. Arslan, 'Quattro lettere di Pietro Visconti a Gian Pietro Ligari', *Rivista Archeologica dell'antica provincia di Como*, 135, 1952, p. 63.

[72] On this point see Pavanello, 'Tutta la vita', p. 52, n. 39.

[73] Mariuz, *Giandomenico Tiepolo*, p. 83.

[74] Cat. 67.

[75] See Gealt and Knox, *Giandomenico Tiepolo*, p. 121, no. 29.

[76] M. Bonicatti, 'Note sul vedutismo veneziano: sulla cultura artistica di Francesco Guardi e di Domenico Tiepolo', *Arte Veneta*, 18, 1964, p. 143.

[77] Cat. 75.

[78] See J. Byam Shaw, *The Drawings of Domenico Tiepolo* (London: Faber and Faber, 1962), pp. 81–2, no. 47.

[79] F. Milizia, *Dizionario delle belle arti del disegno*, 2 vols (Bassano [Remondini], 1797), vol. I, p. 158.

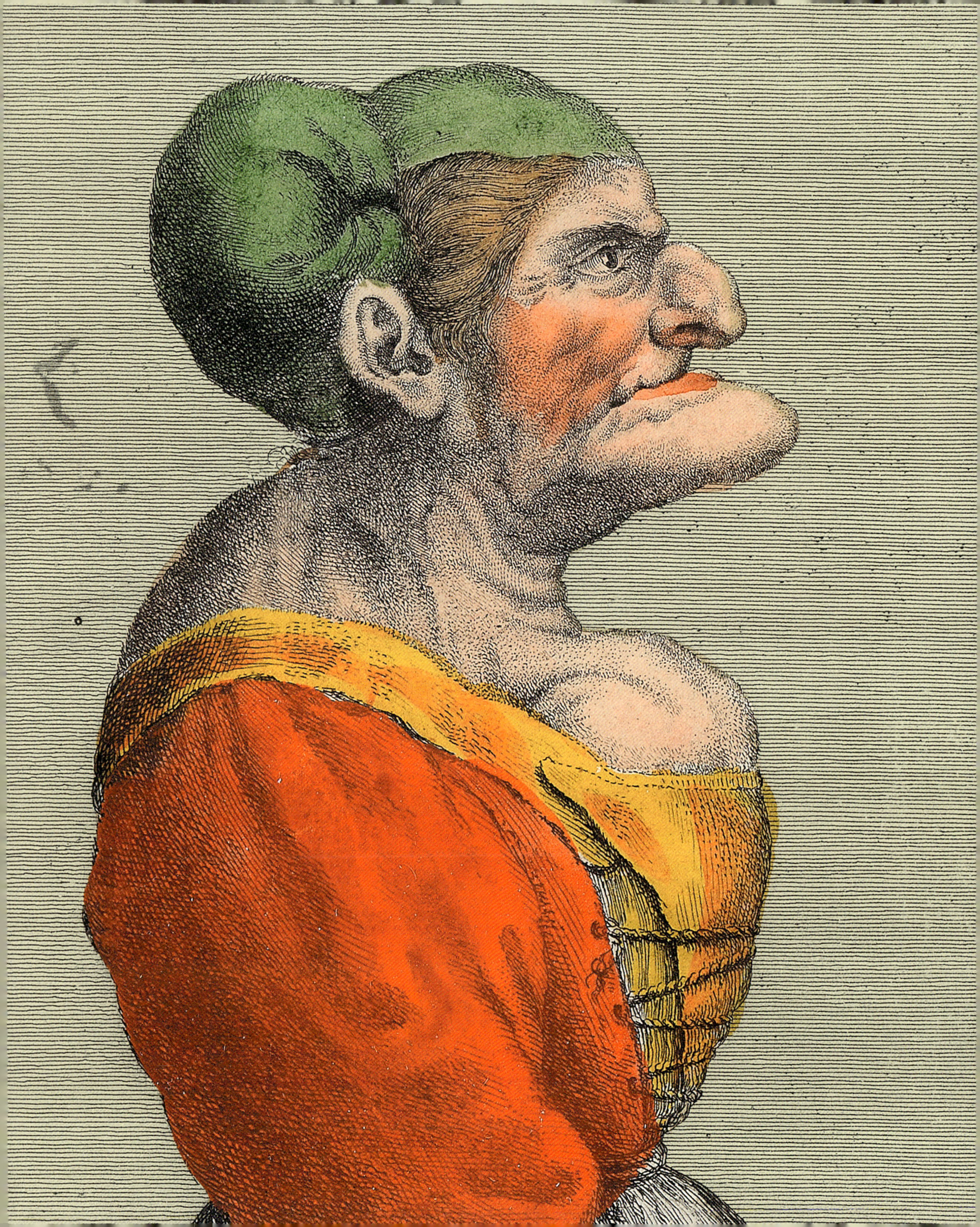

Paola Cordera

The Antiquarian on the Stage of the Great Theatre of Europe

A shrewd expedient for escaping family responsibilities, the pastime that occupies Count Anselmo Terrazzani, the central character in Carlo Goldoni's *La famiglia dell'antiquario* (1750), clearly reflects the typical occupation of a dilettante antiquarian in the eighteenth century, with his predilections and afflictions. If we strip away the author's moral judgements, the character in the play is almost a paradigm of the world of collectors in Venice at the time.

Goldoni's skill as a playwright enables us to enter the Count's chamber, where every object recalls his passion. And his servant Brighella (a stock figure in the Commedia dell'Arte), gives us a clearly mocking description of the 'various fiddly little tables, statues, busts and other ancient things' that require his master to spend (he feels incomprehensibly) huge sums. He observes ironically that the 'study of medals is a matter for highbrows, a beautiful museum honours a house, and I am beloved by the Chevalier, who is noble and has good taste, and that money is always well spent when it is for the honour of a family and of cities'. These brief observations tell us how greatly the individual history of Goldoni's amateur, engaged in his own social ascent, must have reverberated in the wider history of eighteenth-century Venice, and how closely the individual episode inevitably came to be associated with its context. Krzysztof Pomian explains this circumstance: 'The collections in Venice and the Veneto were formed in a more stable social environment and handed down, to a great extent, from one generation to another. For this reason they belonged more to a *gens* than an individual. It all came about as if the objects that composed these collections, above all the paintings, were regarded as the visible expression of the position occupied by each family in the hierarchy . . .'[1]

If it is problematic to attempt to assess the individual's contribution 'to the honour' of the city, the contribution made by collectors and their world to establishing Venice's fame internationally is evident. As Francis Haskell's pioneering studies clearly showed, the Venetian context's inherent cosmopolitan and commercial vocation was closely enmeshed with a protectionist isolation imposed by the establishment.[2] The growing numbers of collectors and the diversification of the

OPPOSITE
Carlo Lasinio
Two grotesque heads of an old woman and man,
c. 1790-1800, detail
Milan, Castello Sforzesco, Ente Raccolta Vinciana, inv. ERV 767

relevant social context should be interpreted in this contradictory setting. Alongside the patriciate, a new type of nobility had emerged as well as a bourgeoisie who were highly sensitive to the new trends in art and taste.

Although the 'traditional' galleries of paintings continued to be considered the 'indispensable corollary of a title of nobility', the spread of collecting led to the development of some specialised collections. In this respect, the Venetian cultural context seems to have matched the observations of the famous naturalist and *secrétaire du roi* Antoine-Joseph Dezailler d'Argenville, regarding the selection and arrangement of a cabinet of curiosities.[3] He was aware that the prototype of a universal collection that he described was a model from which one might draw inspiration, yet without much chance of ever fully realising it in practice. Further defining his own thoughts, he came to the conclusion that the character of a collection was closely bound up with the inclinations of its owner and this led to an inevitable degree of specialisation: 'un Sçavant, par exemple, ne respire que les Livres, un antiquaire ne recherche que les Médailles, un physicien que les expériences, un naturaliste que les productions de la Nature'.[4]

In Dezailler d'Argenville's text we catch a glimpse not only of the creation of specialised collections – *cabinets de tableaux, d'estampes, de desseins, de livres, de médailles & d'autres curiositez* – but also the progressive growth of an antiques market in which the cultural approach had to come to terms with the search for profit. This converged with other activities: for example, it was also noted that the custom of the *curieux* of organising their prints by artists was matched by the activities of dealers.[5] Equally commercial were the restrictions that limited the individual in undertaking a 'certaine dépense pour contenter sa curiosité'.[6] Personal inclinations apart, it was in this milieu that the classificatory approach emerged, accompanied by the sharing of criteria of judgement among some collectors of prints and drawings in eighteenth-century Venice.[7]

The Venetian environment could accommodate a figure like that of the consul and collector Joseph Smith (c. 1674–1770). As Rosie Razzall has noted, Smith was often exposed to criticism by his compatriots because of his commercial interests, which they found it hard to reconcile with the true sensibility of a gentleman connoisseur.[8] Very different was the opinion of Smith's friend Goldoni, who in 1754 dedicated to him the comedy *Il filosofo inglese*: 'Whoever enters your house, finds the most perfect union of all the sciences and all the arts, and you sit in the midst of them not as a lover who contemplates them only, but as a connoisseur devoted to illustrating them. . . Painting, architecture, drawing reign in competition on your walls. Your good taste, your perfect knowledge, have inspired you to choose the finest things, and the courage of your generous soul has moved your hand to acquire them.'[9]

Arranged in his house on the Grand Canal, Smith's collection was described by the writer John Breval (died in 1738) as a significant resource in a city like Venice, which he complained was lacking in libraries and collections 'in the virtuoso way'. Breval seems to have looked with nostalgia to a lost past, recalling the scattered Contarini collection and the Tiepolo collection. Among contemporaries, the only collection considered worthy of the name was that in Casa Sagredo, held to be the largest collection of prints in Europe.[10] His judgement echoed the thought formulated a few decades earlier by the artist Edward Wright (active in the eighteenth century), who had also deplored the lack of access to the collection.[11] This, regrettably for foreign travellers, was a feature common to all Venetian collections even in the early eighteenth century.[12]

Together with a passion for pictures (accumulated over time by several members of the family), Zaccaria Sagredo (1653–1729) had developed a lively interest in graphic works that had led to the formation of a substantial collection, partly through the agency of the Emilian merchant Don Pietro Antonio Toni (1692–1748), a friend of Sebastiano Ricci, Giovanni Battista Piazzetta and Giambattista Tiepolo. Joseph Smith and Anton Maria Zanetti also made use of Toni.[13] The Sagredo collection was housed in the *Camera sopra Canal delli Disegni* and consisted partly of bound tomes – as prescribed by Dezailler d'Argenville – and partly of individually framed sheets hung on the walls. While the collection of paintings was considered worthy of appearing in the *Recueil* of the engraver and art critic Charles-Nicolas Cochin,[14] the collection of prints and drawings was not so favoured. In the 1740s it was even the subject of some criticism,[15] although even by 1726 it could boast various originals by Leonardo from the Casnedi collection in Milan (in addition to a volume of prints by Zanetti). Nevertheless, when the collection was offered for sale by Zaccaria's heirs in 1752, Joseph Smith purchased four volumes of drawings from this prestigious collection. A certain number of Old Master drawings were also acquired by Zanetti. The interest of both connoisseurs in graphic works was accompanied by a complementary passion for sculpture.[16]

More than the reports of foreigners on their travels, it is their letters that tell us of the nature of various collections and of the relations of the owners with other amateurs, revealing the existence of an extended cosmopolitan and international network of intellectuals, collectors and artists. Far from developing new models of collecting, however, the distinctive trait of this system was that it reiterated the elitist model typical of previous aristocratic collections.[17] Naturally, relations between equals were different, bearing witness to the fertile soil that was accumulating in Venice that led to a gradual extension of the practice of collecting.

In this setting, Anton Maria Zanetti di Gerolamo (1680–1767) played a leading role.[18] His painter friend Marco Ricci (1676–1730) has left us this portrait: 'This gentleman has now made a collection of drawings of the first schools and most excellent artists. He draws extremely well, engraves in wood and copper and paints for his own amusement . . . He also has an immense collection of prints and books, as great as could ever be engraved in the world, all ordered and kept with particular propriety and ornament.'[19]

His circle of friends with close ties to the world of opera, as well as collectors and artists, included the painter Rosalba Carriera (1675–1757) and her brother-in-law Giovanni Antonio

Pellegrini (1675–1741),[20] Joseph Smith, the writer and librettist Apostolo Zeno (1668–1750), the painter and composer of burlesque poems Simone Brentana (1656–1742) and the Abbot Antonio Conti (1677–1749).[21] Zanetti's circle gradually spread to other parts of Europe in the first decades of the eighteenth century.[22] Valentine Toutain-Quittelier's studies have shown that Zanetti frequented some French *marchands* such as Claude Jamineau and Philippe Rousseau, the German Johann Jacob Pommer and the French consul Guillaume Le Blond, all connected in different ways to art patronage and collecting in northern Europe.[23]

As is well known, however, it was the relationships established in Venice with the banker Pierre Crozat (1661–1740) in 1715, and the collector and antique dealer Pierre-Jean Mariette[24] in 1718–19 that prompted Zanetti to go to Paris, in the company of Rosalba Carriera and Pellegrini.[25] Mariette was undoubtedly his principal contact in the French capital. Pierre Rosenberg commented 'with regret' that, in his turn, Zanetti 'failed to guide Mariette better in his choices . . . The Venetian representatives is disappointing . . . and one wonders whether Mariette was not poorly advised'.[26] He hints at the possibility that the learned Frenchman had been unwilling to satisfy Zanetti's financial demands. One wonders whether this 'lack of reciprocity' was not so much the result of a failure to do a deal as the consequence of a relationship that was between equals in form alone, not in substance.

From the French capital, Zanetti's journey took him to London and then Flanders before returning home in 1721–2.[27] Pierre Crozat recalled that in London Zanetti had stayed with John Smith, the brother of the famous Joseph.[28] Dr Richard Mead (1673–1754) and the painters Arthur Pond (c. 1705–1758) and Jonathan Richardson (1665–1745) were among those with whom he associated.[29]

With sojourns in the principal centres of the foreign art trade, Zanetti's itinerary was at the same time a reflection of the social and professional level that he had established as a connoisseur. His contacts also included the painter Nicolas Vleughels (1668–1737), the collector Gerhard Michael Jabach (1688–1751),[30] the *abbé* Jean-Antoine de Maroulle (1669/174–1726) and Prince Joseph Wenzel I of Lichtenstein (1696–1772). They were offered drawings or the dedications of works.[31] In this composite mosaic of shared pursuits, their interest in Leonardo's drawings has been studied by Pietro C. Marani, who has proposed the possible existence of a Tuscan–Lombard strand to complement the traditional frame of reference.[32]

Zanetti's visits to the European cities where the circulation of prints was greatest enabled him to take stock of an erudite international context and a potential market, as is shown by his purchase in Paris of Callot's complete œuvre or by the acquisition in London of Lord Arundel's collection. In contact with an extended international milieu, Zanetti refined his critical thinking, at the same time developing the idea of devoting himself to the art of engraving, certainly glimpsing its artistic value, but its financial benefits as well. In this way his fame extended to his position as an art dealer but also as a draughtsman. As Enrico Lucchese has observed, the success of his inventions outside his immediate circle is shown by the drawings of the Roi bequest (now in Vicenza) and the British Museum, together with copies with the subsequent annotations by Francesco Algarotti (1712–1764).[33] Zanetti's work as an agent – acting, for example, towards Bernardo Bellotto (1722–1780) on behalf of the merchant and banker Andrea Gerini (1691–1766),[34] or as the bearer of a miniature of Rosalba Carriera to the Comte de Caylus (1727) – was combined with his role as a patron of the arts, as appears from his relations with Bartolomeo Nazari (1693–1758), Michele Marieschi (1710–1744) and Bernardo Bellotto.

The authority Zanetti had acquired by the middle of the century was immediately reflected in the prominence of the subscribers to his two volumes entitled *Delle antiche statue*.[35] The role he achieved was not that of a mere *passeur de culture* (conveyor of culture) but an anticipator of developments that later became dominant. In this way, he became a frame of reference not just for his contemporaries (and for travellers arriving in Venice) but also for subsequent generations of collectors.[36]

[1] K. Pomian, *Collezionisti, amatori e curiosi: Parigi–Venezia XVI–XVIII secolo* (Milan: Il Saggiatore, 2007), p. 255.

[2] F. Haskell, *Mecenati e pittori: studio sui rapporti tra arte e società italiana nell'età barocca* (Florence: Sansoni, 1985), esp. pp. 377–579; original ed. *Patrons and Painters: A Study in the Relations between Italian Art and Society in the Age of the Baroque* (London: Chatto & Windus, 1963).

[3] 'Lettre sur le choix & l'arrangement d'un Cabinet curieux, écrite par Des-Allier d'Argenville Secrétaire du Roy en la Grande Chancellerie, à M. de Fougeroux, Trésories-Payeur des Rents de l'Hôtel de Ville', *Mercure de France*, June 1727, pp. 1295–330.

[4] Ibid. p. 1330.

[5] 'Quoique ce soit la coûtume de la plupart des curieux de ranger les Estampes par Maîtres, ainsi que le font tous les Marchands'; ibid., p. 1362.

[6] Ibid., p. 1304.

[7] For an overview of the subject see B. Aikema, R. Lauber and M. Seidel, eds, *Il collezionismo a Venezia e nel Veneto ai tempi della Serenissima*, conference proceedings (Venice, 2003; Venice: Marsilio, 2005); S. Mason and L. Borean, *Il collezionismo d'arte a Venezia* (Venice: Marsilio, 2009).

[8] R. Razzall, 'Consul Smith and his Circle', in *Canaletto and the Art of Venice*, ed. R. Razzall and L. Whitaker, exh. cat. (The Queen's Gallery, London, 19 May–12 November 2017; London: Royal Collection Trust, 2017), p. 21.

[9] Goldoni's letter of dedication was printed at the opening of 'Il filosofo inglese', in *Nuovo Teatro Comico dell'Avvocato Carlo Goldoni* (Venice: Pitteri, 1757), vol. I.

[10] 'This is the only branch of Virtue the gentleman is famous for'; J. D. Breval, *Remarks on Several Parts of Europe, Relating Chiefly to their Antiquities and History . . .* (London: H. Lintot, 1738), pp. 229–30.

[11] E. Wright, *Some Observations Made in Travelling. Through France, Italy, &c., in the Years 1720, 1721, and 1722*, 2 vols (London: Tho. Ward and E. Wicksteed, 1730), vol. I, p. 77.

[12] J. Addison, *Remarks on Several Parts of Italy &c in the Years 1701, 1702, 1703* (London: J. R. Tonson & S. Draper, 1705, rev. ed. 1718), p. 65.

[13] On Sagredo's collecting see C. Mazza, *I Sagredo: committenti e collezionisti d'arte nella Venezia del Sei e Settecento* (Venice: Istituto Veneto di Scienze, Lettere ed Arti, 2004); Ketty Gottardo and Giorgio Marini, in Aikema, Lauber and Seidel, *Il collezionismo a Venezia*, pp. 239–58, c259–74 respectively.

[14] C. N. Cochin, *Voyage d'Italie ou recueil de notes sur les ouvrages de peinture et de sculpture . . .*, 3 vols (Paris: C. A. Jombert, 1758–69), vol. 3, pp. 143–52.

[15] On the reservations expressed by the painter Giuseppe Maria Crespi and by Francesco Algarotti concerning the quality of some drawings in the Sagredo collection see Mazza, *I Sagredo*, pp. 99–104.

[16] On these points see G. Tassinari, 'Collezionisti, committenti e incisori di *pietre dure* a *Venezia* nel Settecento', in *Collezionisti e collezioni di antichità e di numismatica a Venezia nel Settecento*, ed. A. Gariboldi, conference proceedings (Trieste, 6–7 December 2019: Trieste: Edizioni Università di Trieste, 2022), pp. 99–211.

[17] On these topics and the accessibility of the collections to a broader public see S. Costa and G. Perini Folesani, *I Savi e gli ignoranti: dialogo del pubblico con l'arte (XVI–XVIII secolo)* (Bologna: Bononia University Press, 2017); S. Costa, *Dal magnifico concerto all'ordinato metodo: collezioni e musei d'Ancien Régime* (Bologna: Bononia University Press, 2019).

[18] On Zanetti as collector see G. Lorenzetti, 'Un dilettante incisore veneziano del XVIII secolo: Anton Maria Zanetti di Gerolamo', in *Miscellanea di Storia Veneta, Reale Deputazione Veneta di Storia Patria* (Venice: R. Deputazione Veneta di Storia Patria, 1917); B. A. Kowalczyk, 'Bellotto and Zanetti in Florence', *The Burlington Magazine*, CLIV (1306), 2012, pp. 24–32.

[19] Marco Ricci to Niccolò Gaburri, Venice, 13 March 1723, in G. Bottari, ed., *Raccolta di lettere sulla pittura, scultura ed architettura, a cura di S. Ticozzi* (Milan: Giovanni Silvestri, 1822), vol. III, p. 129.

[20] On the circle of Rosalba Carriera see esp. F. Zava Boccazzi, 'M.lle Rosalba très vertueuse pentresse', in *Rosalba Carriera 'prima pittrice de l'Europa'*, ed. G. Pavanello, exh. cat. (Palazzo Cini, Venice, 1 September–28 October 2007; Venice: Marsilio, 2007), pp. 15–25; see also Bernardina Sani, 'Note al carteggio di Rosalba Carriera', in ibid., pp. 4–49.

[21] The relationship between Ricci and Zanetti is partly investigated in G. Stefani, *Sebastiano Ricci impresario d'opera a Venezia nel primo Settecento* (Florence: Firenze University Press, 2015).

[22] For an overview of print collections in Europe see C. Hattori, E. Leutrat and V. Meyer, eds, *À l'origine du livre d'art: les recueils d'estampes comme entreprise éditoriale en Europe (XVIe–XVIIIe siècles)* (Cinisello Balsamo [Milan]: Silvana Editoriale, 2010).

[23] V. Toutain-Quittelier, 'Antonio Maria Zanetti à Paris: l'inspiration retrouvée', *La Revue de l'art*, CLVII (3), 2007, pp. 9–22; but see also P. Rosenberg, 'Parigi–Venezia o, piut-

tosto, Venezia–Parigi: 1715–1723', *Atti dell'Istituto Veneto di Scienze, Lettere ed Arti*, CLXI, 2002–3, pp. 1–30.

[24] On Mariette as a collector and scholar see *Le Cabinet d'un grand amateur: P.-J. Mariette 1694–1774*, ed. R. Bacou, exh. cat. (Musée du Louvre, Paris, Galerie Mollien, 1967; Paris: Réunion des Musées Nationaux, 1967). On his collection of Italian drawings and for a bibliography see P. Rosenberg, *Les dessins de la collection Mariette: écoles italienne et espagnole* (Paris: Somogy, 2019). On the Album of caricatures by Leonardo and his followers owned by Mariette see V. Forcione, in *Léonard de Vinci: dessins et manuscrits*, ed. F. Viatte and V. Forcione, exh. cat. (Musée du Louvre, Paris, 5 May–14 July 2003; Paris: Réunion des Musées Nationaux, 2003), pp. 217–27.

[25] For a summary of alternative assumptions and details concerning his stay in Paris see Toutain-Quittelier, *Antonio Maria Zanetti*, pp. 9–22.

[26] On the relations between Mariette and Zanetti and the range of their correspondence, though undocumented, see P. Rosenberg, in M. Magrini, ed., *Anton Maria Zanetti di Girolamo: il carteggio* (Verona: Scripta, 2021), pp. 94–5; see further P. Rosenberg, 'Les dessins vénitiens du XVIII siècle de la collection du Pierre-Jean Mariette', in *Venezia Settecento: studi in memoria di Alessandro Bettagno*, ed. B. A. Kowalczyk (Cinisello Balsamo [Milan]: Silvana Editoriale, 2015), pp. 111–29.

[27] Different theories are formulated by A. Bettagno, ed., *Caricature di Anton Maria Zanetti*, exh. cat. (Fondazione Giorgio Cini, Venice, 1969; Venice: Neri Pozza, 1969).

[28] P. Crozat cited in Razzall, 'Consul Smith', p. 31, n. 39.

[29] Ibid., p. 28.

[30] On the nobleman Gerhard Michael Jabach in the context of Zanetti in Venice see the essay by P. C. Marani here. For an overall picture of his character, also in relation to the work of his famous father Everhard, still fundamental is A. Schnapper, *Curieux du Grand Siècle: collections et collectionneurs dans la France du XVIIe siècle* (1994; Paris: Flammarion, 2005). On his relations with Italy and for a bibliography see A. Sonetti, 'La Città di Colonia a Livorno', *La Nuova Antologia*, 623 (2292), 2019, pp. 230–49.

[31] M. J. Dumesnil, *Histoire des plus célèbres amateurs français et de leurs relations avec les artistes, faisant suite à celle des plus célèbres amateurs italiens* (Paris: Dentu, 1857–8), p. 57.

[32] P. C. Marani, 'Suggestioni leonardesche nella cultura e nelle caricature di Anton Maria Zanetti dell'Album Cini', *Arte veneta*, 73 (2016), 2017, pp. 187–96. On these topics see also E. Lucchese, *L'album di caricature di Anton Maria Zanetti alla Fondazione Giorgio Cini* (Venice: lineadacqua, 2015).

[33] Lucchese, *L'album di caricature*, p. 3. On the reception of Zanetti see also the essay by Marani here.

[34] See most recently for a bibliography *Bellotto e Canaletto: lo stupore e la luce*, ed. B. A. Kowalczyk, exh. cat. (Gallerie d'Italia, Milan, 25 November 2016–5 March 2017; Cinisello Balsamo [Milan]: Silvana Editoriale, 2016), esp. the contribution by B. A. Kowalczyk.

[35] A. M. Zanetti, *Delle antiche statue Greche e Romane, che nell'antisala della libreria di San Marco, e in altri luoghi pubblici di Venezia si trovano*, 2 vols (Venice, 1740–43).

[36] On John Skippe (1741–1812) and his hypothetical encounter with Zanetti, in the context of the history of taste in Venice and London in the eighteenth century, see L. Borean, 'Per il collezionismo grafico tra Venezia e Londra nel Settecento: il caso di John Skippe', *Studi di Memofonte*, 12, 2014, pp. 73–85.

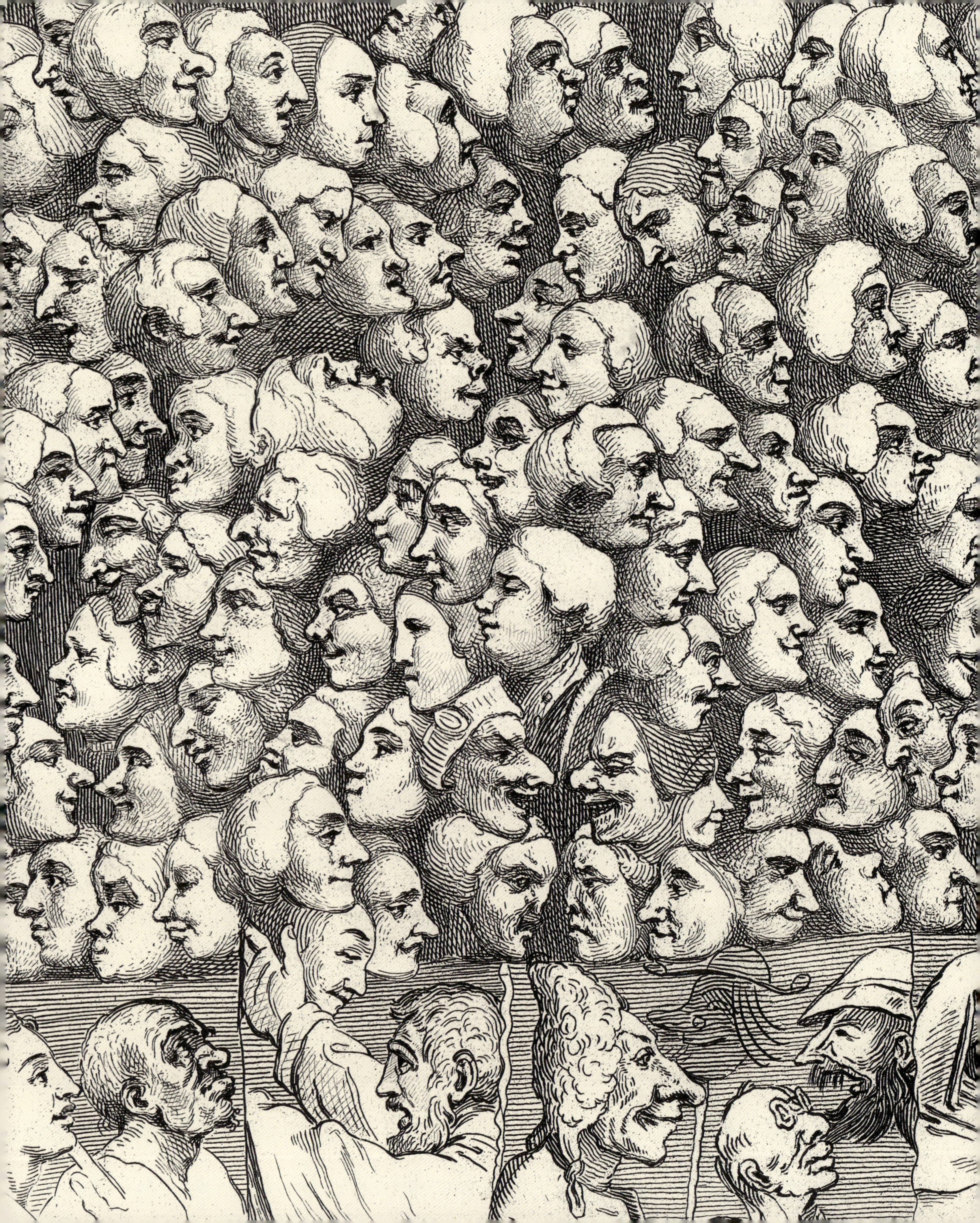

Rosalba Antonelli

The Reception of Leonardo's Character Heads in Eighteenth-Century Engravings: Between Graphic Rendering and Interpretation

opposite
William Hogarth
Characters and Caricaturas, 1743, detail
Milan, Raccolta Achille Bertarelli, vol. FF 44, tav. 52a

During the eighteenth century, the publication of some important suites of engravings derived from original drawings by Leonardo and his school helped spread the genre of grotesque heads and characters among lovers of the fine arts, characterising it as a distinctive strand of his work. Likewise, as renewed versions of Leonardo's models emerged, the theme of grotesque heads reflected significant correspondences in original engraved variants produced by certain artists who were studying character as expressing physiognomic disharmony.

During the seventeenth century, a knowledge of Leonardo's grotesque heads was spread by the etchings of the Bohemian Wenceslaus Hollar (1607–1677).[1] This was a selection of figures produced between 1645 and 1666 after the originals from the rich collection of the English nobleman Thomas Howard, Earl of Arundel (1586–1646), and consisted of etchings the same size as the original drawings grouped by theme and reflecting the engraver's own sensibility.[2]

Etchings of original drawings reproducing their exact size and style was a key point of the *Recueil de testes de caractère & de charges, dessinées par Léonard de Vinci Florentin*.[3] Published in Paris in 1730 by Pierre-Jean Mariette to showcase and promote his drawings, the successful series of etchings reproduced the heads he collected in what is called the Mariette Album.[4] Since some of these male and female heads had already been engraved by Hollar, Mariette conjectured that they came from the Earl of Arundel's highly prized collection.[5] Moreover, in commenting on Hollar's etchings, Mariette took the opportunity to point out, despite the great pains lavished on their execution, a certain failure to attain Leonardo's manner.[6] This work had been entrusted to his engraver friend Anne-Claude-Philippe de Tubières, Comte de Caylus (1692–1765). He was the dedicatee of the introductory text by Mariette himself, who with precise and refined graphic fidelity translated the bizarre, abnormal and sometimes even monstrous heads into this rich selection of physiognomic studies [fig. 1].

The circulation of the two collections by Hollar and Caylus is reflected in their interesting adaptations by such artists as William Hogarth (1697–1764), who etched the print of *Characters*

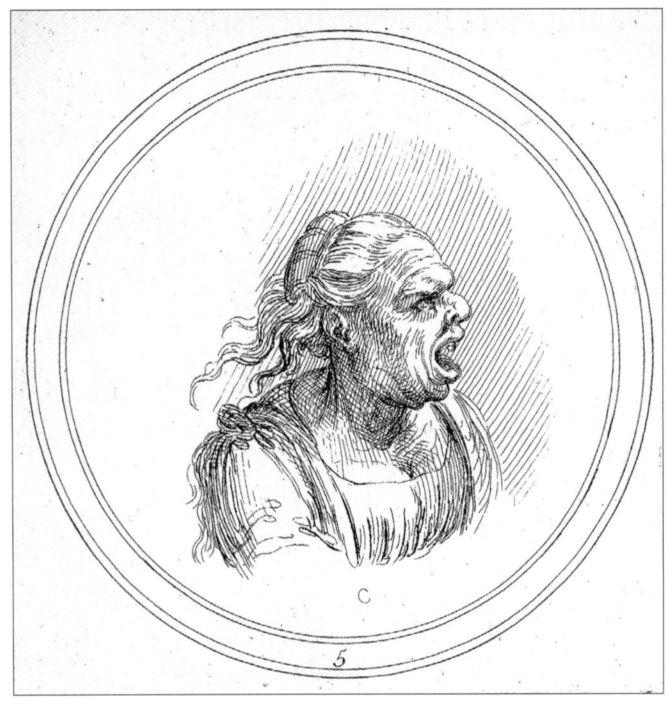

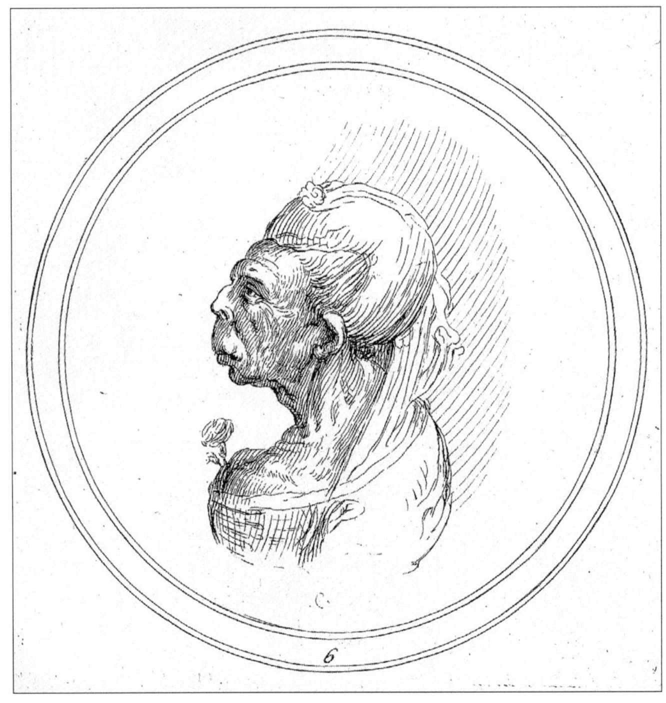

1
Anne-Claude-Philippe de Tubières Comte de Caylus, *Two female grotesque heads*, 1730
Milan, Castello Sforzesco, Ente Raccolta Vinciana, inv. C.III. 39

and Caricaturas published in London in 1743.[7] In the lower section of the plate, following well-known figurative models, such as the studies of Agostino Carracci, Hogarth placed a grotesque male profile by Leonardo,[8] a subject engraved earlier by Hollar and Caylus,[9] next to heads derived from Raphael, Pier Leone Ghezzi and Annibale Carracci [fig. 2]. He again drew on Leonardo's repertoire in the upper band, added in 1764 to the etched and engraved print of *The Bench* (1758).[10] The artist replicated the heads of the apostles in the *Last Supper*, James the Great, Thomas and Andrew (this last present in two versions), reversed and crisply drawn, so exaggerating their noses and mouths as to make them at the same time caricatures,[11] relating their appearance to the theme expressed in the body of the print.

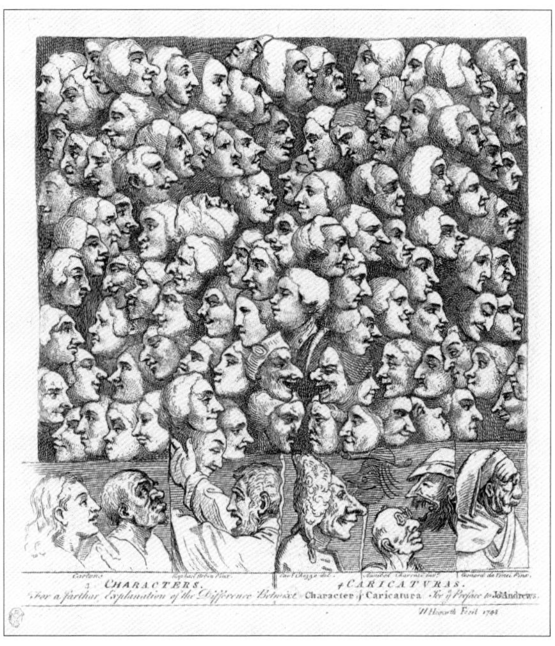

2

2.
William Hogarth
Characters and Caricaturas, 1743
Milan, Raccolta Achille Bertarelli, vol. FF 44, tav. 52a

In Italy, and Lombardy in particular, it is interesting that the theme of caricature was chosen for the meeting of the Accademia dei Trasformati held in Milan on 15 February 1759.[12] In a passage from the *Discorso sopra le caricature* delivered on that occasion, Giuseppe Parini (1729–1799) described two physiognomic types that seem to echo Leonardo's models: 'They were certain lean miseries and consumptives, with their very tight frock coats clinging to their skins; and the others, all with laughing faces, fat and jovial, swathed in certain garments disproportionately loose and left untied at the waist.'[13]

Some twenty years after the reprint of the *Recueil de testes de caractère* in 1767[14] and a decade after the sale of the Mariette collection (1775–6), there was a renewed interest in Leonardo, in which Parini himself had the opportunity to participate in the Biblioteca Braidense.[15] In this period, the circulation of Leonardo's grotesque heads was entrusted to two notable publications issued in Milan in 1784 and 1785 by Carlo Giuseppe Gerli and Girolamo Mantelli. The first of these, *I disegni di Leonardo da Vinci incisi e pubblicati da Carlo Giuseppe Gerli milanese*, presents a significant selection of grotesque heads.[16] At first, Gerli wanted to engrave only drawings of the human figure, 'but then submitted to sage counsellors, who led him to see that, while he could omit a part of the *Caricatures*, since they are extremely numerous, he would do all amateurs a service by publishing some drawings related to other objects',[17] such as machines and inventions, in short 'those contrivances, that for some years now have been as new things coming from England and France', for example the lifebelt in plate XXVII.[18] Nonetheless, *I disegni di Leonardo da Vinci* presents a substantial array of grotesque heads copied from the numerous originals in the Biblioteca Ambrosiana and then brought together by Gerli in fifteen of the sixty-one plates.[19] The subjects depicted are notable for some figures that 'are not far from the natural', such as those in plate XIII, or the people laughing, such as the character in plate XIV, known as *Merlin Cocalio*.[20] But the most strongly caricatured heads are contained in plates XV to XXVII. Their distinctiveness was recognised by Carlo Amoretti, who wrote the introductory text, as lying in the specificity of the exaggerated and abnormal features of the faces of peasants and the aged, which Leonardo sometimes accompanied with extravagant bonnets and hairstyles, depending on the subject, to increase the sense of the ridiculous.[21]

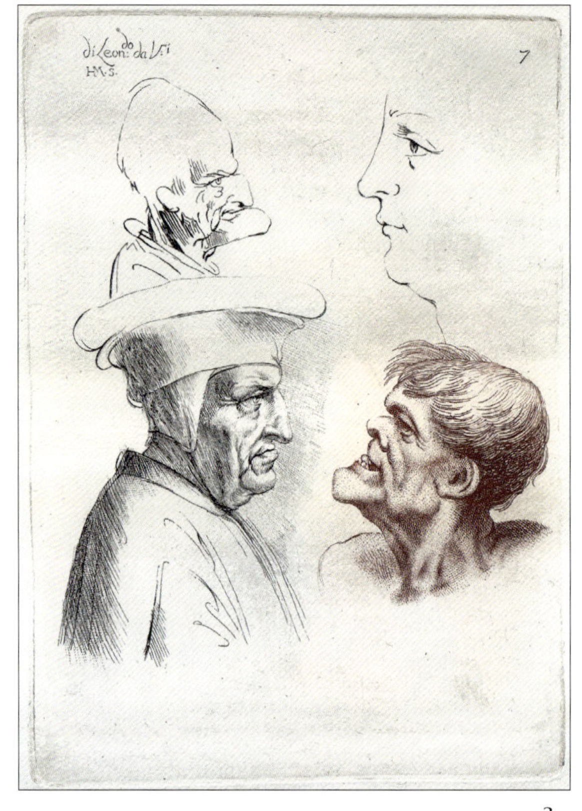

3.
Girolamo Mantelli
Three grotesque male heads and a female profile, 1785
Milan, Castello Sforzesco, Ente Raccolta Vinciana, inv. RV B INF.11

In 1785 Girolamo Mantelli published a new collection of twenty-seven plates in Milan. They were based on thirty-six drawings by Leonardo, again in the Biblioteca Ambrosiana, except for the last three, from the Galleria Arcivescovile in Milan.[22] Although most of the subjects in the *Raccolta di disegni* related to the subject matter here had already been published by Gerli with a general attribution to Leonardo, Mantelli created versions 'of the same size and colour as the originals'.[23] He also adopted the 'crayon manner', an engraving technique that made it possible to render the original handling of the drawing by using coloured inks.[24] The presence of grotesque heads in Mantelli's collection, however, is limited compared to the varied juxtapositions in the previous suite. In many cases the subjects occupy a whole plate individually, though there are some composite plates, such as number 7, where the characters have been represented in ink matching the medium of the original, as in the male head (cod. F 263 inf. 19b) rendered in red ink [fig. 3].

In the last decade of the eighteenth century, Leonardo's caricatured heads, especially those derived from Gerli's publication, were given effective expression in the coloured engraving process

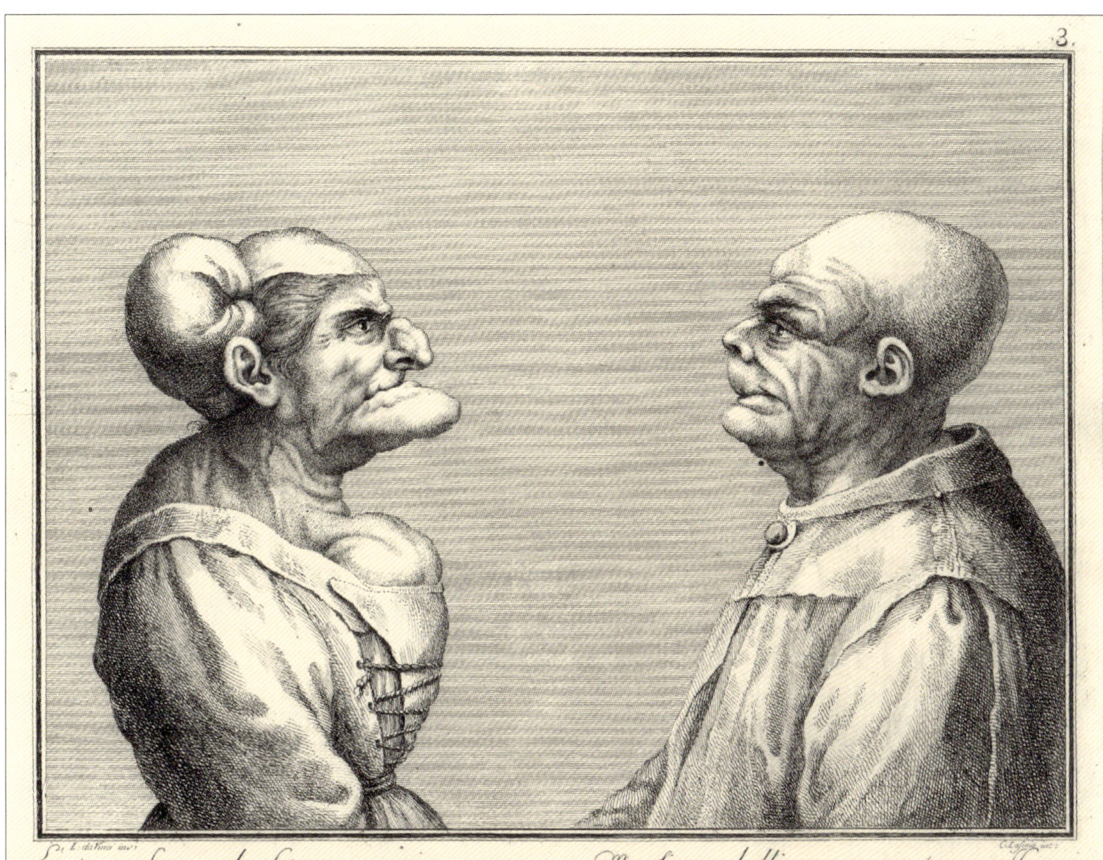

4

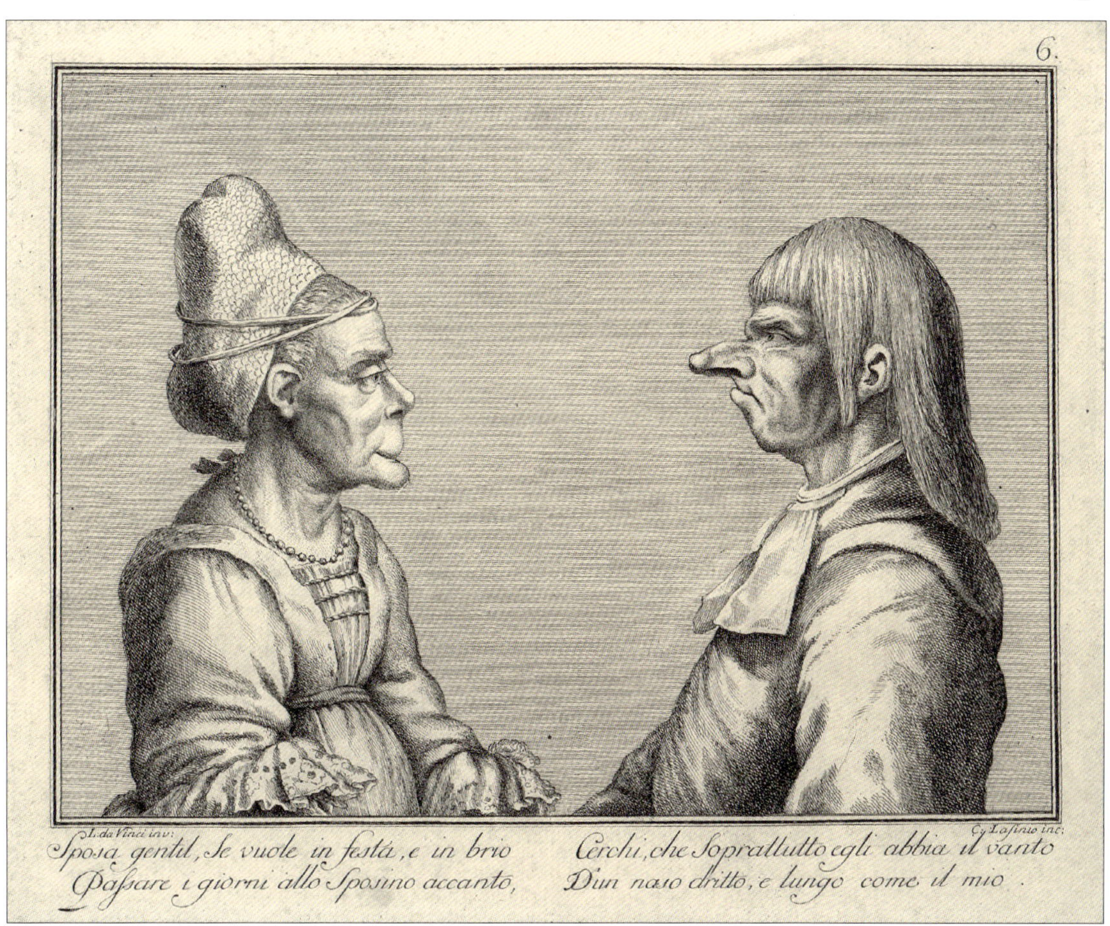

5

4.
Carlo Lasinio
Pair of grotesque heads,
c. 1790
Udine, Gallerie dei Disegni
Stampe dei Musei Civici
di Udine, inv. 1951_S

5.
Carlo Lasinio
Pair of grotesque heads,
c. 1790
Udine, Gallerie dei Disegni
Stampe dei Musei Civici
di Udine, inv. 1954_S_r

developed by Carlo Lasinio (1759–1838) after experimenting with the French engraver Edouard Gautier-Dagoty (1745–1783) living in Florence.[25] With an effect quite similar to watercolour, due to the variety of the chromatic range of the plates and the possibility of adding finishing touches with a brush,[26] Lasinio issued twelve etched plates depicting unlikely married couples who declaim burlesque mottos about the beauty and joys of marriage, with ironic allusions to their grotesque bodily appearance. The series, moreover, includes uncoloured plates, such as the suite of six specimens from the Musei Civici of Udine,[27] which bring out most fully the figurative qualities achieved by Lasinio in working on Leonardo's models [figs 4 and 5], mainly based on Gerli's engravings of 1784, which circulated at the same time in a French translation.[28] Lasinio's interest in Leonardo's grotesque heads is also reflected in a small corpus of watercolour drawings, which was on the market in 2013,[29] consisting of four copies of grotesque heads, three of them certainly derived from the suite engraved by Caylus.[30]

The last series of collections of heads engraved after Leonardo in the eighteenth century – not overlooking the new London edition of Hollar published in 1786 by John Clarke (1756–1815),[31] notable for its dry, terse handling – with the suite *Imitations of Original Designs by Leonardo da Vinci . . . in His Majesty's Collection* issued by John Chamberlaine (1745–1812) in London in 1796.[32] It is a valuable series of etchings after originals in the English royal collection (indiscriminately attributed to Leonardo da Vinci),[33] largely the work of Francesco Bartolozzi (1728–1815), a painter and engraver active among the founding members of the Royal Academy in London.[34] This series was also mentioned and praised by Giuseppe Bossi (1777–1815) for the 'way in which those [drawings] of the great masters should be published'.[35] This distinctive rendering was achieved by stippling, a technique perfected by Bartolozzi through experiments in the crucible of London[36] to imitate the effect of the original, through the use of a toothed wheel (called a rocker) with black or red ink, an effect seen before in the plates in Mantelli's suite of engravings.

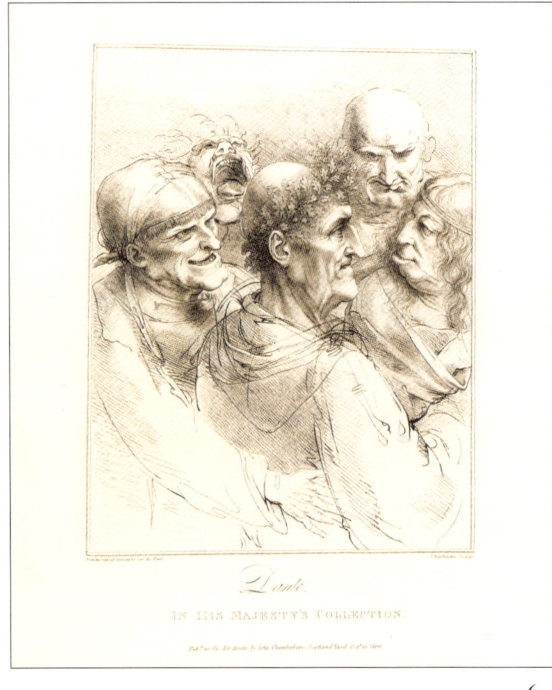

6

6.
Francesco Bartolozzi
Five grotesque heads – 'Dante', 1806
Wolfenbüttel, Herzog August Bibliothek, inv. Xd FM 23.20 (23)

Bartolozzi's technical sensibility appears particularly in certain subjects of the suite, such as plate VII37, a version of Leonardo's striking *Five grotesque heads* (Windsor,

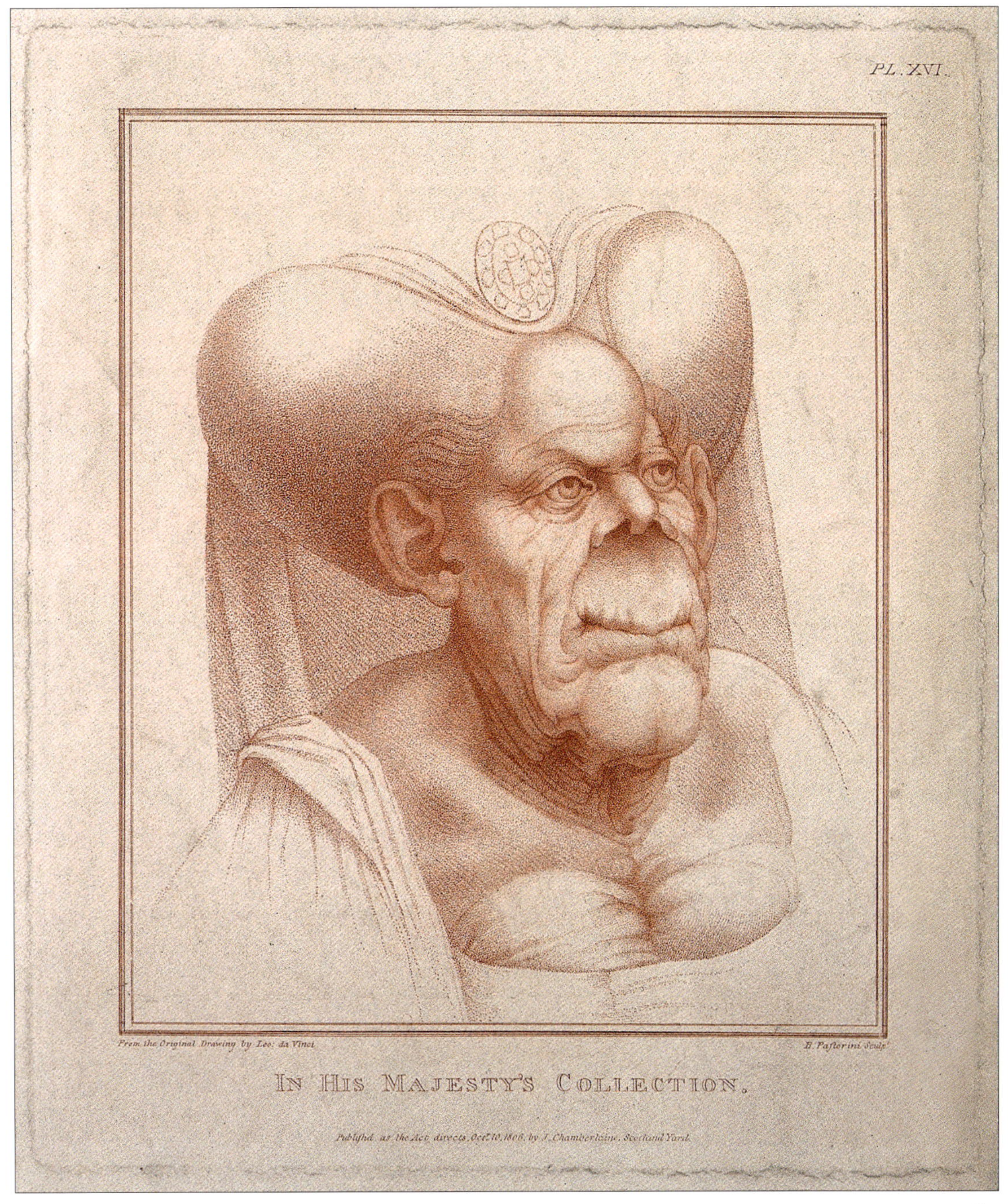

7

7.
Benedetto Pastorini
Grotesque bust of an old woman wearing a large escoffin with a wimple, 1806
London, Wellcome Collection
Wellcome Library, inv. no. 3232i

Royal Library, inv. no. 12495r) previously engraved by Hollar. This specimen of Bartolozzi's etching, entitled *Dante,* with the heads facing in the correct direction, transposes the original with precise graphic equivalents, without adding or integrating in the lightly sketched parts [fig. 6].[38] Plate XVI, depicting *Four grotesque figures of old people,* presents a composition of grotesque male and female profiles by Benedetto Pastorini (1746–1806?) with stippling in red ink,[39] similar to plate XV, dominated by the majestic *Grotesque bust of an old woman wearing a large escoffin with a wimple* [fig. 7],[40] printed with effective chiaroscuro passages and physiognomic details faithful to the original (Windsor, Royal Library, inv. no. 12492).[41]

In Bartolozzi's independent output, finally, we can still trace some stylistic formulas put into circulation by Leonardo's models. This is not difficult to grasp, for example, in the engraving *The Alderman's Feast* after a drawing by Nathaniel Dance (1735–1811).[42] Another is the refined portrait of the musician Thomas Arne made in 1782, whose profile can be seen as caricature because of the prominent eyes, the accentuation of the nose and the upward curve of the lower lip.[43] Finally, caricature inspired by Leonardo's models is reflected in the singular *Bust of a man with profile facing right* engraved by Bartolozzi in 1799 (British Museum, inv. 1928.0313.284).[44] Although the subject cannot be identified, this profile, with its allusion to Leonardo's grotesque heads, offers a significant starting point to record the spread of certain figurative models expressed in refined and prized engravings, and developed in diversified and original artistic works.

[1] See A. Perissa Torrini, ed., *Leonardo disegnato da Hollar*, exh. cat. (Fondazione Pedretti, Vinci, 16 December 2018–5 May 2019; Poggio a Caiano: C. B. Edizioni, 2018).

[2] On this point see M. Melani, 'Leonardo e Hollar in scala 1:1', in ibid., pp. 77–105, esp. the comparison between the engraving and Leonardo's drawing *Five grotesque heads* (Windsor, inv. RL 12495r), pp. 92–3, 132–3.

[3] *Recueil de testes de caractère de charges, dessinées par Léonard de Vinci Florentin et gravées par M. le Cte. de C.* [Comte de Caylus] (Paris: J. Mariette, 1730). On this work see V. Forcione, in *Léonard de Vinci: dessins et manuscrits*, ed. F. Viatte and V. Forcione, exh. cat. (Musée du Louvre, Paris, 5 May–14 July 2003; Paris: Réunion des Musées Nationaux, 2003), pp. 228–36, no. 74; Forcione, in *Leonardo da Vinci: Master Draftsman*, ed. C. C. Bambach, with contributions by C. C. Bambach et al., exh. cat. (The Metropolitan Museum of Art, New York, 22 January–30 March 2003; New York: The Metropolitan Museum of Art; New Haven and London: Yale University Press, 2003), pp. 702–22, no. 138; for the 1767 reprint see R. Antonelli, in *La Cène de Léonard de Vinci pour François Ier, un chef-d'œuvre en or et soie*, ed. P. C. Marani, exh. cat. (Amboise, Château du Clos Lucé, 7 June–2 September 2019; Paris: Skira, 2019), pp. 208–9, no. 50.

4 *Album de Caricature*, Paris, Musée du Louvre, Département des Arts Graphiques, inv. RF 28725-RF 28785. See V. Forcione, 'L'album du Louvre: les grotesques de Léonard de Vinci, originaux, dispersion, copies, estampes', in Viatte and Forcione, *Léonard de Vinci*, pp. 206–16, 217–27, no. 73; Forcione, in Bambach, *Leonardo da Vinci*, pp. 680–702, no. 137; Antonelli, in Marani, *Cène de Léonard de Vinci*, pp. 206–7, nos 48–9.

[5] Recent studies consider the grotesque heads in the Mariette Album to be copies by a Dutch artist; Forcione, 'L'album du Louvre', p. 214.

[6] P.-J. Mariette, 'Lettre sur Leonard de Vinci, peintre florentin, à Monsieur le C. De C.', in *Recueil de testes*, p. 5.

[7] William Hogarth, *Characters and Caricaturas*, 1743, etching, second state of two, 230 × 206 mm (copperplate), Milan, Raccolta Achille Bertarelli, Vol. FF 44, pl. 52a. See C. Salsi, in *L'anima e il volto: ritratto e fisionomica da Leonardo a Bacon*, ed. F. Caroli, exh. cat. (Palazzo Reale, Milan, 30 October 1998–14 March 1999; Milan: Electa, 1998), pp. 370–71; C. C. McPhee and N. M. Orenstein, eds, *Infinite Jest: Caricature and Satire from Leonardo to Levine*, exh. cat. (The Metropolitan Museum of Art, New York, 13 September 2011–4 March 2012; New York: The Metropolitan Museum of Art; New Haven and London: Yale University Press, 2011), pp. 32–3, n. 11.

[8] For the grotesque figure by Leonardo formerly in the Arundel collection, see M. W. Kwakkelstein, in *Leonardo da Vinci: The Language of Faces*, ed. M. W. Kwakkelstein with M. Plomp, exh. cat. (Teylers Museum, Haarlem, 5 October 2018–6 January 2019; Bussum: Thoth, 2018), pp. 130–31, no. 24.

[9] *Recueil de testes*, fol. 29, fig. 32.

[10] *The Bench/ Of the Different Meaning of the Words Character, Caracatura and Outrè in Painting and Drawing*, which contains, on a separate plate, a long explanatory text on the difference between caricature and character (London, British Museum n. inv. S,2.139).

[11] See the entry on *La corte* in *William Hogarth: dipinti, disegni, incisioni*, ed. A Battagno, exh. cat. (Fondazione Giorgio Cini, Venice, 26 August–12 November 1989; Venice: Neri Pozza, 1989), p. 65, no. 108.

[12] R. Negri, 'Il Parini a una serata dei Trasformati: il "Discorso sopra le caricature"', *Lettere italiane*, XVII, 2, April–June 1965, pp. 191–205; G. Dell'Aquila, 'Intenti satirici e omaggio alla tradizione nell'onomastica pariniana del Discorso sopra le caricature', Tenth International Conference of Onomastica & Letteratura Proceedings (Pisa, 19–20 February 2004), *Il Nome nel testo: rivista internazionale di onomastica letteraria*, VII, 2005, pp. 31–47.

[13] G. Parini, 'Discorso sopra le caricature', in *Poesie e prose, con appendice di poeti satirici e didascalici del Settecento*, ed. L. Caretti (Milan and Naples: Ricciardi Editore, 1951), p. 580.

[14] *Recueil de charges et de têtes de différents caractères, gravées à l'eau forte d'après les desseins de Leonard de Vinci, Précédé d'une lettre de M. Mariette sur ce peintre florentin. Nouvelle edition, revue et augmentée per l'auteur* (Paris: C. A. Jombert, 1767). For the editions of the *Recueil* see M. V. Guffanti, 'Il conte di Caylus e le caricature di Leonardo', *Raccolta Vinciana*, XXIX, 2001, pp. 303–16.

[15] Francesco Reina, curator of Parini's works, recorded the poet's interest in writing about the composition of the *Last Supper*, studied with his friend and colleague Giuseppe Franchi (1731–1806); see P. Frassica, 'Appunti sul linguaggio figurativo del Parini dal "Giorno" ai "Soggetti"', *Aevum*, L (5–6), September–December 1976, p. 584. Franchi kept the copy of the *Last Supper* from the Charterhouse of Pavia, important for its close resemblance to the original, for which see P. C. Marani, *'Bella quanto l'originale istesso': la copia del Cenacolo della Royal Academy di Londra. Vicende, fortuna, attribuzione* (Florence: LoGisma, 2016).

[16] C. G. Gerli, *Disegni di Leonardo da Vinci incisi e pubblicati da Carlo Giuseppe Gerli milanese* (Milan: Giuseppe Galeazzi regio stampatore, 1784).

[17] C. Amoretti, 'Ragionamento intorno ai disegni di Leonardo da Vinci compresi in questo volume', in Gerli, *Disegni di Leonardo da Vinci*, p. 3.

[18] Ibid., p. 11.

[19] The first systematic work of recognition and comparison between the original drawings and Gerli's engravings was carried out by L. Cogliati Arano, *Disegni di Leonardo e della sua cerchia alla Biblioteca Ambrosiana di Milano* (Milan: Arcadia/Electa, 1981), pp. 113–25.

[20] Imitator of Leonardo, *Studi fisionomici*, pen and brown ink, 167 × 197 mm, Milan, Biblioteca Ambrosiana, cod. F. 263 inf. 98. See Cogliati Arano, *Disegni di Leonardo*, p. 15, no. 27.

[21] C. Amoretti, 'Spiegazione delle tavole', in Gerli, *Disegni di Leonardo da Vinci*, p. 10.

[22] G. Mantelli, *Raccolta di disegni incisi da Girolamo Mantelli di Canobio sugli originali esistenti nella biblioteca ambrosiana di mano di Leonardo Da Vinci e de suoi scolari lombardi dedicata a sua eccellenza Gilberto Borromeo Arese* (Milan, 1785), n.p.

[23] Subscription sheet, *Agli Amatori delle Belle Arti, Catalogo delle Stae finora uscite alla luce, e tratte in egual grandezza e colore dagli originali* [1785], London, Royal Academy of Arts, inv. 18/1272.

[24] On this subject see B. Spadaccini, 'La pietra rossa nelle stampe che imitano i disegni', in *Disegni a pietra rossa: fonti, tecniche e stili 1500–1800 ca.*, ed. L. Fiorentino and M. W. Kwakkelstein, conference proceedings (Florence, Istituto Olandese di Storia dell'Arte, 18–19 September 2019; Florence: Edifir, 2021), pp. 223–36.

[25] On Lasinio and Dagoty see F. Borroni Salvatori, 'Carlo Lasinio e gli autoritratti di Galleria', *Mitteilungen des Kunsthistorischen Institutes in Florenz*, 28, 1984, pp. 112–15.

[26] For the print technique used by Lasinio, see also L. Lanzeni, 'Ancora su Carlo Lasinio e gli autoritratti di Galleria', *Mitteilungen des Kunsthistorischen Institutes in Florenz*, 43 (2–3), 1999, p. 665; G. Coccolini et al., 'La serie di ritratti di pittori celebri del Gabinetto Disegni e Stampe del Museo Correr: un problema di restauro', *OPD Restauro*, 19, 2007, p. 51.

[27] Carlo Lasinio, *Coppie caricate leonardesche*, plates 1–6, coloured etching, Gallerie dei Disegni Stampe dei Musei Civici di Udine, inv. 1949 S-1954 S, c. 1790.

[28] C. J. Gerli, *Desseins de Léonard de Vinci gravés par Charles Joseph Gerli Milanois* (Milan 1784).

[29] Carlo Lasinio, four caricatures by Leonardo: 1 *Caricature of a male figure in hat*, pen and brush with red ink wash, 147 × 115 mm; 2 *Caricature of a man with a prominent lip*, pen and brush, red ink wash, 151 × 119 mm; 3 *Female caricature with rose between the breasts*, pen and brush, red ink wash, 142 × 100 mm; 4 *Caricature of a woman in a hat*, pen and brush, red ink wash, 153 × 105 mm; 'Stampe, disegni, carte geografiche e vedute', Florence, Gonnelli Libreria Antiquaria/Casa d'Aste, auction no. 12, 17–18 May 2013, lot 623.

[30] Three subjects correspond to plates 10, 13 and 34 of the *Recueil de testes*.

[31] *Characaturas by Leonardo da Vinci, from Drawings by Wincelslaus Hollar, out of the Portland Museum. Published as the Act Directs Nov.r 1 1786 by John Clarke* (London, 1786).

[32] *Imitations of Original Designs by Leonardo da Vinci. Consisting of Various Drawings of Single Figures, Heads, Compositions, Horses, and Other Animals; Optics, Perspective, Gunnery, Hydraulics, Mechanics; and in Particular of Very Accurate Delineations, with a Most Spirited Pen, of a Variety of Anatomical Subjects. In His Majesty's Collection, Published by John Chamberlaine, Keeper of The King's Drawings and Medals, And F.S.A* (London: W. Bulmer and Co., 1796). Some of the drawings in the suite are found in A. Vesme and A. Calabi, *Francesco Bartolozzi: Catalogue des estampes et notice biographique d'après les manuscrits de A. De Vesme entièrement réformés et complétés d'une étude critique par A. Calabi* (Milan: Guido Modiano, 1928), pp. 525–8, nos 2085–101. For the suite, see R. Antonelli, in Marani, *Cène de Léonard*, pp. 210–12, nn. 51–3.

[33] The title page is dated 1796 while the seventeen plates of the collection have different publication dates: 1 September 1795 (plate I); 1 March 1796 (plate V), 11 April 1796 (plate VI); 13 May 1796 (plate IV); 1 October 1796 (plate II, III); October 1803 (plate XII); 10 October 1806 (plates VII–XI, XII–XVII). Bartolozzi engraved the first six plates (not numbered, dated 1795 or 1796), while some of the plates in the final group are by the engravers Peltro William Tomkins, Robert Shepster and Benedetto Pastorini, with the exception of the tenth, which lacks the engraver's name. For the complete series, see C. Alberici, 'Leonardo e l'incisione: qualche aggiunta', *Raccolta Vinciana*, XXIV, 1992, pp. 28–47, which presents the restored copies in the Dipartimento delle Stampe, Biblioteca Nazionale, Florence (Pal. 10-B-A-7-11).

[34] On Bartolozzi as engraver see A. Calabi, 'Francesco Bartolozzi', *Bollettino d'arte del Ministero della Pubblica Istruzione*, 22, 1928–9, pp. 103–21; A. Petrucci, 'Francesco Bartolozzi', in *Dizionario biografico degli Italiani*, vol. 6, 1964, pp. 793–6.

[35] G. Bossi, *Del Cenacolo di Leonardo da Vinci. Libri Quattro by Giuseppe Bossi, painter* (Milan: Dalla Stamperia Reale, 1810), pp. 69–70.

[36] The stippling technique is used in seventeen plates dated 1796 and 1806.

[37] See the copy in the Herzog August Bibliothek in Wolfenbüttel, etching, 361 × 303 mm (plate), 1806, Wolfenbüttel, Herzog August Bibliothek, inv. Xd FM 23.20 (23).

[38] This title does not appear in the collection in Vesme and Calabi, *Francesco Bartolozzi*; it can be identified in the entry 'Groupe de cinq bustes' by Leonardo da Vinci, p. 526, no. 2091; Alberici, 'Leonardo e l'incisione', p. 34, fig. 17.

[39] Ibid., p. 42, fig. 26.

[40] Ibid., fig. 25.

[41] For the drawing by Leonardo, see M. W. Kwakkelstein, in Kwakkelstein with Plomp, *Leonardo da Vinci*, pp. 133–4, no. 27.

[42] Francesco Bartolozzi, engraving, 275 × 213 mm (plate), 347 × 257 mm (sheet), Rome, Calcografia di Stato, Fondo Corsini, inv. S-FC67427; see *Francesco Bartolozzi: incisore delle Grazie*, ed. B. Jatta, exh. cat. (Villa Farnesina, Rome, 27 October–17 December 1995; Museo Nacional de Arte Antiga, Lisbon, 27 January–29 September 1996; Rome: Artemide, 1995), p. 141, no. 55.

[43] For the profile of Arne, see B. Brumana, 'Francesco Bartolozzi (1728–1815) incisore della musica', *Esercizi: musica e spettacolo*, XX, n.s., 2006–7, pp. 37–8, 59, fig. 6; on Bartolozzi's caricatures, pp. 42–6. Bartolozzi's engravings of William Hogarth's satirical drawings are also noteworthy.

[44] London, British Museum, etching, oval inserted in a rectangle, 300 × 236 mm, 'F. Bartolozzi R. A. Sculps. 1799'. The subject is not present in Vesme and Calabi, *Francesco Bartolozzi*.

49.

Recueil de testes de caractère & de charges dessinées par Leonard de Vinci Florentin & gravée par M. le C de C.
Paris, J. Mariette Rue de St. Jacques aux Colonnes d'Hercules, 1730
Paper volume, 293 × 211 mm
Milan, Castello Sforzesco, Ente Raccolta Vinciana, inv. RV C. III. 39

Published in Paris in 1730, the *Recueil* stands out for its monographic approach to Leonardo's grotesque heads etched by Anne-Claude-Philippe de Tubières, Comte de Caylus (1692–1765). The volume opens with the *Lettre sur Leonard de Vinci* (Mariette 1730, pp. 1–22), an introductory text on Leonardo's life and works by the publisher Pierre-Jean Mariette (1694–1774) dedicated to his friend the etcher, and it closes with a list of etchings derived from Leonardo's drawings and paintings. Of the fifty-eight etchings, fifty-two reproduce the originals owned by the Parisian publisher of the so-called Mariette Album, regarded as autograph works (Forcione 2003, pp. 217–27, no. 73; Antonelli, in Marani 2019, pp. 206–7, nos 48, 49) and today recognised as copies after Leonardo (Forcione, in Bambach 2003, pp. 680–702, no. 137). The first twenty-six plates in the suite reproduce pairs of heads in the album, distinguished by a number and the engraver's initial, 'C.[aylus]', placed in the body of the etching. Mariette included twelve etchings based on Leonardo's grotesque heads in other collections, such as that 'du Cabinet du Roy' (copy no. 55; Paris, Musée du Louvre, Département des Arts Graphiques, inv. 2249), Crozat (nos 56–9 and the closing plate) and the Hickman collection (no. 46). A copy of the 1730 edition of the *Recueil* was present in Anton Maria Zanetti's library (Marani 2017, pp. 190–91), serving as a fundamental collection for the reception and dissemination of the theme of Leonardo's grotesque heads in Venice in the eighteenth century. The printed edition of 1730 must have been preceded by an earlier print run and followed by at least two others (Guffanti 2001, pp. 303–16): a German edition of 1750 traced by Steinitz (Steinitz 1974, p. 22; Forcione 2003, p. 238, cat. 75) and a third reprinted again in Paris in 1767 by Jombert (Antonelli, in Marani 2019, pp. 208–9, no. 50).

RA

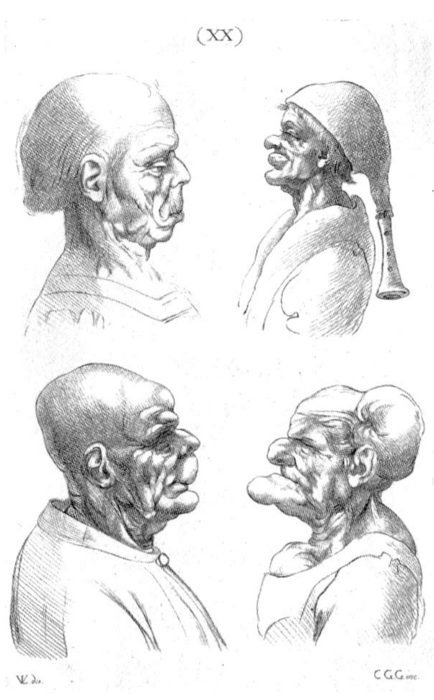

1. *Recueil de testes de caractère & de charges dessinées par Leonard de Vinci Florentin & gravée par M. le C de C.*, Paris 1730

Bibliography:
Guffanti 2001, pp. 303–16; Forcione 2003, pp. 206–36; Forcione, in Bambach 2003, pp. 702–22, no. 138; Villata 2013, no. 18; Antonelli, in Marani 2019, pp. 208–9, no. 50.

50.

Page 33 of the Zanetti Album, nine sheets glued on paper, c. 523 × 385 mm, each framed with a double line in sepia ink

Marco Ricci (1676–1730)
Sebastiano Ricci, third decade of the eighteenth century
Pen, graphite sketch, sepia ink on paper, 294 × 203 mm

Anton Maria Zanetti (1680–1767)
Lucrezia Basadonna Mocenigo, third decade of the eighteenth century
Pen and light sepia ink on paper, 73 × 64 mm

Rosalba Carriera, c. 1730
Pen, graphite sketch, light sepia ink on paper, 90 × 69 mm

Margherita Pio of Savoy, third decade of the eighteenth century
Pen and sepia ink on paper, 74 × 64 mm

Maddalena Salvai, 1721
Pen and light sepia ink on paper, 89 × 54 mm

Juana Moura de Moncada y Corte Real, third decade of the eighteenth century
Pen and sepia ink on paper, 76 × 62 mm

Francesca Vanini Boschi, after 1728
Pen and sepia ink on paper, 65 × 57 mm

Marietta Correr, third decade of the eighteenth century
Pen and sepia ink on paper, 71 × 58 mm

Anastasia Robinson, 1721
Pen and light sepia ink on paper, 89 × 54 mm

Venice, Fondazione Giorgio Cini, Gabinetto dei Disegni e delle Stampe, inv. 36556–36564

Portly and elderly, Sebastiano Ricci stands full-length at the centre of a comic circle of eight female half-busts. Anton Maria Zanetti di Girolamo mounted them on the sheet and added most of the inscriptions before the album was recorded in his *Indice dei Libri* of 1744 (see Lucchese 2015, p. 13), with the purpose

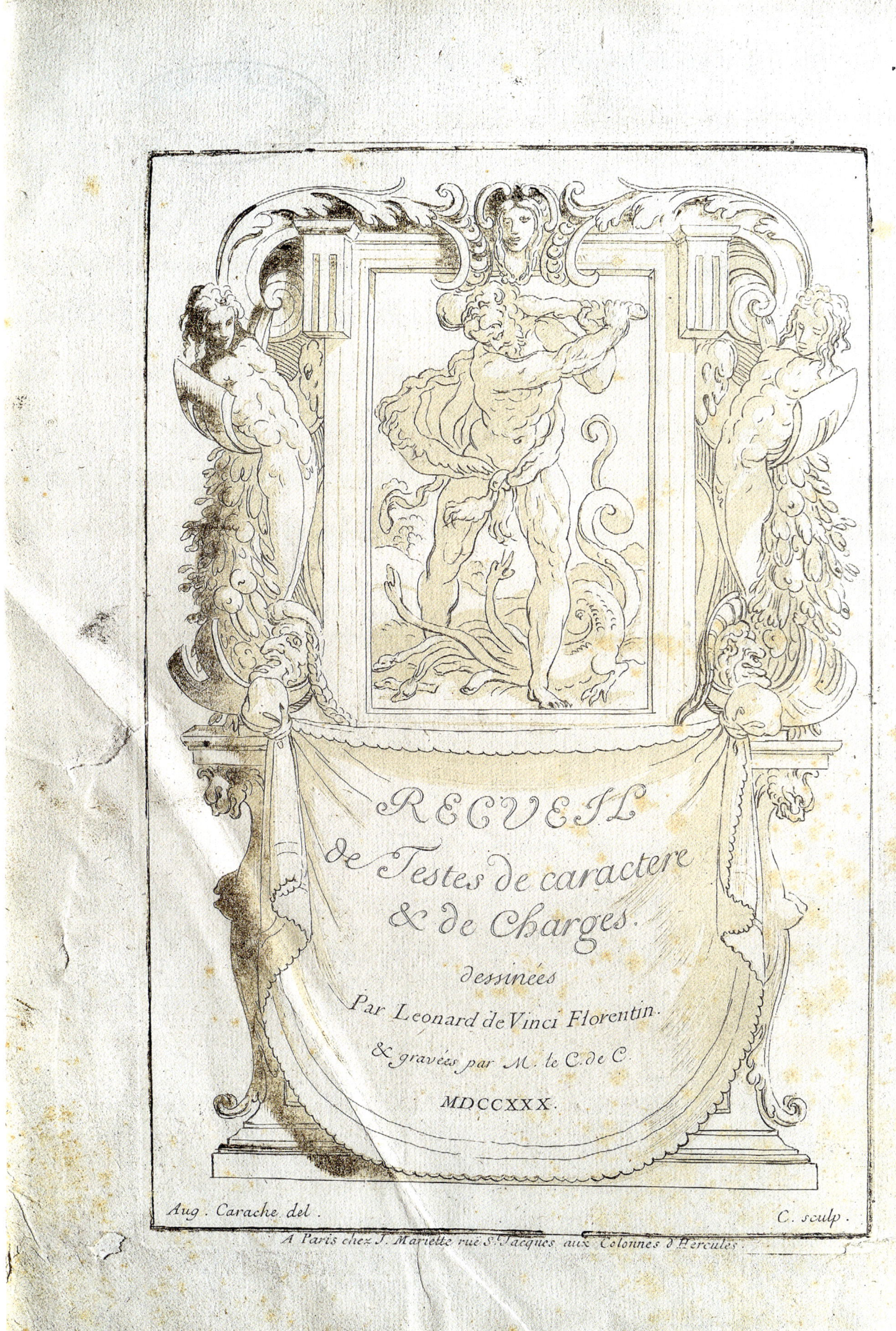
RECVEIL
de Testes de caractere
& de Charges.
dessinées
Par Leonard de Vinci Florentin.
& gravées par M. le C. de C.
MDCCXXX.
Aug. Carache del.
C. sculp.
A Paris chez J. Mariette rue S.t Jacques aux Colonnes d'Hercules.

49.

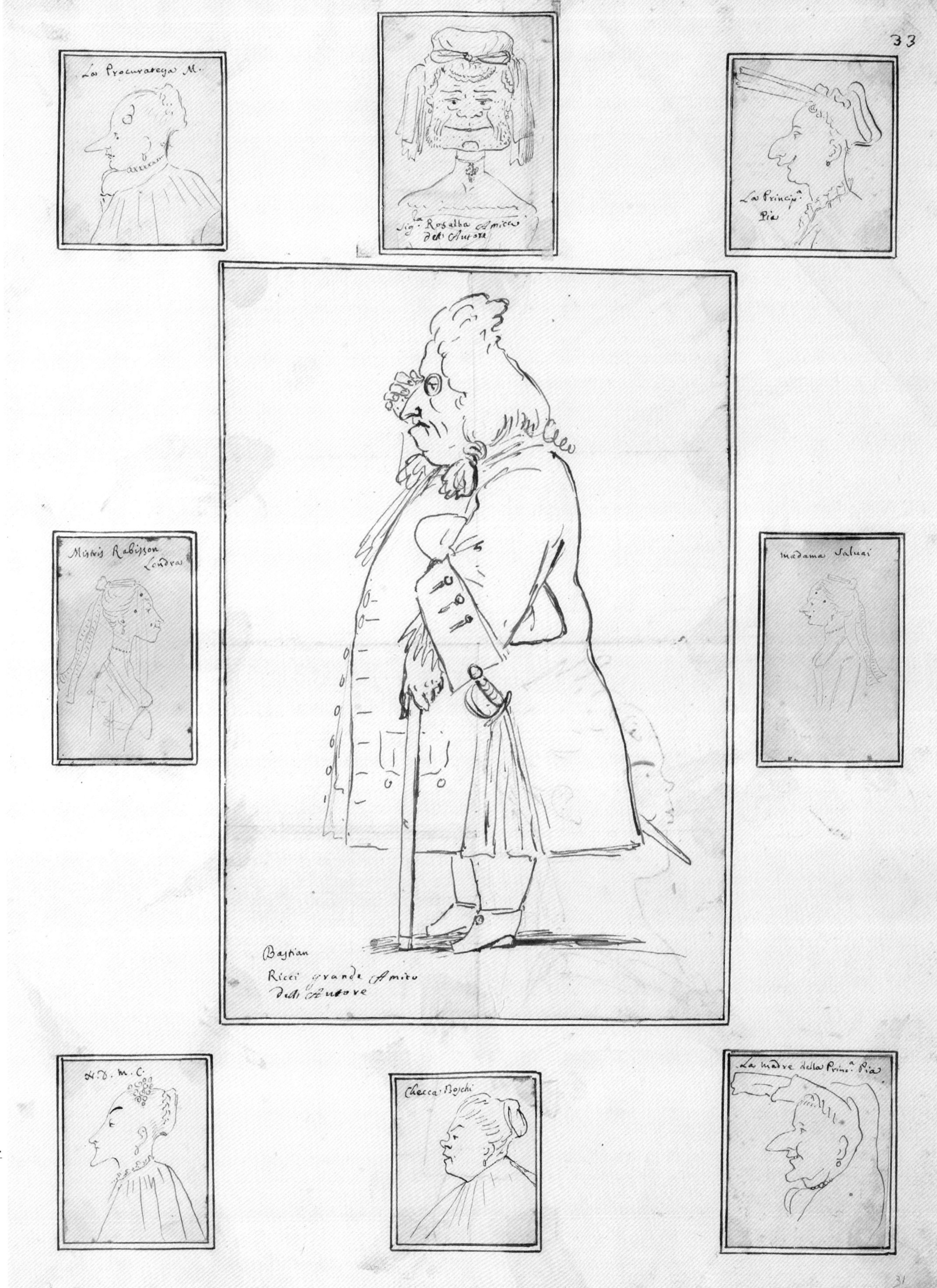

50.

of pillorying the passion of his painter friend for women (Stefani 2015, pp. 20–26). On the reverse of the central sheet, folded as if it had originally been in an envelope, the drawing of the large head of a lady with a retroussé nose acquires the value of an emblematic watermark. 'Bastian Ricci', as we read at bottom left in Zanetti's hand, points his pince-nez at the daring *décolleté* of 'Mistris Rabisson Londra', the singer Anastasia Robinson, well known in her time for being 'at the same time a prude and a kept mistress' (Wortley Montagu 1966, p. 37). On the other side is 'Madama Salvai', a soprano who specialised – even outside the theatre, one might say, given her place on the page – in the roles of 'donna secunda' (Highfill, Burnim and Langhans 1991) at the Royal Academy of Music, closely associated with Handel. The female images date from Zanetti's stay in London in the summer–autumn of 1721, while we can plausibly date the 'Sig.ra Rosalba', pasted above *Sebastiano Ricci*, to some ten years later. It is an irreverent representation of 'how grudging nature was in external gifts' (Zanetti 1771, p. 448). His close friendship since youth with Anton Maria and the album's originally private purpose (Lucchese 2015, p. 103) made possible the witty and cruel portrait of the 'Author's Lady Friend', in the words of Francesco Albergati Capacelli, a posthumous annotator of the collection (ibid., pp. 17–18). He also added, next to the inscription by Zanetti beneath Ricci, the information 'a close friend of the author'. In the lower register, in the middle, is the caricature of another virtuoso, the Venetian singer 'Checca Boschi', who sang the title role in Handel's *Agrippina* on December 1709 at the Teatro di San Giovanni Grisostomo (Selfridge-Field 2007, pp. 292–3). She was an 'excellent contralto' (Fassini 1914, p. 34), probably shown here after her definitive return in 1728 to her homeland with her husband and colleague Giuseppe Boschi. The corners of the page are kept for the grotesque profiles of aristocratic women: at left, 'M. the procurator's wife' and 'N.D.M.C.', acronyms that conceal the names of two Venetian patrician ladies who, in the first decade of the eighteenth century were ranked among the most beautiful in the city and portrayed by Rosalba Carriera: the 'wife of the Procurator Moceniga' and the 'charmante Marietta Correra' in the letters to the artist (Sani 1985, vol. I, pp. 167, 180). Zanetti's pen depicted them as the parodies of a faded or only legendary beauty. On the right 'Princess Pia', namely Margherita Pio of Savoy, who married her second husband, the patrician Pietro Zen, in Venice in 1692, and at the same time was the lover of Cardinal Ottoboni in Rome. She is recorded as in business in 1713–14 with Antonio Pellegrini and his wife Angela Carriera, then in Dusseldorf. Below her appears 'The mother of Princess Pia', who in 1683 married her second husband, Domenico Contarini, the Venetian ambassador to the imperial court, who died in 1696. She was very strong-willed in her political sympathies and is said to have raised her children with many a good thrashing (Veronese 2012, p. 108, n. 5).

The image in the central drawing derives from a similar *Sebastiano Ricci* in the Smith Album assigned to Marco Ricci (Croft-Murray 1957, p. 157, no. 2). It is identical, except for the detail of the right arm, to the 'Sebastian Ricci lost in thought' in the Zanetti Album, also by the subject's nephew (Lucchese 2015, pp. 300–01, no. 51.III). These images are still endowed with a certain urge towards verisimilitude, which in the present specimen veers towards caricature: the head has been enlarged, the curl of the wig is curiously turned up, the curved nose overhangs a toothless mouth, the torso is compressed, the coat opens like a flag on his belly and his back is marked by curvature of the spine, while the legs are turned into two logs anatomically unconnected with the rest of the body. The metamorphosis is rendered with a firm and lively handling in the redrawing, never losing sight of the space, the volume and the succession of planes in the deformation, coinciding with the first of Marco Ricci's three graphic styles that can be made out in the English album (Croft-Murray 1957, p. 146).

Zanetti, whose witty spirit must have shared in the development of such a comic image, wanted to work both on the impulses of Marco's uncle, and – at a higher level of interpretation – on the power of art to transcend reality. He achieved this by emphasising the figure of Rosalba at the top of the page, posed frontally as in her portraits, beside the distorted profiles that depict good likenesses of her famous subjects. Anton Maria distinguished his friend Rosalba's ability, described later by his nephew of the same name (Zanetti 1771, p. 448), to make 'the natural, although in itself defective, painted by her hands, appear beautiful, without departing from likeness or the truth'. These last qualities are also present, like the other side of the same coin, in the highly distinctive genre of caricature.

EL

Bibliography

Bettagno, in Bettagno 1969, pp. 67–9, nos 156–64; Bettagno 1970, pp. 107–8; Viatte 1970, p. 92; Webster 1970, p. 114; Vivian 1971, fig. IV; Bettagno, in Bettagno 1972, pp. 38–41, nos 46–54; Bettagno 1976a, p. 53; Bettagno 1976b, pp. 85–6; Croft-Murray 1980, p. 75; Dean, in Sadie 1980, vol. III, p. 74, vol. XVI, pp. 75, 434; Sani 1985, vol. I, p. 253, n. 3; Blanchard and de Cande 1986, p. 297; Highfill, Burnim and Langhans 1991, pp. 24–5, 193–4; Scarpa Sonino 1991, p. 29; Lowerre 1995, pp. 220–23, 226; Prosperi Valenti Rodinò 1992a, p. 119; Caroli 1995, fig. 67; Sponzilli, in Caroli 1998, p. 369; Zava Boccazzi 1998, p. 77; Montecuccoli degli Erri and Pedrocco 1999, pp. 67–8; Dean, in Sadie 2001, vol. XXI, p. 473, vol. XXII, p. 183; Del Torre, in Bettagno and Magrini 2002, pp. 25–6, no. 31; Foglia, in Caroli 2003, pp. 458, 461; Rosenberg 2005, p. 124; Mehler 2006, p. 110; Pasian, in Pavanello 2007a, pp. 82–3, no. 1, pp. 86–7, no. 3; Pavanello 2007b, pp. 63–4; Sani 2007b, pp. 258, 282; Barcham 2009, pp. 154–5; Llewellyn, in Llewellyn 2009, pp. 76–7, n. 209, p. 166, n. 486; Lucchese, in Pavanello 2010, pp. 48–9, no. 1; Veronese 2012, pp. 114–15; Lucchese 2015, pp. 208–17, nos 31.I–31.IX; Stefani 2015, p. 25; Marani 2017, p. 187; Sani 2021, p. 11.

51.
Imitator of Marco Ricci
(Maestro del Ricciolo?)
Sebastiano Ricci, third quarter
of the twentieth century
Pen and sepia ink over pinkish ochre
wash on paper, 200 × 130 mm
Milan, private collection

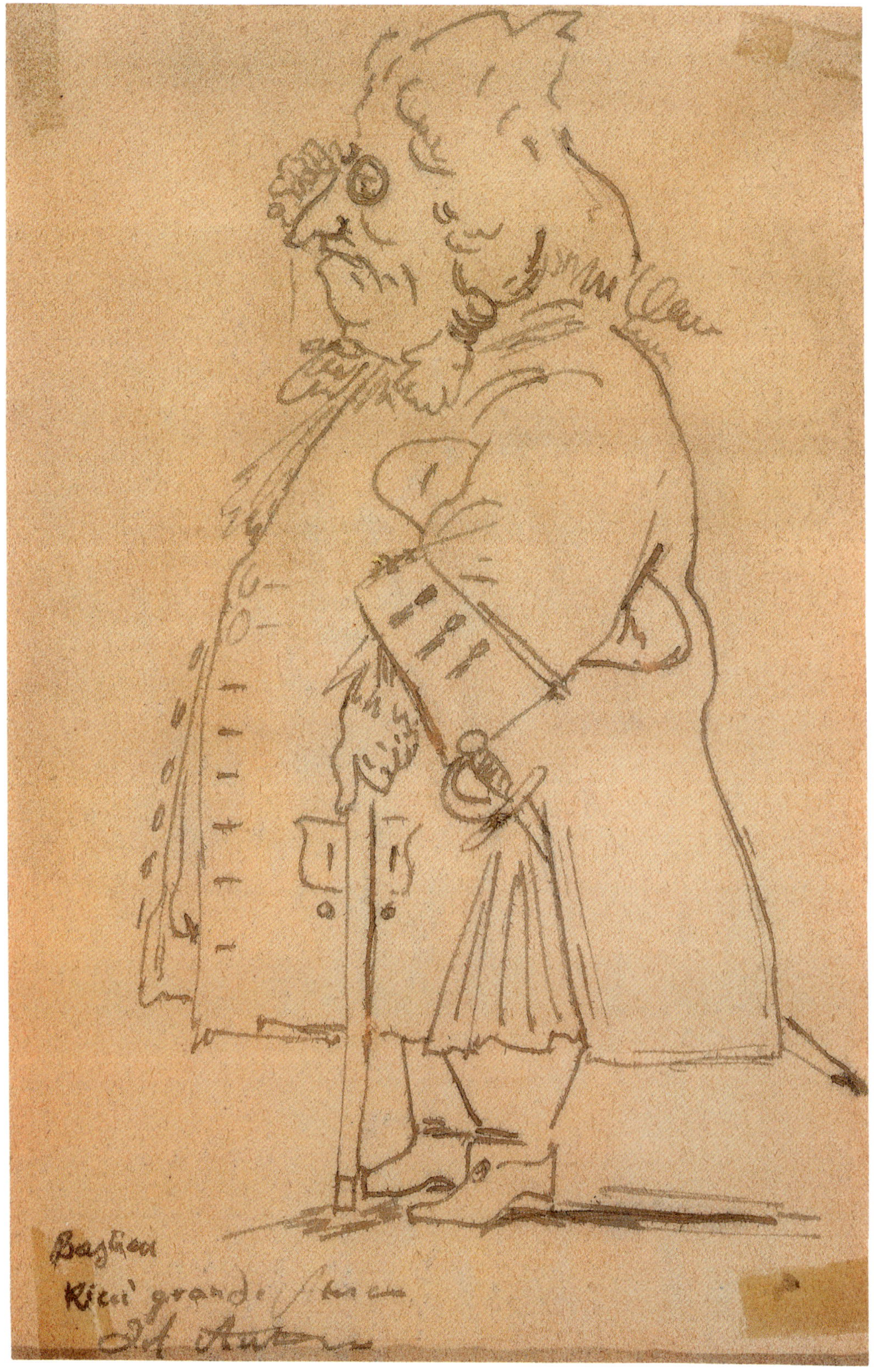

This is the replica on a smaller scale of the central caricature, by Marco Ricci, from page 33 of the Zanetti Album [cat. 50], which repeats – also in the various spellings of Anton Maria Zanetti and Francesco Albergati Capacelli – the inscription 'Bastian Ricci a close friend of the author'. Compared to the prototype, the line is more schematic, for example in the details of the feet or the wig, which here touches the upper edge of the sheet, while Sebastiano's already substantial bulk is increased. This working method and the use of prepared paper do not match the drawings attributable to Marco or the tracing made by Anton Maria Zanetti after works by his friend present in the Smith Album or the copies taken later for his collection by Francesco Algarotti. Considering that the Zanetti Album came into the possession of the Polish Count Zamoyski by the end of the eighteenth century (Lucchese 2015, p. 18) and returned to Venice only in the summer of 1968 (*Un acquisto eccezionale* 1968), followed first by the exhibition at the Fondazione Giorgio Cini (Bettagno 1969) and then a facsimile reproduction of it (Bettagno 1970), this was a work drawn from the reproduction. This might agree with a possible attribution to the artist called the Maestro del Ricciolo (Marani 2017), otherwise known as Giuseppe Latini, active in Rome and Milan (see Zavatta 2019). Among his fake drawings by Guardi, Canaletto and Tiepolo, he also produced a group of caricatures, sometimes accompanied by pseudo-inscriptions (ibid., pp. 130–31), a distinctive feature of his work. At other times – as in the case of a couple in the Fondazione Cini previously owned by Giuseppe Fiocco (Moretti, in Pavanello 2005, pp. 306–7, nos 513, 514) – they lack inscriptions and are in a format with clipped corners, like the sheets by Tiepolo. His adoption of a model different from the more profitable Tiepolo and the faithful transcription of the caption suggest that this drawing was intended as a sincere tribute to the invention – at the time regarded as by Zanetti (Bettagno, in Bettagno 1969, p. 68, no. 160) – of perhaps the most authentic portrait of Sebastiano Ricci, like Latini a pleasure-seeker and forger.

EL

Bibliography
Marani 2017, pp. 187–8.

52.

Marco Ricci (1676–1730)
Count Sava, 1720
Pen and sepia ink on paper,
143 × 191 mm
Private collection
[work not on display]

Represented on the other side of this sheet is a *Mountain landscape*, its chronology supposed to date from 'around 1710, when the lines were rigid and the hatching formed by parallel strokes' (*Antichi disegni* 2005). It appears to coincide with the artist's stay in England (Scarpa Sonino 1991, pp. 60–61) and seems to be stylistically earlier than the image on the verso, with its soft graphic handling. It has been identified (Lucchese 2015, 2018) as a variant of the caricature in the Zanetti Album also on display [cat. 55], in turn drawn on the back of a version, again by Marco Ricci, of *Daniele Antonio Bertoli with the famous Pattatocco*. These two characters arrived in Venice in late November 1726 on the way to Rome and returned to Vienna in late July of the following year (Lucchese 2022, p. 78). It is a likeness of the Serbian nobleman Sava Lukich Vladislavich, known as Il Raguseo, who was in Venice from 1 August 1716 as the 'agent of Muscovy' and a 'private knight'. On 19 September 1720 he married the patrician Virginia Trevisan at San Stae and was confirmed a count in late March 1722 by the Senate of the Serenissima shortly before leaving for Russia (Androsov 1999, pp. 68–9, 72–3). Absent from Venice for most of 1717 and 'from the first months of 1720 for two years' (ibid., p. 74), 'Count Sava Wladislavich' was the dedicatee of the operatic libretto *La verità in cimento* set to music by Antonio Vivaldi. It was first performed with sets devised and painted by the brothers Giuseppe and

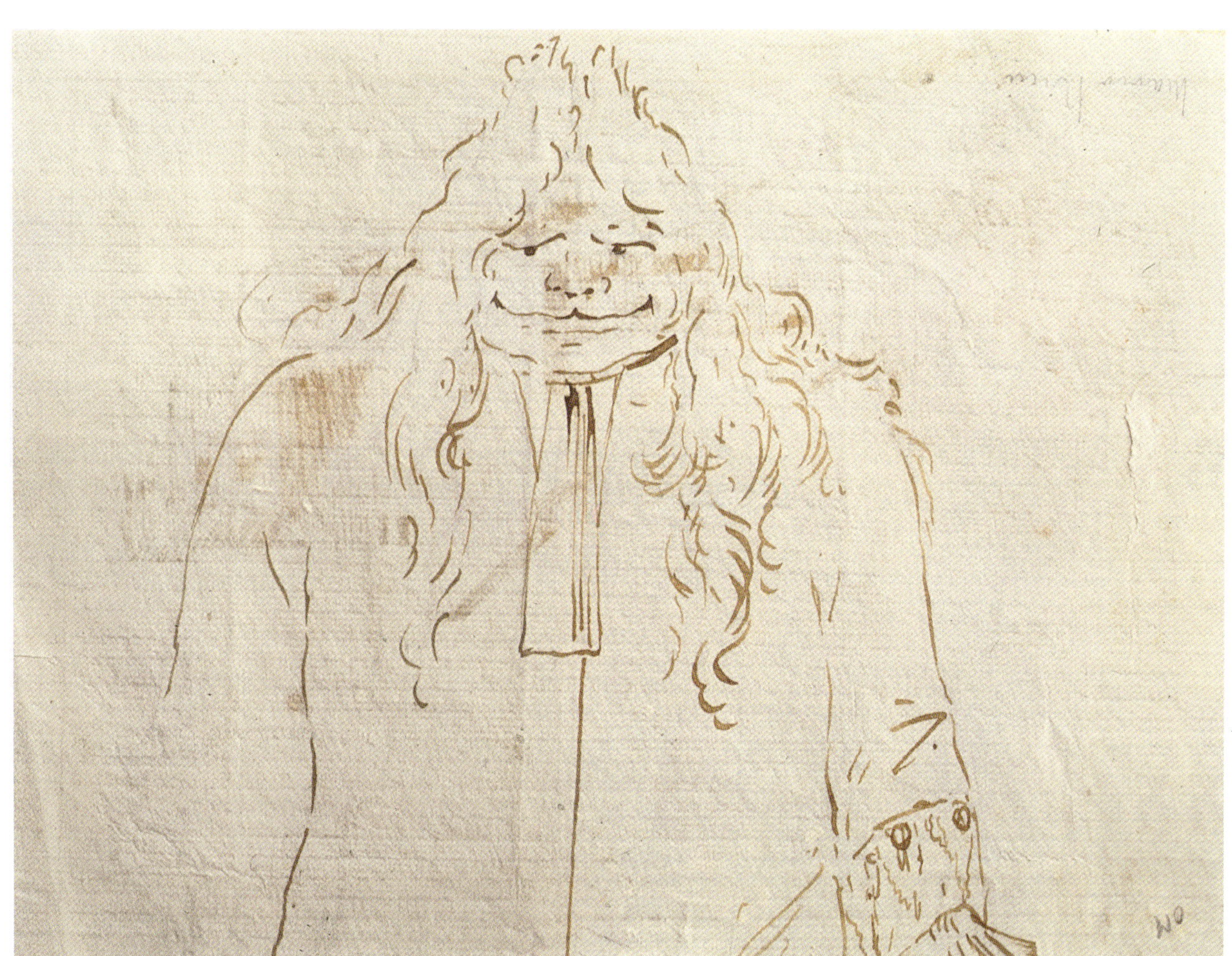

52.

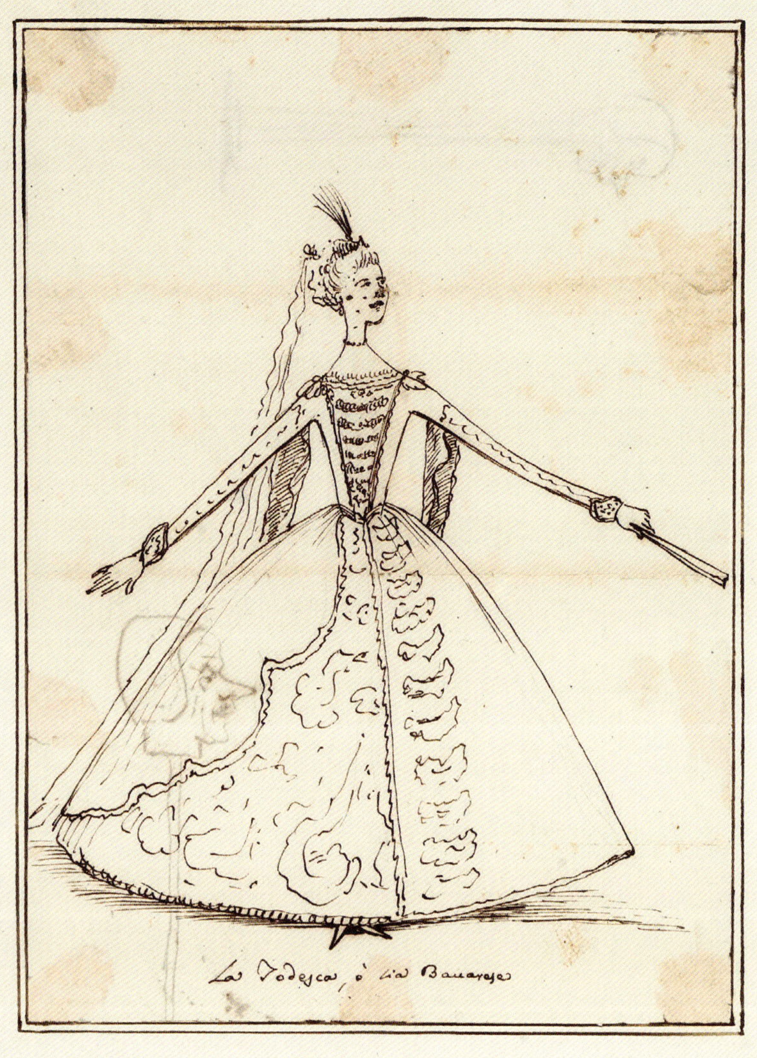

53.

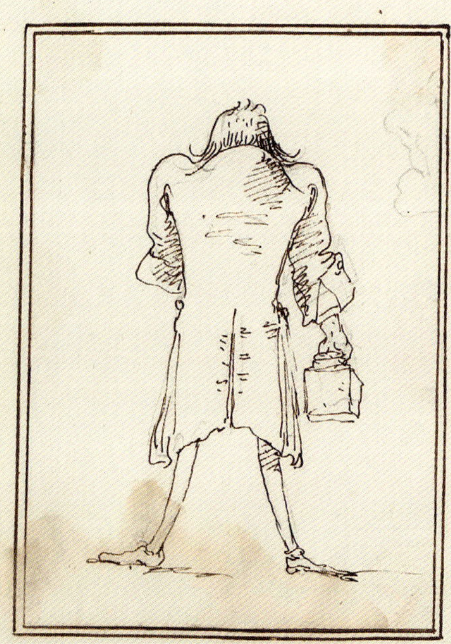

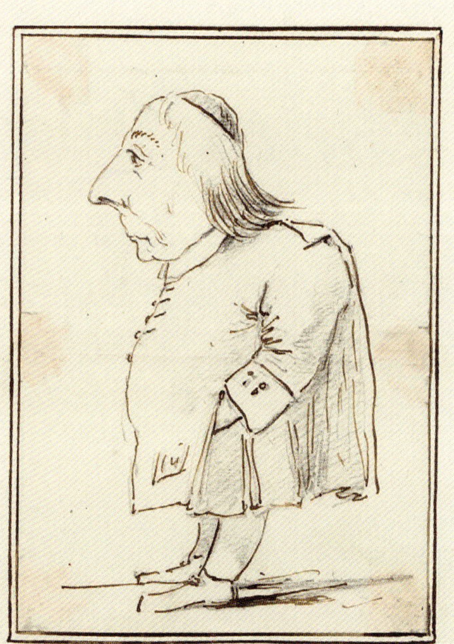

Domenico Valeriani – who received from Marco Ricci 'the most necessary counsels' (Zanetti 1771, p. 531) – at the Teatro Sant'Angelo on 26 October 1720 (Selfridge-Field 2007, p. 355). It is likely that on the occasion of this performance, a month after his wedding to a member of the Venetian patriciate, and so at the time of Sava's greatest public prominence, Ricci directed his witty attention towards the corpulent character, representing him in the pair of caricatures considered here. They are both drawn on the reverse of a composition of a different date, and on another sheet of the Zanetti Album with *Count Sava* depicted from behind (Lucchese 2015, pp. 279–80, no. 41.III).

EL

Bibliography
S. Scarpa, in *Antichi disegni* 2005, pp. 130–31; Lucchese 2015, pp. 270–71; Lucchese 2018, p. XIV.

53.

Page 62 of the Zanetti Album, three sheets glued on paper, c. 523 × 385 mm, each framed with a double line in sepia ink

Anton Maria Zanetti (1680–1767)
Josepha Pirker, called La Tedesca, 1733
Pen, graphite sketch, sepia ink on paper, 266 × 196 mm

Caricature of a hunchbacked man from behind, sixth decade of the eighteenth century (?)
Pen, graphite sketch, sepia ink on paper, 152 × 109 mm

Caricature of a hunchbacked priest, in profile facing left, fifth decade of the eighteenth century
Pen, graphite sketch, sepia ink on paper, 153 × 108 mm

Venice, Fondazione Giorgio Cini, Gabinetto dei Disegni e delle Stampe, inv. 36693–36695

On the larger sheet, beneath the lady with elongated arms, appears the inscription 'La Todesca, o'sia Bavarese' ('the German or Bavarian lady') while on the reverse of the sheet is drawn twice a mannequin wig-holder with a sarcastic expression, which appears in another caricature in the Zanetti Album (Lucchese 2015, pp. 296–7, no. 50.III). Thanks to the inscription we can identify the singer who played the Aztec Teutile in Vivaldi's *Montezuma* first staged on 14 November 1733 at the Teatro Sant'Angelo in Venice (Selfridge-Field 2007, p. 437), while the two small men in the lower register of the page are unidentified. The first of these, shown from behind, perhaps a sacristan with a bag for offerings, might also reappear as the grotesque profile dotted with graphite along the upper right-hand margin. As the page is mounted, it seems that the second caricature is a sort of ridiculous projection of the common physical defects of the drawing alongside. In reality, his garments suggest that this hunchbacked dwarf is a priest. For this last invention, Pietro C. Marani (2017) recalled the influence of the series of *Varie figure gobbe* engraved in 1616 by Jacques Callot, whose complete works Zanetti had acquired during his stay in Paris in 1720–21. His well-known passion for graphic art is again evident in the *Caricature of a priest* by the use of parallel graphite hatching to reproduce chiaroscuro in imitation of the effect in etching. This is an exception in his drawings, usually rather simplified in pen and ink without a watercolour wash and intended above all to achieve the effect of caricature in the form of an apparent scrawl (see Lucchese 2015, p. 3). The care in rendering the shadows and so the volumes on the ungainly body of the ecclesiastic demonstrates the influence of the caricatures of similar grotesque figures 'heightened by a noble style, just like any other drawing' (Mariuz, in Pavanello 2004, p. 31) by Giambattista Tiepolo, with whom Anton Maria was in contact at the time when the painter's *Capriccios* added to his *Chiaroscuri* of Castle Howard from 1742 (Bettagno 1998, p. 40).

EL

Bibliography
Bettagno, in Bettagno 1969, p. 99, nos 293, 294; Bettagno 1970, p. 115; Lucchese 2015, pp. 309–10, nos 56.I–56.III; Marani 2017, pp. 190–91.

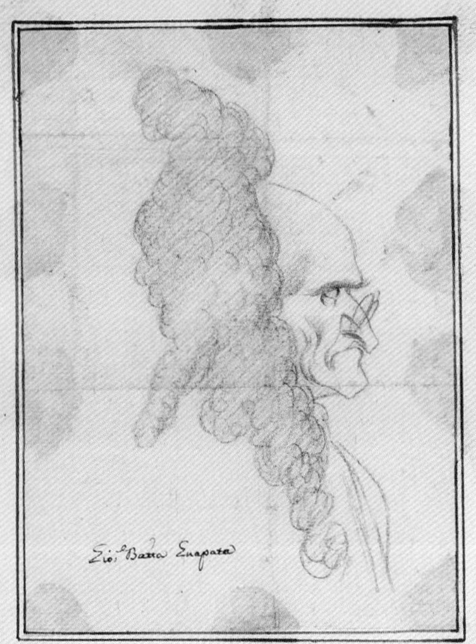
Gio: Batta Zuapata

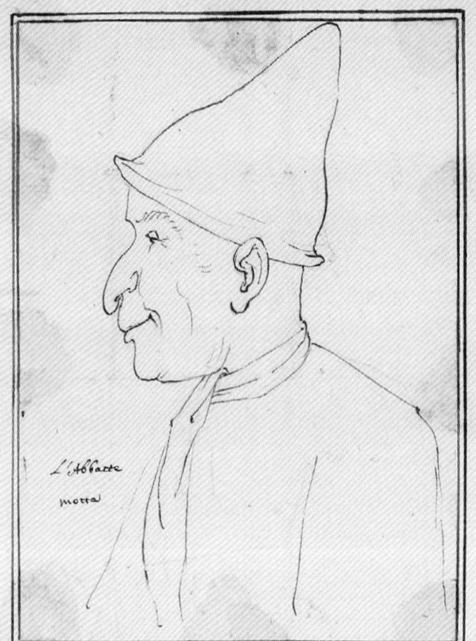
L'Abbatte
motta

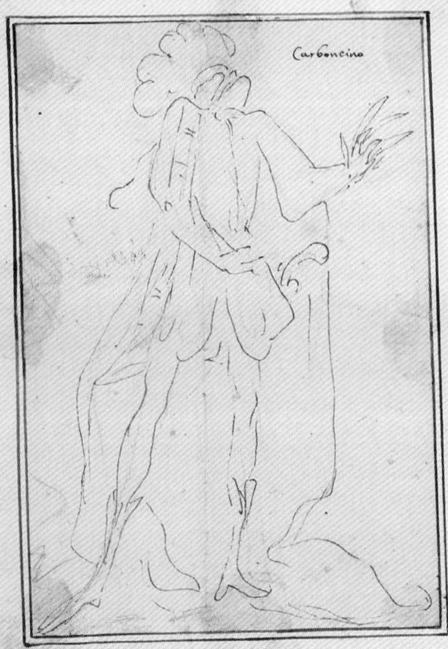
Carboncino

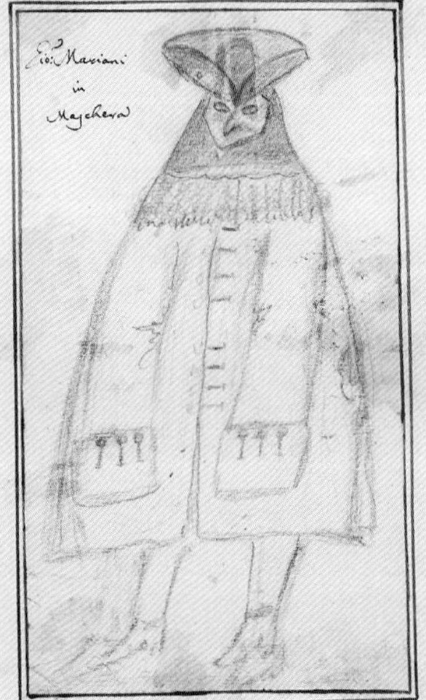
Gio: Mariani
in
Maschera

54.

Page 50 of the Zanetti Album,
four sheets glued on paper,
c. 523 × 385 mm, each framed
with a double line in sepia ink

Anton Maria Zanetti (1680–1767)
Giovanni Battista Ruberti known as Gnapata, fourth decade of the eighteenth century
Graphite on paper, 179 × 134 mm

Giuseppe Motta, 1727
Pen, graphite drawing, sepia ink on paper, 181 × 132 mm

Giovanni Mariani in costume with a mask, after 1705
Graphite on paper, 183 × 105 mm

Marco Ricci (1676–1730)
Giovanni Battista Carboni, called Carboncino, 1703
Pen, drawing in red pencil, sepia ink, graphite on paper, 153 × 108 mm

Venice, Fondazione Giorgio Cini, Gabinetto dei Disegni e delle Stampe, inv. 36655–36658

This page of the Zanetti Album stands out from the others by the different techniques used. 'Gio: Batta Gnapata', the former singer Ruberti, so called for his big nose (Bettagno, in Bettagno 1969, p. 50), appears on another sheet of the volume while 'prompting in the opera' (Lucchese 2015, pp. 151–2, n. 16.IV). He also performs this function in a caricature by Marco Ricci in the Smith Album (Croft-Murray 1957, p. 159, no. 15). Ricci was responsible for another drawing (ibid., no. 21), which concentrates, as here, on his characteristic profile, in the Windsor one without the ridiculous wig towering over a wide forehead. Through a work in graphite comparable to Zanetti's drawings for the *Dactyliotheca* (Lucchese 2015), his physical defects were heightened to create a caricatural medal, in a tradition reminiscent of Leonardo (Marani 2017). Zanetti owned his collection of Leonardo's heads engraved in 1730 from the collection of his friend Pierre-Jean Mariette (ibid., p. 190; Lucchese 2015, pp. 5, 13). Possible comparisons with Leonardo's caricatured figures, of which a version by Lomazzo is on display [cat. 25], also draw on the half-length representation of the profile opposite (Marani 2017), 'The Abbot Motta', datable to the year when he defrayed the cost of the altar for an altarpiece by Antonio Pellegrini in San Vidal in Venice. Zanetti was a witness at Pellegrini's wedding and his associate (Lucchese 2022). The idea of mounting the drawings opposite each other appears to be a further confirmation that contrasts between 'monstrous faces' were favoured in Leonardo's work, mentioned moreover in a posthumous gloss by Francesco Albergati Capacelli on the Zanetti Album (Marani 2017, p. 188).
While the upper half of the sheet is devoted to faces, in the lower half Anton Maria pasted a pair of drawings mocking the bodies of a star singer on the stage and a family member at Carnival time. The first, with its skilful, terse and nervous handling, is by Marco Ricci: 'Carboncino' was probably portrayed in the part of Farnace at the Teatro Sant'Angelo from 19 November 1703 (Selfridge-Field 2007, p. 259) and it would be one of the earliest caricatures of the Venetian eighteenth century. Next to it, the silhouette of Zanetti's brother-in-law looks like a live sketch, attracted by the enigma behind every mask.

EL

Bibliography

Bettagno, in Bettagno 1969, p. 91, nos 255–8; Bettagno 1970, p. 113; Bucciarelli 2000, p. 143; Lucchese 2015, pp. 285–7, nos 45.I–45.IV; Marani 2017, pp. 191–3; Lucchese 2022, pp. 80–81.

55.

Page 41 of the Zanetti Album, eight sheets glued to paper, c. 523 × 385 mm, each framed with a double line in sepia ink

Marco Ricci (1676–1730)
Count Sava, 1720
Pen and sepia ink on paper, 237 × 170 mm

Iseppo Sartor known as Cagnana, third decade of the eighteenth century (?)
Pen and sepia ink on paper, 184 × 98 mm

Tonina dalla commare, end of the second decade of the eighteenth century
Pen, graphite sketch, sepia ink on paper, 146 × 98 mm

Anton Maria Zanetti (1680–1767)
Youthful self-portrait in caricature, from behind, first decade of the eighteenth century
Pen, graphite sketch, sepia ink on paper, 133 × 93 mm

Don Bartolomeo, fifth decade of the eighteenth century
Pen, graphite sketch, sepia ink on paper, 100 × 82 mm

La Tamagnina, early fourth decade of the eighteenth century (?)
Pen, graphite sketch, sepia ink on paper, 137 × 99 mm

Antonio Denzio, 1717 (?)
Pen, graphite sketch, sepia ink on paper, 146 × 95 mm

Benedetto Baldassari known as Benedettino, 1718
Pen, graphite sketch, sepia ink on paper, 119 × 70 mm

Venice, Fondazione Giorgio Cini, Gabinetto dei Disegni e delle Stampe, inv. 36632–36640

The page is divided into three registers with the related comic 'stories'. Standing out at the centre is the bulk of Sava Lukich Vladislavich, drawn, like his other image [cat. 52], by Marco Ricci at Vivaldi's *La verità in cimento* dedicated to the Serbian count on the occasion of his wedding in Venice. The sheet, annotated by Zanetti, was reused by Ricci on the back to draw the caricature of his friend Daniele Antonio Bertoli and his dog, who arrived in

41

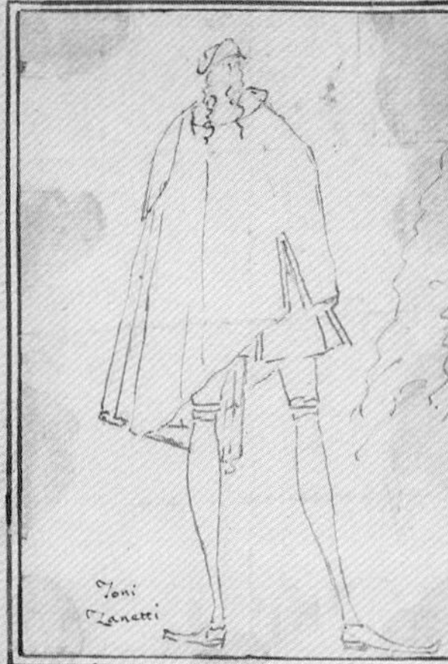

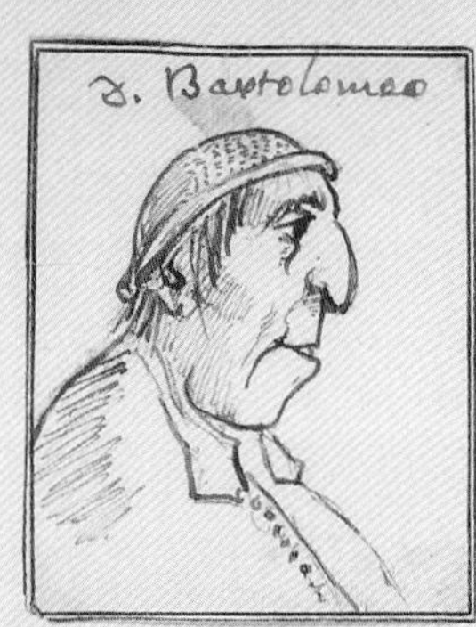

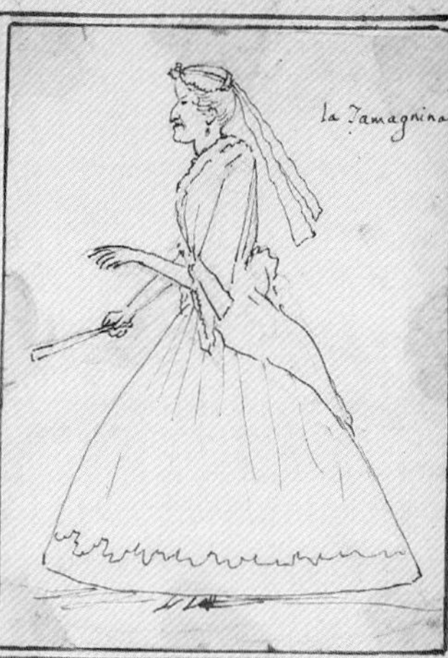

Sonetto

Spassiza la Città certo ceruello,
che ueste Drappi neri alla Spagnolla
Cauei grisi, e la barba Cauriola
da Diogene porta un gran Capello
Nell' operar, bisbetico Ceruello
Camina à salti, e par una Cariola
L'è sempre in Ziro come ua la Mola
o' in Oration mental da Beccarello
La notte, e'l Zorno hà el Cul pien de farende
e per le Conuertie e per le Zitelle
uuol far da Salamon, e niente intende
Và à dessensar el pan in Callesella
per la Fraterna; in soma lui pretende
rottar in terra e in Ciel Tedia da stella
chi uolesse conoscer stò Fanchiana
questo è Iseppo Sartor, detto Cajnang

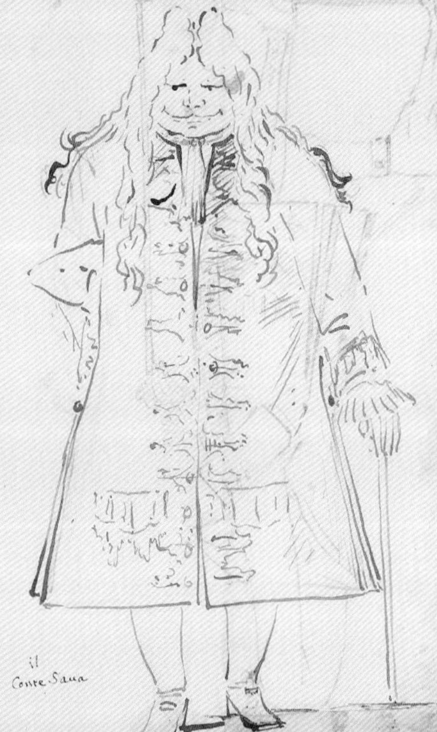

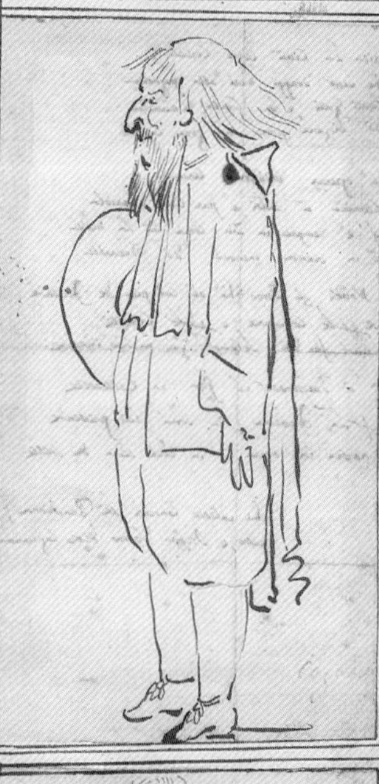

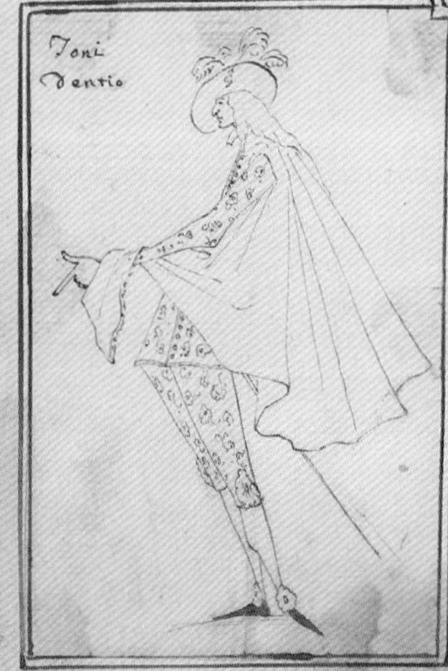

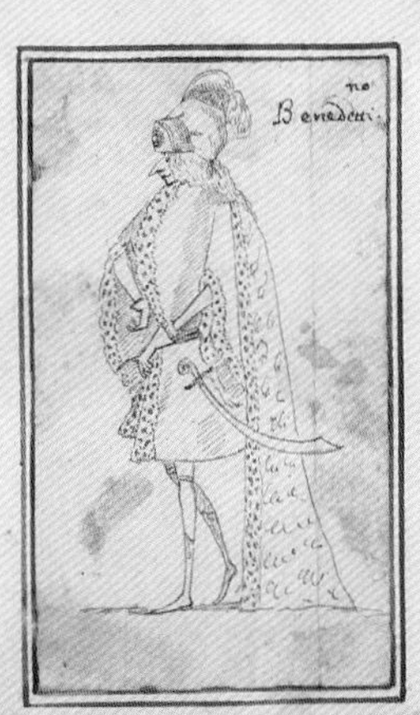

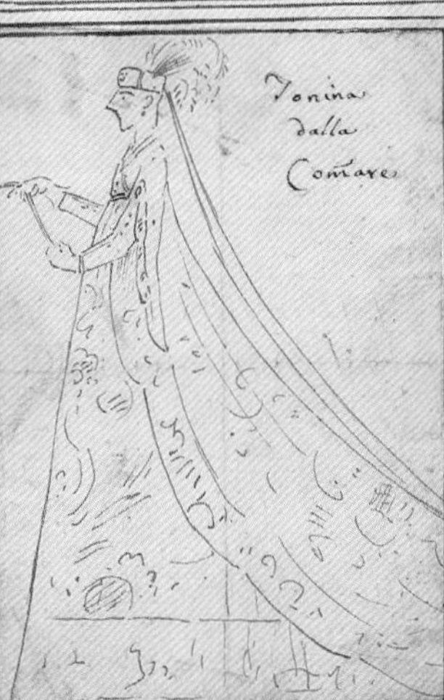

55.

Venice at the end of November 1726 on the way to Rome and returned to Vienna at the end of July 1727 (Lucchese 2022, p. 78). To the right of 'Count Sava' Anton Maria glued 'Cagnana', as if he were a servant in relation to his master, transcribing on the other side, directly on the support, the sonnet by Giorgio Baffo (Dazzi 1956, p. 241) covered by the caricature, originally folded to fit in a small envelope. The richness of the lines of the drawing, intended for Marco, renders the impression of a 'shrewish brain', with 'black drapery in Spanish style, grey hair, and a goat's beard', with a hat 'in the style of Diogenes' under his arm, represented as 'Panchiana' or a teller of tall tales (Boerio 1829, p. 401). Above this scene, a comic conversation piece begins with Zanetti in a youthful self-portrait, influenced by Ricci's handling but with his typical stylistic abbreviations and taste for anatomical deformity. He is viewed from behind at a safe distance from the priest, with a rather unintelligent air, in the company of an unpleasant lady, whose probable nickname indicates 'a turd already become mouldy from old age' as well as a person 'who has more years than she shows' (Alunno 1550, p. 165). Below this, a procession of dandies moves towards the binding of the volume, as if to flee from such inelegant circumstances. The leader is 'Toni Dentio', perhaps in the role of the governor of Hungary in *L'innocenza riconosciuta* performed on 27 October 1717 at the Teatro Sant'Angelo (Selfridge-Field 2007, p. 334), followed by 'Benedittino' as Omiro, the son of the Parthian king in *Farnace*, first performed at the Teatro San Cassiano on 11 January 1718 (ibid., p. 338), and a singer with a train to her dress portrayed by Marco. This is Antonia Cavazzi or, more likely, her colleague Antonia Pellizzari.

EL

Bibliography
Bettagno, in Bettagno 1969, pp. 84–7, nos 232–40; Bettagno 1970, p. 111; Scarpa Sonino 1991, p. 27; Dalle Fusine and Androsov 1993, p. 164; Mancini, Muraro and Povoledo 1996, p. 23; Androsov 1999, pp. 64, 73–4; Barcham, in Venice 2004, p. 93; Milada 2008, p. 85; Strohm 2008, plate 1; Androsov 2015, pp. 189, 195, n. 2; Lucchese 2015, pp. 268–74, nos 39.I–39.IX; Lucchese 2018, p. XIV.

56.

Giambattista Tiepolo (1696–1770)
Caricature of a standing figure wearing a bautta *with a muff, in profile facing left*, 1755–60
Pen and black ink, brush and black ink wash on paper with oblique cuts at the corners, outlined in pen, mounted, 162 × 116 mm
Milan, Castello Sforzesco, Gabinetto dei Disegni, inv. Au. B 2482

The figure in this caricature wears the typical Venetian eighteenth-century carnival costume known as a *bautta*, which in its commonest form comprised a black cloak, hood, white mask with a prominent nose, leaving the lower half of the face uncovered, and a tricorn on his head. Giambattista Tiepolo interpreted this invention in several sheets of caricatures, where the detail of the fur muff always appears, as here (compare the two sheets in the Robert Lehman collection at the Metropolitan Museum in New York, inv. 1975.1.452 and inv. 1975.1.454; Venice 2004, pp. 142–3, nos 83, 85, with the figure as here in profile, and the full-face version in the Musei Civici in Trieste, inv. 2092; Venice 2004, p. 133, no. 56, with the figure depicted frontally).
The personage is subtly caricatured here. The presence of the mask even denies an identity to the face and the comedy arises from the contrast between the excessive billowing of the short cloak that accentuates the body of the figure and the slenderness of the lower limbs, with their peculiar curvature.
Within the context of the well-known dynamics of the reuse by Giandomenico Tiepolo of some of his father's inventions in drawn or painted scenes of Venetian life, Arnalda Dallaj (in Venice 2004) identified as a possible derivation from this figure a character on the right in the *Puppet Theatre in the Nuns' Parlour* (formerly in the Beuderley collection, then Ottawa, National Gallery, in Succi 1988, p. 54).
The critical reception of the drawing, added to the civic collections in 1900 as a donation from Gustavo Frizzoni (for a note on the acquisition see cat. 57), began relatively late (Morassi 1955), but it is interesting that this sheet was selected to represent Giambattista Tiepolo's graphic works in volume XXVII of the series in the Istituto Alinari in Florence devoted to the masters of caricature from Leonardo to Tiepolo (Corti 1979). The whole nucleus of drawings by Tiepolo exhibited here, coming from the Gabinetto dei Disegni in the Castello Sforzesco, bears a long-established dating to the second half of the 1750s, at a time close to the decoration of Villa Valmarana in Vicenza in 1757.

AA

Bibliography
Morassi 1955, p. 148, no. 41b, plate 41b; Corti 1979, p. 31, no. 35b; A. Dallaj, in Venice 2004, p. 128, n. 48; Loisel 2018, p. 107, no. 73b.

57.

Giambattista Tiepolo (1696–1770)
Caricature of man in a tricorn hat viewed frontally, 1755–60
Pen and black ink, brush and ink wash on paper with oblique cuts at the corners, outlined in pen and partly mounted, 177 × 129 mm
Milan, Castello Sforzesco, Gabinetto dei Disegni, inv. Au. B 2483

This drawing in black ink, with confident handling depicting a figure frontally with head slightly bowed, but clearly characterised in his physiognomy, can be compared in technique, style and angle of the face with a drawing in the Boijmans Museum in Rotterdam today assigned to Giambattista Tiepolo (inv. I.155; Venice 2004, p. 123, no. 41), formerly believed to be by Giandomenico.
The drawing is distinguished from the other caricatures in the Milanese nucleus at the Castello Sforzesco by the greater care in describing the layers of the clothes, probably favoured by the frontal point of view; the dense watercolours define the figure's position in space, with a source of light on the right.
Among the sets of Tiepolo's caricatures that began in the nineteenth century and entered public collections in Europe, the one in the Gabinetto dei

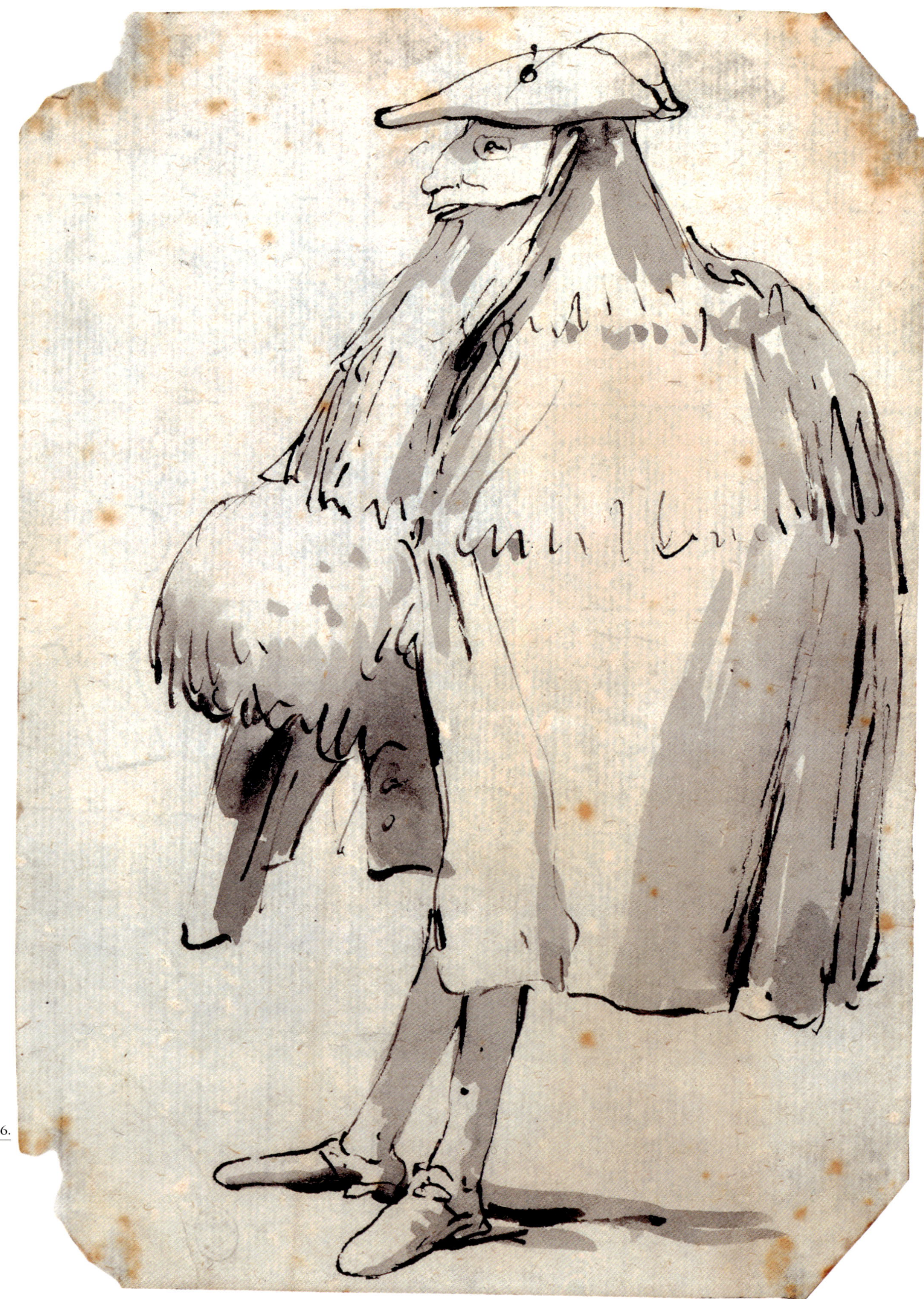

56.

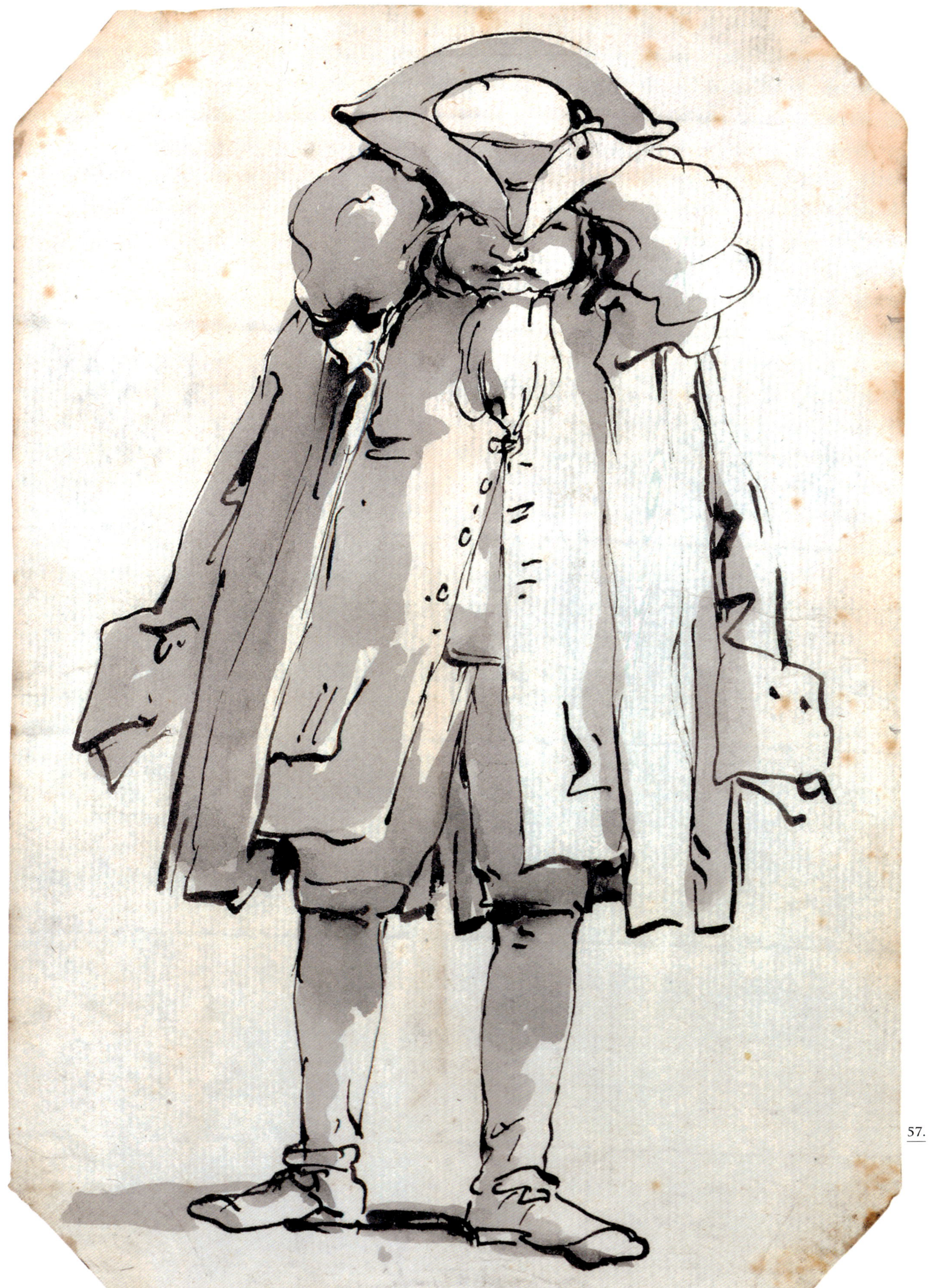

57.

Disegni of the Castello Sforzesco in Milan is among the oldest, with its acquisition recorded in 1900 as a donation from the art critic and collector Gustavo Frizzoni. Four of the eight sheets that entered on that occasion had belonged to the famous connoisseur Giovanni Morelli (in addition to cats 59, 60, 62, inv. Au. B 2489, here fig. p. 00), as shown by his ink stamp in the lower right-hand corner (Lugt 1902) and photographs of them in two 1880s editions of drawings in his collection. In Morelli's will and as executed by Frizzoni, the drawings were added to the civic collections in Milan. The four that lack Morelli's stamp [cats 56–8, plus inv. Au. B 2485], appear to have belonged to Frizzoni, although to judge from the identical features of the works (oblique cuts at the corners, outlines on the sheets redrawn in pen and the mounting on grey cardboard), it seems likely that the two sets were acquired at the same time (G. Bora, in Morelli 1994, p. 229).

AA

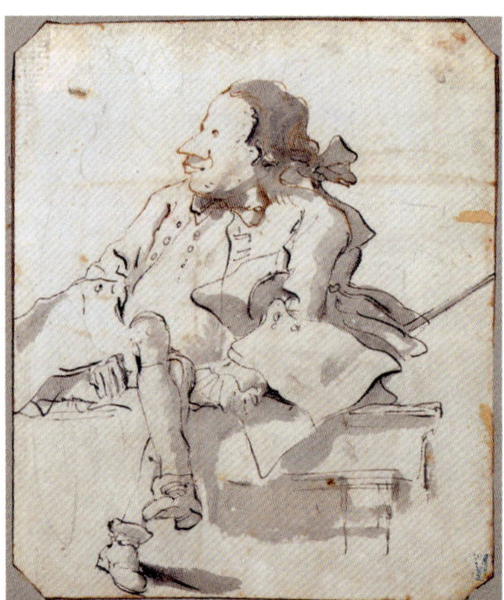

2. Giambattista Tiepolo, *Caricature of seated gentleman, facing left*, 1755–60
Milan, Castello Sforzesco, Gabinetto dei Disegni, inv. Au. B 2489

Bibliography

Rizzi 1965, p. 84, no. 53; Rizzi 1971, II, p. 37, no. 47; A. Perissa Torrini, in Venice 1995, p. 427, no. 147; A. Dallaj, in Venice 2004, pp. 128–30, no. 47.

58.

Giambattista Tiepolo (1696–1770)
Caricature of prelate reading, seated, in profile facing left, 1755–60
Pen and brown and black ink, brush and ink wash on paper with oblique cuts at the corners, outlined in pen and partly mounted, 173 × 140 mm
Milan, Castello Sforzesco, Gabinetto dei Disegni, inv. Au. B 2484

The typological variety of the set of Tiepolo's caricatures that belonged to Gustavo Frizzoni and Giovanni Morelli, donated in 1900 to the municipality of Milan, includes the figure of a prelate, identified by the skullcap and a long tunic. Sitting on a bench, he holds some sheets of paper in one hand and his spectacles in the other. The position in profile brings out the marked curvature of his back, while his drooping head, perpendicular to his torso, heightens the grotesque outlines of the face, with long, flattened nose and protruding chin.
Morelli and Frizzoni were forward-looking collectors, at a time when this strand of Tiepolo's work was not yet well known. It is likely that as early as 1881 the Tiepolos owned by Morelli were present in the historic exhibition organized at the Poldi Pezzoli Museum with drawings from several important private collections. There is no catalogue of the exhibition, but its content can now be reconstructed through a review by Frizzoni published in several issues of *L'Art: revue hebdomadaire illustrée*, which is also interesting because it is one of the first signs of the critical reception of these works linked to the name of Tiepolo: 'Elles semblent indiquer ce fait nouveau que Tiepolo le père aurait eu du goût pour la caricature; on en voit la trace dans certaines figures d'hommes bossus et difformes, tantôt isolées, tantôt réunies en groupes, faites à l'aquarelle sur nature d'après des citoyens de la sérénissime République, qui de son temps ont dû sans doute une certaine notoriété à leur extérieur et à leur nature un peu bizarres. Tiepolo réussissait dans ce genre aussi bien que dans les sujet épiques et historiques' (Frizzoni 1881, p. 42).
Unlike Tiepolo's other caricatures in the Morelli-Frizzoni set, this sheet has not attracted the interest of critics, except in very recent times.

AA

Bibliography

A. Dallaj, entry, in Venice 2004, pp. 128–30, no. 50; Pisot 2019, p. 321, no. 68, p. 284, no. 68.

59.

Giambattista Tiepolo (1696–1770)
Caricature of a gentleman seated, in profile facing left, 1755–60
Pen and brown and black ink, brush and wash in brown and black ink on paper with oblique cuts at the corners, outlined in pen and mounted, 166 × 122 mm
Milan, Castello Sforzesco, Gabinetto dei Disegni, inv. Au. B 2486

In the variety of human types that Giambattista Tiepolo identifies in his gallery of caricatures, the principal figure in this sheet is that of the gentleman, here identified by his short wig, elegant bow tie and the sword hanging from his belt. His character is conveyed by the composed pose, in contrast to the tricorn hat that has landed upside down on the floor, and his immense head with upturned nose and rapt expression. In recalling the figure in this drawing, which he cites for comparison with a caricature in the Musei Civici of Trieste (inv. 2086), Giorgio Vigni called it 'that malicious type' (Vigni 1942, p. 74 sub no. 247).
Like cats 60 and 62, the sheet comes from Giovanni Morelli's collection, as certified by the ink stamp of the Milanese connoisseur affixed near the bottom right-hand corner (Lugt 1902) and its photograph in two nineteenth-century publications dealing with the

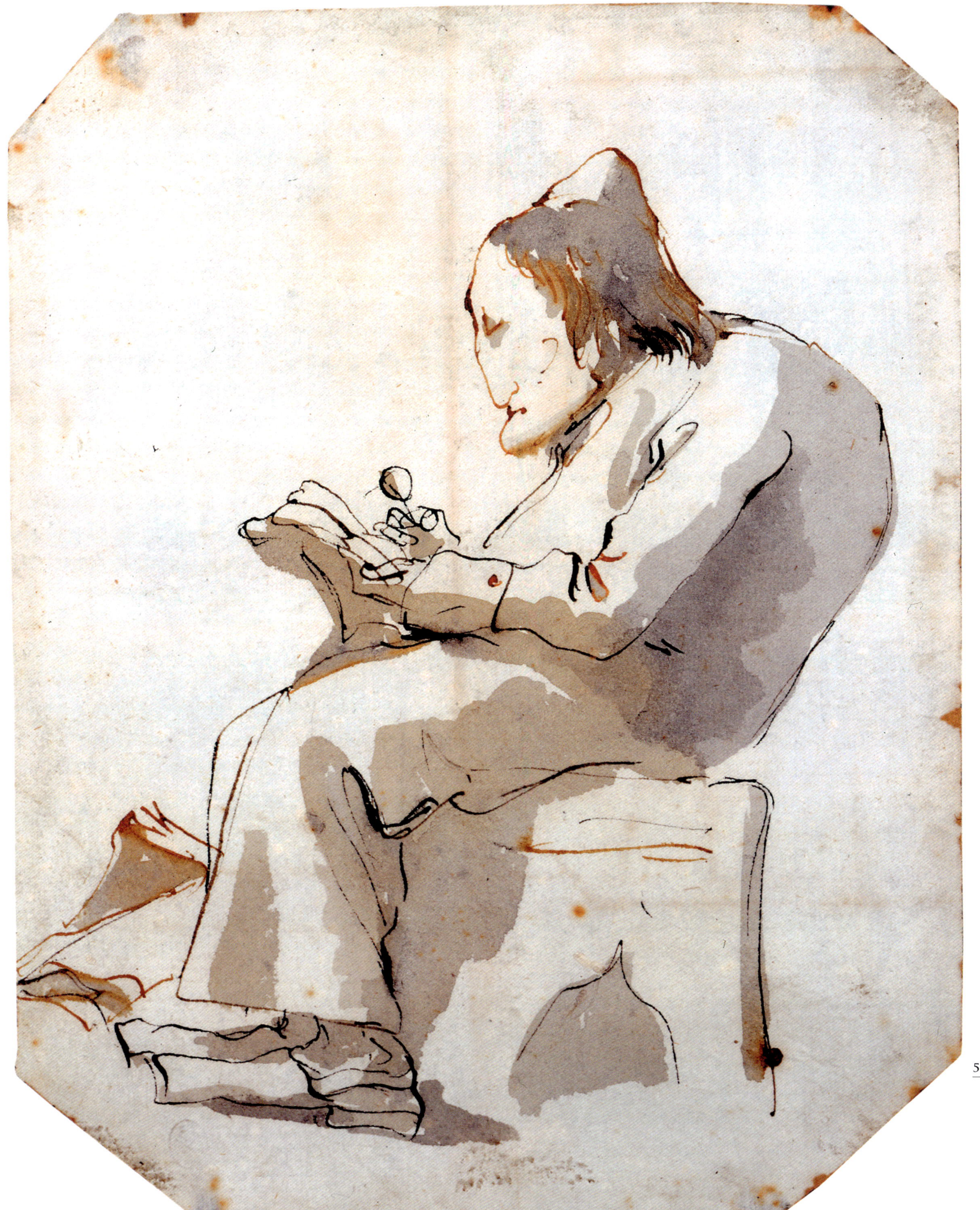

58.

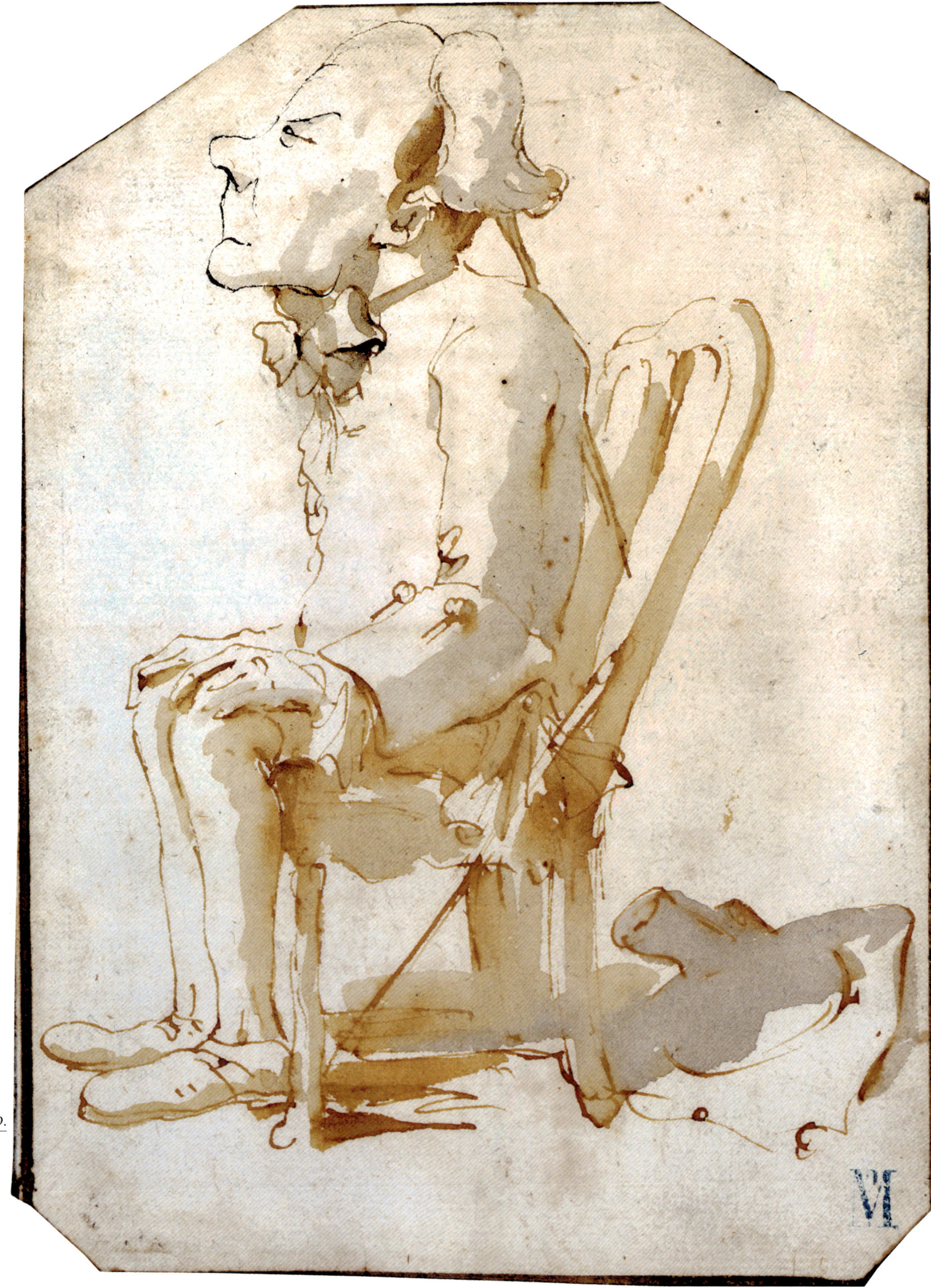

59.

drawings he owned. In the *Collezione di quaranta disegni scelti dalla raccolta del senatore Giovanni Morelli*, Gustavo Frizzoni commented on the plates reproducing these caricatures: '[Tiepolo's] drawings are now scattered to the four winds; except that in the four sketches presented here he reveals a side of his genius that we believe to be lesser known, namely expressive of his abilities as a fine caricaturist. In this way he refutes in his own case, just as Leonardo could have done in his day, the claim of those who assert that the genre of humour is wholly lacking in Italian art of past centuries. What refined observation is contained in these few lines of ink and sepia, and with what good humour it represents certain purely eighteenth-century personages and their characters, now bold now timid, always burlesqued and exaggerated! In these effective and confident touches, the lion's claw appears clearly' (Frizzoni 1886, comment on plates XXX and XXXI).

AA

Bibliography

Morelli 1882, plate; Frizzoni 1886, plate XXXI; Sack 1910, pp. 245, 258; *Giovanni Morelli* 1987, p. 61, no. 33; Bora 1988, pp. 234–8, no. 89, p. 289, no. 137; G. Bora, in Morelli 1994, pp. 228–30, no. III.168, 333 fig. III.168; A. Dallaj, in Venice 2004, pp. 126–7, no. 44.

60.

Giambattista Tiepolo (1696–1770)
Caricature of a hunchback standing, in profile facing left, 1755–60
Pen and brown ink, brush and brown ink wash on paper with oblique cuts at the corners, with outlines in pen and partly mounted, 159 × 116 mm
Milan, Castello Sforzesco, Gabinetto dei Disegni, inv. Au. B 2487

The figure of the hunchback, wrapped in a large cloak, with long, loose hair and his hat in his hand, is characterised by the eldest of the Tiepolo family with a few pen strokes. It is one of the inventions that have met with the widest interest from critics in the set of eight caricatures by Tiepolo originating in the Morelli-Frizzoni collection preserved in the Gabinetto dei Disegni at the Castello Sforzesco (for information on this acquisition, see cat. 57).
The sheet belonged to the art critic Giovanni Morelli, as shown by the blue ink stamp with the initial 'M' and small 'o' (Lugt 1902) and its reproduction in two nineteenth-century editions of drawings in the Morelli collection (Morelli 1882 and Frizzoni 1886).
The drawing is often mentioned as an effective example of the reuse of isolated figures by Giambattista Tiepolo in the compositions of his son Giandomenico, and consequently as evidence that the father's caricature albums were kept in the family workshop. A figure with identical features, depicted turning his back on the main scene, can be made out at the extreme left of a drawing that formerly belonged to Tomás Harris and then the Duc de Talleyrand, now in a private collection, entitled *Meeting during a walk* (pen and watercolour, 285 × 420 mm; Byam Shaw 1962, p. 489, no. 72, plate 72). The only variant consists in the position of the shadow, here projected in front of the figure, while in Giandomenico's sheet it stretches behind the man.

AA

Bibliography

Morelli 1882, plate; Frizzoni 1886, plate XXXI; Sack 1910, pp. 245, 258, fig. 256; Rizzi 1965, pp. 83–4, no. 52; Rizzi 1971, p. 35, no. 46; Pignatti 1972, plate LV; Bora 1988, pp. 234–8, no. 90, 289, no. 138; G. Bora, in Morelli 1994, pp. 228–30, no. III.169; A. Perissa Torrini, in Venice 1995, p. 426, no. 146; A. Dallaj, in Venice 2004, pp. 123, 126, n. 43; Loisel 2018, p. 107, no. 73a.

61.

Giambattista Tiepolo (1696–1770)
Caricature of a hunchbacked man with spectacles, seated and in profile, with a book in his hand, 1754–62
Pen, black ink and grey wash on paper, 202 × 151 mm
Private collection

Like the *Caricature of a hunchbacked man standing and in profile* [cat. 65], to which the reader is referred for further information, and another pair of drawings on display [cats 66, 67], the sheet was part of the *Tomo terzo de caricature*, placed seventh in the album. Detached from the page it was originally pasted on, it was auctioned by Christie's in London in 1943 as lot 242g. Purchased by Callman, it then passed to Max Walter, Elsie Walter, Anne Clark, Artemis (an antiquarian gallery that exhibited it in London in November 1990, no. 33) and Pietro Scarpa, before reaching its present location (Knox, in *Antichi disegni* 2005). The conjecture that this is a cleric by the presence of a 'conical hat' (ibid.) is difficult to decide, both by the shape of the headgear, closer to a domestic cap than a *rochet* or *zucchetto*, and above all by the fact that he is wearing a gentleman's garments rather than a cassock. The curious character, with a slightly foolish smile and with spectacles flattened, like his nose, on his face, might be – given the large book in his lap – a learned pedant or rather a teacher, by analogy with a drawing in the Lehman collection (Knox, in Byam Shaw and Knox 1987, p. 130, no. 103), depicted seated on a wooden chair, as far as his hump and stomach like Pulcinella allow. He shares this pose, despite

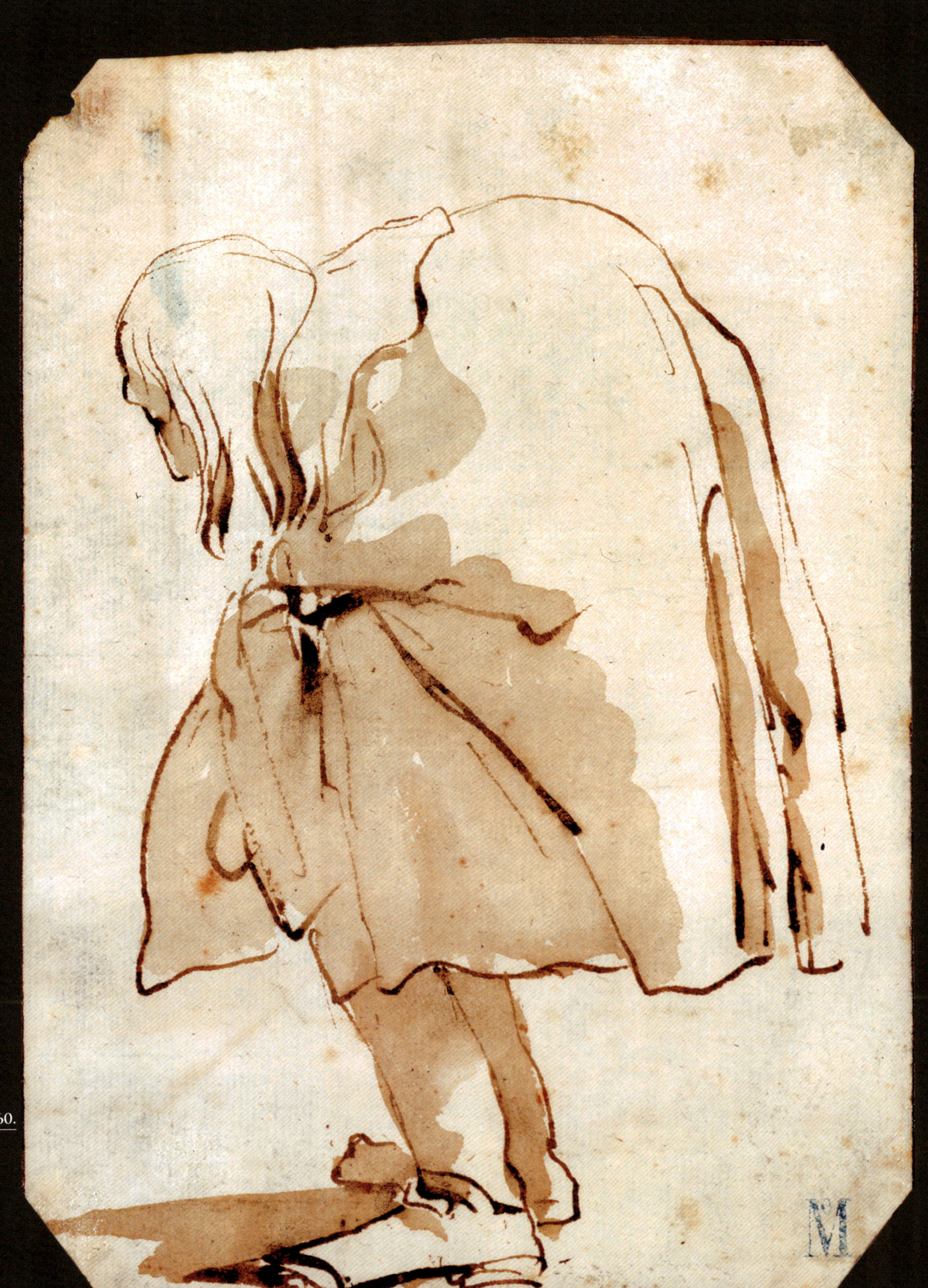

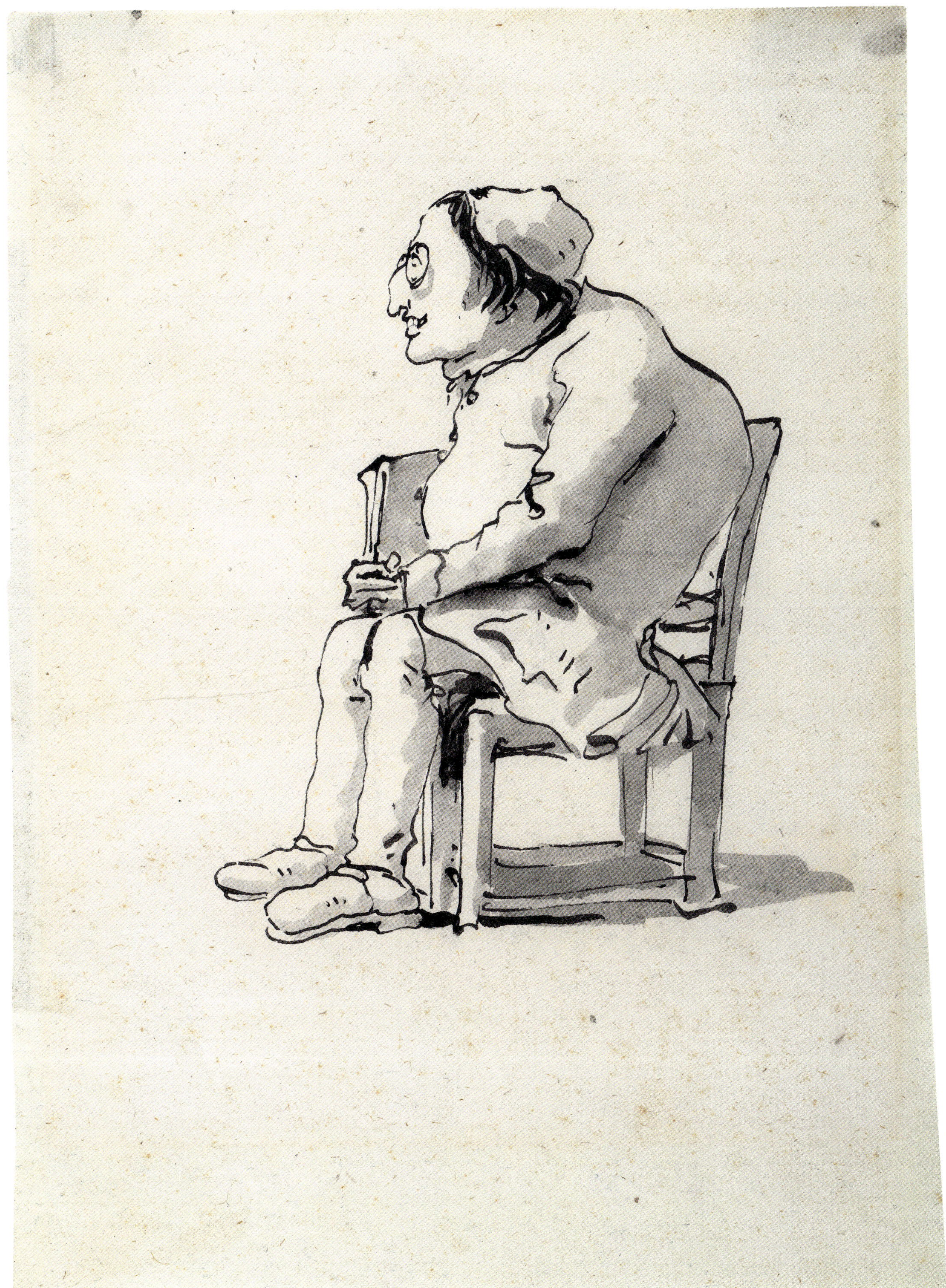

61.

the difficulties of remaining on the chair, with other Tiepolo caricatures on display [cats 58, 59, 62, 74].
Rather than producing a humorous portrait of a specific person, Giambattista Tiepolo sought through a refined stylistic handling, identical to that used in his major works, to represent a ridiculous body, to be included in that inventory of types of figures that is the *Tomo terzo de caricature*, a singular gallery of 'universal types and characters of the human fauna: the fat, the thin, the pleasure-seeking priest, the elderly curmudgeon, etc.'
Satirical intent is absent, namely the purpose of reforming by mockery. The violence of the deformity brings out the superiority of art over nature even in relation to ugliness. The purpose is to show that there exists 'a beauty of deformity' (Mariuz 1971, p. 83).

EL

Bibliography
Knox, in *Antichi disegni* 2005, pp. 145, 156–7.

62.

Giambattista Tiepolo (1696–1770)
Caricature of gentleman in a wig, seated, in profile facing right, 1755–1760
Pen and black ink, brush and black ink wash on paper, mounted,
165 × 140 mm
Milan, Castello Sforzesco, Gabinetto dei Disegni, inv. Au. B 2488

Of Tiepolo's eight caricatures in the Gabinetto di Disegni at the Castello Sforzesco, three represent gentlemen seated in a variety of poses (in addition to cats 58, 59, the *Caricature of a gentleman seated with his legs crossed*, inv. Ow. B 2489, here fig. 2 on p. 156). In this sheet the subject is characterised by a tall thick wig that falls over the curve of his shoulders behind, bringing out his marked hump, while in front it descends along the forehead to form a diagonal with the man's angular profile; one hand rests on his knee while the other displays a sheet of paper folded in half with a few lines of writing on it. Although the features are clearly shown, it should be remembered that Tiepolo is never known to have depicted a specific individual, unlike Anton Maria Zanetti before him, but only an amused representation of a human type.
Compared to most of Tiepolo's caricatures, which generally focus only on the figure, a distinctive aspect of this drawing is its summary evocation of some parts of the background, set in an interior, with a low table where the man seems to have placed his hat, conjured up with a few lines and skilful use of ink wash.
The ink stamp with the letters 'Mo' (Lugt 1902) records the drawing's provenance in Giovanni Morelli's collection, which it entered before 1882, when it was reproduced in heliotype by the Venetian photographer-editor Giovanni Battista Brusa in *Raccolta di disegni originali dei più celebri artisti tratti dalla scelta collezione del senatore Giovanni Morelli in Milano* (for information on the Morelli-Frizzoni set of drawings, see cat. 57).
As noted by George Knox (Knox 2005, p. 149) the only such example known to him in all Tiepolo's caricatures, the sheet in the Gabinetto dei Disegni in the Castello Sforzesco served as a model for another version, identical and autograph, in a private collection [cat. 74].

AA

Bibliography
Morelli 1882, plate; Frizzoni 1886, plate XXX; Sack 1910, p. 258; Rizzi 1965, p. 84, no. 55; *Giovanni Morelli* 1987, p. 61, no. 31; Bora 1988, pp. 234–8, no. 91, 289, no. 139; G. Bora, in Morelli 1994, pp. 228–30, no. III.170; A. Dallaj, in Venice 2004, p. 127, no. 45; Pisot 2019, p. 321, no. 69, 285, no. 69.

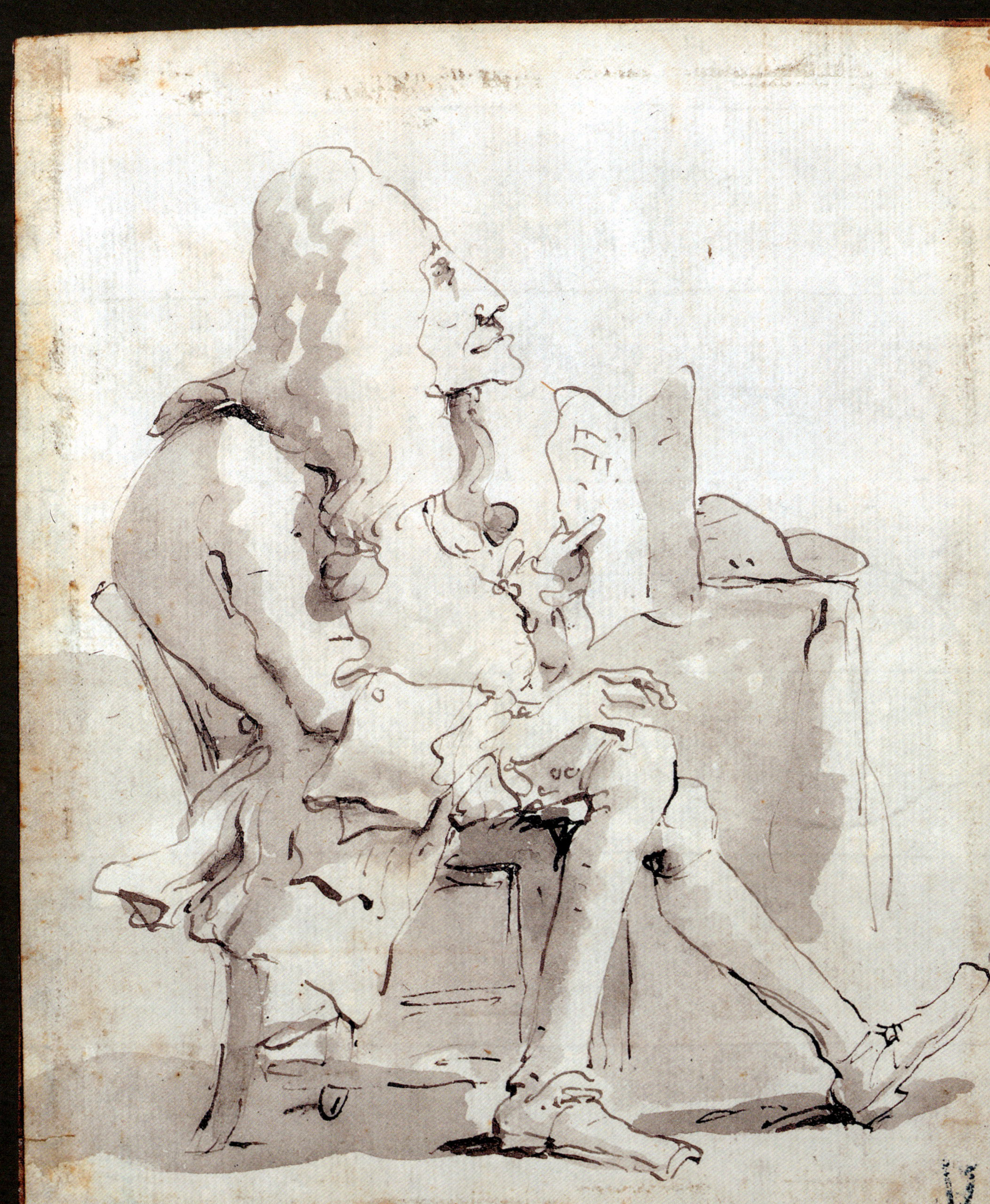

62.

63.

Giambattista Tiepolo (1696–1770)
Caricature of a priest with spectacles, standing in profile, sixth decade of the eighteenth century
Pen, black ink and grey wash on paper with clipped corners, 201 × 122 mm, traces on the edges of the outer frame of sepia ink, on the lower side also inside the paper
Private collection

Made known by Pietro Scarpa (1983) with the title *The abbot*, this pen and ink bears on the verso at the top the modern inscription in capitals 'G. B. Tiepolo'. The provenance 'Mme Z. Birtschansky, Paris; auction Dr. Pierre Pobé, Basel 1979 (no. 95)' is said to 'clearly date from the twenties, before Janos Scholz had had the opportunity to see the Sacchetto collection' (Knox, in *Antichi disegni* 2005). This means that the 'about 140 sheets, which – so the saying goes – once belonged to the Valmarana family' (Scholz 1960, p. 64) seen 'some years ago' by that scholar before the exhibition of the Wallraf drawings formerly in the possession of the Valmarana family (Morassi, in Morassi 1959, p. 56, nos 76–87), were in the possession of the Sacchetto family in Padua. From these last Giuseppe Fiocco (in Fiocco 1955, p. 29, no. 75) received three caricatures mounted on brown paper, with clipped edges and traces of framing along the perimeter of the sheet (Knox, in Pavanello 2005, pp. 253–4, nos 412–14). The reconstruction is not confirmed in Scholz's account, which does not mention the Sacchetto family. The drawing in question could certainly come from that collection, in which it was thought that 'all the caricatures were trimmed, with traces of an outline and the corners clipped, not recorded before World War II' (Knox, in *Antichi disegni* 2005, p. 144). But it should also be remembered that the sheets by Tiepolo with this specific form appear in nineteenth-century collections, for example in most of the drawings donated by Gustavo Frizzoni to the Civiche Raccolte d'Arte of the Castello Sforzesco in Milan, exhibited here [cats 56–60]. They also appear in the pair of caricatures in Theodore Correr's bequest (1830) to the museum of that name in Venice (Knox 2004b, p. 121), which is the oldest example of these particular works.
The theme of mockery of ecclesiastics with which Venice was teeming was dear to Anton Maria Zanetti. Perhaps partly because of this precedent, Giambattista Tiepolo created an unforgettable gallery of priests and friars. This figure, bespectacled and rapacious in the nose, expression and hunched body, which reappears among the spectators of Giandomenico's *Puppet Theatre* (Gealt and Knox 2005), proves to be a sort of grotesque antithesis to the chubby and placid *Profile of a religious* in the École Nationale Supérieure des Beaux-Arts in Paris (Knox, in Venice 2004, p. 133, no. 54).

EL

Bibliography
Scarpa 1983, pp. 70–71, 76; Gealt and Knox 2005, p. 126, no. 31; Knox, in *Antichi disegni* 2005, pp. 164–5.

64.

Giambattista Tiepolo (1696-1770)
Caricature from behind of a fat man standing, with tricorn, sword and stick, sixth decade of the eighteenth century
Pen and black ink, grey watercolour on paper with clipped corners, 172 × 106 mm, glued and framed along the perimeter with sepia ink on the sheet, 250 × 200 mm, with a thick rectangular frame drawn not far from the outer edge in sepia ink. Two horizontal graphite sections appear on the backing sheet just below the ends of the lower edge of the drawing, with another vertical line on the drawing paper, bordering the right edge at the shoulder of the figure, probably made when mounting the drawing.
Private collection

It should be identified with lot 325 sold by Christie's in London on 26 March 1963 (p. 80): 'Caricature of a Man, standing, seen from behind, in tricorne hat, short-skirted coat and sword.' It was then one of the seventeen drawings purchased at auction by Stephen Spector (Knox, in *Antichi disegni* 2005), formerly among the thirty-two caricatures in the Paul Wallraf collection reported four years earlier by Antonio Morassi (in Morassi 1959, p. 56, nos 76–87) with the provenance 'Conti Valmarana di Vicenza' and the date 1757, the same as Tiepolo's frescoes in the family's villa (ibid., p. 59). In this respect, Janos Scholz (1960, p. 64) recalled that he had seen almost all this group of about 140 sheets years earlier. The present drawing, formerly in Pietro Scarpa's collection (Knox, in *Antichi disegni* 2005), is connected with the *Caricature from behind of a fat man*, in the same technique and finely executed, in the Lehman collection at the Metropolitan Museum, New York (Knox, in Venice 2004, p. 142, no. 81), formerly also in the Wallraf collection. There the man with the long pigtail holds the tricorn under his arm; he no longer has a walking stick and shows his right hand with index finger outstretched. The American sheet bears on the back the words 'Tiepoletto veneziano 1760', which reappear, the first two words abraded, also on the

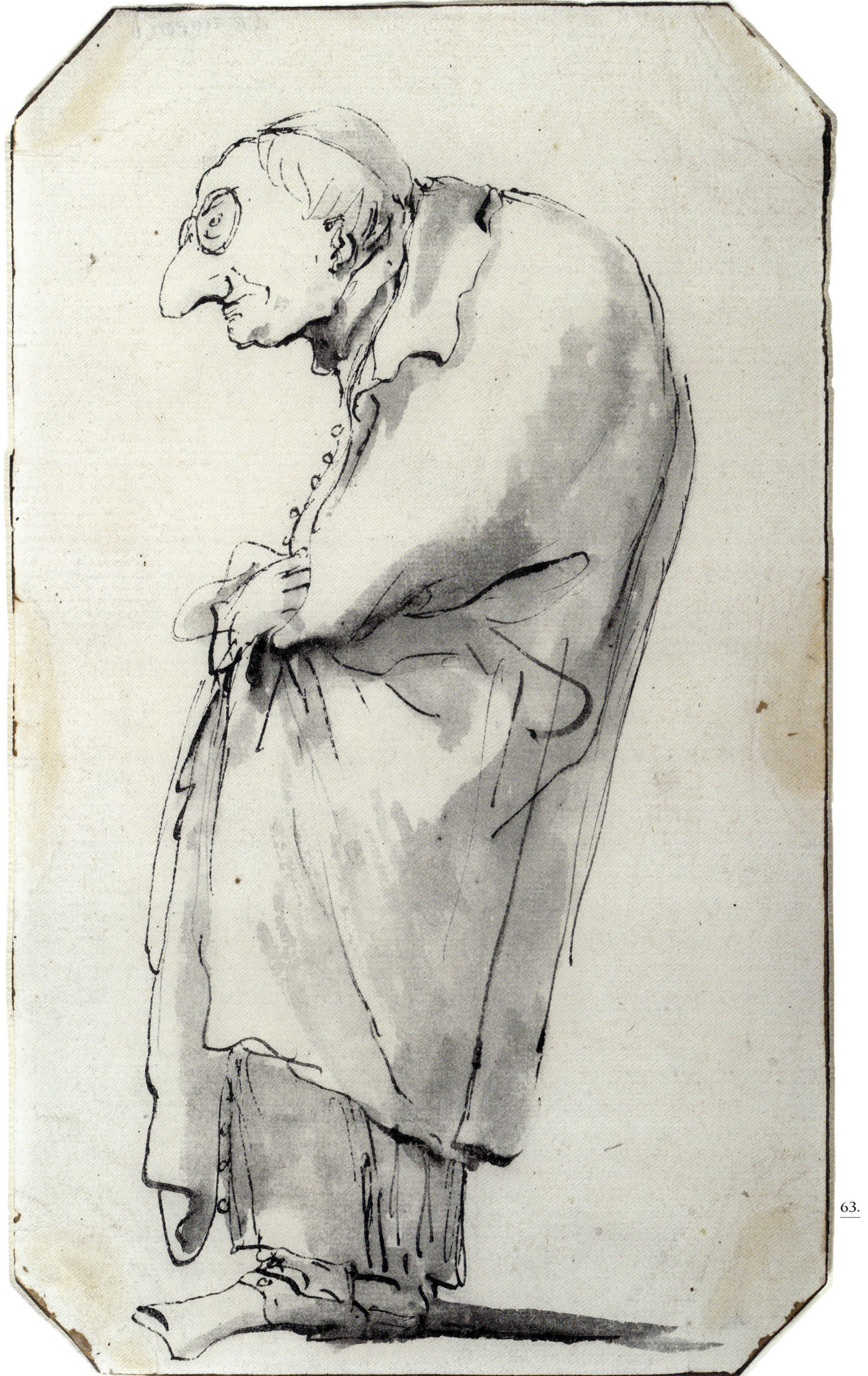

63.

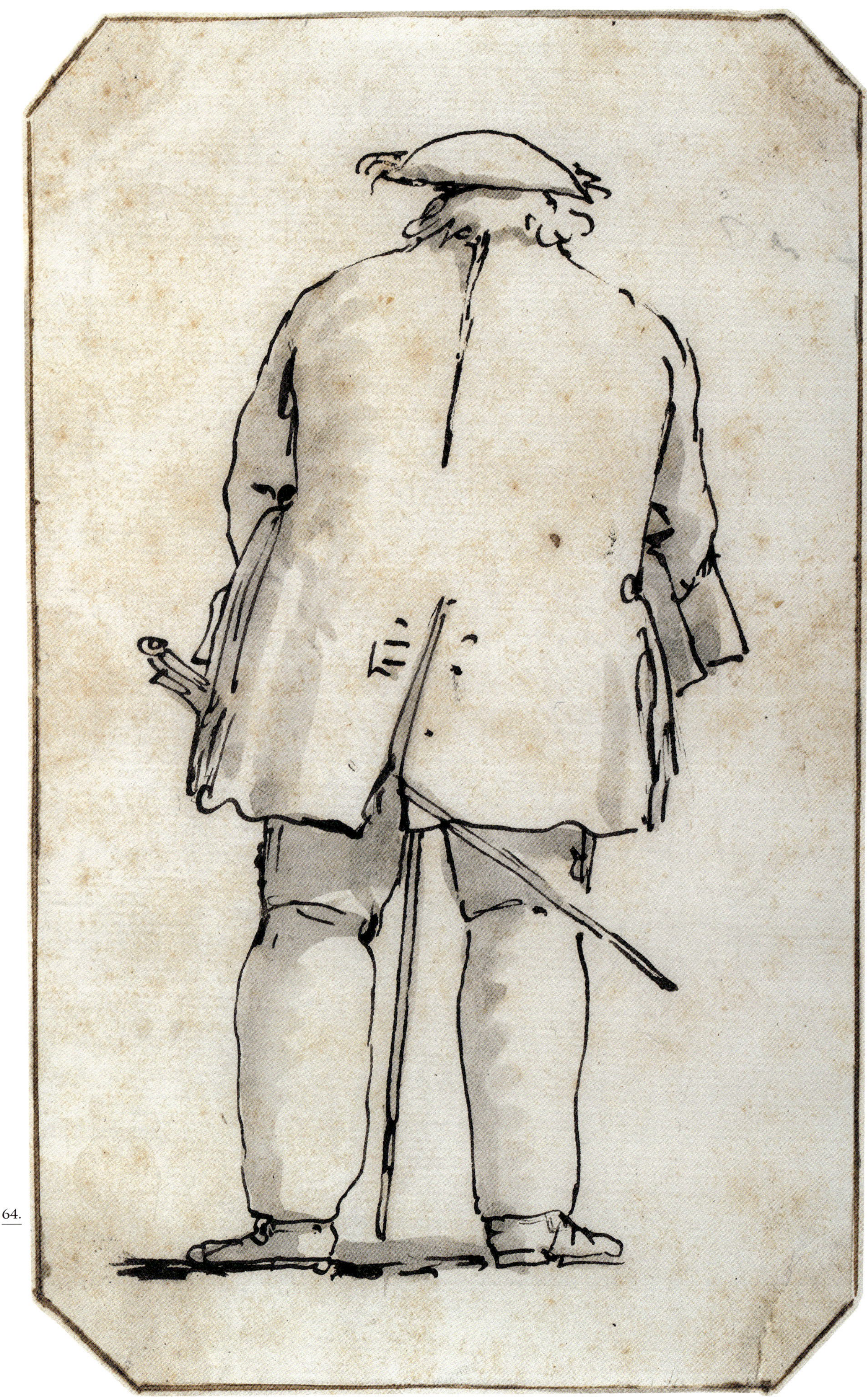

64.

back of the work under review (at the bottom right, just below a stamp, with writing in French by an export office), a common feature of the series (Knox, in Byam Shaw and Knox 1987, pp. 126–7, no. 97). It must have been mounted and probably bound in an album in the early nineteenth century, judging from the backing paper of the central sheets (Knox 2004b, p. 120), the handwriting of the inscriptions described and the fact that Teodoro Correr's 1830 bequest contained a pair of caricatures with the same octagonal format (ibid., p. 121). Finally, some drawings were used by Giandomenico in the 1790s for his *Scenes of contemporary life*, probably remaining 'in Tiepolo's studio until his death (in 1804)' (ibid., p. 120). In this case, the figure appears, with smaller legs, among the audience of the *Charlatan* in the Morgan Library and Museum, New York (see Gealt and Knox 2005, p. 121, no. 30).

EL

Bibliography

Shaack 1962, no. 62; Knox, in *Antichi disegni* 2005, pp. 143, 152–3.

65.

Giambattista Tiepolo (1696–1770)
Caricature of hunchback man standing and in profile, with tricorn and sword, 1754–62
Pen, black ink and grey wash on paper, 201 × 139 mm
Private collection

This was lot 249f at Christie's London auction on 9 April 1943, where it was purchased by Rosenberg. It was presented again by the same auction house in New York on 10 January 1990, lot 80, and then, through Pietro Scarpa in May of that year reached its current location. The first of these sales was due to the dismemberment of the *Tomo terzo de caricature*, in which the present sheet was in ninety-fourth place, consisting of 106 drawings mounted in pairs on fifty-three pages, then owned by Arthur Kay and coming from an auction of Dowell's books in Edinburgh on 25 March 1925 (lot 1004), where it was purchased by the local bookseller John Grant. Previously, it seems 'that it had belonged to the Breadalbane family collection, which it had entered from the collection formerly at Langton House at Duns, Berwickshire' (Knox, in *Antichi disegni* 2005). From the period photographs, at the Witt Library in London, the pages of the album appeared on brown paper; unfortunately there is no reproduction of the original cover with the title, which would place the *Tomo terzo* 'within the series of albums that were created in Tiepolo's studio before the family left for Madrid in 1762', with the consequent dating of the corpus to 1754–62 (Knox 2004b, p. 121). Three other sheets in the exhibition have the same provenance [cats 61, 66, 67].
Again in this magnificent caricature it is through a 'noble style, as in all the other drawings', suited to 'serious' subjects, that Tiepolo lampoons an ungraceful appearance, 'the revelation of the mocking *truth* of individuals as opposed and complementary to the sublime *fiction* of stories, fables, allegories' (Mariuz, in Pavanello 2004, p. 31). Giambattista had attained these results in his drawings of Pulcinella, a figure who is only once present in *Tomo terzo* (Knox 2004b, p. 121). While 'Pulcinella, the archetype of a physically flawed man, was the means to attain the world of caricature, an operation of unmasking, to reveal humanity as a body' (Pavanello 2004, p. 29), in this image, and in all Tiepolo's other similar images, the being in the flesh has passed into a caricatural apotheosis, not so much mocked as creating imaginative masks of the world.

EL

Bibliography

Knox, in *Antichi disegni* 2005, pp. 145, 154–5.

66.

Giambattista Tiepolo (1696–1770)
Caricature of a hunchback man standing in profile, with a tricorn in his hand and a sword, 1754–62
Pen, clear watercolour sepia ink and bistre on paper, 197 × 142 mm
Private collection

Together with three other sheets on display [cats 61, 65, 67], this drawing was in the *Tomo terzo de caricature*, in which fifty-three pages were bound with 106 drawings pasted to them (the present was in fifty-eighth place), formerly at Langton House, Duns, Berwickshire, and then in the Breadalbane family. It was bought by the antiquarian John Grant at the Dowell auction house in Edinburgh on 25 March 1925 (lot 1004) and sold with the unbound caricatures from the book by Arthur Kay at Christie's in London on 9 April 1943. The work in question was lot 246j. It was purchased by the Arcade Gallery in London (which also bought cat. 67), and passed to William M. Milliken, then in Sotheby's auctions of 21 March 1974 (lot 106) and 11 December 1975 (lot 32). It was also exhibited at the Cleveland Museum of Art in 1970 at the *Fiftieth Anniversary Exhibition 1919–1969* (Knox, in *Antichi disegni* 2005). At the Witt Library in London there are some period photographs documenting the original state of the pages of the *Tomo terzo*, with the caricatures in pairs mounted one above the other on brown

65.

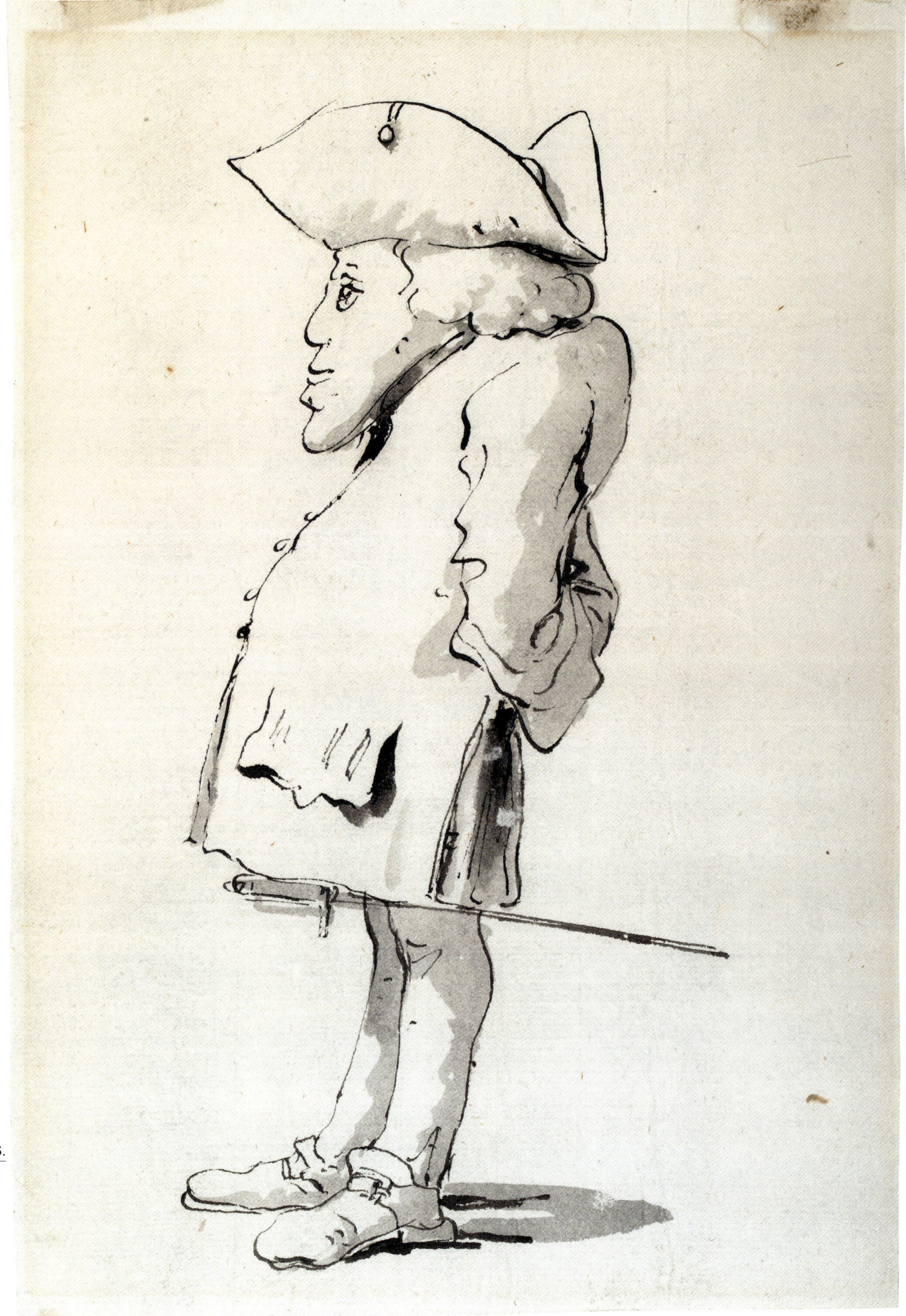

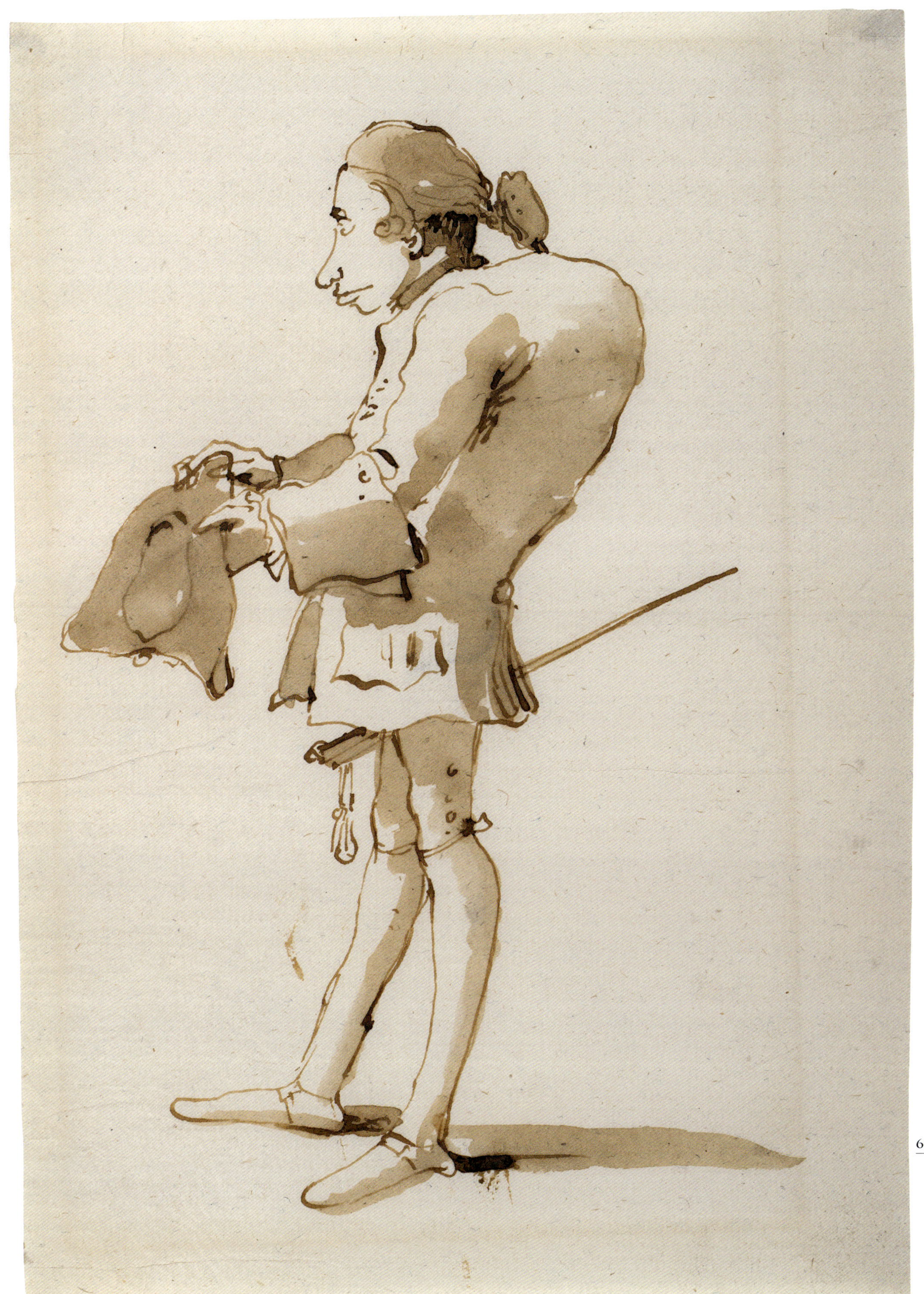

66.

sheets. It is supposed that the volume was made before the Tiepolo family departed for Spain in March 1762: 'the drawings seem to date back from the years 1754–1762' (Knox 2004b, p. 121). The assumption that the young hunchback is a soldier, because of 'his short jacket and sword' (Knox, in *Antichi disegni* 2005) is doubtful since, for example, the character's dress seems the same as that of the contemporary leisured 'beau' in the so-called *Picnic* by Giandomenico Tiepolo (Schulze Altcappenberg, in Venice 2004, pp. 174–7, no. 117).
A superb graphic work by Giambattista, the present caricature depicts the grotesque deformity of a human body with a highly refined technique, using bistre to clot the ink wash in the more shadowy areas, in a manner comparable to two drawings, here on display [cats 58, 59], from the Gabinetto dei Disegni in the Castello Sforzesco in Milan.

EL

Bibliography
Knox, in *Antichi disegni* 2005, pp. 145, 162–3.

67.

Giambattista Tiepolo (1696–1770)
Caricature of a thin man standing and in profile, with tricorn hat and sword, 1754–62
Pen, black ink and grey wash on paper, 203 × 130 mm
Private collection

This was originally the seventy-fourth drawing in the *Tomo terzo de caricature*, the album dismembered by Christie's in London for auction on 9 April 1943. The sheet is identifiable as lot 248b of the auction, purchased by the London Arcade Gallery. It entered the collection of Mrs Becker in New York, from which it was sold by Christie's on 10 January 1990, as lot 84, entering Pietro Scarpa's collection in May of the same year before reaching its present collocation (Knox, in *Antichi disegni* 2005). The last two changes of ownership were shared with another caricature on display [cat. 65], also from *Tomo terzo*, and to which the reader is referred for information about the history of the volume and its hypothetical chronology. Two further drawings with the same earlier origin are exhibited here [cats 61, 66].
The ridiculously geometric profile of the lanky gentleman is rendered with a rapid line, balanced by masterful layers of ink wash to give texture and light to the figure isolated on the paper, so resolving the contrast between the naturalism of the lower part – feet, legs and shadows – and the terse representation of the bust, darkened along the back and side, and the head surmounted by a narrow crumpled tricorn hat. This formal coherence is Tiepolo's hallmark in the history of the genre. The drawing repeats the linear abstractions of Anton Maria Zanetti, whose summa is the *Beautiful Maid in Ca' Vezzi* (Lucchese 2015, pp. 195–6, no. 28.IX), and Francesco Fontebasso (see Berra 2009, pp. 124–8), in the tradition of the Carracci's 'objectual physiognomy' (ibid., p. 93). In it Giambattista stresses his original position as a mocking cataloguer of universal human types in the *Tomo terzo* and other similar collections (see Knox 2004b). In its relentless classification of men with wizened silhouettes and features schematised beneath absurd headgear, the drawing is close to the figure in the sheet formerly in the Valmarana and Paul Wallraf collections, now in the Lehman collection at the Metropolitan Museum, New York (Knox, in Venice 2004, p. 142, no. 84).
In 1791 Giandomenico Tiepolo reused this invention of his father's in *The Picture Show* in the Thaw collection at the Morgan Library and Museum, New York (Gealt and Knox 2005).

EL

Bibliography
Gealt and Knox 2005, p. 121, no. 29; Knox, in *Antichi disegni* 2005, pp. 145, 158–9.

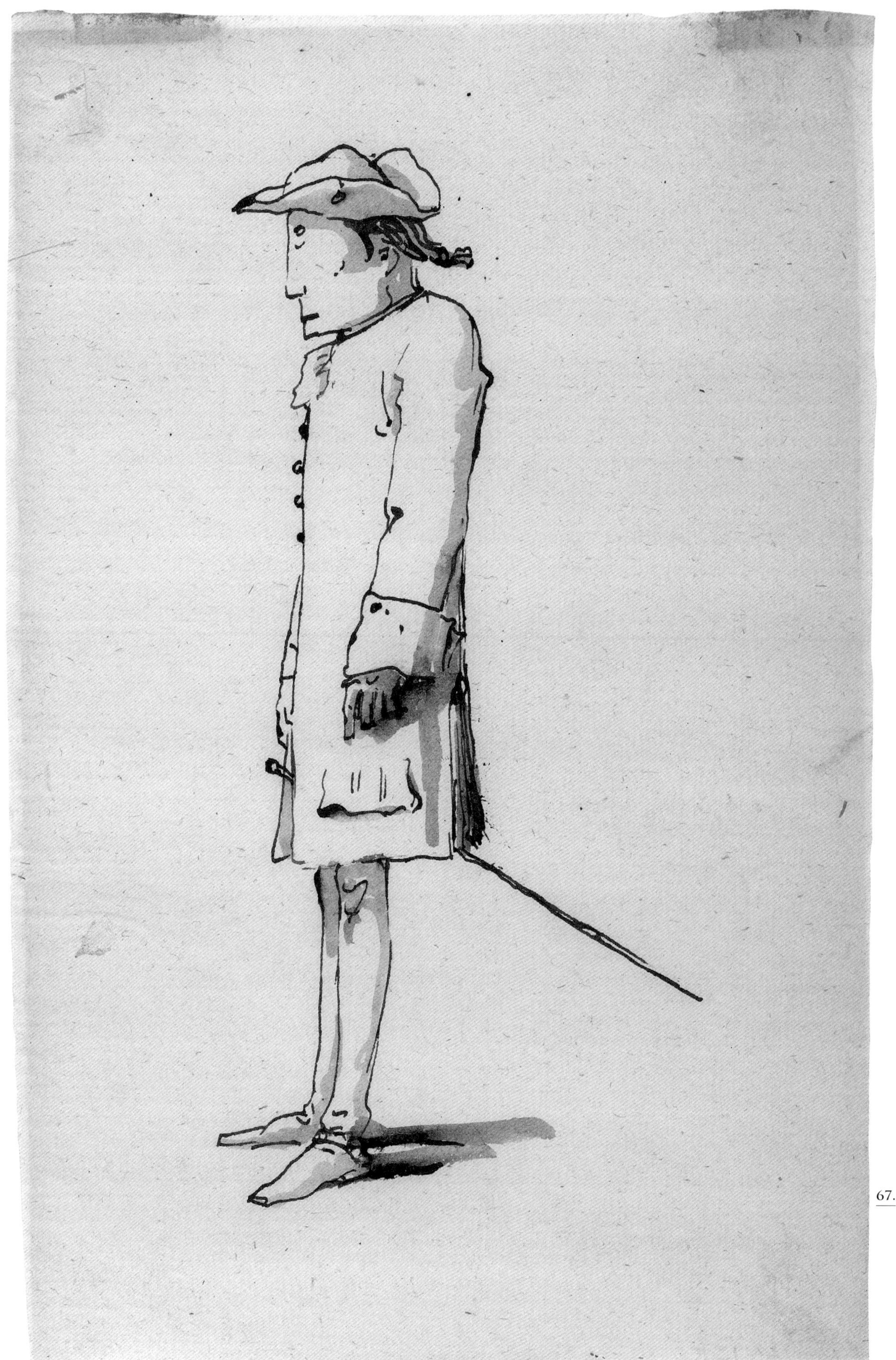

67.

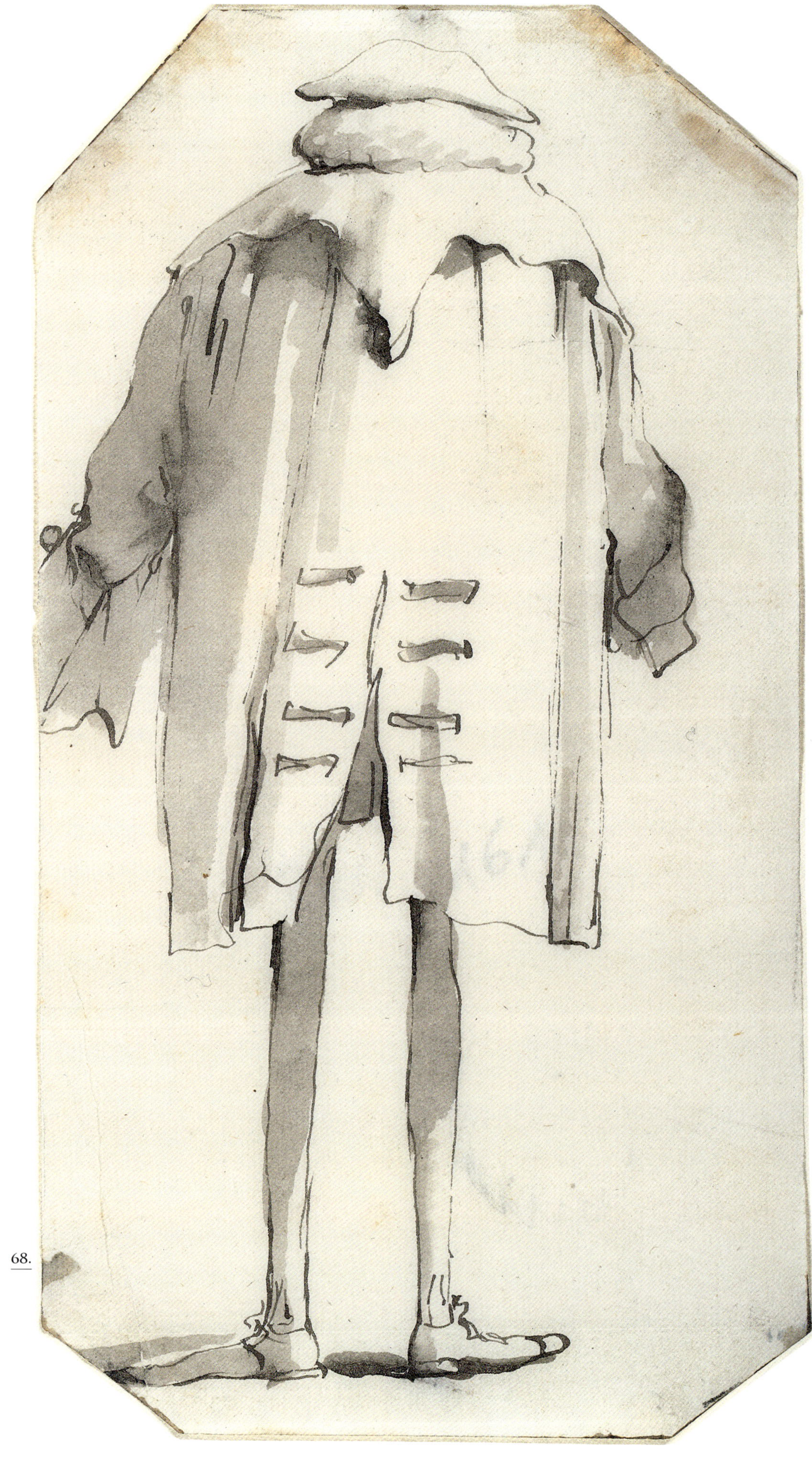

68.

68.

Giambattista Tiepolo (1696-1770)
Caricature from behind of a thin man and a hunchback standing,
sixth decade of the eighteenth century
Pen, black ink and grey watercolour, bistre, on paper with clipped corners, 184 × 105 mm, traces of the frame in sepia. Graphite marks visible along the upper margin, the left lateral margin and the right lower oblique margin, probably made during the mounting of the drawing on a lost backing paper
Private collection

George Knox (in *Antichi disegni* 2005) conjectures a provenance for this drawing in the collection of the Counts Sacchetto in Padua, named by Giuseppe Fiocco (1955, p. 29, no. 75) as the previous owners of one of his caricatures, mounted on brown paper, with clipped edges and traces of a frame (Knox, in Pavanello 2005, pp. 253–4, nos 412–14). The irregular octagonal format is therefore analogous to that of the thirty-two caricatures in the Paul Wallraf collection made known, with provenance from the Counts Valmarana of Vicenza, by Antonio Morassi (1959, p. 56, nos 76–87). These must have been part of a larger set of about 140 sheets (Scholz 1960, p. 64). There is however, no firm evidence for the idea that 'all the trimmed caricatures, with traces of an outline and clipped corners, not recorded before the Second World War' (Knox, in *Antichi disegni* 2005, p. 144) come from the Sacchetto collection. Even though 'the name Sacchetto is associated with the drawings in the Wallraf auction in 1933' (Knox 2004b, p. 121), there are no direct links with the caricatures formerly in the Valmarana collection (ibid.). It is more likely that the dispersal of these octagonal sheets in various collections began not long after Giandomenico Tiepolo's death in 1804, at least starting from Teodoro Correr's Venetian bequest in 1830.
An exponent of a rich Tiepolesque repertoire of hunchbacks exemplified by various drawings on display, the character with spindly legs seen from behind has immense feet that closely resemble the shoes in a similar *Caricatural self-portrait* by Anton Maria Zanetti at the Fondazione Giorgio Cini (Lucchese 2015, pp. 293–4, no. 48.II). While the latter, perfectly and incoherently parallel to the plane of vision, imitates a child's scrawl, here the virtuosity of the pen and ink wash gives shape and light to a figure created as a work of art rather than a humorous masterpiece.

EL

Bibliography
Knox, in *Antichi disegni* 2005, pp. 160–61.

69.

Giambattista Tiepolo (1696-1770)
Frontal caricature of a thin man cloaked and standing, with tricorn hat and muff,
sixth decade of the eighteenth century
Pen, black ink and grey watercolour on paper with clipped corners, 170 × 85 mm, glued on a sheet, 190 × 100 mm; on the lower edges of the drawing paper, traces of the frame in sepia ink
Private collection

Considered of probable provenance in the Sacchetto collection, this drawing mounted on paper judged to be of the eighteenth century has also made it possible to conjecture 'its inclusion in the Valmarana Album' (Knox, in *Antichi disegni* 2005). This last assumption can be confidently discarded by comparison with a sheet in the collection that was formerly in the Wallraf collection [here cat. 64]. It is observed that the pages of the caricatures reported by Antonio Morassi (1959, p. 56, nos 76–87) from the 'Counts Valmarana in Vicenza' are larger and above all have a double frame drawn in sepia ink, the outer one about twenty millimetres from the edge of the larger sheet, the other running along the perimeter of the paper with the image. Even if one imagines a cut-out of the original page, the absence of the continuous frame around the caricature excludes a link with the Valmarana series. Observing instead that at the bottom left a piece of the toe of the shoe and the shadow of the character have been arbitrarily cut out, we can deduce that the caricature was larger and that it was trimmed and mounted on a sheet differing from the original mounting. This would explain the absence of inscriptions or other markings on the back, of the kind found in the example from the Wallraf and Valmarana collections.
The idea of a man like a beanpole swathed in heavy garments, with a huge muff forming a pendant to the wig had already appeared in the caricatural profile of the singer *Benedetto Baldassari called Benedettino*, of whom another ridiculous image can be seen in the exhibition [cat. 55], portrayed walking in a Venetian street by Anton Maria Zanetti and Marco Ricci in the winter of 1718

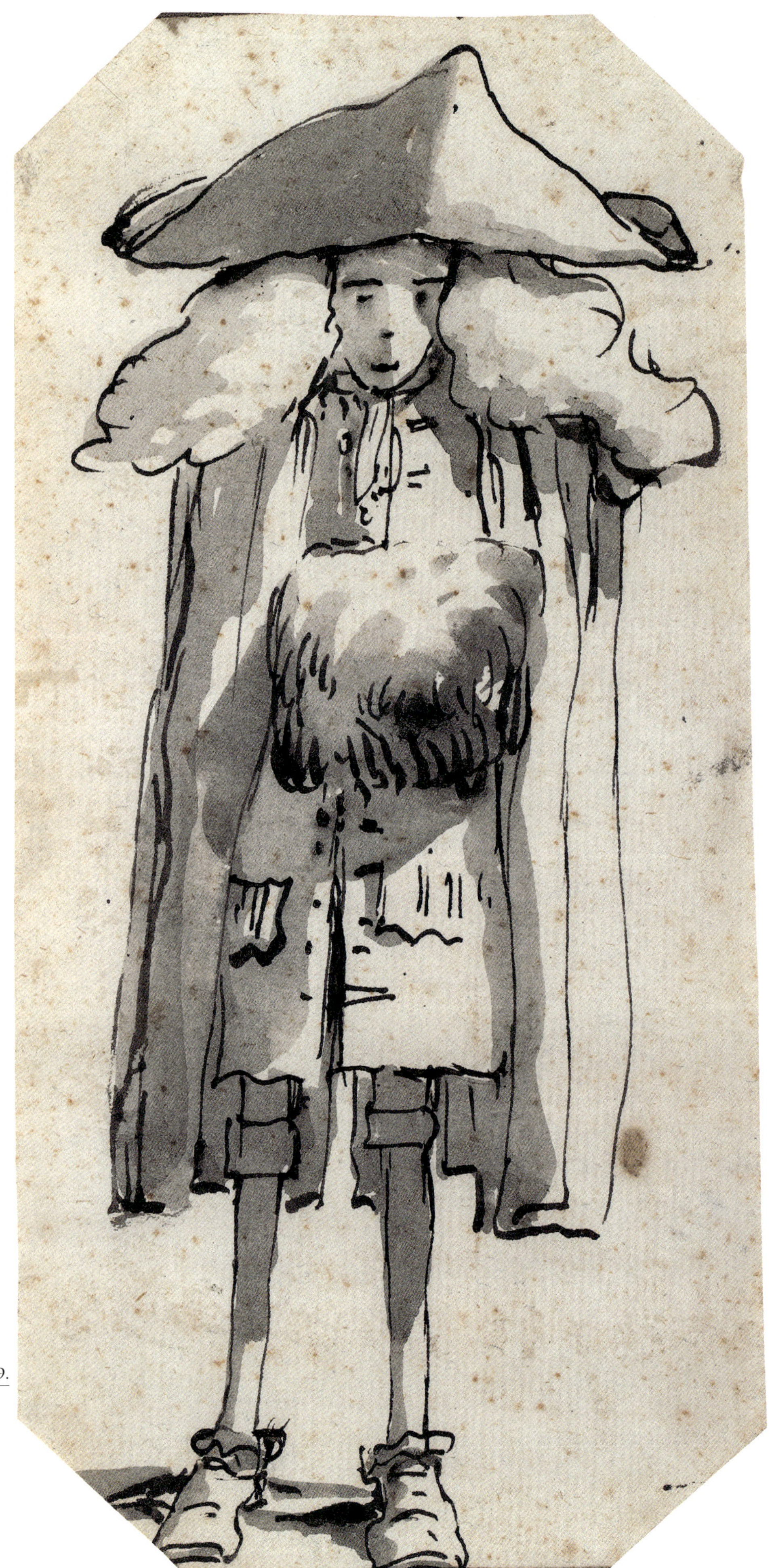

69.

(Lucchese 2015, pp. 233–4, no. 33.VIII). Here, however, in addition to the frontal view and the invention of the gigantic tricorn on top of an equally outsize wig, the artist not only used flickering pen strokes to evoke the slender figure, but also thickened the wash to mark the volumes and chiaroscuro effects, conferring notable graphic execution on a figure whose facial features are no more than a simple set of lines and dots.

EL

Bibliography
Knox, in *Antichi disegni* 2005, pp. 164–5.

70.

Giambattista Tiepolo (1696–1770)
Caricature of a hunchback standing seen from behind, sixth decade of the eighteenth century
Pen, sepia and bistre wash on paper with clipped corners, 189 × 110 mm, framed in sepia, mounted on brown paper, 203 × 122 mm
Private collection

The rigid backing of the drawing bears the stamp of a Parisian shipping company, a cutting from the page of a French sales catalogue with the reproduction of the work (lot 35) and the label of the Christie's auction held in London on 3 July 2018, where the drawing was offered as lot 26. Since it is clipped at the corners, eliminating parts of the shadows drawn below, and perhaps also ancient marks or inscriptions (Byam Shaw 1970, pp. 239, 241, n. 14), with the perimeter marked by a sepia frame and mounted on a sheet of brown paper, the caricature could come from the Sacchetto collection in Padua (Knox, in *Antichi disegni* 2005, p. 144), from which Giuseppe Fiocco (in Fiocco 1955, p. 29, no. 75) acquired three works (Knox, in Pavanello 2005, pp. 253–4, nos 412–14). The attribution to Giambattista rests on the extraordinary stylistic quality apparent in the depiction of the figure, presumably a dwarf, with a valgus deformity and wearing a large wig that spreads over his hump. With skilful pen strokes, from which the ink wash and bistre broaden out to create space and volumes, Tiepolo seems to point a spotlight on the deformed figure captured on paper 'in a pitiless, dazzling loneliness', like an 'attack from behind. The figure caricatured is unaware of the violence he suffers from our gaze' (Mariuz, in Pavanello 2004, p. 29), which sees the most ridiculously hideous aspects of humanity embodied in an extremely attractive graphic style, so exalting 'the superiority of art over nature' (Mariuz 1971, p. 83). In this drawing Tiepolo seems to merge two human types captured by his pen in a sheet at the Biblioteca Comunale in Treviso, perhaps formerly owned by Francesco Algarotti (Pavanello 2004, p. 26), and another at the Civico Museo Sartorio in Trieste (Knox, in Venice 2004, p. 123, no. 42, p. 135, no. 62). The latter collection contains a sheet with an image comparable to the present one, for which a dating to the eighteenth century has been suggested (ibid., p. 133, no. 60).

EL

Bibliography
Unpublished.

71.

Giambattista Tiepolo (1696-1770)
Caricature from behind of a thin man standing, sixth decade of the eighteenth century
Pen, black ink and grey watercolour, bistre, on paper with clipped corners, 184 × 105 mm, framed in sepia
Private collection

At the top left appears, written in pen in the same ink apparently as the frame, the number '41' underlined. It does not seem to match the style of numbering of some works from the Wallraf-Valmarana collections – represented by a pair of drawings in this exhibition [cats 64, 72] but lacking the number – in the upper right-hand corner of the backing sheet. For this last collection, however, the conjecture of a limited numerical sequence 'between 1 and 32 has to be excluded, so it is clearly the remainder of a small but elegant album' (Knox, in *Antichi disegni* 2005, p. 144), since one copy bears the number '38' (Knox, in Byam Shaw and Knox 1987, p. 127, no. 98); and Janoz Scholz (1960, p. 64) records that almost the whole group originally amounted to about 140 sheets.
The drawing comes from the collection of Eugene V. Thaw, auctioned at Christie's in London on 30 October 2018 (lot 258), as documented by a label on the back. It depicts a man with stick-like legs and sharp collarbones that seem to exist to support a strange cloud-shaped wig, with wash shading that makes it almost resemble a storm.
In his study of Giambattista Tiepolo as caricaturist, Max Kozloff (1961) reflected on the sheet, then still in the Thaw collection, and the other examples of

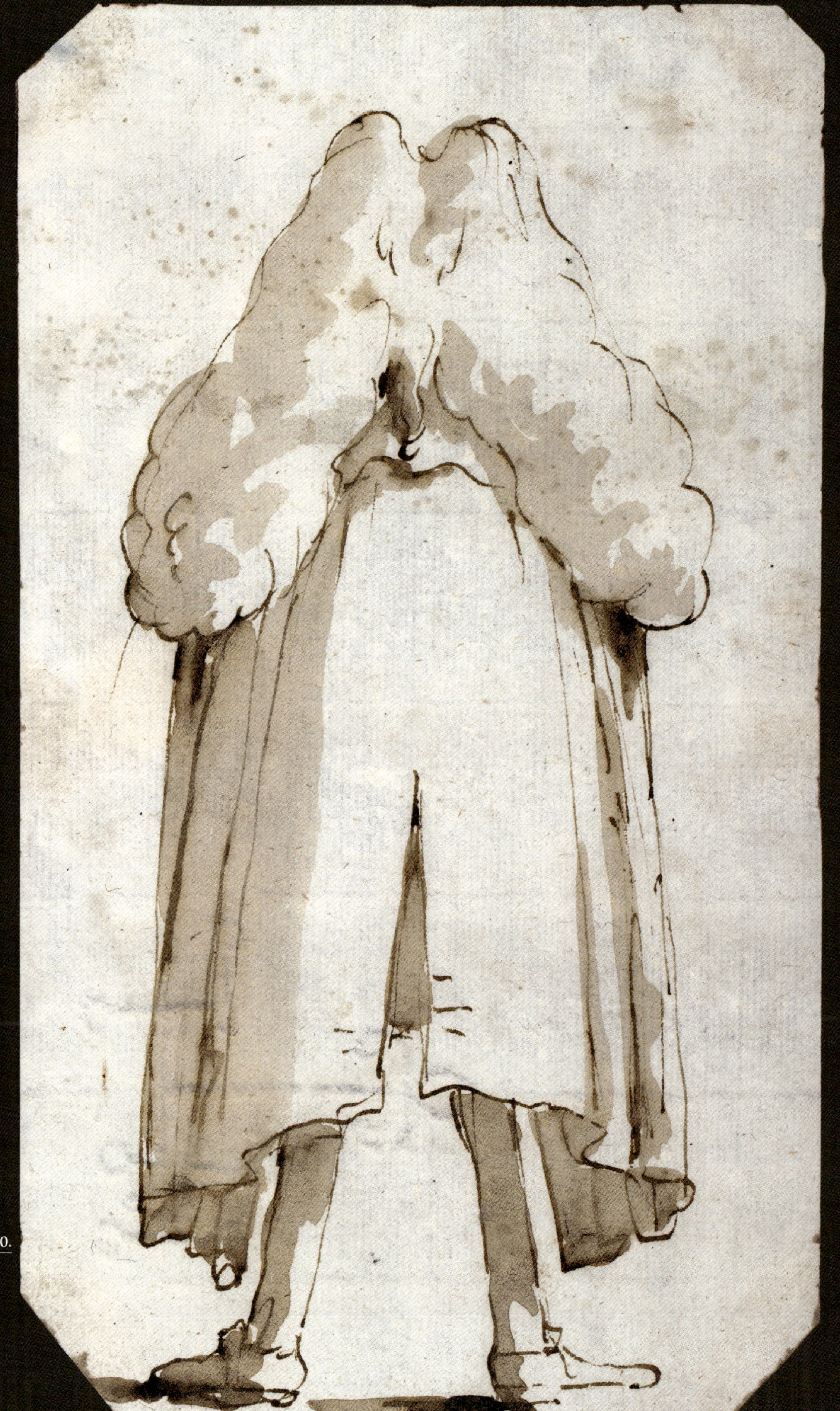

70.

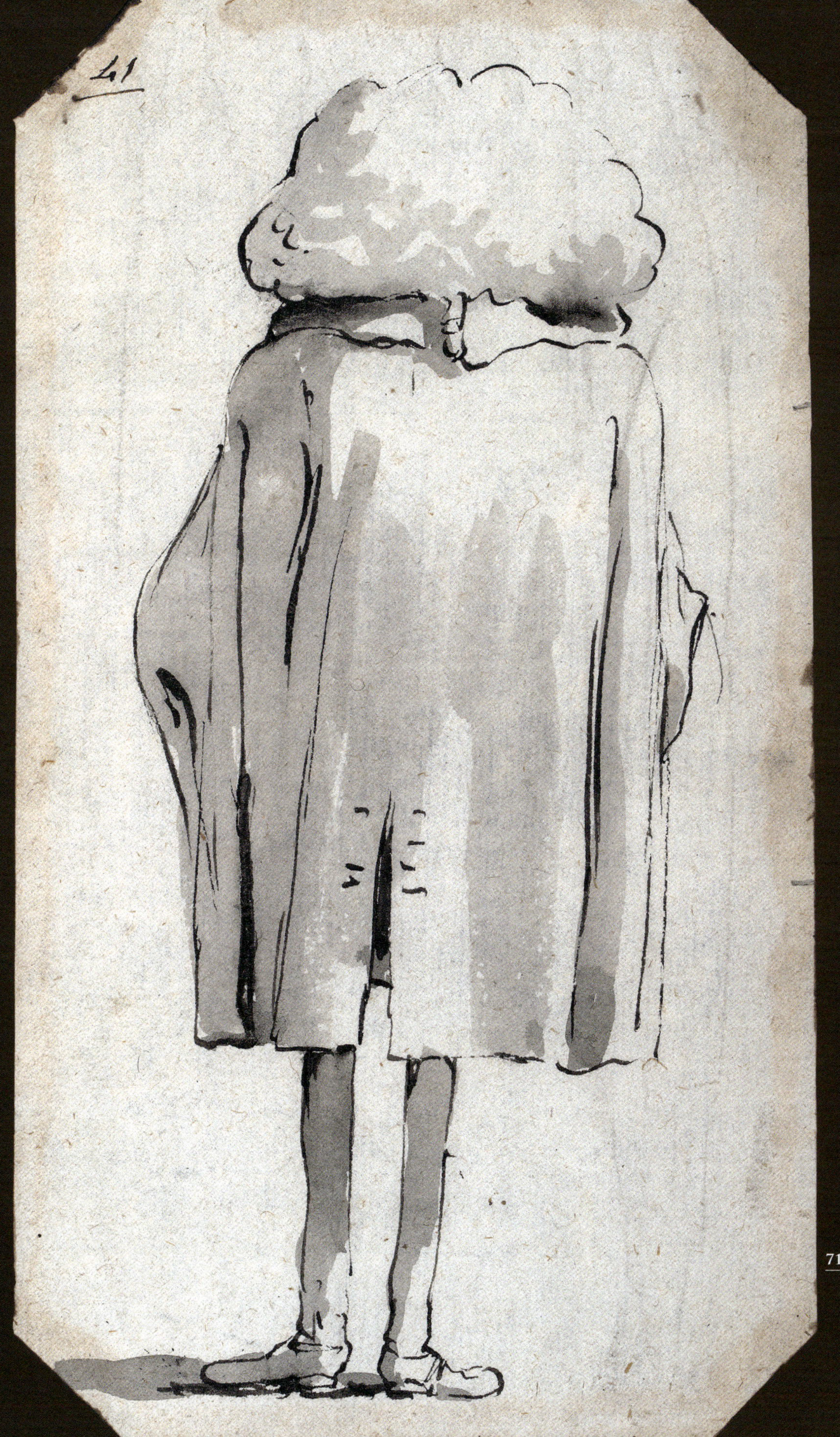

71.

figures depicted from behind, 'the opposite of the human façade'. Although finding remote precedents in Mantegna's figures in the Venetian context, they had their eighteenth-century humorous turning point in the drawings of Marco Ricci and a partial source in the figures in Canaletto's *vedute* (and those by Luca Carlevarijs, it might be added). The back, the scholar observes, is conceived to record and then magnify every weakness or peculiarity of the figures, as in a purely formal exercise, in which the artist mocks without being ensnared by the defects of the face, the classic target of the figurative genre that is the subject of the present exhibition. In a certain sense, Tiepolo's genius discovered the potential of the 'still life of caricature', giving his figures viewed from behind the status of still lifes and so performing the necessary change of paradigm by which we appreciate them as authentic works of art.

EL

Bibliography

Kozloff 1961, p. 33.

72.

Giambattista Tiepolo (1696–1770)
Caricature of an ecclesiastic from behind, sixth decade of the eighteenth century
Pen, black ink and grey watercolour, bistre, on paper with clipped corners, 191 × 116 mm, with traces of the frame in sepia and glued to a sheet, 255 × 183 mm, which has a frame in sepia ink parallel to the right and at a short distance from the drawing paper, while a second frame, thicker and hexagonal in form, is drawn at a short distance from the outer edge in sepia. Graphite lines appear on the support page near the top edge of the inner paper, on the far left, and along its right side, in the middle and below, probably made when the drawing was being mounted
Private collection

Direct observation suggests that the drawing paper has been detached and then reattached to the same support, but without matching it to the lines of the inner sepia frame. The horizontal folds (but not the vertical folds) visible at a short distance from the upper and lower edges of the page are similar to the caricature formerly in the Wallraf-Valmarana collection on display [cat. 64], which has similar graphite marks, probably made while mounting the drawing, and above all the same double lines in ink of the two linear frames of the backing, though the outer one differs in form. It therefore appears likely that the present drawing is the 'Caricature of a Man, standing, seen from behind, wearing a belted gown and a cap', lot 322 sold by Christie's in London on 26 March 1963 (p. 79 of the catalogue) in the Paul Wallraf sale, or another similar one among the some 140 Valmarana drawings seen by Janos Scholz (1960, p. 64). That the figure in the long garment clasped at the waist by a belt and with a cap on its head is an ecclesiastic, perhaps an Augustinian monk, is borne out by comparison with a caricature wearing similar garments in the Lugt collection at the Fondation Custodia in Paris. This was formerly attributed to Giandomenico Tiepolo and then restored, on the recommendation of Pietro Scarpa, to Giambattista Tiepolo (Byam Shaw, in Byam Shaw 1981, p. 74, no. 84). The artist is undoubtedly the elder of the Tiepolos, given the confident handling, fluid and sustained as his imagination. The form of the neck here is different, as well as the way the attention of the artist concentrates on the pitiless depiction not of the projecting ears, as in the figure in Paris, but on the even more hunched back, into which the man's head is sunk, and his coarse, grotesque shoes. Mischievous rather than vindictive (Kozloff 1961, p. 33), Giambattista draws caricatures by integrating them into the style of his most solemn work, 'just as the farcical interlude can be inserted in the heroic drama', demonstrating that 'art is capable of praise as of mockery, evokes angels and dwarfs, stirs feeling and laughter and reveals, in the implacable truth of its light, the great fiction of everything' (Mariuz 1971, p. 83).

EL

Bibliography

Unpublished.

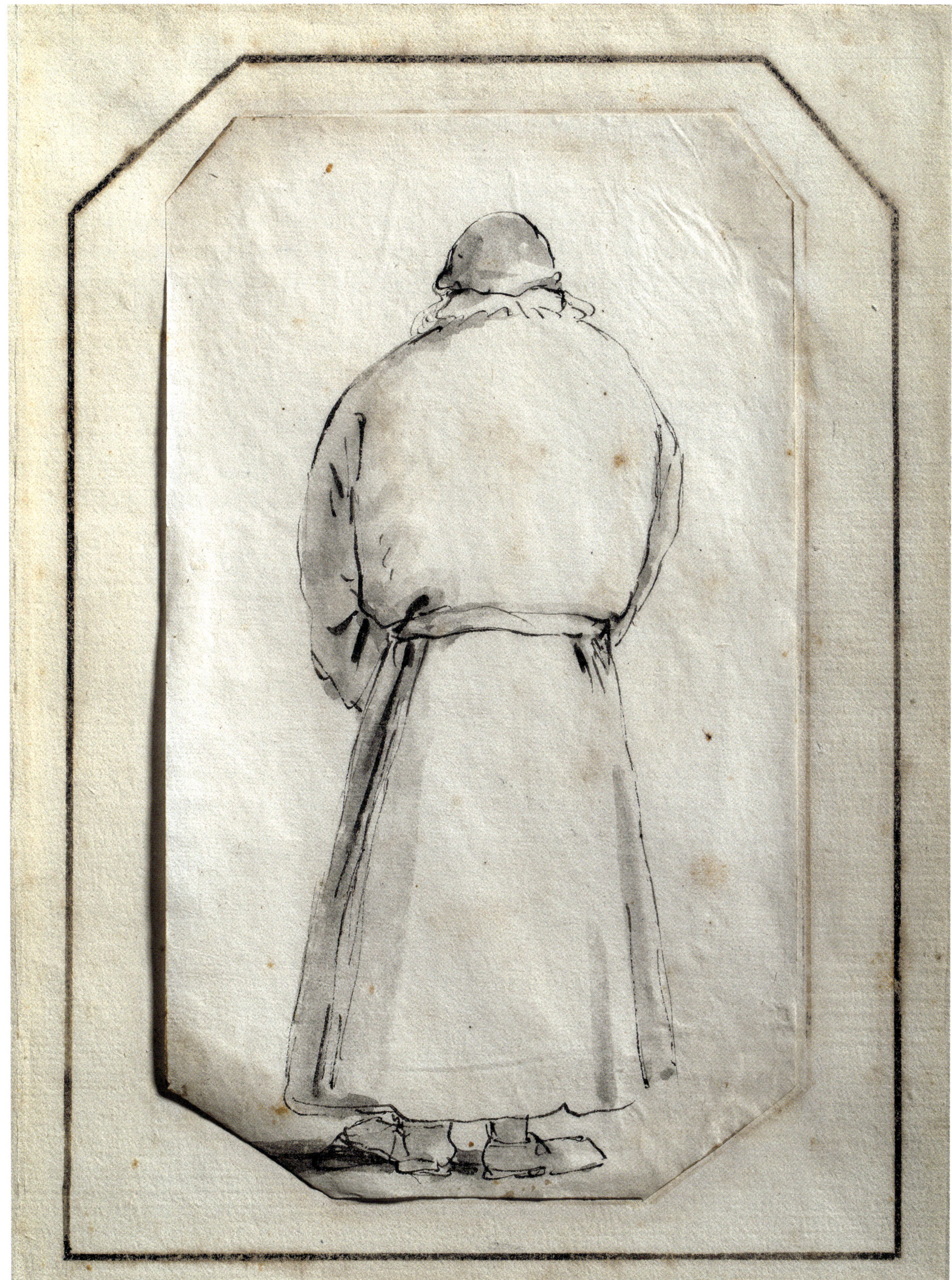

72.

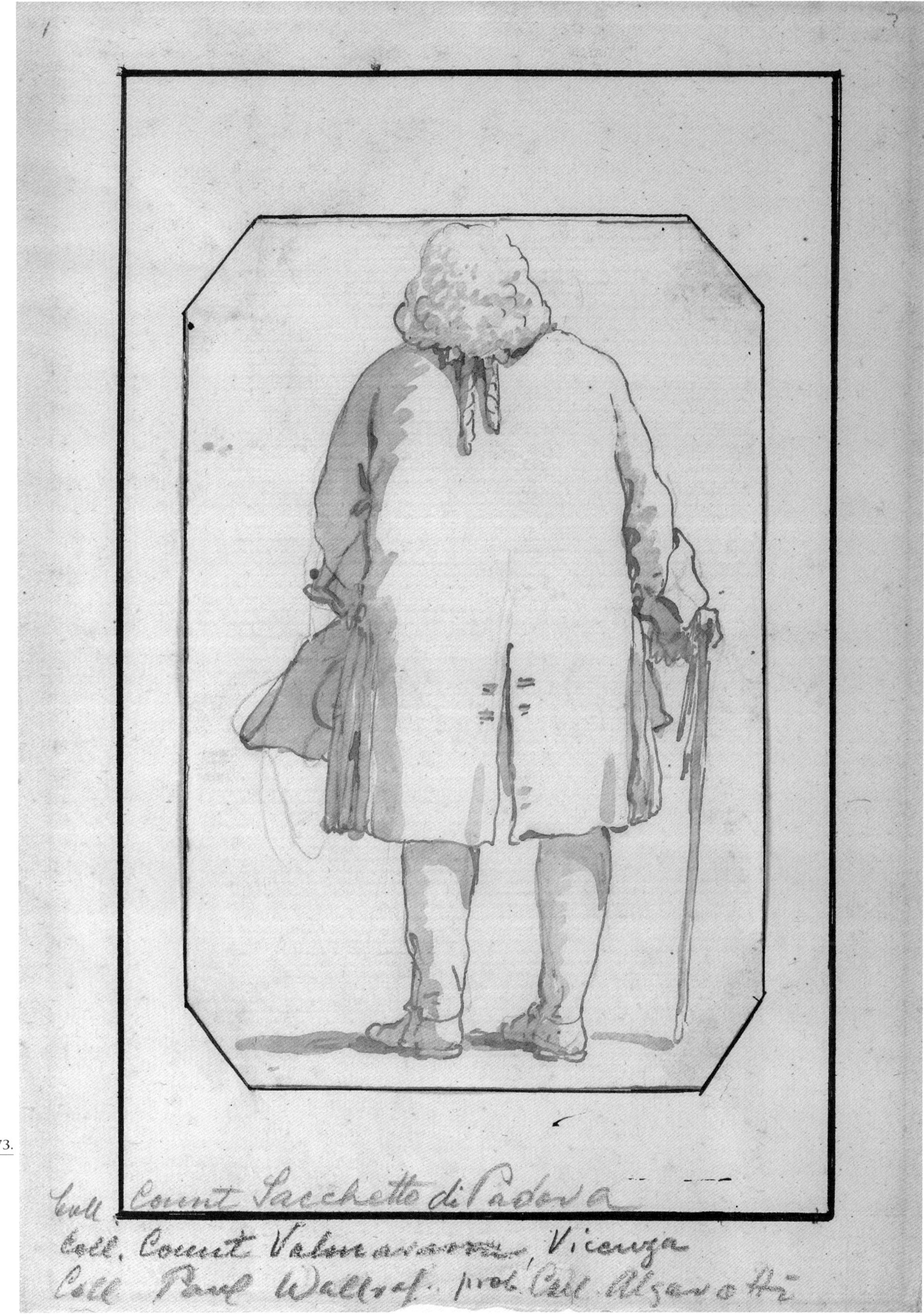

73.

73.

Workshop of Giambattista Tiepolo
Caricature of a fat man from behind, with tricorn hat and stick in hand,
sixth decade of the eighteenth century
Pen, graphite sketch, sepia ink wash on paper with the corners clipped, 154 × 106 mm, with traces of framing along the edges in sepia at the top right, on the right side at the bottom, partly covered by the black ink of the outer frame, along the successive oblique side and all the lower edge and on the upper half of the left-hand side. The drawing is pasted to a sheet, 338 × 225 mm, which frames its perimeter, with a line in black ink; a second rectangular linear frame, executed in several overlapping sections of black ink, runs a few millimetres from the edges of the page
Private collection

At the bottom left, in three lines in pencil, in a modern hand: 'Coll. Count Padua Bag/ Coll. Count Valmarana, Vicenza/ Coll. Paul Wallraf prob. Coll. Algarotti'. This is a combination of knowledge and theories about the origin of Tiepolo's caricatures with their corners clipped, perhaps to remove ancient marks or inscriptions (Byam Shaw 1970, pp. 239, 241, n. 14), or resulting from being torn from other pages (Byam Shaw, in Byam Shaw 1981, p. 74, no. 84), or only to create an effect of regularity in a mass of materials on supports of different forms, such as the scrap of paper of a figure in costume in Trieste (Resciniti 2021, pp. 508–9, no. 237). While the works from the Sacchetto collection are connected to the caricatures in the Fondazione Giorgio Cini (Knox, in Pavanello 2005, pp. 253–4, nos 412–14), the Wallraf and Valmarana collections are related to the group to which two sheets on display here belong [cats 64, 72]. They have the double frames on the page in sepia and not black ink, especially not above the previous one in sepia of the octagon with the drawing. Finally, the provenance from the Algarotti collection rests on the report from 1854 of '"two large books" with a "copious collection of humorous drawings by Tiepolo": they might have been albums of caricatures or the two valuable collections of large drawings made by Domenico' (Knox, in *Antichi disegni* 2005, p. 141). The inscription is repeated, except for the last note, on another caricature, formerly owned with the present one by the London antiquarian Stephen Ongpin, both attributed to Giambattista Tiepolo. The drawing on display was sold on 2 July 2019 by Christie's in London (lot 67), adding among the origins the Parisian Galerie Pardo and its acquisition (1972) by Eileen and Herbert C. Bernard of New York. It is similar to a sheet in the Museo Correr, considered to be by Giandomenico (Pavanello 2004, p. 52, n. 39) or Giambattista (Knox, in Venice 2004, p. 144, no. 93). With too many uncertainties to be the father's and unlike the only youthful caricature reliably by his son (ibid., no. 91), it appears to be by the workshop. Perhaps it can be classed as a copy, as another sheet on display definitely is [cat. 74].

EL

Bibliography
Unpublished.

74.

Early copy after Giambattista Tiepolo
Caricature of a man seated and in profile, with a sheet of paper in his hand,
after 1750–60
Pen, black ink, grey wash, bistre on paper with clipped corners, 220 × 170 mm, framed in sepia ink
Private collection

Interpreted also as a 'musician, seated in his chair, following a melody that he hears only in space, ready to fix it on the sheet music he holds in his hand, while the other drums rhythmically on his knee' (Scarpa 1983), this drawing has been recognised as an autograph work by Tiepolo and as a 'faithful copy, line by line, of a sheet preserved in the Civiche Raccolte d'Arte in the Castello Sforzesco in Milan' (Knox, in *Antichi disegni* 2005), also on display [cat. 62]. In comparison, the present caricature is half as large again, with more fluent drawing. A comparison of some details of the execution – mouth, both hands, back and forearm – shows how the work under review simplifies its model in Milan, yet remains faithful to Tiepolo's manner. The stylistic closeness and the use of bistre, absent from the original, favour the idea that this was an exercise by the workshop, in which it was required to render, as far as possible, the freshness of execution of the original, replicating even the master's *pentimenti*, for example in the details of the ends of the back legs of the chair. The drawing can therefore be placed in a formative practice documented at the Kupferstichkabinett in Berlin (see Schulze Altcappenberg 1996, pp. 77–85, nos 57–64), but which represented subjects from 'history painting'. The exception exhibited here, evidence of the importance of the genre of caricature to Tiepolo, also in the training of other artists, finds a parallel in the sheet in the Victoria and Albert Museum, London, assigned to the workshop (Knox 1960, p. 93, no. 311). That represents, this time on a smaller scale, the image of the *Elderly Couple* in the Metropolitan Museum, New York, attributed with some uncertainty to Giambattista (Knox, in Venice 2004, p. 144, no. 90), but also doubtfully attributed to his son Lorenzo (Byam Shaw 1970, p. 239,

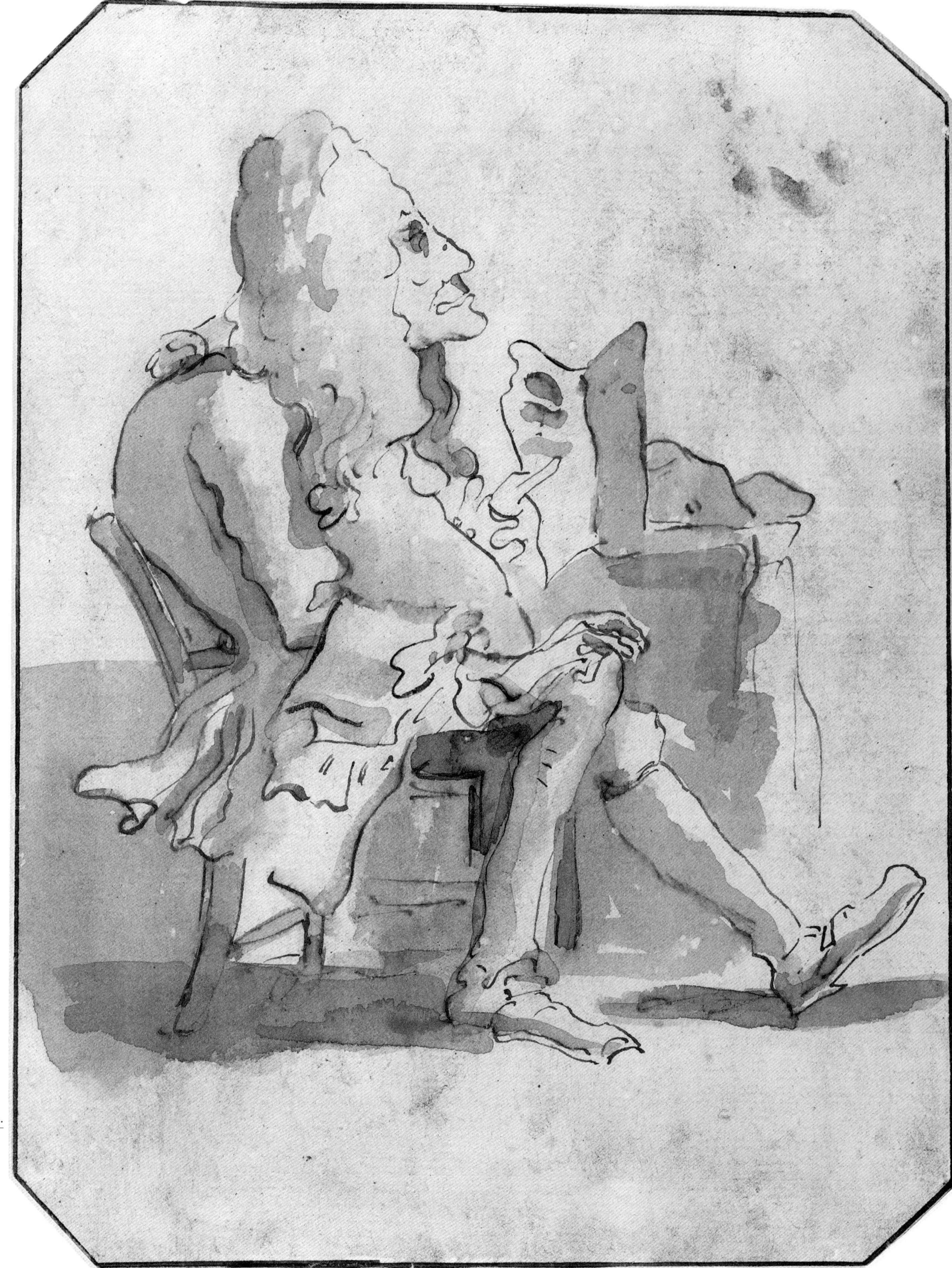

74.

n. 11). While we do not have any caricatures reliably by Lorenzo (see Knox, in Venice 2004, pp. 136–7, no. 66), there is the sheet in New York by his brother Giandomenico (ibid., p. 144, no. 91), the work of a young caricaturist who imitated his father's style with talents superior to those displayed in our drawing.

EL

Bibliography
Scarpa 1983, pp. 70, 75–6; Knox, in *Antichi disegni* 2005, pp. 168–9.

75.

Giandomenico Tiepolo (1727–1804)
Frontal caricature of man in the form of a bird, standing cloaked, c. 1790
Pen, sepia wash and bistre, traces of graphite marks on the cloak and on the figure's left leg, on paper, 200 × 170 mm, glued to paper, 249 × 151 mm, on which is drawn an outline in black chalk about 10 mm from the central sheet. In the same black chalk, lines were drawn, to guide the mounting of the drawing, inside the support of the drawing, about halfway along the upper, lower and left-hand sides (where there are also traces of black chalk in the upper part of the margin), and also on the backing, at bottom left and top right, a short distance from the sheet with the drawing
Private collection

On the larger sheet, at the bottom right, the inscription 'Tiepolo' in a late nineteenth-century or early twentieth-century hand; the absence of the characteristic clipped corners seems to exclude its presumed 'almost certain' provenance from the Sacchetto collection as well as the observation that the mount recalls the Valmarana sheets (Knox, in *Antichi disegni* 2005), given the differences with the sheets of that origin exhibited here [cats 64, 72]. The conjecture that the strange character depicted frontally with a bird's beak for a nose and claws instead of feet is a 'plague doctor' (Scarpa 1983) is groundless. Their dress was very different from the volatile metamorphosis of a man in a small wig, large round staring eyes and arms concealed by the layers of the cloak to evoke wings, complying with the Carracci's 'approach to physiognomy, transferring the human likeness to animals' (Bellori 1672, p. 75). Published as by Giambattista, the drawing has been associated with Janos Scholz's observation (1960, p. 64), in the case of the Valmarana drawings, of the differences in the manner and quality between the Tiepolos' various caricatures, suggesting the intervention of other hands in addition to those of Giambattista and Giandomenico (Knox, in *Antichi disegni* 2005), to whom the zoomorphic image should be assigned. His characteristic stylistic features are the tremulous handling of the outline, thicker than his father's, and the uniform application of the wash, as well as the inconsistency in the construction of the figure, specifically at the point where the legs should join the body. The unusual subject finds parallels in Giandomenico's drawings and aesthetic, for example in the *Studies of an eagle's head* in Naples (Knox, in Udine–Bloomington 1996, p. 185, no. 115). His work as a caricaturist in his father's orbit is not fully clarified (see Pavanello 2004, p. 52, n. 19), being based on two signed drawings in the Metropolitan Museum in New York (see Knox, in Venice 2004, p. 144, nos 91, 92), marking the poles within which we can place the sheet here displayed. In the roughness of the handling and inventive singularity, it is close to the drawing depicting a trio of monkeys, two of them in the form of skeletons (Byam Shaw 1962, pp. 81–2, no. 47), in the Morgan Library and Museum, New York.

EL

Bibliography
Scarpa 1983, pp. 69–70, 76; Knox, in *Antichi disegni* 2005, pp. 170–71.

76.

Imitator of Tiepolo
Caricature of an old man with spectacles and a stick, late nineteenth to early twentieth century
Pen, sepia wash on paper, 171 × 100 mm, with black ink frame drawn at a short distance from the edge and closed at each corner by another line in the same ink to form a triangle
Private collection

The triangles at the four corners are meant to replicate in some form the sheets by Tiepolo actually clipped at the corners. One edge of the paper has peeled off along the lower edge, tearing a piece, now recomposed, of the figure's right foot. The elderly man in a tailcoat with a sort of skull cap on his head leans on a stick with the other hand in his

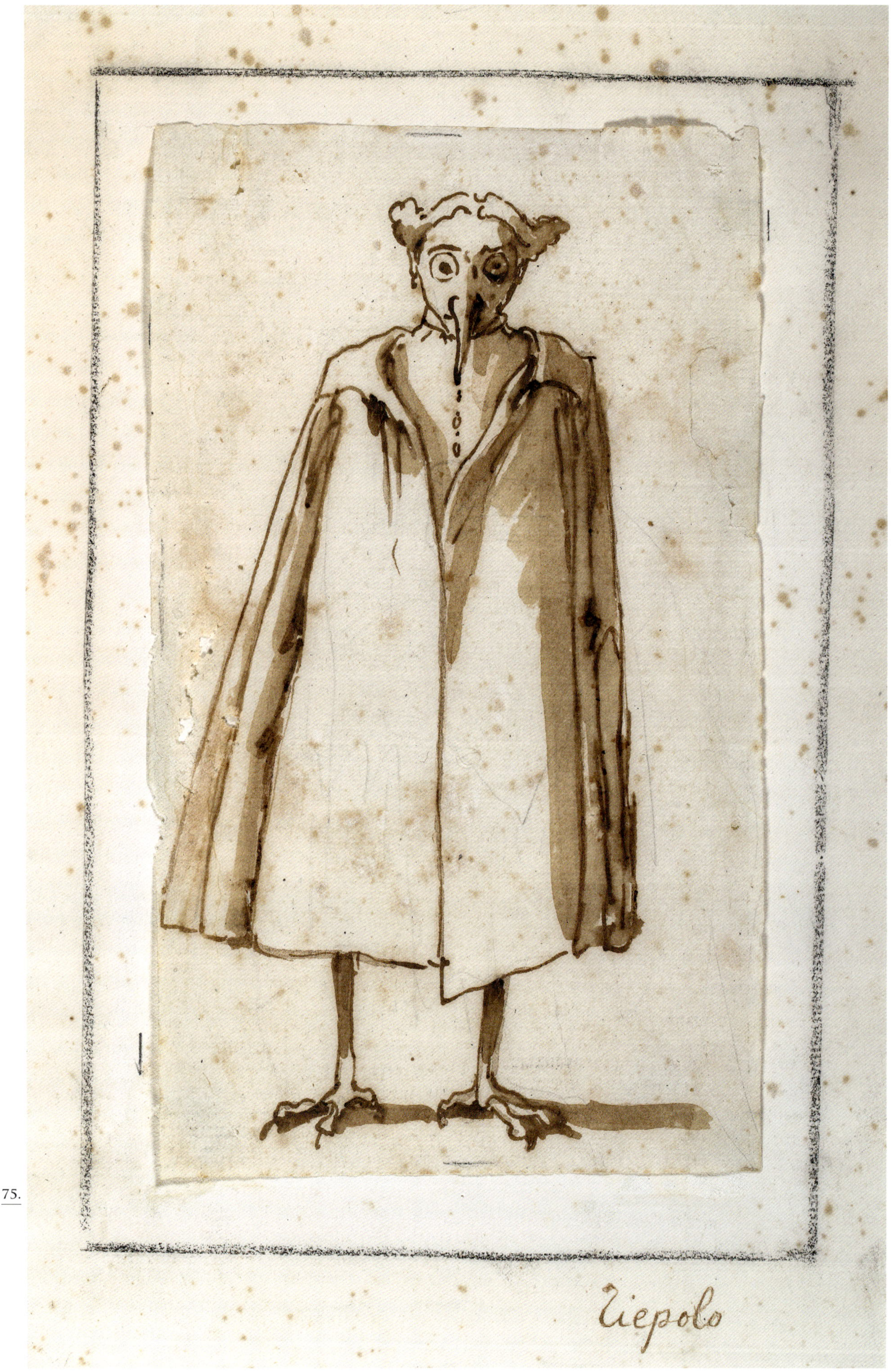

75.

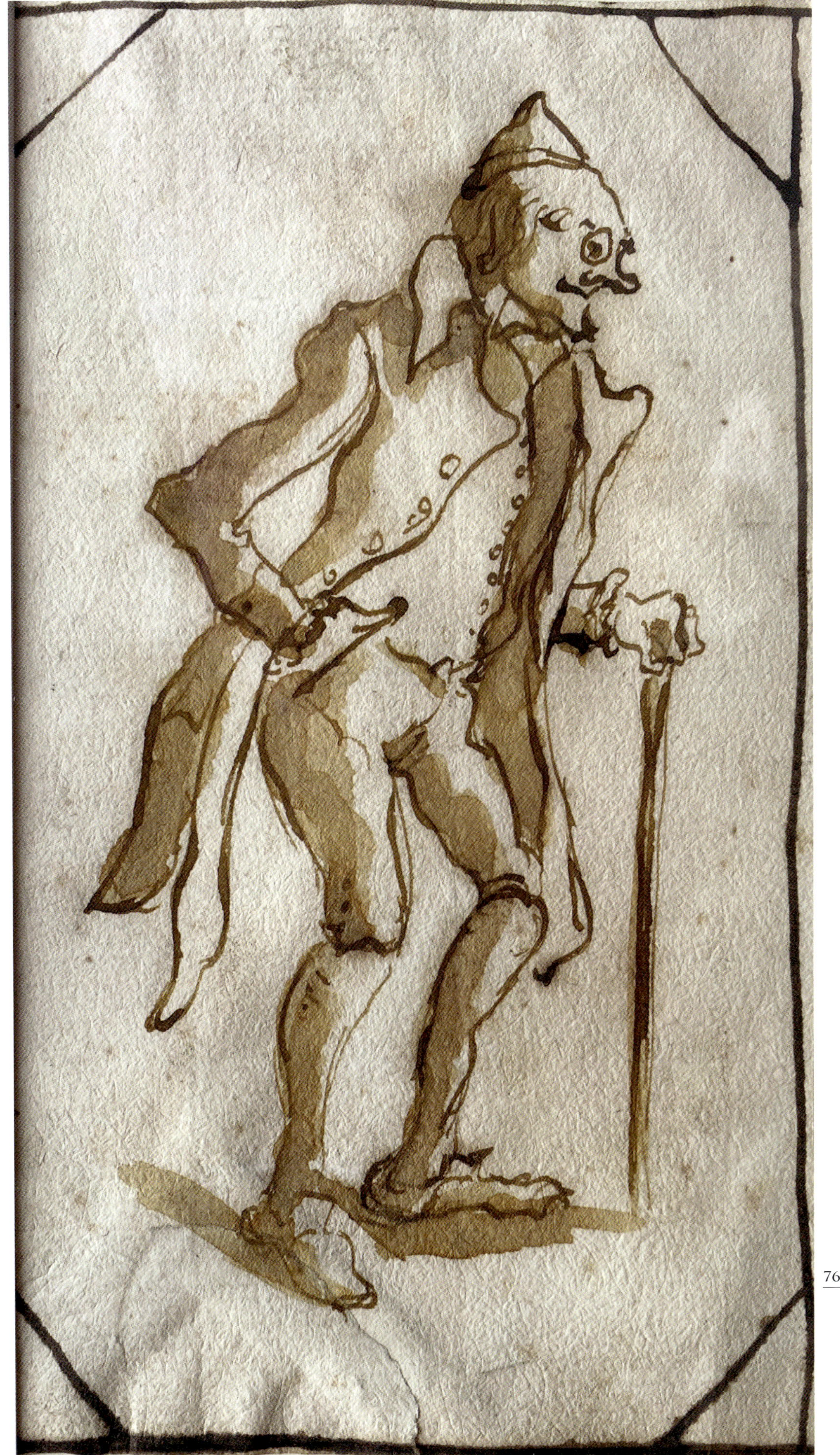

76.

trouser pocket. The accentuation of this detail is inconsistent with the work of Giambattista and also Giandomenico, to whom the drawing has been attributed. Taken with the generally mediocre execution both in the pen strokes and the wash shading, inconsistent and flat, this removes the work from the group of caricatures most closely linked to Tiepolo and his sons. For these reasons, it seems correct to judge it as the work of a later imitator, bearing testimony to the reception of these extraordinary graphic inventions, such as the *Pulcinella with a stick*, curiously assigned to the 'École vénitienne vers 1800, suiveur de Pier Leone Ghezzi', auctioned at the Hôtel Drouot in Paris by Thierry Maigret, on 20 May 2022, lot 56. It seems to rework in a minor key the same subject represented in the single sheet with the depiction of this figure in the *Tomo terzo de caricature* (see Knox, in Venice 2004, p. 106, no. 24).

EL

Bibliography
Unpublished.

77.

Gianantonio Guardi (1699–1760)
View from behind of a gentleman and lady standing, wearing the bauta,
second half of the sixth decade of the eighteenth century
Pen, graphite lines, sepia wash on paper, 212 × 160 mm, with frame in sepia ink close to the margin
Private collection

At the bottom left, in a badly damaged area of the paper, the inscription 'Guardi' is written in pen and ink, with the first three letters retraced. The name is repeated, in a better state, on the back of the sheet, just below the number '45' in graphite and diagonally towards the upper right-hand corner, visible in transparency on the recto above the gentleman's tricorn hat. It is similar to the 'signature (?)' of *Gianantonio Guardi* behind *The vision of St Rose* in the Hermitage (Morassi 1975, p. 84, no. 26) and the inscription 'eighteenth-century, but not autograph' of the *Venetian Admiral received by the Sultan* in Oxford (ibid., pp. 33, 99, no. 115). The present inscriptions were, however, considered erroneous (Scarpa 1983), and the work was assigned to Giambattista Tiepolo for its 'clear and confident handling' (Scarpa, in *Antichi disegni* 2005).

The masked couple appears several times in the catalogue of his son Giandomenico. Among his earliest paintings, they are found at the sides of a Pulcinella in the Brescian frescoes of 1754–5 (Cogliati Arano 1998, vol. I, pp. 426–7, vol. II, p. 141, fig. 14), in a mirror pose in the coeval *Tooth-Puller* in the Louvre (Loire 2017, pp. 342–4) and with other variations in the following series in the Museu de Arte in Barcelona (Mariuz 1971, pp. 111–12). Among the drawings, in addition to the *Charlatan* formerly in the Talleyrand collection (see Byam Shaw 1962, p. 87, no. 27), the *Group of figures in costume and two Pulcinellas* in Trieste, attributed to him, is associated with a sheet by Giambattista Piranesi in Hamburg dating from the latter's stay in Venice in 1745–7 (Knox, in Venice 2004, pp. 104–5, nos 20, 21), rather than an earlier stay in 1744 (Pavanello 2004, p. 23). The female figure with the fan and the mask on the tricorn hat, but accompanied by a Pulcinella, appears in the drawing by Giambattista formerly in the Plaut collection (Knox, in Knox 1970, no. 85) at the Morgan Library (inv. 1996.58), evoked for comparison with the work on display (Scarpa, in *Antichi disegni* 2005). This, however, is less rich in chiaroscuro, with the liquid ripples of the lines alien to Tiepolo's handling. These features lead the lettering to be reconsidered, even if apocryphal, and link the drawing to Guardi as a copyist also of drawings (see Barcham 2021), with comparisons with the *St. Sebastian* in the British Museum by Giovanni Segala and the replica in Vienna, with variations, of the 1757 ceiling by his brother-in-law for Ca' Rezzonico (see Morassi 1975, pp. 81, 87, nos 31, 45).

EL

Bibliography
Scarpa 1983, pp. 70, 76–7; Scarpa, in *Antichi disegni* 2005, pp. 172–3.

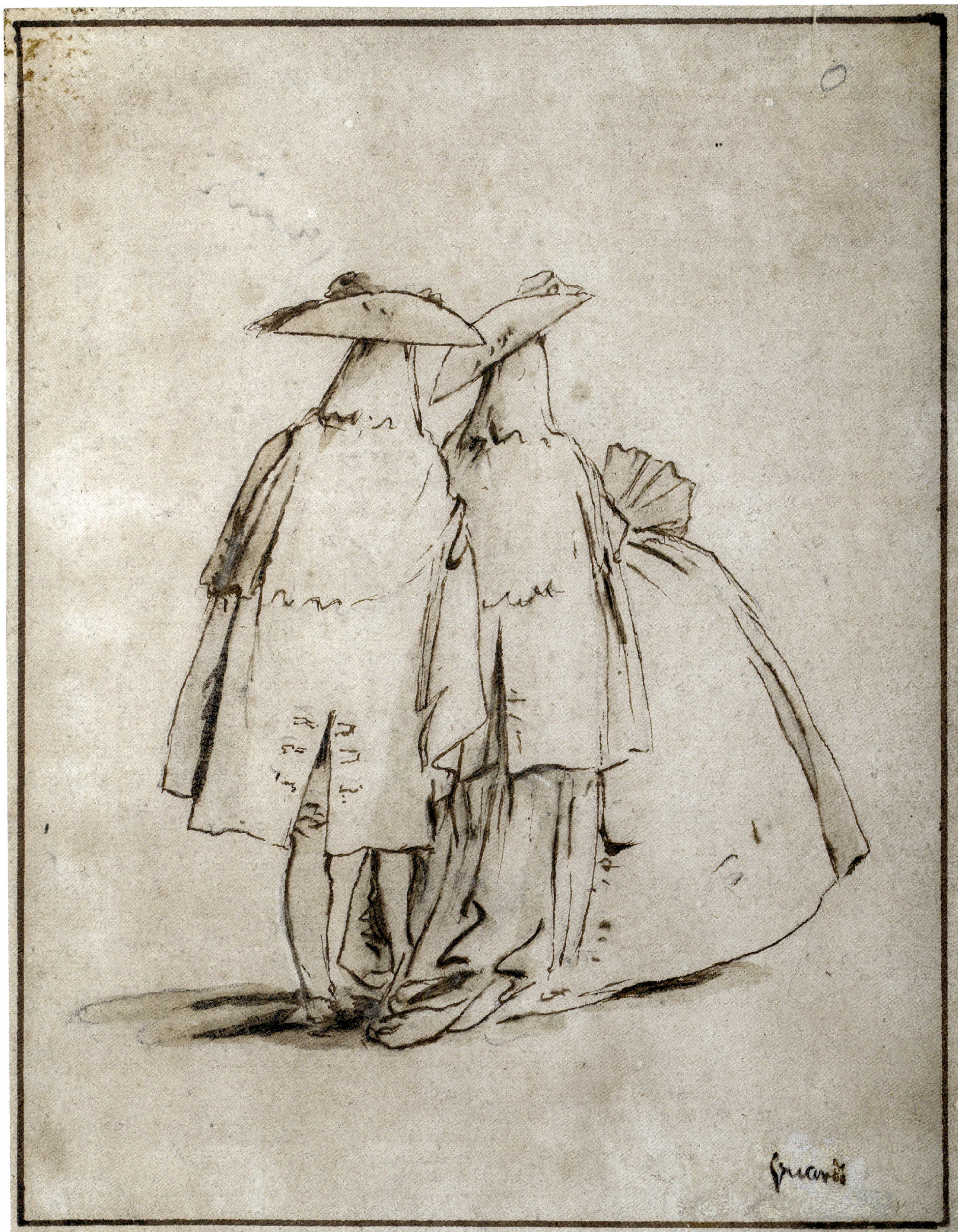

77.

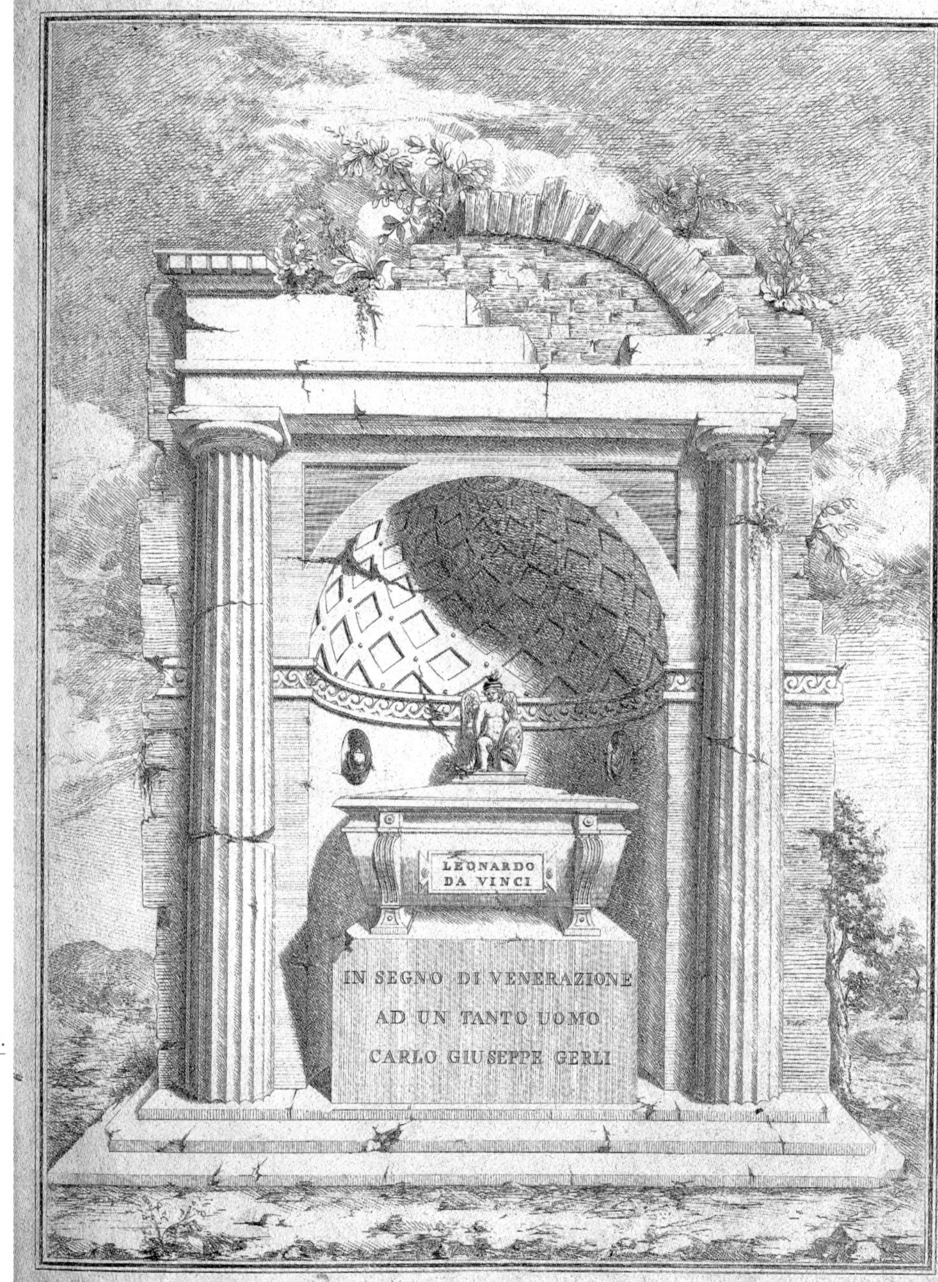

78.

78.
Carlo Giuseppe Gerli
Disegni di Leonardo da Vinci incisi e pubblicati da Carlo Giuseppe Gerli Milanese
Milan, Giuseppe Galeazzi regio stampatore, 1784
Paper volume, 448 × 293 mm
Milan, Castello Sforzesco, Ente Raccolta Vinciana, inv. B. Inf. 15

With the exception of the frontispiece, an original etching by the engraver depicting an imaginary funerary monument to Leonardo, the suite consists of sixty-one plates signed 'C. G. G. inc.' reproducing a selection of drawings also ascribed to Leonardo and distinguished by the monogram 'VL dis.', the latter not present on the original sheets and therefore probably the invention of the engraver. The first forty-five plates render drawings from the Biblioteca Ambrosiana (Cogliati Arano 1980b, pp. 113–25; Mara 2010, pp. 74–118), while the last sixteen engravings, distinguished by an asterisk next to the Roman numeral, derive from the drawings in the collection of Venanzio De Pagave, notable 'not by quantity but by incomparable merit' (Amoretti 1784a, p. 3). These sheets were later purchased by Giuseppe Bossi (1777–1815) and are now preserved at the Gallerie dell'Accademia in Venice (Nepi Sciré and Perissa Torrini 2003). The description of the individual plates, based on the advice of learned connoisseurs and collectors (Mara 2017, pp. 399–400), is the work of Carlo Amoretti (Amoretti 1784a; Amoretti 1784b). It explains the decision to engrave little-known drawings by Leonardo rather than the caricatures already widely represented by Hollar and Caylus (Amoretti 1784a, p. 3), although the presence of Leonardo's grotesque heads predominates, showing that this genre was generally admired by collectors and recognised as a distinctive trait of Leonardo's art. The simultaneous publication of the French translation of Amoretti's text assisted Gerli's collection to circulate more widely, especially by the rich selection of Leonardo's grotesque and caricatural heads. In this way they provided a figurative model for other artists, such as the engraver Carlo Lasinio of Treviso (1759–1838), who around 1790 used some of these profiles to form bizarre pairs of ridiculous characters (Alberici 1984b, p. 131, nos 202–4).

RA

Bibliography
Cogliati Arano 1980b, pp. 113–25; Cogliati Arano 1982, pp. 92–3, nos 1–30; Alberici 1984b, pp. 131–2, nos 190–94; Bora 1991, p. 208–12, fig. 14; Forcione, in Paris 2003, pp. 238–41, nos 76, 77; Mara 2017, pp. 395–407.

79.
Wenceslaus Hollar (1607–1667)
Characaturas by Leonardo da Vinci from Drawings by Wenceslaus Hollar out of the Portland Museum, published as the Act directs November 1 1786 by John Clarke, Antwerp [?], Portland Museum, 1786
Paper volume, 271 × 210 mm
Milan, Castello Sforzesco, Ente Raccolta Vinciana, inv. D.IV.1

Added to the Raccolta Vinciana in 1908, this book contains a selection of plates of Leonardo's 'teste caricate' by the Bohemian engraver Wenceslaus Hollar (1607–1677). Published in 1645 and reprinted in 1648 and then 1666, this collection was again published by John Clarke (1756–1815) in 1786.
Hollar was able to see Leonardo's originals (now Royal Collection, Windsor Castle) between 1636 and 1644, when he was in the service of the diplomat and collector Thomas Howard (1585–1646), 21st Earl of Arundel. The repertoire he composed contributed arouse renewed interest in Leonardo's studies of physiognomy in the English-speaking world (for which see the essay by Antonelli in this volume).

PC

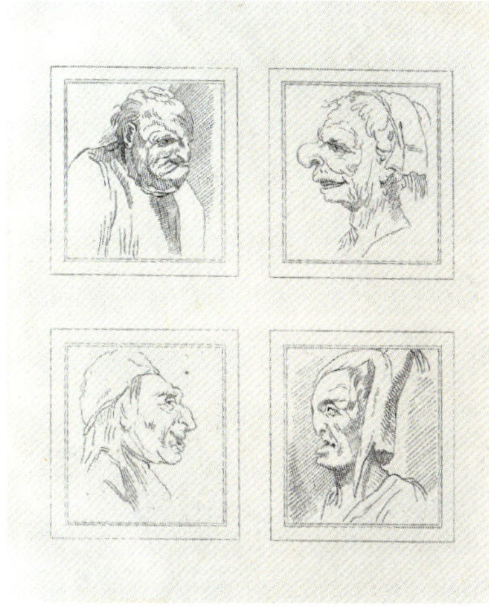

3. Wenceslaus Hollar, *Characaturas by Leonardo da Vinci from Drawings by Wenceslaus Hollar out of the Portland Museum*, Antwerp 1786

Bibliography
Elenco e analisi 1909, p. 36; Guerrini 1990, vol. I, p. 126; Pennington 1982, p. 272; Villata 2013, pp. 64–5, no. 19.

79.

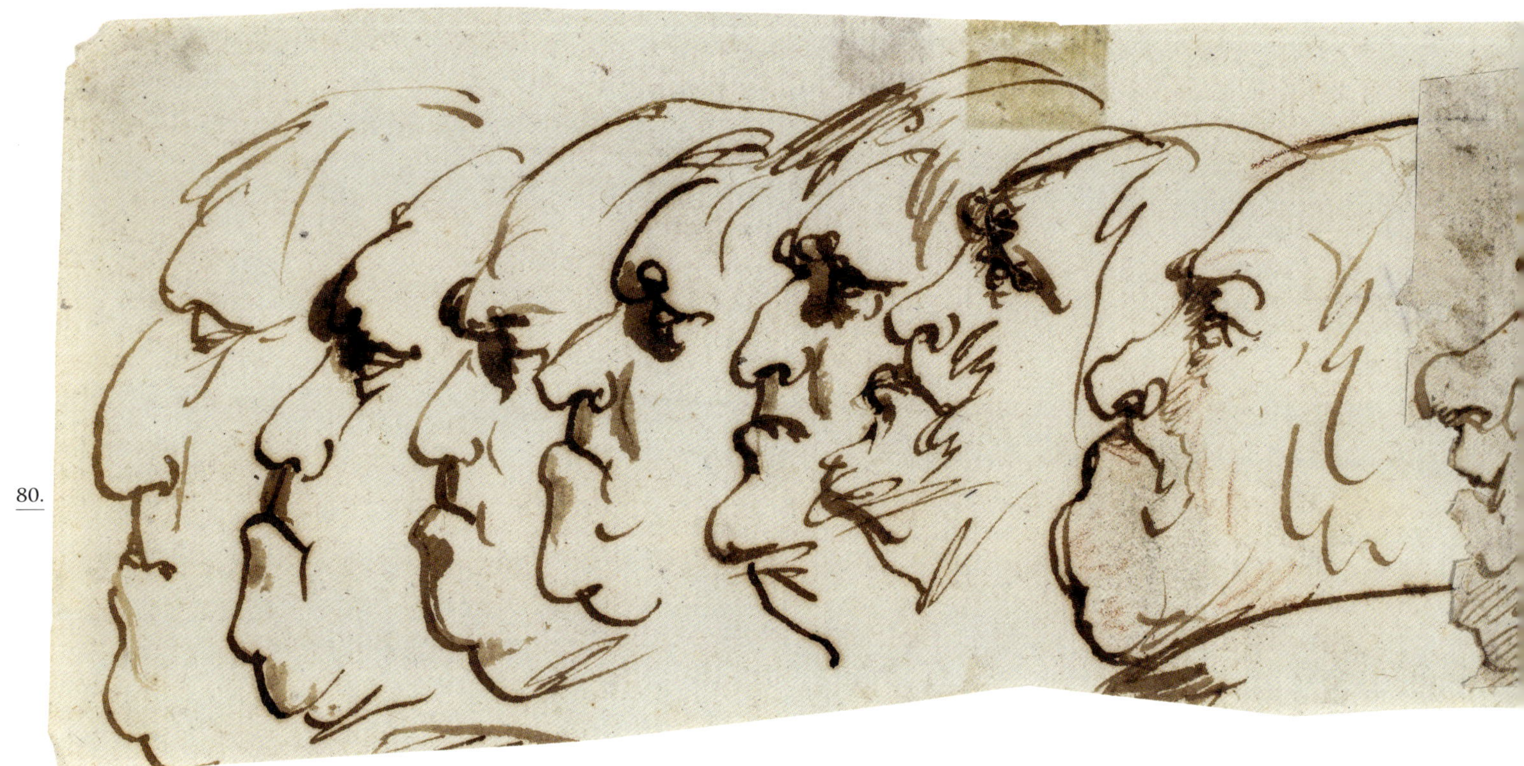

80.

81.

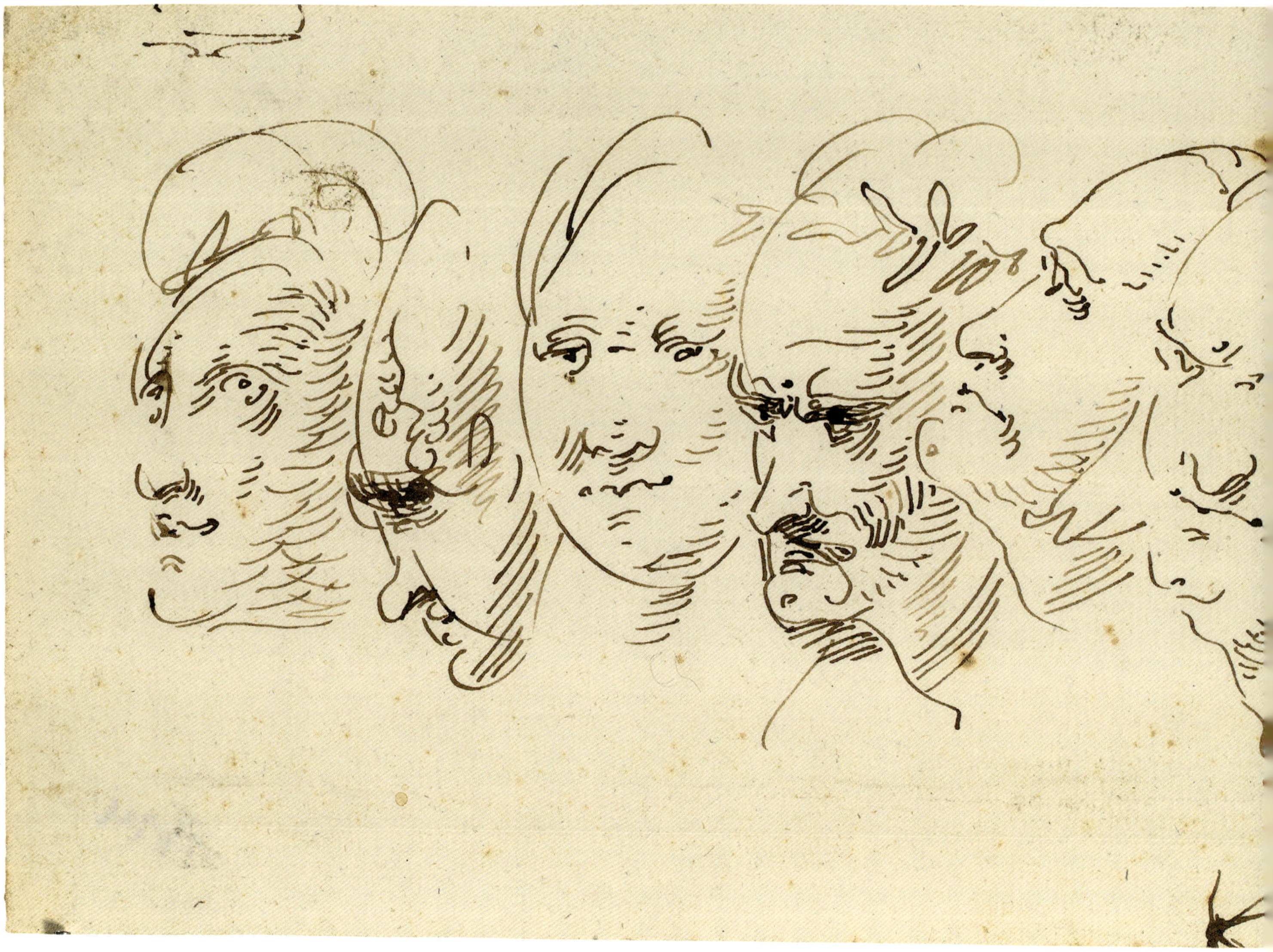

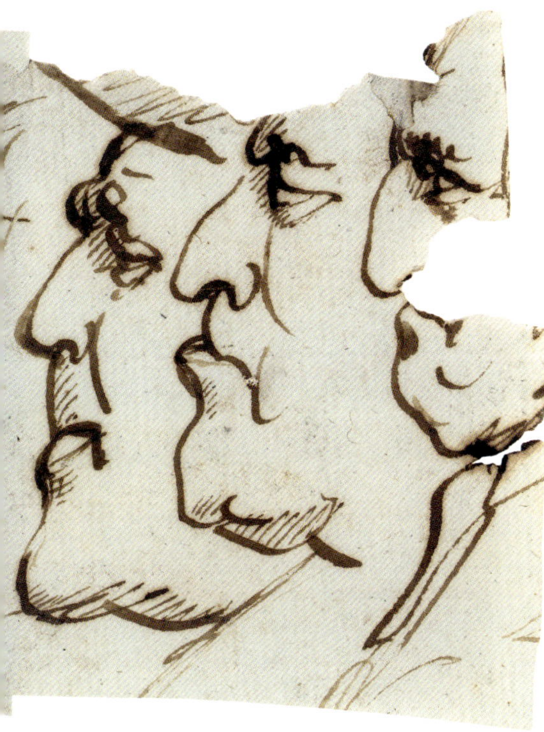

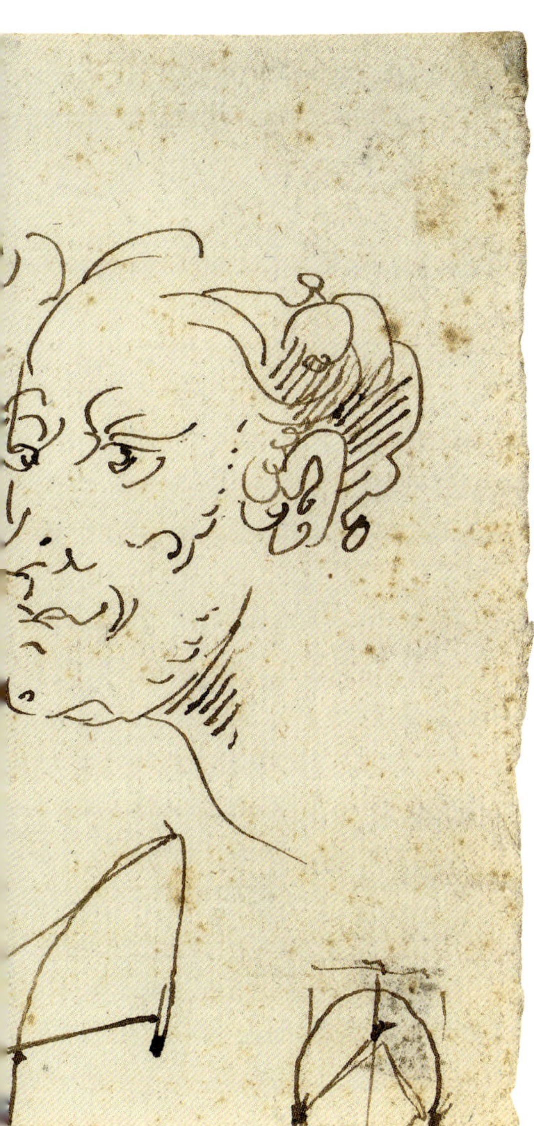

80.
Circle of Carlo Marchionni (1702–1786)
Eleven caricatural profiles of men, mid-eighteenth century
Pen and sepia on paper with red pencil highlights, 80 × 235 mm
Private collection

Two different strips of paper are pasted together to compose a single image. After the seventh face from the left, the only one that has red pencil highlights, the backing continues for a few millimetres to connect the next profile; its lower part has been cut out, from the nostrils to the chin, to ensure continuity in the sequence. The state of preservation is poor, especially in the right-hand section. The acidity of the ink has corroded parts of the last figure, which is not very legible, partly because of the tear that runs along the upper side, so deleting details of the figures in second-last (the forehead) and third-last (a broad-brimmed hat) place. The irregularity of the margins and lack of corners to the left suggest that originally the drawing may have been pasted over another sheet.
The work was published with an attribution to Pier Leone Ghezzi and compared with the Chatsworth *Procession* (*Antichi disegni* 2005). Despite the rapid handling in pen, the Chatsworth drawing (Jaffé 1994, p. 76) does not deviate from that 'firm and incisive line' (Prosperi Valenti Rodinò 2015, p. 39), absent from this work, that is characteristic of the Roman artist's work as a professional caricaturist, even in graphic works of very similar conception, such as the *Caricature of the organist Felicetto* of 1710 (Rostirolla 2001, pp. 274–5, no. 14).
Rather than a 'certain coarseness and formal heaviness' (*Antichi disegni* 2005), in the *Eleven profiles* we find a summary approach that can be compared to the series of faces and variations that Marchionni, bearing in mind the model of Ghezzi (Prosperi Valenti Rodinò 2015, p. 63), created in his sketches from life, 'on pieces of paper of all kinds 'and with an 'informal and anti-academic spirit'. He concentrated on capturing ridiculous details 'through a cinematographic succession of the same face' (ibid., p. 76), a method that sometimes went so far as to alter the features (Debenedetti 2016, pp. 28–32), attaining results of comic vividness not unlike those of the drawing. This can therefore be considered a product of Roman figurative culture in the mid-eighteenth century, influenced by the taste for caricature of the architect of Villa Albani.

EL

Bibliography
Antichi disegni 2005, pp. 128–9.

81.
Giuseppe Bernardino Bison (1762–1844)
Seven heads, 1800–31
Pen and sepia ink on paper, 119 × 239 mm
Private collection
[work not on display]

On the back of the sheet, in the middle in pencil, 'Bison' is written in modern cursive, probably the same hand that wrote again in pencil, in the lower right-hand corner, inverted in relation to the previous wording, the figure '3000'. Although abraded, the black ink stamp in the upper right-hand corner is identifiable as that of the collection of the Udinese physician and writer on art Tito Miotti (1913–2002), important for the many drawings by Bison. It consists of a rampant lion holding a flower within a circle (Lugt 4259). It is placed not far from the initial 'B.' followed by a full stop, which seems to have been written in the sepia of the drawing on the recto and in the known writing of the painter. Exhibited in Udine in 1962, the work was recorded by Aldo Rizzi (1976) as still in the Miotti collection at Tricesimo in Friuli, but this provenance is no longer mentioned by Scarpa (*Antichi disegni* 2005).
With the ease of touch typical of this master, who worked at the turning point between two centuries and two civilisations, the sheet depicts a row of faces juxtaposed with different facial expressions without any real caricatural purpose but expressive of 'character'. While respecting Emilian and Venetian iconographic precedents, the drawing belongs to the neoclassical aesthetic, in which

'simplicity, elegance and correctness exclude excess, the *grotesque*' (Milizia 1797, vol. I, p. 158).

EL

Bibliography

Rizzi 1962, p. 68; Rizzi 1976, p. 37, no. 121; Scarpa, in *Antichi disegni* 2005, pp. 128–9.

82.

Pietro Antonio Novelli (1729–1804)
Sixteen figures, last decade
of the eighteenth century
Pen and sepia ink on paper clipped at
the corners, 93 × 145 mm
Private collection

The caricatural aspect of the composition, noted in the previous entry, seems to be present with various degrees of attenuation in only seven (almost all in the front row) of these figures, three depicted half-length, the others only with their faces turned to our left, except for the one in profile at the other end of the sheet. Some of them wear ruffs, one couple wear conical hats rather lower than the one worn by Pulcinella, a character represented by Novelli in a drawing formerly in the Rutishauser collection (Favilla and Rugolo 2006, p. 206). Rather than caricatures, the figures could be better understood as 'character heads' or fantasy heads, a case that would explain the influence of 'possible north-European figurative prototypes' (Scarpa, in *Antichi disegni* 2005). This appears in the second row of the group, reflecting the reception of Rembrandt in eighteenth-century Venetian figurative taste, which Pietro Antonio Novelli also explored – for example, in a pair of sheets in Warsaw (Mrozinska, in Mrozinska 1958, pp. 62–3, nos 70, 71). Moreover, oblique and cross-hatching to render shadows reveal the artist's practice as an engraver. In this field, his reversed graphic reproductions of Jacques Callot's dwarfs are also known, completed 'with captions of burlesque verses, salacious and frequently scurrilous' (Tomezzoli 2005, pp. 136–7). They were composed by the painter, who also wrote playful poetic verses (see Rigoli 1983). According to his friend Giuseppe Avelloni, 'he was also very charming in describing the caricatures of some figures, both real and fabulous' (in Favilla and Rugolo 2006, p. 206). To the last category seem to belong the figures crowded onto the sheet on display, some corpulent to the point of overwhelming monstrosity. Their mocking and hostile tone makes them seem, rather than heirs of the Tiepolesque caricatures, images taken from disturbing nightmares at the dawn of the contemporary age.

EL

Bibliography

Scarpa, in *Antichi disegni* 2005, pp. 124–5.

83.

Carlo Lasinio (1759–1838)
Grotesque couple with a man
with a long nose, c. 1790–1800
Colour etching, 262 × 190 mm
Milan, Castello Sforzesco, Ente
Raccolta Vinciana, inv. ERV 768

84.

Carlo Lasinio (1759–1838)
Pair of grotesque heads, c. 1790–1800
Colour etching, 370 × 260 mm
Milan, Castello Sforzesco, Ente
Raccolta Vinciana, inv. ERV 764

85.

Carlo Lasinio (1759–1838)
Two grotesque heads of an old woman
and man, c. 1790–1800
Colour etching, 373 × 262 mm
Milan, Castello Sforzesco, Ente
Raccolta Vinciana, inv. ERV 767

These three etchings come from a rare and extraordinary series of twelve colour plates by the engraver Carlo Lasinio of Treviso (1759–1838), each depicting a pair of Leonardo's grotesque profiles. Studying the ten copies in the Raccolta Bertarelli in Milan (Albo E 169, plates 1–10) belonging to this series, Clelia Alberici identified the collection of engravings by Carlo Giuseppe Gerli (*Disegni di Leonardo da Vinci incisi e pubblicati da Carlo Giuseppe Gerli milanese*), published in Milan in 1784, as the model used by Lasinio (Alberici 1984b, pp. 131–2). Distinguished by a number placed at the top right, the three specimens here correspond to plates 1, 3 and 6 and belong to a group of five engravings in the Ente Raccolta Vinciana (Villata, in Villata 2013, p. 25, ill. p. 21; Marani 2017, p. 193, fig. 12), which includes the two missing specimens from the Bertarelli series, namely plates 9 and 10. Each panel presents two profiles facing each other, one female and one male, all attributed to Leonardo da Vinci. The two figures (except for plate 6 which has been trimmed) are matched with two witty comments with a burlesque and allusive tone on the beauty and joys of marriage that are rather droll considering the figures' obvious physical deformities. The etching technique used by Lasinio, perfected by the French artist Jacques-Fabien Gautier d'Agoty (1716–1785), made it possible to produce coloured prints by pulling copies from multiple plates for each colour (Cassinelli Lazzeri 2004, p. XIII). This gave the etching a watercolour effect whose chromatic range could vary in the individual figures of the couples depicted. It can be observed how the fields of colour in the clothes and headgear (brilliant and perfectly preserved in these examples) are highly varied and diversified, even in relation to the same subject, as shown by comparison with the six plates sold by Gonnelli in 2020 (*Stampe disegni & dipinti Libri, manoscritti & autografi*, Libreria Antiquaria Gonnelli, auction no. 28, 26–8 May 2020, lot 179), and the eleven plates recently sold by Bassenge (*Druckgraphik des 15. bis 19. Jahrhunderts*, Bessange, 1 June 2022, lot 5264).
As already indicated by Alberici, Lasinio was a 'copyist' of the grotesque heads engraved by Gerli (1984, pp. 131–2), deriving his subjects faithfully from those present in the Milanese suite and described by Carlo Amoretti (1784b, pp. 9–16). Amoretti himself observed that Leonardo, dissatisfied with the strangeness of the heads, increased their ridiculousness 'with the dress, with the headgear above all, and with the hairstyles adapted to the character of the

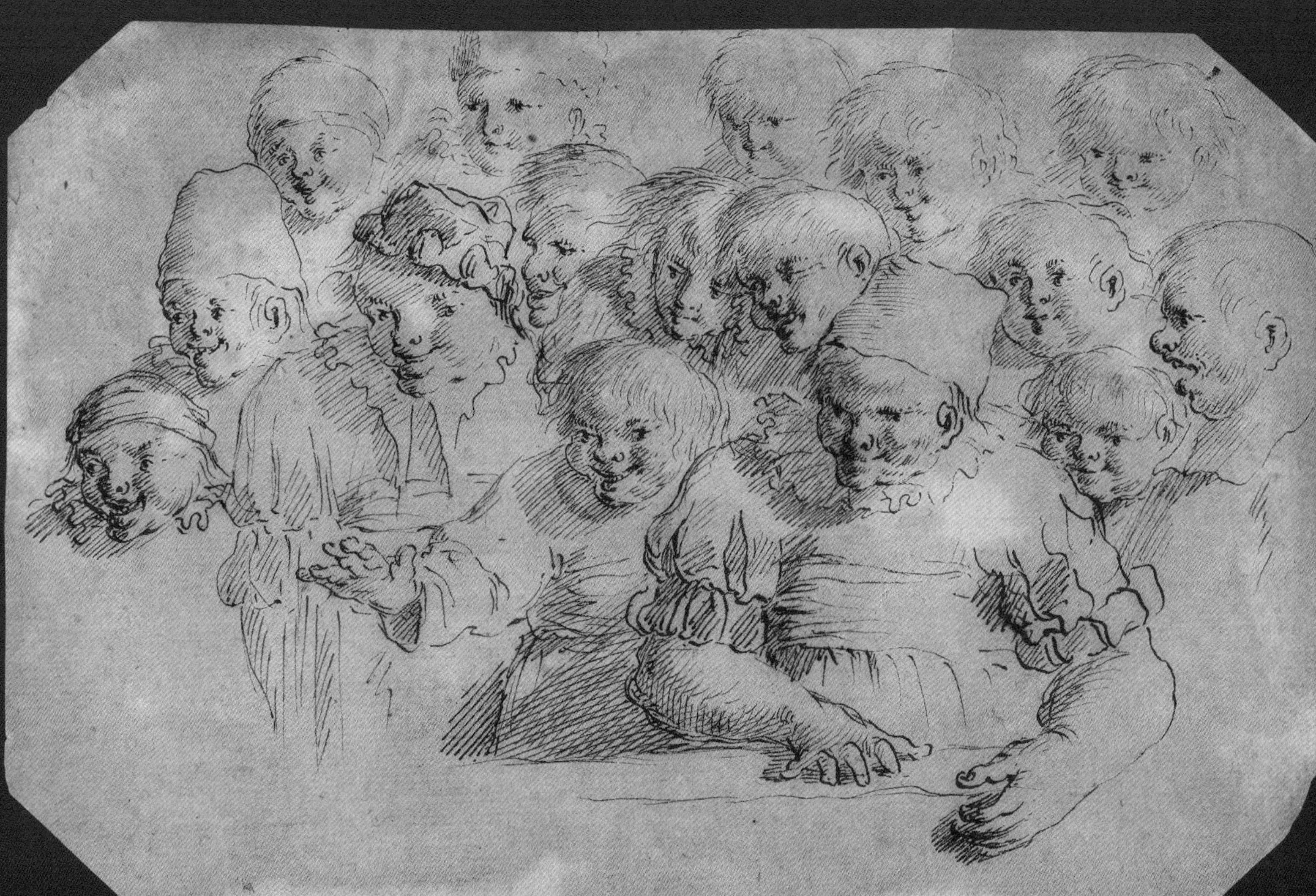

82.

83.

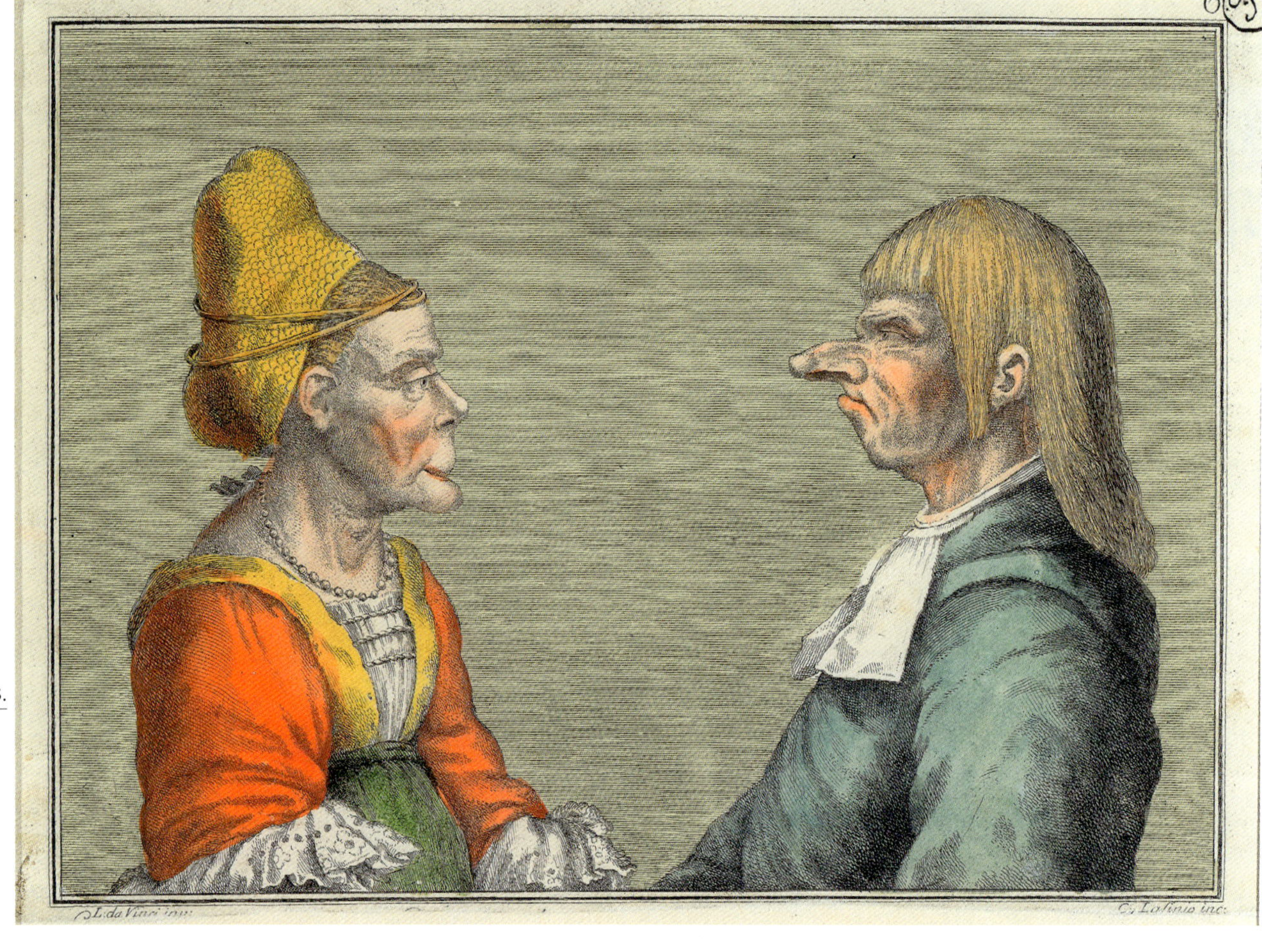

face' (Amoretti 1784b, p. 10). It is precisely these aspects that Lasinio accentuated and ridiculed in the assortment of his loving couples. For example, the hat of the figure in plate 1 (inv. ERV, 764) with an odd hanging feather and armour, is included by Gerli in plate XIX as a translation of the drawing in cod. F 274 inf. 40 recto in the Ambrosiana. This figure is matched with the female figure reversed present in Gerli's plate XVII and derived from the drawing cod. F 274 inf. 41 verso in the Ambrosiana. The figure is reinterpreted by Lasinio in his characterisation of the bust opposite, while taking some hints from Hollar's engraving of the same subject. Hence the differences between Lasinio's etching and Gerli's (seen in the greater characterisation of the deformities of mouths and noses and in the particular care in the rendering of the garments, which in the female forms barely conceal the deformed physique) reflect a certain harmony with Hollar's engravings, which circulated widely and were republished by John Clarke (1756–1815) in 1786. Then the two elderly figures in plate 3 (inv. ERV 767) are significantly paired with the licentious motto 'And we do everything between ourselves', despite their combined age of 160. This comes close to the double meaning in the motto missing from plate 6 (inv. ERV 768), which alludes to the husband's long nose. Of this series, finally, it is worth mentioning the circulation of non-coloured specimens, such as the six plates in the Museo Civico of Udine (inv. 1949 S–1954 S, plates 1–6), not recorded in registers devoted to the artist, like the series presented here. Depending on the technique used, in stylistic terms, the production of Lasinio's plates based on Leonardo could be close to the suite printed in Florence in c. 1790–95 of the *Dodici ritratti di persone facete che servano a divertire il pubblico fiorentino* (Alberici 1984b, p. 131), also related to the theme of ridicule and known both in a coloured version (*à la poupée*) and black and white (Cassinelli Lazzeri 2004, p. XVIII). A certain correspondence, at least thematically, should also be sought in the suite *Lo sposalizio di Marfisa*, ten unbound plates without a frontispiece drawn by Giuseppe Piattoli (1748–1834). Here the figures with their 'grotesque faces set on tiny bodies' are related to a popular tradition in the genre running from Callot and Baccio del Bianco to Ghezzi and Zanetti (Berra 2009, pp. 120–21), while revealing certain thematic and stylistic similarities with William Hogarth as well as Gian Domenico Tiepolo (D'Amelio 2015, p. 54).

RA

Bibliography

Alberici 1984b, pp. 131–2; Alberici 1984a, pp. 139–10, nos 202–4; Villata 2013, p. 25, ill. p. 21; Marani 2017, p. 192, fig. 12.

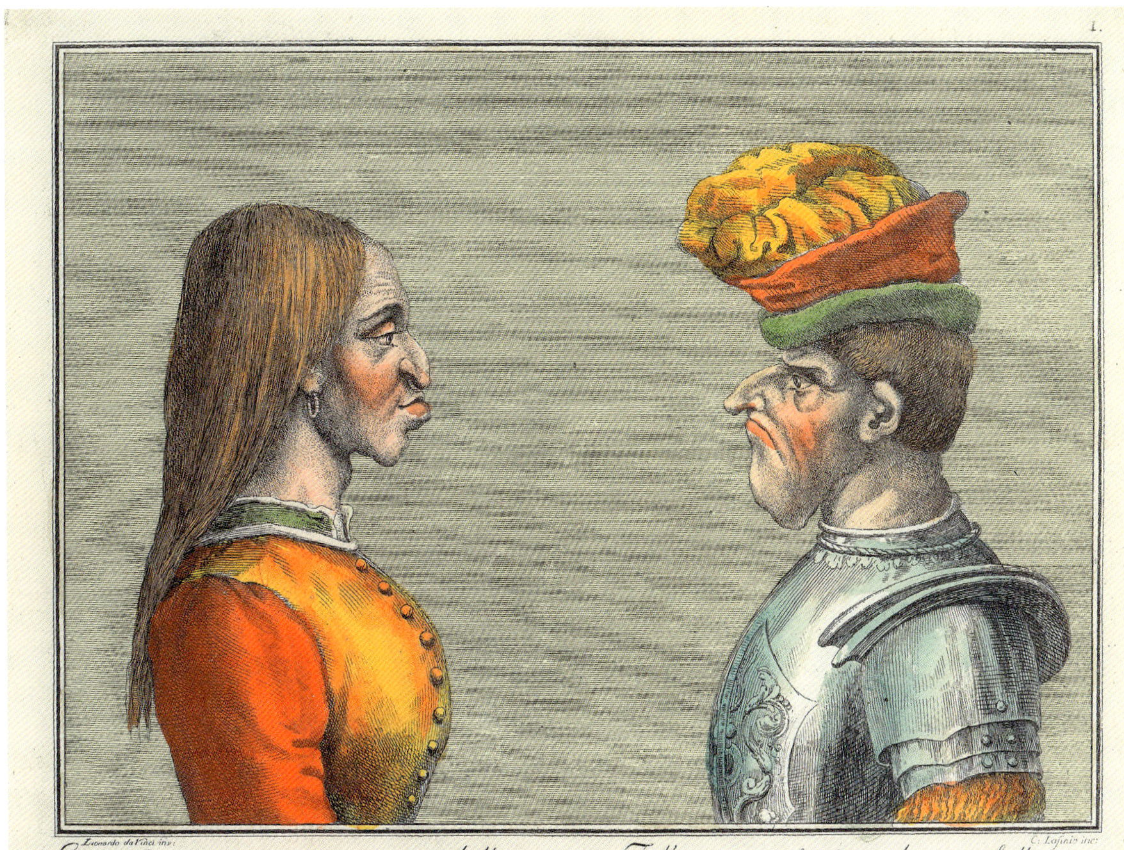
1.
Leonardo da Vinci inv:
C. Lasinio inc:
Io Son Guerrierò non temer mia bella;
Difenderò la tua beltade in campo:
Tu l'Amor mio sarai, tu la mia Stella,
Ed io per te sarò fulmine e lampo.

84.

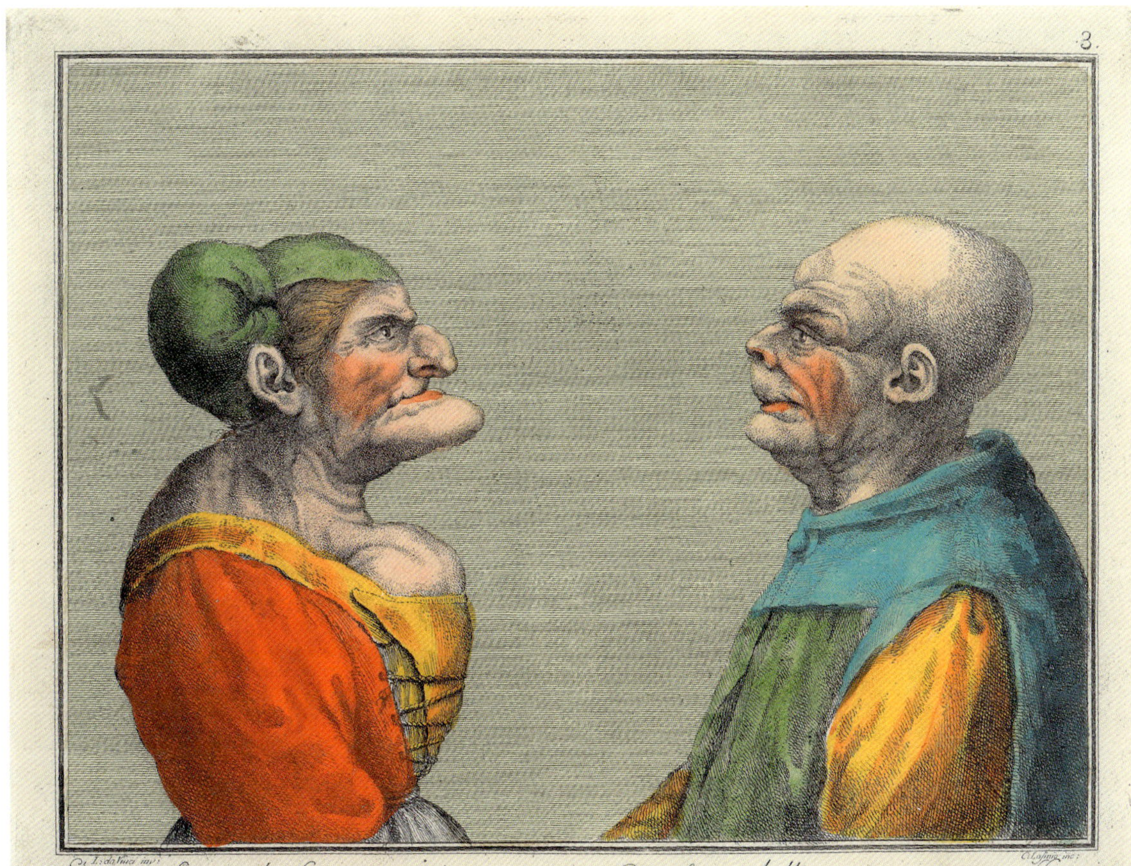
3.
L. da Vinci inv:
C. Lasinio inc:
E vero, o Sposa, che fra me, e voi
Abbiamo in tutti due censessantanni;
Ma siamo belli ancora, e senza affanni,
E ogni cosa facciamo fra di noi.

85.

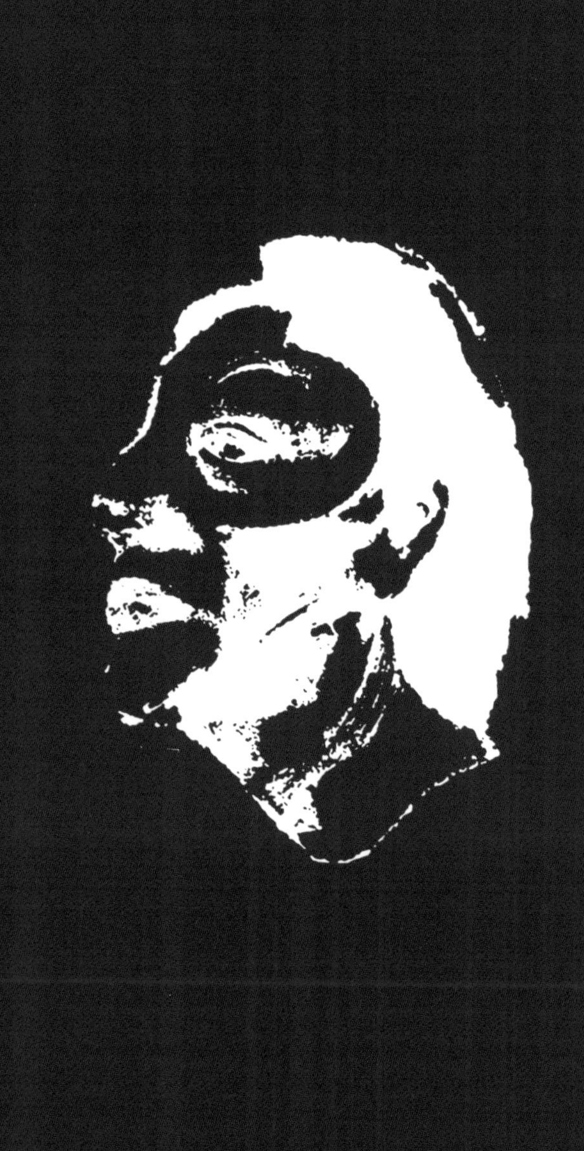

Bacon's Metamorphoses

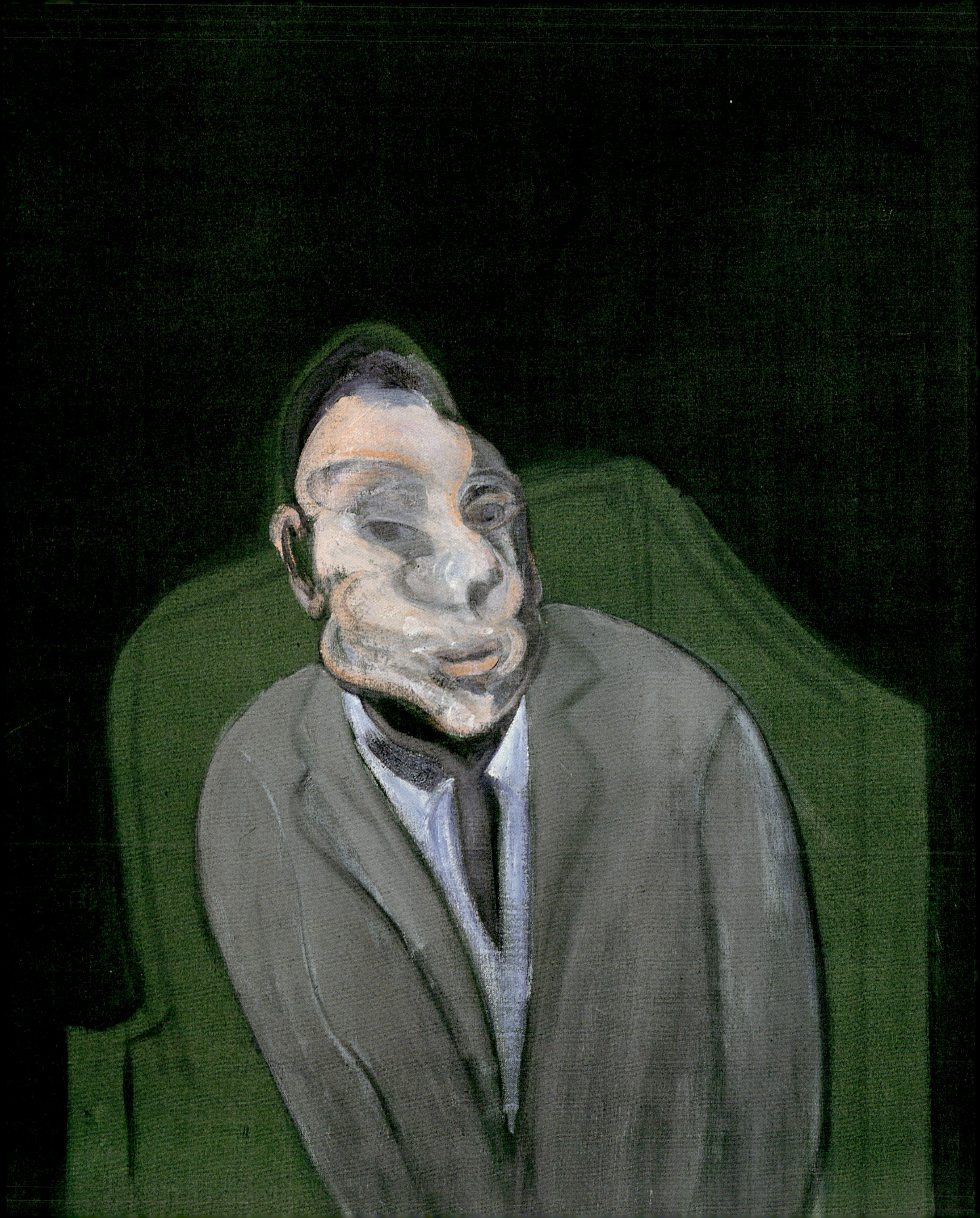

Calvin Winner

Francis Bacon's Portraiture: An Act of Portrayal

This short essay explores Francis Bacon's engagement with portraiture, an artistic genre of rich and ancient tradition. Francis Bacon (1909–1992) painted a range of subjects memorialising those closest to him, from small head studies to large-scale triptychs. Collectively, these works question traditional definitions of the genre and blur the boundaries of realism, expressionism, figuration and abstraction. Bacon's portraits were never concerned with likeness and even less that they might flatter the sitter. On the contrary, he was nervous about what he described as the 'injury' he might inflict on his intended subjects. 'I terribly don't want to make freaks', he once said.[1] Nor did they have the *joie de vivre* of a Cubist portrait by Picasso, playfully depicting one of his lovers. Bacon strived to make portraits as intense psychological exercises in the manner of Rembrandt. He understood that it was a fruitless and even a hopeless task in the wake of Modernism. And yet, like Rembrandt, he wanted to capture the essence or, rather, the presence of his subject – something beyond surface appearance or a mimetic likeness. In Bacon's case, portraits could also be physiological in their exploration of the body and more specifically the human head. Bacon was prepared to distort, even brutalise the image far from everyday appearance. This in his mind only served to bring it back to a recording of the appearance and 'onto the fact more violently'.

His subject for portraits included artist friends such as Lucian Freud and Isabel Rawsthorne. Importantly, there was also the confessional portrayal of long-term relationships – Peter Lacy in the 1950s, George Dyer in the 60s and John Edwards in the 70s and 80s. In addition, he made an extensive exploration of the female body through his friend and model Henrietta Moraes. Further to these was the close circle of friends, collectors, writers or acquaintances, such as Lisa and Robert Sainsbury, Michel Leiris, Muriel Belcher and John Hewett. Their portraits serve us now as a window into the biography of the artist, and through portraiture we share his loves, his despair, grief and pain. With very few exceptions (particularly Robert and Lisa Sainsbury), Bacon preferred to work from photographs, and in the case of Moraes, prints that Bacon commissioned

OPPOSITE
Francis Bacon
Head of a Man (Self-Portrait), 1960
Norwich, Sainsbury Centre for Visual Arts, University of East Anglia, inv. UEA 35

from the photographer John Deakin. Bacon explained how he frequently chose to distance himself from his sitters, painting from photographs and memory, so that he could be free and less inhibited by the presence of what were most often his closest friends. In this way he felt he was protecting his subject from any perceived 'injury' that he might inflict through his expressive interpretation.[2] This gave him the freedom to distort and not be restricted to capturing a polite likeness. Michel Leiris in 1967 described his portraits as carrying the signs of his actions rather as a person's flesh bears the scars of an accident or an attack.[3] This was a form of caricature that served to return the sitter to the fact in a more intense form of realism. Drawing on the art of the past, Bacon often made responses to portraits by earlier artists, for example Velázquez, Rembrandt, Van Gogh and William Blake, which pay homage while at the same time challenging assumptions of what a portrait was or could be.

Bacon used the term 'portrait' or sometimes 'study' tentatively in titles. His first identified portrait, painted in 1951, was of his friend the artist Lucian Freud. Soon after he started a series of seven paintings known as the *Man in Blue*. His 1955 portrait of Robert Sainsbury followed this format of the anonymous man in blue. The suit has no colour other than the ground, so that only the ghostly face, shirt and tie emerge from the darkness, as he summoned the spirit of the sitter. The portrait of Robert Sainsbury was the only time Bacon agreed to a commission, in this instance from Lisa Sainsbury. The series of portraits of Lisa herself take a more hieratical form, verging on a pharaonic appearance. Peter Lacy was Bacon's partner from 1952 until his decline and death in 1962. Their relationship was complicated, at times violent. Lacy is often portrayed confident and alert as Bacon explored the physicality of his body. However, there are also more tender and intimate portrayals of Lacy sleeping. George Dyer, Bacon's partner for the rest of the 1960s, became the subject of perhaps Bacon's greatest exploration of masculinity and the male body. Most significant are the series in memorial known as the 'Black Triptychs' (1972–4), imbued with tragedy after Dyer's death in 1971. John Edwards became a prominent subject from the mid-1970s until Bacon's death in 1992.

Three Studies for Portrait of Isabel Rawsthorne, 1965 (Norwich, University of East Anglia, Sainsbury Centre) is one of twenty paintings of this artist friend. Although they had known each since 1946, Bacon did not make his first painting of Isabel until 1961 and then painted her more frequently in the mid-1960s. Their friendship was deep, lasting and may even have been intimate. The portraits of Isabel demonstrate his virtuoso manipulation of flesh through the medium of oil paint. His concentration on the face lends an intensity to the subject through the expressive paintwork, as if the skin has been flayed and flesh laid bare. Image and paint become impossible to separate or, as Bacon explained, 'A complete interlocking of image and paint, so that the image is the paint and vice versa. Here the brushstroke creates the form and does not simply fill it in'.[4]

The portraits of Henrietta Moraes reveal Bacon's confidence and mastery in large-scale triptychs.

It is in the portrait studies of Moraes where we see perhaps his greatest exploration of the female body. They are also some of Bacon's most brutal attacks on the human body – vulnerable and truncated bodies that writhe and squirm and whose strange beauty is a guilt-ridden pleasure. Such large-scale compositions allowed Bacon fully to explore the physiology of the body. In contrast, the small and intense triptychs focus solely on the head as disembodied apparition in a succession of small canvases of floating heads, sightly under life-size, that he painted from the beginning of the 1960s. The self-portrait, which had captivated the masters Bacon most admired, was explored periodically. Often small and intense they focus solely on the face, which he stated he 'loathed'. In one of the many interviews with the artist recorded by the critic David Sylvester, Bacon characteristically explained away self-portraits as something of a last resort, stating: 'people around me have been dying like flies and I've nobody else left to paint but myself'.[5] This of course is a partial truth yet nevertheless they are an ultimate expression of his commitment to a new kind of portraiture. Bacon's first acknowledged self-portrait appeared in the mid-1950s. Thereafter portraits became a central theme for the artist, one to which he returned again and again. Most often they were painted with the aid of photographs, or in the case of self-portraits a mirror: 'I look at myself in the mirror', he remarked to David Sylvester. They were a daily reminder of aging and time, as Bacon liked to recall Cocteau's remark: 'Each day in the mirror I watch death at work.'

[1] Francis Bacon quoted in John Russell, *Francis Bacon*, rev. and updated ed. (London: Thames and Hudson, 1993), p. 99.

[2] David Sylvester, *The Brutality of Fact: Interviews with Francis Bacon* (London: Thames and Hudson, 1990), p. 41.

[3] *Francis Bacon: Recent Paintings*, 1967, text by Michel Leiris (London: Marlborough Fine Art, 1967), p. 17.

[4] Bacon quoted in *Matthew Smith: Paintings from 1909 to 1952* (London: Tate Gallery, 1953), p. 12.

[5] Sylvester, *Brutality of Fact*, p. 129.

86.
Francis Bacon (1909–1992)
Three Studies for Portrait of Isabel Rawsthorne, 1965
Oil on canvas, triptych,
47 × 115.5 cm in all
Norwich, Sainsbury Centre for Visual Arts, University of East Anglia,
inv. UEA 37

This painting was purchased by Robert and Lisa Sainsbury from Marlborough Fine Art, London, in 1965. It was donated by them to the Sainsbury Centre, University of East Anglia, in 1973 as part of the original gift to the Centre. There is an inscription on the back of the left canvas, '3 studies of portrait Isabel Rawsthorne 1965', in Francis Bacon's hand.
Three Studies for Portrait of Isabel Rawsthorne is one of twenty paintings by Bacon in which his friend Isabel Rawsthorne is the subject. Some are full-length portraits while others are smaller diptychs and triptychs, sometimes with multiple sitters. This example was the first triptych, of which he went on to produce five (three including this one in 1965 alone). Bacon and Isabel spent a great deal of time together in 1965, the year Alberto Giacometti, Isabel's friend, was in London for his first Tate Gallery exhibition (Winner 2016, p. 75). This painting was one of two that Bacon showed at his exhibition at the Marlborough that year. Two years later, in 1967, Bacon displayed six portraits of Isabel at his next Marlborough exhibition. In the 1960s she and Henrietta Moraes succeeded Lisa Sainsbury as Bacon's most important female sitters.
The triptych presents three views of Isabel: frontal in the centre panel, turned towards the centre in the left panel and in profile facing left in the right panel. Photographs of Isabel by John Deakin now in the Francis Bacon Studio Archive (Hugh Lane Gallery, Dublin) demonstrate how Bacon could physically manipulate photographs of the sitter, selectively torn, creased, folded and crumpled, distorting the features in ways that Bacon could transfer to paint. But despite the distortions it is remarkable how he was able to retain a likeness of his subject. The painting shows Bacon at the height of his powers, combining masterly technique while locking in the essence of the sitter. The application of paint and brushwork is assured and confident, often showing the imprint of a cloth. Each canvas has pinholes at each corner, suggesting that they were painted prior to stretching. The small-scale triptych of heads became an established format in the 1960s and Bacon went on to produce more than forty, claiming that he was inspired by police file photographs (Jacobi 2020, p. 235). As well as Isabel, a number of other close friends were painted in this format, including his partner George Dyer, Lucian Freud, John Hewitt, Henrietta Moraes and Muriel Belcher. Bacon confessed that 'I see every image all the time in a shifting way and almost in shifting sequence (Sylvester 2003, p. 20, interview I, 1962). He tended to use photographs taken by Deakin as source material rather than working from life, commenting to David Sylvester that, 'I find it easier to work [from photographs] than actually having their presence in the room' (Sylvester 2003, p. 36).
Isabel Rawsthorne (née Nicholas) was an artist and friend of Bacon, whom she had known since the 1940s. She attended Liverpool Art School and won a scholarship to the Royal Academy Schools. In London, she met the sculptor Jacob Epstein, entered his household as a studio assistant and modelled for him. Determined to be an artist in her own right, she left London for Paris. In 1935, she met Alberto Giacometti and they quickly became close friends, resulting in the first sculpture bust of her made in 1936 (Winner 2016, p. 57). Isabel's remarkable beauty was both an asset and a distraction from her own

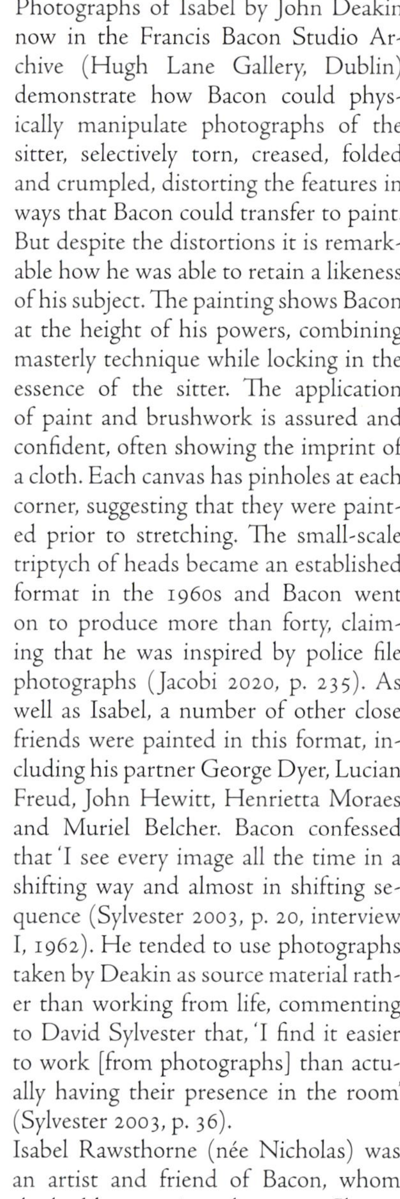

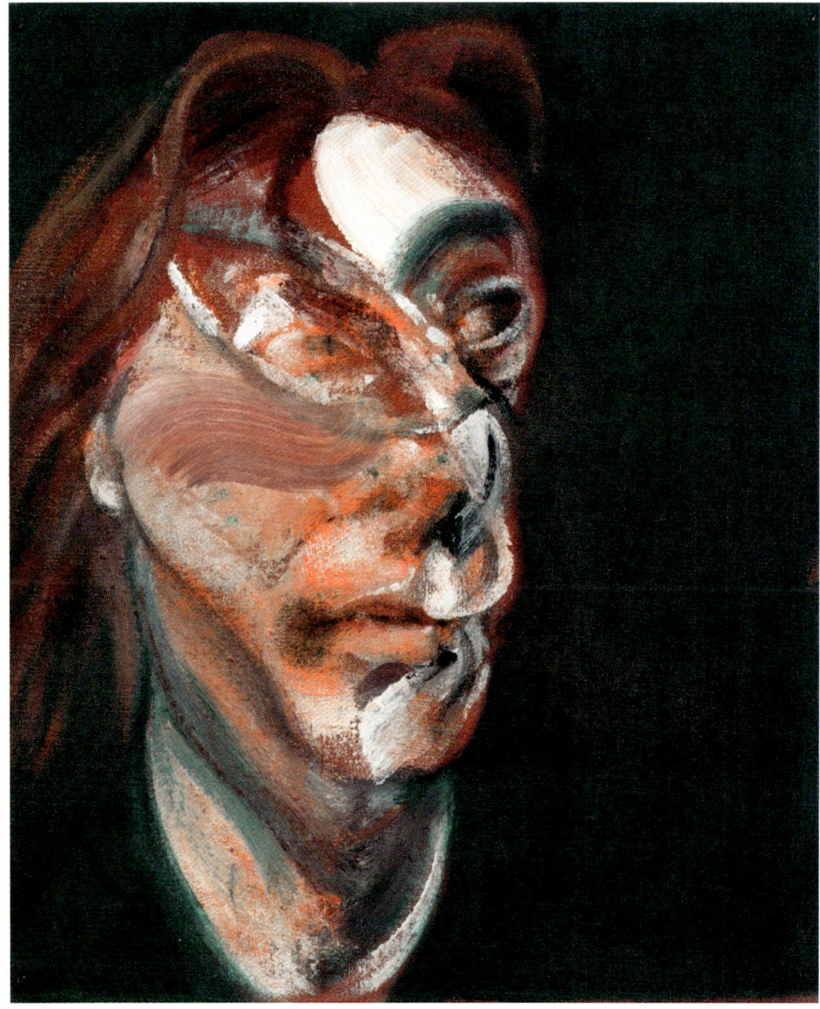

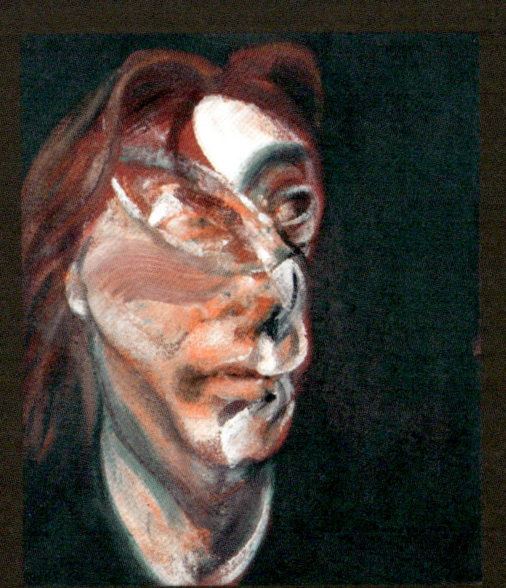

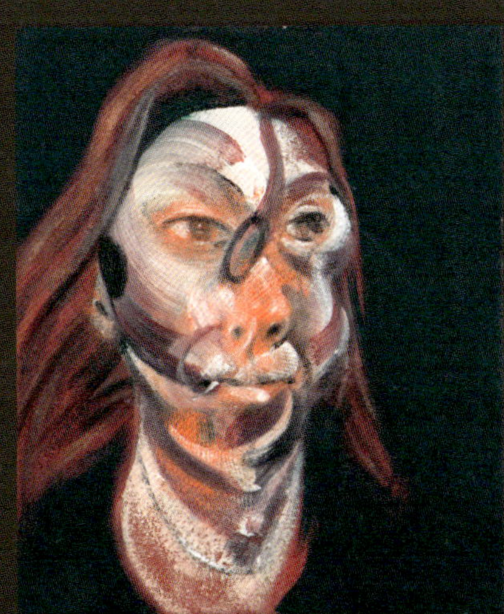

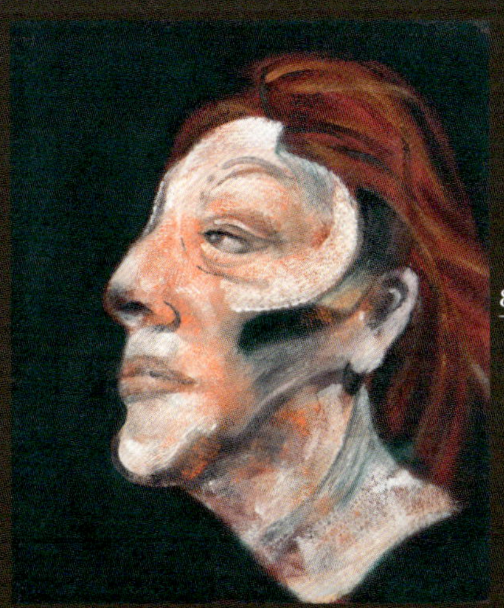

86.

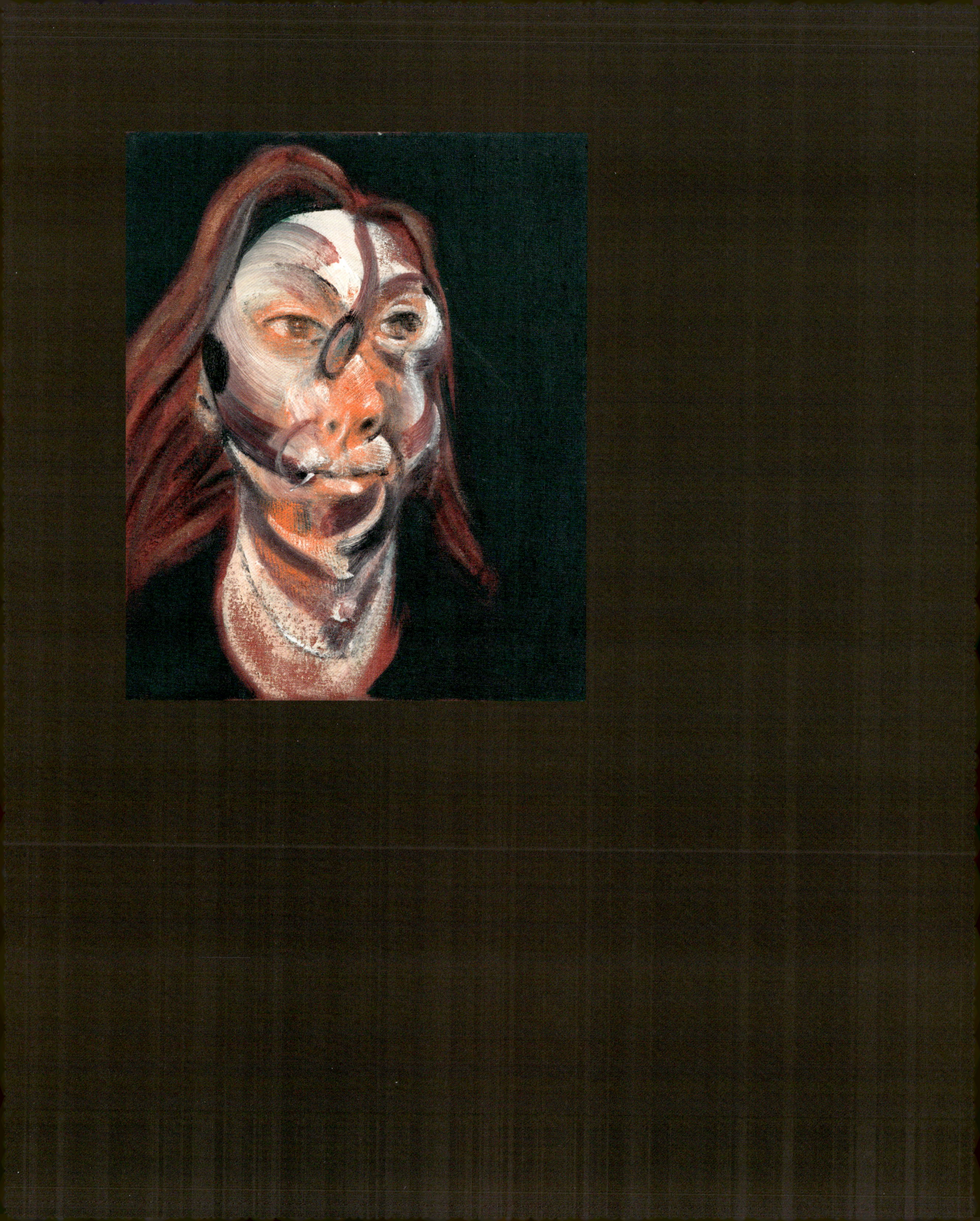

quest to become an artist and she frequently gained the attention of other artists who wished to paint her, notably André Derain and Pablo Picasso who both painted multiple portraits of her in 1936. She was in Paris until the outbreak of the Second World War when she was forced to return to the UK. During the war she worked in intelligence and 'black' propaganda for a clandestine department of the British government.
After the war, Isabel briefly returned to Paris and met up with Giacometti, but their rekindled romance was brief. In November 1946, Isabel and Bacon met for the first time, in Paris, via the photographer and artist Peter Rose Pulham, with whom she was living (Jacobi 2020, p. 234). Bacon had travelled from Monte Carlo, his then home, to Paris to see an exhibition of Balthus's works. Isabel and Bacon must have subsequently become friends as they spent the Christmas of 1948 together after they had both resettled in London (Jacobi 2020, p. 235). They may also have met up regularly at the famous private members club the Gargoyle, which was still popular with artists and writers in post-war London. The two artists became close and possibly intimate, as Bacon revealed in his very last interview in March 1992, for *Paris Match* (Jacobi 2020, p. 278). Isabel's exhibition at Erica Brausen's Hanover Gallery opened in February 1949, with the catalogue forward written by Rose Pulham. Bacon had his first exhibition at the Hanover Gallery in November that year. In 1950, Isabel, Bacon, Lucian Freud and Giacometti were included in the exhibition *London–Paris: New Trends in Painting and Sculpture* at the Institute of Contemporary Arts (ICA), London, which acknowledged the links between the two capitals and the growing movement of British and French artists across the Channel.
For most of Isabel's artistic career she was known as Isabel Lambert after her marriage to the musician and critic Constant Lambert in 1947. She had further exhibitions at the ICA in 1951 and 1954 and at the Hanover Gallery in 1959, who also represented Bacon until 1960. In 1968, she had an important show at Marlborough Fine Art. Bacon (who had been represented by

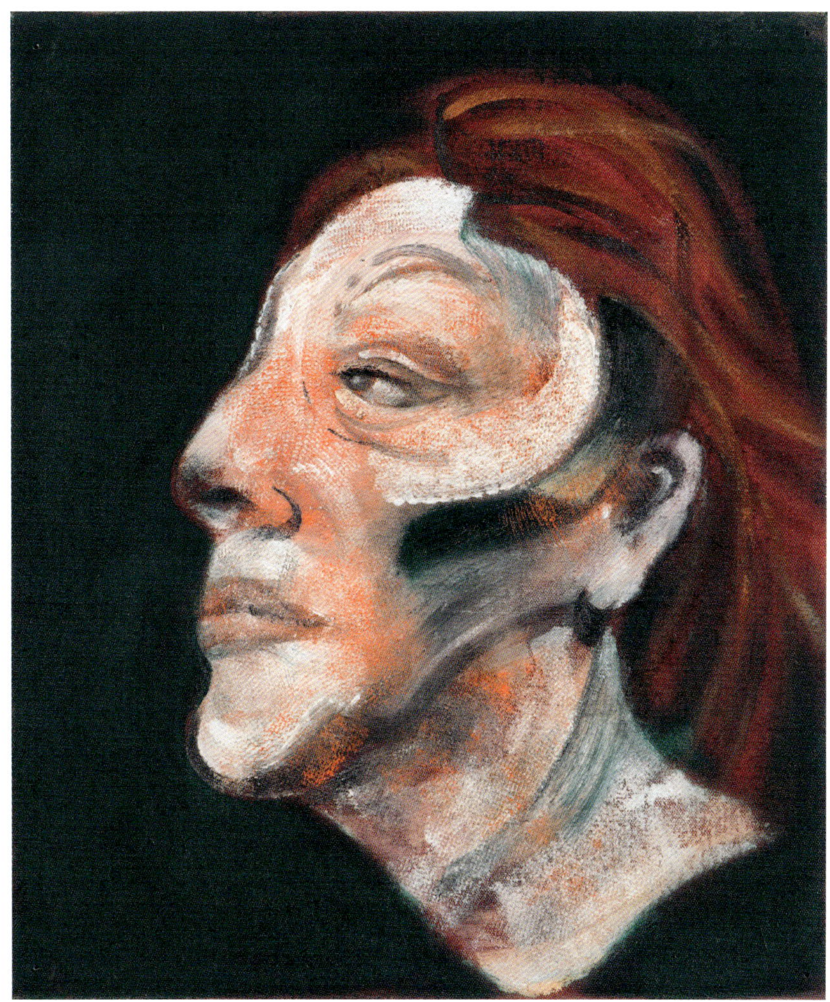

Marlborough since 1960) was photographed attending the show.
It is perhaps surprising that having met in 1946, Bacon did not make his first painting of Isabel until 1961 (destroyed by fire in 1966), some fifteen years later. He made his last painting of her in 1983.

CW

Bibliography

Sylvester 2003, pp. 20, 36; Winner 2016, pp. 57, 75; Jacobi 2020, pp. 234, 235, 278.

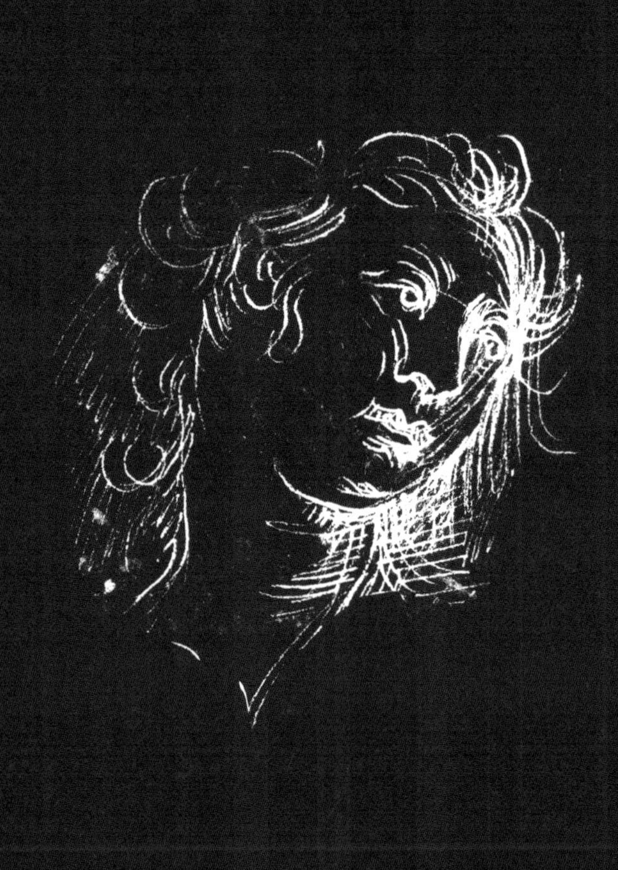

Bibliography

1517
Folengo 1517
[T. Folengo], *Merlini Cocai poëta e Mantuani Liber Macaronices*, Venetiis in aedibus Alexandri Paganini

1550
Alunno 1550
F. Alunno, *Le ricchezze della lingua volgare*, Vinegia: in casa de' figliuoli di Aldo

1557
Azzaiolo 1557
[F. Azzaiolo], *Dal Primo libro de Villotte alla Padoana*, Venezia: appresso Antonio Gardano

1584
Lomazzo 1584
G. P. Lomazzo, *Trattato dell'arte de la pittura di Gio. Paolo Lomazzo Milanese pittore*, Milan: Gottardo Pontico

1586
Della Porta 1586
G.B. Della Porta, *De Humana Physiognomia*, Sorrento: Giuseppe Cacchi

1587
Lomazzo 1587
G. P. Lomazzo, *Rime... divise in sette libri . . . intitolate Grotteschi... con la vita del auttore descritta da lui stesso in rime sciolte*, Milan: Gottardo Pontio

1590
Lomazzo 1590
G. P. Lomazzo, *Idea del tempio della pittura di Gio. Paolo Lomazzo pittore*, Milan: Gottardo Pontio

1672
Bellori 1672
G. P. Bellori, *Le vite de' pittori, scultori et architetti moderni*, Rome: Successor al Mascardi

1681–1728
Baldinucci 1681–1728
F. Baldinucci, *Notizie de' professori del disegno da Cimabue in qua*, Florence: per Santi Franchi, vol. V; Florence, 1974, vol. V, pp. 32–3

1705 [1718]
Addison 1705 [1718]
J. Addison, *Remarks on Several Parts of Italy &c in the Years 1701, 1702, 1703*, London: J. R. Tonson & S. Draper

1722
Richardson 1722
J. Richardson, *An Account of Some of the Statues, Bas-reliefs, Drawings and Pictures in Italy, Ec. with Remarks by Mr. Richardson, Sen. and Jun.*, London: Knapton

1727
Lettre sur le choix 1727
'Lettre sur le choix & l'arrangement d'un Cabinet curieux, écrite par Des-Allier d'Argenville Secrétaire du Roy en la Grande Chancellerie, à M. de Fougeroux, Trésories-Payeur des Rents de l'Hôtel de Ville', *Mercure de France*, June, pp. 1295–330

1730
Caylus 1730
Recueil de testes de caractère et de charges, dessinées par Léonard de Vinci Florentin et gravées par M. le Cte. de C., Paris: J. Mariette

Mariette 1730
P.-J. Mariette, 'Lettre sur Leonard de Vinci, peintre florentin, à Monsieur le C. de C.', in *Recueil de testes de caractère de charges, dessinées par Léonard de Vinci Florentin et gravées par M. le Cte. de C.*, Paris: J. Mariette, pp. 1–22

Wright 1730
E. Wright, *Some Observations Made in Travelling. Through France, Italy, &c., in the Years 1720, 1721, and 1722*, 2 voll., Tho. Ward and E. Wicksteed, London 1730.

1738
Breval 1738
J. D. Breval, *Remarks on Several Parts of Europe, Relating Chiefly to their Antiquities and History...*, London: H. Lintot

1739
Zanotti 1739
G. Zanotti, *Storia dell'Accademia Clementina di Bologna*, 2 vols, Bologna: Lelio dalla Volpe

1740–1743
Zanetti 1740–1743
A. M. Zanetti, *Delle antiche statue Greche e Romane, che nell'antisala della libreria di San Marco, e in altri luoghi pubblici di Venezia si trovano*, 2 vols, Venice: s.e.

1757-1780
Nuovo Teatro Comico 1757–1780
Nuovo Teatro Comico dell'Avvocato Carlo Goldoni, 15 vols, Venice: Francesco Pitteri

1758–1769
Cochin 1758–1769
C. N. Cochin, *Voyage d'Italie ou recueil de notes sur les ouvrages de peinture et de sculpture...*, 3 vols, Paris: C. A. Jombert

1767
Mariette 1767
Recueil de charges et de têtes de différents caractères, gravées à l'eau forte d'après les desseins de Leonard de Vinci. Précédé d'une lettre de M. Mariette sur ce peintre florentin. Nouvelle édition, revue et augmentée per l'auteur, Paris: C. A. Jombert, Pris

1771
Zanetti 1771
[A. M. Zanetti], *Della pittura veneziana e delle opere pubbliche de' veneziani maestri. Libri V*, Venice: Giambattista Albrizzi

1784
Amoretti 1784a
C. Amoretti, 'Ragionamento intorno ai disegni di Leonardo da Vinci compresi in questo volume', in C. G. Gerli, *Disegni di Leonardo da Vinci incisi e pubblicati da Carlo Giuseppe Gerli milanese*, Milan: presso Giuseppe Galeazzi regio stampatore, pp. 3–8

Amoretti 1784b
C. Amoretti, 'Spiegazione delle Tavole', in C. G. Gerli, *Disegni di Leonardo da Vinci incisi e pubblicati da Carlo Giuseppe Gerli milanese*, Milan: presso Giuseppe Galeazzi regio stampatore, pp. 3–8, 9–16

Gerli 1784a
C. G. Gerli, *Disegni di Leonardo da Vinci incisi e pubblicati da Carlo Giuseppe Gerli milanese*, Milan: presso Giuseppe Galeazzi regio stampatore, Milan

Gerli 1784b
C. J. Gerli, *Desseins de Léonard de Vinci gravés par Charles Joseph Gerli Milanois*, Milan

1785
Mantelli 1785
G. Mantelli, *Raccolta di disegni incisi da Girolamo Mantelli di Canobio sugli originali esistenti nella biblioteca ambrosiana di mano di Leonardo da Vinci e de suoi scolari lombardi dedicata a sua eccellenza Gilberto Borromeo Arese*, Milan

1786
Characaturas by Leonardo da Vinci 1786
Characaturas by Leonardo da Vinci, from Drawings by Wincelslaus Hollar, out of the Portland Museum. Published as the Act Directs Nov.r 1 1786 by John Clarke, London, 1786

1795–1796
Lanzi 1795–1796
L. Lanzi, *Storia pittorica dell'Italia dell'ab. Luigi Lanzi*, Bassano: Remondini, vol. II

1796
Chamberlaine 1796
Imitations of Original Designs by Leonardo da Vinci. Consisting of Various Drawings of Single Figures, Heads, Compositions, Horses, and Other Animals; Optics, Perspective, Gunnery, Hydraulics, Mechanics; and in Particular of Very Accurate Delineations, with a Most Spirited Pen, of a Variety of Anatomical Subjects. In His Majesty's Collection, Published by John Chamberlaine, Keeper of The King's Drawings and Medals, and F.S.A, London: W. Bulmer and Co.

1797
Milizia 1797
F. Milizia, *Dizionario delle belle arti del disegno*, 2 vols, Bassano: [Remondini]

1810
Bossi 1810
G. Bossi, *Del Cenacolo di Leonardo da Vinci: libri quattro di Giuseppe Bossi pittore*, Milan: Dalla Stamperia Reale

1822
Bottari and Ticozzi 1822
M. G. Bottari and S. Ticozzi, *Raccolta di lettere sulla pittura, scultura e architettura*, 8 vols, Milan: Giovanni Silvestri

1829
Boerio 1829
G. Boerio, *Dizionario del dialetto veneziano*, Venice: Andrea Santini e figlio

1841
Malvasia 1841
C. C. Malvasia, *Felsina Pittrice: vite de' pittori bolognesi*, 2 vols, Bologna: Guidi all'Ancora

1845
Catalogue d'une collection 1845
Catalogue d'une collection d'estampes anciennes d'après et par des peintres et graveurs... provenant de la Succession de Dominique Tiépolo, Peintre Vénitien, Paris: Vinchon Imprimeur

1854
Selvatico 1854
P. Selvatico, *Catalogo delle opere d'arte contenute nella Sala delle Sedute dell'I. R. Accademia di Venezia*, Venice: Naratovich

1855
Vallardi 1855
G. Vallardi, *Disegni di Leonardo da Vinci posseduti da Giuseppe Vallardi dal medesimo descritti ed in parte illustrati*, Milan: Tipografia di Pietro Agnelli

1857–1858
Dumesnil 1857–1858
M. J. Dumesnil, *Histoire des plus célèbres amateurs français et de leurs relations avec les artistes, faisant suite à celle des plus célèbres amateurs italiens*, Paris: Dentu

1870
Catalogo della Raccolta 1870
Catalogo della Raccolta di disegni autografi antichi e moderni donata dal prof. E. Santarelli alla R. Galleria di Firenze, Florence: Cellini

1881
Frizzoni 1881
G. Frizzoni, 'Exposition de dessins de maîtres anciens au Palais Poldi Pezzoli, à Milan pendant le primptemps et l'été de 1881', in *L'Art: revue hebdomadaire illustrée*, 7, 1881, pp. 193–8

1882
Morelli 1882
G. Morelli, *Raccolta di disegni originali dei più celebri artisti tratti dalla scelta collezione del senatore Giovanni Morelli in Milano*, Venice: G. B. Brusa

1884
Uzielli 1884
G. Uzielli, 'Disegni di Leonardo conservati nella R. Accademia di Venezia', in *Ricerche intorno a Leonardo da Vinci*, second series, Rome: Salviucci , 1884, pp. 273–82

1886
Frizzoni 1886
G. Frizzoni, *Collezione di quaranta disegni scelti dalla raccolta del senatore Giovanni Morelli, riprodotti in eliotipia, ed illustrati dal Dr. Gustavo Frizzoni*, Milan: Ulrico Hoepli

1899
Müntz 1899
E. Müntz, *Léonard de Vinci: l'artiste, le penseur, le savant*, Paris: Librairie Hachette, Paris

1903
Loeser 1903
C. Loeser, 'Note intorno ai disegni conservati nella R. Galleria di Venezia', *Rassegna d'arte*, 3 (12), December, pp. 177–84

1904
Beltrami and Fumagalli 1904
L. Beltrami and C. Fumagalli, *Disegni di Leonardo e della sua scuola alla Biblioteca Ambrosiana*, Milan: Stabilimento Montabone

1905
Strong 1905
A. Strong, *Critical Studies and Fragments*, London: Kessinger

1909
'Elenco e analisi' 1909
'Elenco e analisi delle pubblicazioni pervenute alla Raccolta dal luglio 1908 al luglio 1909', *Raccolta Vinciana*, V, pp. 13–81

1910
Sack 1910
E. Sack, *Giambattista und Domenico Tiepolo: ihr Leben und ihr Werke*, Hamburg: H. V. Clarmanns Kunstverlag

1914
Fassini 1914
S. Fassini, *Il melodramma italiano a Londra nella prima metà del Settecento* (Bibliotheca Musica Bononiensis, III, 63), Turin: Fratelli Bocca

1917
Lorenzetti 1917
G. Lorenzetti, 'Un dilettante incisore veneziano del XVIII secolo: Anton Maria Zanetti di Gerolamo', in *Miscellanea di Storia Veneta, Reale Deputazione Veneta di Storia Patria*, Venice: R. Deputazione Veneta di Storia Patria

1926
Parker 1926
K. T. Parker, 'Cesare da Sesto', *Old Master Drawings, a Quarterly Magazine for Students and Collectors*, 1(1), June, pp. 36–7

1928
Vesme and Calabi 1928
A. Vesme and A. Calabi, *Francesco Bartolozzi: catalogue des estampes et notice biographique d'après les manuscrits de A. de Vesme entièrement réformés et complétés d'une étude critique par A. Calabi*, Milan: Guido Modiano

1928–1929
Calabi 1928–1929
A. Calabi, 'Francesco Bartolozzi', *Bollettino d'arte del Ministero della Pubblica Istruzione*, 22, pp. 103–21

1931
Bodmer 1931
H. Bodmer, *Leonardo: Des Meisters Gemaelde und Zeichnungen*, Stuttgart and Berlin: Deutsche Verlags-Anstalt

Moschini 1931
V. Moschini, 'Disegni del tardo Cinquecento e del Seicento all'Accademia di Venezia', *Bollettino d'arte*, 25(2), pp. 70–83

Verga 1931
E. Verga, *Bibliografia Vinciana*, 2 vols, Bologna: Zanichelli

1932
Alcsuti 1932
C. Alcsuti, 'Donato Creti pittore bolognese', *Il Comune di Bologna*, IX, pp. 17–32

1935-1956
Ortolani 1935–1956
G. Ortolani, ed., *Tutte le opere di Carlo Goldoni*, 14 vols, Milan: Arnoldo Mondadori

1939
Venturi 1939
A. Venturi, ed., *I manoscritti e i disegni di Leonardo da Vinci pubblicati dalla R. Commissione Vinciana. Disegni*, folder V, *Disegni dal MCDLXXXIX al MCDXCIX*, with 59 plates, Rome: Danesi

1942
Vigni 1942
G. Vigni, *Disegni del Tiepolo*, Padova: Le Tre Venezie, 1942

1946
Lucerna 1946
Italienische Kunst: Ambrosiana, Mailand, Meisterwerke aus oberitalienischen Kirchen, Museen und Privatsammlungen, exh. cat. (Lucerne, Kunstmuseum, 6 July–31 October 1946), Lucerne

1947
Mahon 1947
D. Mahon, *Studies in Seicento Art and Theory*, London: Warburg Institute

1949
Heydenreich 1949
L. H. Heydenreich, *I disegni di Leonardo da Vinci e della sua scuola conservati nella Galleria dell'Accademia di Venezia*, Florence: Lange, Domsch & Co.

1950
Popham and Pouncey 1950
A .E. Popham and P. Pouncey, *The Fourteenth and Fifteenth Centuries: Italian Drawings in the Department of Prints and Drawings in the British Museum*, London: Trustees of the British Museum

1951
Parini 1951
G. Parini, 'Discorso sopra le caricature', in L. Caretti, ed., *Poesie e prose, con appendice di poeti satirici e didascalici del Settecento*, Milan and Naples: Ricciardi Editore, pp. 572–88

1952
Arslan 1952
E. Arslan, 'Quattro lettere di Pietro Visconti a Gian Pietro Ligari', *Rivista Archeologica dell'antica provincia di Como*, 135, pp. 63–72

Wittkower 1952
R. Wittkower, *Carracci Drawings at Windsor Castle*, London: Phaidon

1953
Suida 1953
W. Suida, *Bramante pittore e il Bramantino*, Milan: Ceschina

1954
Geiger 1954
B. Geiger, *I dipinti ghiribizzosi di Giuseppe Arcimboldi: pittore illusionista del Cinquecento (1527–1593)*, with a note on Arcimboldo as a musician by L. Levi and epilogue by O. Kokoschka, Florence: Vallecchi

Gombrich 1954
E. H. Gombrich, 'Leonardo's Grotesque Heads: Prolegomena to their Study', in Comitato per le Onoranze a Leonardo nel Quinto Centenario della Nascita, ed., *Leonardo: saggi e ricerche*, presentation by A. Marazza, Rome: Istituto Poligrafico dello Stato, pp. 197–219

1954–
New Hollstein German 1954–
New Hollstein German Engravings, Etchings and Woodcuts, 1400–1700, 48 vols, Rotterdam: Sound & Vision Publishers

1955
Fiocco 1955
G. Fiocco, ed., *Cento antichi disegni veneziani* (Cataloghi di mostre, 1), exh. cat. (Venice, Fondazione Giorgio Cini), Venice: Neri Pozza

Legrand and Sluys 1955
F.-C. Legrand and F. Sluys, *Arcimboldo et les arcimboldesque*, Paris: Editions d'art André de Rache

Morassi 1955
A. Morassi, *G.B. Tiepolo: His Life and Work*, London: Phaidon, 1955

Pirrotta 1955
N. Pirrotta, '"Commedia dell'Arte" e opera', *The Musical Quarterly*, XLI(3), pp. 305–24

1956
Dazzi 1956
M. Dazzi, ed., *Il fiore della lirica veneziana*, vol. II: *Seicento e Settecento*, Venice: Neri Pozza

Tours–Paris 1956
Dessins et manuscrits de Léonard de Vinci, ed. A. Corbeau, G. Nicodemi and F. Bérence, exh. cat. (Tours, Musée des Beaux-Arts, 23 June–1 October 1956; Paris, Musée Jacquemart André, 16 October–30 November 1956), Amboise: Ambrosiana, Musées de France, Galeries d'Italie

1957
Alfons 1957
S. Alfons, *Giuseppe Arcimboldo: En biografisk och ikonografisk studie*, Malmö: Allhems Förlag

Croft-Murray 1957
E. Croft-Murray, 'Venetian Caricatures', in A. Blunt and E. Croft-Murray, eds, *Venetian Drawings of the XVII and XVIII Centuries in the Collection of Her Majesty the Queen at Windsor Castle*, London: Phaidon Press, pp. 137–83

1958
Mrozinska 1958
M. Mrozinska, ed., *Disegni Veneti in Polonia* (Cataloghi di mostre, 7), exh. cat. (Venice, Fondazione Giorgio Cini), Venice: Neri Pozza

Steinitz 1958
K. T. Steinitz, *Leonardo da Vinci's Trattato della Pittura, Treatise on Painting: A Bibliography of the Printed Edition*, Copenhagen: Munksgaard

1959
Morassi 1959
A. Morassi, ed., *Disegni Veneti del Settecento nella collezione Paul Wallraf* (Cataloghi di mostre, 9), exh. cat. (Venice, Fondazione Giorgio Cini), Venice: Neri Pozza

Roli 1959
R. Roli, 'Donato Creti (1671–1749)', *Arte antica e moderna*, 7, pp. 328–41

1960
Geiger 1960
B. Geiger, *Die skurrilen Gemälde des Giuseppe Arcimboldi (1527–1593)*, Wiesbaden: Limes

Knox 1960
G. Knox, *Catalogue of the Tiepolo Drawings in the Victoria and Albert Museum*, London: Her Majesty's Stationery Office

Scholz 1960
J. Scholz, 'Notes on Old and Modern Drawings. Sei-Settecento Drawings in Venice: Notes on Two Exhibitions and a Publication', *The Art Quarterly*, XIII (1), pp. 52–68

1961
Bacou 1961
R. Bacou, ed., *Dessins des Carrache: XXVIII exposition du Cabinet des dessins*, Paris: Réunion des Musées Nationaux

Berenson 1961
B. Berenson, *The Drawings of the Florentine Painters* (1938), Chicago: University of Chicago Press

Kozloff 1961
M. Kozloff, 'Caricatures of Giambattista Tiepolo', *Marsyas: Studies in the History of Art*, X, 1960–61, pp. 13–33

1962
Byam Shaw 1962
J. Byam Shaw, *The Drawings of Domenico Tiepolo*, London: Faber and Faber

Levey 1962
M. Levey, 'Two Footnotes to any Tiepolo Monograph', *The Burlington Magazine*, CIV, 708, March 1962, pp. 118–19

Nielsen 1962
R. Nielsen, 'Azzaiolo, Filippo', in *Dizionario biografico degli Italiani*, vol. IV, Rome: Istituto della Enciclopedia Italiana

Rizzi 1962
A. Rizzi, ed., *Cento disegni del Bison*, exh. cat. (Udine, Loggia de Lionello, 21 December 1962–6 January 1963), Udine: Tip. Doretti

Roli 1962
R. Roli, 'I disegni di Donato Creti agli Uffizi', *Bollettino d'arte*, XLVII, pp. 241–50

Schaack 1962
E. van Schaack, *Master Drawings in Private Collections*, New York: Lambert-Spector

1964
Bonicatti 1964
M. Bonicatti, 'Note sul vedutismo veneziano: sulla cultura artistica di Francesco Guardi e di Domenico Tiepolo', *Arte Veneta*, 18, pp. 135-46

Petrucci 1964
A. Petrucci, 'Bartolozzi, Francesco', in *Dizionario biografico degli Italiani*, vol. VI, Rome: Istituto della Enciclopedia Italiana, pp. 793–6

1965
Negri 1965
R. Negri, 'Il Parini a una serata dei Trasformati: il "Discorso sopra le caricature"', *Lettere italiane*, XVII(2), April–June, pp. 191–205

Omodeo 1965
A. Omodeo, ed., *Mostra di stampe popolari venete del '500*, exh. cat. (Florence, Gabinetto dei Disegni e delle Stampe delle Gallerie degli Uffizi 20), Florence: Leo S. Olschki

Rizzi 1965
A. Rizzi, *Disegni del Tiepolo*, exh. cat. (Udine, Loggia del Lionello, 10 October–14 November 1965), Udine: Tipografia Doretti, 1965

1966
Cogliati Arano 1966
L. Cogliati Arano, *Disegni di Leonardo e della sua cerchia alle Gallerie dell'Accademia*, exh. cat. (Venice, Gallerie dell'Accademia, 10 September 1966–28 February 1967), Venice: Stamperia di Venezia

Marabottini 1966
A. Marabottini, ed., *Le arti di Bologna di Annibale Carracci*, Rome: Edizioni dell'Elefante

Wortley Montagu 1966
M. Wortley Montagu, *The Complete Letters*, ed. R. Halsband, vol. II, Oxford: Clarendon Press

1967
Bacou 1967
R. Bacou, *Le cabinet d'un grand amateur: P.-J. Mariette 1694–1774: dessins du XVe siècle au XVIIIe siècle*, ed. R. Bacou, exh. cat. (Paris, Musée du Louvre, Galerie Mollien, 1967), Paris: Musée du Louvre

Kris 1967
E. Kris, *Ricerche psicoanalitiche sull'arte*, Turin: Einaudi

Roli 1967
R. Roli, *Donato Creti*, Milan: M. Spagnol

1968
'Un acquisto eccezionale' 1968
'Un acquisto eccezionale', *Notiziario di San Giorgio*, 35, July–December, pp. 36–7

Ciardi 1968
R. P. Ciardi, *Giovanni Ambrogio Figino*, Florence: Marchi & Bertolli

1968–1969
Clark and Pedretti 1968–1969
K. Clark with C. Pedretti, *The Drawings of Leonardo da Vinci in the Collection of Her Majesty the Queen at Windsor Castle*, 2nd ed. rev., 3 vols, Oxford: Phaidon

1969
Bettagno 1969
A. Bettagno, ed., *Caricature di Anton Maria Zanetti* (Cataloghi di mostre, 29), exh. cat. (Venice, Fondazione Giorgio Cini, 1969), Vicenza: Neri Pozza

1970
Arcangeli 1970
F. Arcangeli, *Natura ed espressione nell'arte bolognese-emiliana*, Bologna: Alfa

Bettagno 1970
A. Bettagno, ed., *Caricature di Anton Maria Zanetti: disegni della Fondazione Giorgio Cini*, Venice: Pirelli, Milan, and Fondazione Giorgio Cini

Byam Shaw 1970
J. Byam Shaw, 'The Biron Collection of Venetian Eighteenth-Century Drawings in the Metropolitan Museum', *Metropolitan Museum Journal*, 3, pp. 235–58

Knox 1970
G. Knox, *Tiepolo: A Bicentenary Exhibition 1770–1970. Drawings, mainly from American Collections, by Giambattista Tiepolo and the Members of his Circle*, exh. cat. (Cambridge, MA, Fogg Art Museum, 14 March–3 May 1970) Cambridge, MA: Fogg Art Museum, Harvard University

Richter 1970
J. P. Richter, *The Literary Works of Leonardo da Vinci* (1883), 2 vols, New York: Phaidon Press

Viatte 1970
F. Viatte, 'Caricatures d'Anton Maria Zanetti', *Revue de l'art*, 9, pp. 92–3

Webster 1970
M. Webster, 'Caricature di Anton Maria Zanetti', *Arte illustrata*, 25–6, pp. 113–14

1971
Bora 1971
G. Bora, *Disegni di manieristi lombardi*, Vicenza: Neri Pozza

Mariuz 1971
A. Mariuz, *Giandomenico Tiepolo* (Profili e saggi di arte veneta IX), Venice: Alfieri

Posner 1971
D. Posner, *Annibale Carracci: A Study in the Reform of Italian Painting around 1590*, London: Phaidon

Rizzi 1971
A. Rizzi, ed., *Mostra del Tiepolo*, exh. cat. (Udine, Villa Manin di Passariano, 27 June–31 October 1971), 2 vols, Milan: Electa

Vivian 1971
F. Vivian, *Il console Smith mercante e collezionista*, Vicenza: Neri Pozza

1972
Bettagno 1972
A. Bettagno, ed., *Venetian Drawings of the Eighteenth Century: An Exhibition in Aid of the Venice in Peril Fund* (Cataloghi di mostre, 34), exh. cat. (London, Heim Gallery, 26 January–26 February 1972), Vicenza: Neri Pozza

Pignatti 1972
T. Pignatti, *Tiepolo: disegni*, Florence: La Nuova Italia

1973
Pedretti 1973
C. Pedretti, *Leonardo da Vinci: Studies for a Nativity and the 'Mona Lisa Cartoon' with Drawings after Leonardo from the Elmer Belt Library of Vinciana: Exhibition in Honour of the Elmer Belt, M.D. on the Occasion of His Eightieth Birthday*, (Center for Medieval and Renaissance Studies, 6), Los Angeles: UCLA

1973–1975
Lomazzo 1973–1975
G. P. Lomazzo, *Scritti sulle arti*, ed. R. P. Ciardi, 2 vols, Florence and Pisa: Centro Di

1974
Leonardo da Vinci 1974
Leonardo da Vinci, *Scritti letterari: nuova edizione accresciuta con i manoscritti di Madrid*, ed. A. Marinoni, Milan: BUR Rizzoli

Steinitz 1974
K. T. Steinitz, *Pierre-Jean Mariette and the Comte de Caylus and their Concept of Leonardo da Vinci in the Eighteenth Century*, Los Angeles: Zeitlin & Ver Brugge

1975
Morassi 1975
A. Morassi, *Guardi: tutti i disegni di Antonio, Francesco e Giacomo Guardi*, Venice: Alfieri

1976
Bettagno 1976a
A. Bettagno, 'The Birth of a New Collection', *Apollo*, 173, July, pp. 48–53

Bettagno 1976b
A. Bettagno, 'Precisazioni su Anton Maria Zanetti, il Vecchio Sebastiano e Marco Ricci', in *Sebastiano Ricci e il suo tempo*, conference proceedings (Udine, Passariano, 26–28 May 1975), Milan: Electa, pp. 85–95

Frassica 1976
P. Frassica, 'Appunti sul linguaggio figurativo del Parini dal "Giorno" ai "Soggetti"', *Aevum*, L(5–6), September–December, pp. 565–87

Rizzi 1976
A. Rizzi, *Disegni del Bison*, Udine: Del Bianco

Tempesti 1976
F. Tempesti, 'Introduzione', in *Maestri della caricatura: Leonardo, Aspertini, Michelangelo, Parmigianino, Passarotti, Zuccari, Carracci, Guercino, Callot, Bernini, Bocchi, Crespi, Ferretti, Ghezzi, Zanetti, Tiepolo etc.*, ed. L. Corti, Florence: Istituto Alinari, pp. 5–17

1977

Roli 1977
R. Roli, *Pittura bolognese 1650–1800: dal Cignani ai Gandolfi* (Fonti e testi per la storia di Bologna e delle Province emiliane e romagnole 6), Bologna: Alfa

Ruggeri 1977
U. Ruggeri, *Maestri lombardi del Seicento: Procaccini, Salmeggia, Moncalvo, Cerano, Morazzone, Fiammenghini, Tanzio, Daniele Crespi, Barbelli, Gherardini, Ceresa, Nuvolone, Ghitti*, Florence: Alinari

1978–1979

Zava Boccazzi 1978–1979
F. Zava Boccazzi, 'Nicolò Cassana a Venezia', *Atti dell'Istituto Veneto di Scienze, Lettere ed Arti*, CXXXVII, 1978–9, pp. 611–34

1979

Corti 1979
L. Corti, *Maestri della caricatura. Leonardo, Aspertini, Michelangelo, Parmigianino, Passarotti, Zuccari […]*, Florence: Istituto Alinari, 1979

Neilson 1979
N. W. Neilson, *Camillo Procaccini: Paintings and Drawings*, New York: Garland

Pedretti 1979
C. Pedretti, 'An Unpublished Leonardo Drawing', *Master Drawings*, XVII, pp. 24–8

Tempesti and Corti 1979
L. Corti, ed., and F. Tempesti, intro., *Maestri della caricatura: Leonardo, Aspertini, Michelangelo, Parmigianino, Passarotti, Zuccari, Carracci, Guercino, Callot, Bernini, Bocchi, Crespi, Ferretti, Ghezzi, Zanetti, Tiepolo etc.*, Florence: Alinari

1980

Cogliati Arano 1980a
L. Cogliati Arano, ed., *Disegni di Leonardo e della sua cerchia alle Gallerie dell'Accademia*, exh. cat. (Venice, Gallerie dell'Accademia, May–June 1980), Milan: Electa

Cogliati Arano 1980b
L. Cogliati Arano, 'Indicazioni dei disegni fonte per le incisioni del Gerli', in *Disegni di Leonardo e della sua cerchia alle Gallerie dell'Accademia*, ed. L. Cogliati Arano, exh. cat. (Venice, Gallerie dell'Accademia, May–June 1980), Milan: Electa, pp. 113–27

Croft-Murray 1980
E. Croft-Murray, *An Album of Eighteenth Century Venetian Operatic Caricatures formerly in the Collection of Count Algarotti*, exh. cat. (Toronto, Art Gallery of Ontario, 20 September–9 November 1980), Toronto: Art Gallery of Ontario

Pedretti 1980
C. Pedretti, in K. D. Keele and C. Pedretti, *Leonardo da Vinci: Corpus of Anatomical Studies in the Collection of Her Majesty the Queen at Windsor Castle*, New York: Harcourt Brace & Jovanovich, vol. II, p. 860

Sadie 1980
S. Sadie, ed., *The New Grove Dictionary of Music and Musicians*, 20 vols, London: Macmillan, London

1981

Byam Shaw 1981
J. Byam Shaw, ed., *Disegni veneti della collezione Lugt* (Cataloghi di mostre, 44), exh. cat. (Venice, Fondazione Giorgio Cini), Vicenza: Neri Pozza

Cogliati Arano 1981
L. Cogliati Arano, *Disegni di Leonardo e della sua cerchia alla Biblioteca Ambrosiana di Milano*, critical apparatus, Milan: Arcadia/Electa

1982

Bean 1982
J. Bean, *15th and 16th Century Italian Drawings in The Metropolitan Museum of Art*, with L. Turcic, New York: The Metropolitan Museum of Art

Cogliati Arano 1982
L. Cogliati Arano, 'I disegni di Leonardo e della sua cerchia', in *Leonardo all'Ambrosiana: il Codice Atlantico. I disegni di Leonardo e della sua cerchia*, ed. A. Marinoni and L. Cogliati Arano, exh. cat. (Milan, Biblioteca Ambrosiana, 1982), Milan: Electa, pp. 92–157

Milan 1982
Leonardo all'Ambrosiana: il Codice Atlantico. I disegni di Leonardo e della sua cerchia, ed. A. Marinoni and L. Cogliati Arano, exh. cat. (Milan, Biblioteca Ambrosiana, 1982), Milan: Electa

Nepi Scirè 1982
G. Nepi Scirè, *Storia della collezione dei disegni*, Milan: Electa

Pennington 1982
R. Pennington, *A Descriptive Catalogue of the Etched Work of Wenceslaus Hollar (1606–1677)*, Cambridge: Cambridge University Press

Rossi 1982
Grafica del '500: 2° Milano e Cremona, ed. F. Rossi, exh. cat. (Bergamo, Accademia Carrara, 2 April–30 June 1982), Bergamo: Poligrafiche Bolis

1983

Bacou 1983
R. Bacou, *I grandi disegni italiani della collezione Mariette al Louvre di Parigi*, Cinisello Balsamo (Milan): Silvana Editoriale

Rigoli 1983
P. Rigoli, 'Una scherzosa disfida sui vini della Valpolicella ne "La Cogeide" di G. B. Maffei', *Annuario storico della Valpolicella*, 1982–3, pp. 79–84

Scarpa 1983
P. Scarpa, 'La caricatura veneziana e Giambattista Tiepolo', *Ligabue Magazine*, II(3), pp. 66–77

Scrase 1983
D. Scrase, 'A Sidelight on the Artistic Personality of Count Carlo Lasinio', *Master Drawings*, XXI(1), pp. 32–6, ills 107–11

1984

Alberici 1984a
C. Alberici, ed., *Leonardo e l'incisione: stampe derivate da Bramante dal XV al XIX secolo*, exh. cat. (Milan, Castello Sforzesco, January–April 1984), Milan: Electa

Alberici 1984b
C. Alberici, 'Incisioni derivate da disegni di Leonardo', in *Leonardo e l'incisione: stampe derivate da Bramante dal XV al XIX secolo*, ed. C. Alberici, exh. cat. (Milan, Castello Sforzesco, January–April 1984), Milan: Electa, pp. 129–32

Borroni Salvatori 1984
F. Borroni Salvatori, 'Carlo Lasinio e gli autoritratti di Galleria', *Mitteilungen des Kunsthistorischen Institutes in Florenz*, 28, pp. 109–32

Coleman 1984
R. Coleman, *Renaissance Drawings from the Ambrosiana*, exh. cat. (Washington D.C., National Gallery of Art, 12 August–27 October 1984), South Bend, Ind.: University of Notre Dame

De Grazia 1984
D. de Grazia, *Le stampe dei Carracci con i disegni, le incisioni, le copie e i dipinti connessi*, Bologna: Alfa

1985

Fanti 1985
M. Fanti, 'Le chiese sulle mura', in G. Roversi, ed., *Le mura perdute: storia e immagini dell'ultima cerchia fortificata di Bologna*, Casalecchio di Reno (Bologna): Grafis, pp. 97–124

Haskell 1985
F. Haskell, *Mecenati e pittori: studio sui rapporti tra arte e società italiana nell'età barocca*, Florence: Sansoni; original ed. *Patrons and Painters: A Study in the Relations between Italian Art and Society in the Age of the Baroque* (London: Chatto & Windus, 1963)

Pedretti 1985
C. Pedretti, in K. D. Keele and C. Pedretti, *Leonardo da Vinci: corpus degli studi anatomici nella Collezione di Sua Maestà la Regina Elisabetta II nel Castello di Windsor*, Florence: Giunti, vol. III, p. 863

Pedretti and G. Dalli Regoli 1985
C. Pedretti and G. Dalli Regoli, *I disegni di Leonardo da Vinci e della sua cerchia, nel Gabinetto disegni e stampe della Galleria degli Uffizi a Firenze*, Florence: Giunti Barbera

Sani 1985
B. Sani, *Rosalba Carriera: lettere, diari, frammenti* (Accademia Toscana di Scienze e Lettere 'La Colombaria', 'Studi', LXXI), 2 vols, Florence: Leo S. Olschki

Strappini 1985
L. Strappini, 'Croce', in *Dizionario biografico degli Italiani*, vol. XXXI, Rome: Istituto della Enciclopedia Italiana

1986

Blanchard and de Cande 1986
R. Blanchard and R. de Cande, *Dieux et divas de l'opera*, vol. I: *Des origins à la Malibran*, Paris

Gombrich [1976] 1986
E. H. Gombrich, *The Heritage of Apelles: Studies in the Art of the Renaissance*, Ithaca and New York 1976, pp. 57–75; Italian ed. *L'eredità di Apelle: studi sull'arte del Rinascimento*, Turin: Einaudi

Mariuz 1986
A. Mariuz, 'I disegni di Pulcinella di Giandomenico Tiepolo', *Arte Veneta*, XL, 1986, pp. 265–73

Pescarmona 1986
D. Pescarmona, ed., *Disegni lombardi del Cinque e Seicento della Pinacoteca di Brera e dell'Arcivescovado di Milano*, exh. cat. (Milan, Pinacoteca di Brera, 1986), Florence: Cantini

1987

Arquié-Bruley, Labbé and Bicart-Sée 1987
F. Arquié-Bruley, J. Labbé and L. Bicart-Sée, *La collection Saint-Morys au Cabinet des Dessins du Musée du Louvre*, 2 vols, Paris: Réunion des Musées Nationaux

Bora 1987
G. Bora, 'Per un catalogo dei disegni dei leonardeschi lombardi', *Raccolta Vinciana*, XXII, pp. 139–82

Byam Shaw and Knox 1987
J. Byam Shaw and G. Knox, *The Robert Lehman Collection*, vol. VI: *Italian Eighteenth-Century Drawings*, New York and Princeton: The Metropolitan Museum of Art and Princeton University Press

Giovanni Morelli 1987
Giovanni Morelli da collezionista a conoscitore, exh. cat. (Bergamo, Accademia Carrara, 4 June - 31 July 1987), Bergamo: Accademia Carrara

Hulten 1987
P. Hulten, ed., *Effetto Arcimboldo: trasformazioni del volto nel sedicesimo e ventesimo secolo*, exh. cat. (Venice, Palazzo Grassi, 15 February–31 May 1987), Milan: Bompiani

Marani 1987a
P. C. Marani, *Leonardo e i leonardeschi a Brera*, Florence: Cantini

Marani 1987b
P. C. Marani, 'Fortuna dei leonardeschi lombardi nelle esposizioni milanesi', in *Disegni e dipinti lombardi dalle collezioni milanesi*, ed. G. Bora et al., exh. cat. (Milan, Palazzo Reale, 27 November 1987–31 January 1988), Milan: Electa, pp. 158–61

Milan 1987
Disegni e dipinti leonardeschi, ed. G. Bora et al., exh. cat. (Milan, Palazzo Reale, 27 November 1987–31 Janaury 1988), Milan: Electa

Perissa Torrini 1987
A. Perissa Torrini, *Disegni del Figino*, Milan: Electa

1987–1993

Jaffé 1987–1993
M. Jaffé, *Old Master Drawings from Chatsworth: A Loan Exhibition from the Devonshire Collection, organized and circulated by the International Exhibitions Foundation*, exh. cat. (1987–8 and 1993), Alexandria, Vt.: International Exhibitions Foundation; London: British Museum Press

1988

Bora 1988
G. Bora, *I disegni della collezione Morelli*, Bergamo: Credito Bergamasco

Levey 1988
M. Levey, *Giambattista Tiepolo: la sua vita, la sua arte*, Milan: Arnoldo Mondadori

Succi 1988
D. Succi, ed., *I Tiepolo: virtuosismo e ironia*, exh. cat. (Mirano, Venice, Barchessa Villa 25 April, 11 September–30 November 1988), Turin: U. Allemandi

1989

Baltrušaitis 1989
J. Baltrušaitis, *Aberrations: An Essay on the Legend of Forms*, trans. R. Miller, Cambridge, MA: MIT Press

Bettagno 1989
A. Bettagno, ed., *William Hogarth: dipinti, disegni, incisioni*, exh. cat. (Venice, Fondazione Giorgio Cini, 26 August–12 November 1989), Venice: Neri Pozza

Bora 1989
G. Bora, 'Da Leonardo all'Accademia della Val di Bregno: Giovan Paolo Lomazzo, Aurelio Luini e i disegni degli accademici', *Raccolta vinciana*, XXIII, pp. 73–101

Moro 1989
F. Moro, 'Giovanni Agostino da Lodi ovvero l'Agostino di Bramantino: appunti per un unico percorso', *Paragone*, 473, pp. 22–61, figs 36–53b

New York 1989
Important Old Master Paintings: Devotion and Delight, ed. R. B. Simon and F. Dabell, exh. cat. (New York, Pietro Corsini, 3 November–1 December 1989), New York: Pietro Corsini

1990

Cassinelli Lazzeri 1990
P. Cassinelli Lazzeri, 'Temi caricaturali nella produzione incisoria di Carlo Lasinio', *Critica d'arte*, LV, 2–3, pp. 66–73

Ghirardi 1990
A. Ghirardi, *Bartolomeo Passerotti pittore: catalogo generale*, Rimini: Luisè

Guerrini 1990
M. Guerrini, *Bibliotheca Leonardiana (1493–1989)*, 3 vols, Rome: Editrice Bibliografica

Marani 1990
P. C. Marani, *Leonardo e i leonardeschi nei musei della Lombardia*, Milan: Electa

Sylvester 1990
D. Sylvester, *The Brutality of Fact: Interviews with Francis Bacon*, London: Thames and Hudson

1991

Bora 1991
G. Bora, 'I disegni dei leonardeschi e il collezionismo milanese: consistenza, fortuna, dispersione', in *I leonardeschi a Milano*, ed. M. T. Fiorio and P. C. Marani, conference proceedings (Milan 25–6 September 1990), Milan: Electa, pp. 206–17

Caroli 1991
F. Caroli, *Leonardo: studi di fisiognomica*, Milan: Leonardo

Highfill, Burnim and Langhans 1991
P. H. Highfill Jr., K. A. Burnim and E. A. Langhans, *A Biographical Dictionary of Actors, Actresses, Musicians, Dancers, Managers and Other Stage Personnel in London 1660–1800*, vol. XIII, Carbondale: Southern Illinois University Press

Maiorino 1991
G. Maiorino, *The Portrait of Eccentricity: Arcimboldo and the Mannerist Grotesque*, University Park: Pennsylvania State University Press

Parronchi 1991
A. Parronchi, 'Inganni d'ombre', *Achademia Leonardi Vinci: Journal of Leonardo Studies and Bibliography of Vinciana*, IV, pp. 52–6

Ricardi 1991
F. Ricardi, 'Traccia da Leonardo ai Sacri Monti', in *Leonardo a Milano: fortuna e collezionismo*, ed. M. T. Fiorio and P. C. Marani, conference proceedings (Milan, 25–26 September 1990), Milan: Electa, pp. 141–6

Scarpa Sonino 1991
A. Scarpa Sonino, *Marco Ricci*, Milan: Berenice

1992
Alberici 1992
C. Alberici, 'Leonardo e l'incisione: qualche aggiunta', *Raccolta Vinciana*, XXIV, pp. 9–53

Bora 1992
G. Bora, 'I leonardeschi a Venezia tra anticlassicismo e "maniera moderna"', in *Leonardo & Venezia*, ed. G. Nepi Scirè and P. C. Marani, exh. cat. (Venice, Palazzo Grassi, March–July 1992), Milan: Bompiani, pp. 111–35

Cogliati Arano 1992
L. Cogliati Arano, *Leonardo e la rappresentazione della terza età*, XXXI Lettura Vinciana (Vinci, 15 April 1991), Florence: Giunti

Humfrey 1992
P. Humfrey, 'I rapporti fra Leonardo e la pittura veneziana nella storiografia', in *Leonardo & Venezia*, ed. G. Nepi Sciré and P. C. Marani, exh. cat. (Venice, Palazzo Grassi, March–July 1992), Milan: Bompiani, pp. 37–43

Mazza 1992a
A. Mazza, '"Eracle e Cerbero": un affresco di Creti diciassettenne in Palazzo Fava ed altre opere giovanili', *Arte a Bologna: bollettino dei musei civici d'arte antica*, 2, pp. 97–123

Mazza 1992b
A. Mazza, *La pittura a Bologna nella seconda metà del Seicento*, in *La pittura in Emilia e in Romagna: il Seicento*, ed. A. Emiliani, vol. I, Bologna: Credito Romagnolo, pp. 219–77

Prosperi Valenti Rodinò 1992a
S. Prosperi Valenti Rodinò, 'Anton Maria Zanetti', in *Il disegno: i grandi collezionisti*, Cinisello Balsamo (Milan): Amilcare Pizzi, pp. 116–19

Prosperi Valenti Rodinò 1992b
S. Prosperi Valenti Rodinò, 'Jean-Pierre Mariette', in *Il Disegno, i grandi collezionisti*, Cinisello Balsamo (Milan): Amilcare Pizzi, pp. 133–9

Venice 1992
Leonardo & Venezia, ed. G. Nepi Scirè and P. C. Marani, exh. cat. (Venice, Palazzo Grassi, March–July 1992), Milan: Bompiani

1993
Brummer 1993
H. H. Brummer, 'The editio princeps of Leonardo da Vinci's Treatise on painting dedicated to Queen Christina', *Achademia Leonardi Vinci*, 6, pp. 117–25

Carracci 1993
A. Carracci, *Diverse figure al numero di ottanta, disegnate di penna nell'hore di ricreatione da Annibale Carracci intagliate in rame e cavate dagli originali da Simone Guilino Parigino dedicate a tutti i virtuosi et intendenti della professione della pittura e del disegno*, Lodovico Grignani, Roma 1646 (anastatic reprint: Editori delle Marche, Ancona 1993)

Dalle Fusine and Androsov 1993
C. Dalle Fusine and S. O. Androsov, 'O portrietach Savvy Vladislavič-Ragunzinskogo', in *Stranicy istorii zapadnoevropejskoj skul'ptury*, ed. S. O. Androsov, St Petersburg: Gosudarstvennyi Ermitaž. Nauč.

Di Giampaolo 1993
M. Di Giampaolo, *Disegni emiliani: Gallerie dell'Accademia di Venezia*, Milan: Electa

Isella 1993
D. Isella, ed., *Rabisch: Giovan Paolo Lomazzo e i Facchini della Val di Blenio*, Turin: Einaudi

Lomazzo 1993
G. P. Lomazzo, *Rabisch*, ed. D. Isella, Turin: Einaudi

Trutty-Coohill 1993
P. Trutty-Coohill, 'The Spencer Collection of Grotesques and Caricatures after Leonardo', *Arte Lombarda*, 105–7, pp. 48–52

Trutty-Coohill and Pedretti 1993
P. Trutty-Coohill, ed., and C. Pedretti, intro., *The Drawings of Leonardo da Vinci and His Circle in the American Collections*, exh. cat., Florence: Giunti

1994
Jaffé 1994
M. Jaffé, ed., *The Devonshire Collection of Italian Drawings: Roman and Neapolitan School*, London: Phaidon

Kwakkelstein 1994
M. W. Kwakkelstein, *Leonardo da Vinci as a Physiognomist: Theory and Drawing Practice*, Leiden: G. & B. Intl

Morelli 1994
Mo. Giovanni Morelli collezionista di disegni: la donazione al Castello Sforzesco, Cinisello Balsamo (Milan): Silvana Editoriale

1995
Caroli 1995
F. Caroli, *Storia della fisiognomica: arte e psicologia da Leonardo a Freud*, Milan: Leonardo

Jatta 1995
B. Jatta, ed., *Francesco Bartolozzi: incisore delle Grazie*, exh. cat. (Rome, Villa Farnesina, 27 October–17 December 1995; Lisbon, Museo Nacional de Arte Antiga, 27 January–29 September 1996), Rome: Artemide

Leonardo da Vinci 1995
Leonardo da Vinci, *Libro di Pittura, Codice Urbinate Latino 1270 nella Biblioteca Apostolica Vaticana*, ed. C. Pedretti, transcript. C. Vecce, Florence: Giunti

Lowerre 1995
K. Lowerre, 'Beauty, Talent, Virtue and Charm: Portraits of Two of Handel's Sopranos', *Imago Musicae*, IX/XII, 1992–5, pp. 205–44

Marani 1995
P. C. Marani, in *The Touch of the Artist: Master Drawings from the Woodner Collections*, ed. M. Morgan Grasselli, exh. cat. (Washington D.C., National Gallery of Art, 1 October 1995–28 January 1986), New York: Harry N. Abrams, pp. 80–83

Mazza 1995
A. Mazza, 'Momenti della fortuna di Simone Cantarini nella pittura bolognese del secondo Seicento', in *Disegni marchigiani dal Cinquecento al Settecento*, ed. M. di Giampaolo and G. Angelucci, conference proceedings (Monte San Giusto, 22–23 May 1992), Florence: Medicea, pp. 87–101

Paliaga 1995a
F. Paliaga, 'Quattro persone che ridono con un gatto', *Achademia Leonardi Vinci*, 8, pp. 143–57

Paliaga 1995b
F. Paliaga, 'Giovanni Ambrogio Brambilla, "Le teste di carattere" di Leonardo e la Commedia dell'Arte', *Raccolta Vinciana*, XXVI, pp. 219–54

Venice 1995
Splendori del Settecento veneziano, ed. G. Nepi Sciré and G. Romanelli, exh. cat. (Venice, Museo del Settecento Veneziano – Ca' Rezzonico, Gallerie dell'Accademia, Palazzo Mocenigo, 26 May–30 July 1995), Milan: Electa

1996

Garzoni [1585] 1996
T. Garzoni, *La piazza universale di tutte le professioni del mondo*, Venice: Giovan Battista Somasco, 1585; Florence: Olschki

Mancini, Muraro and Povoledo 1996
F. Mancini, M. T. Muraro and E. Povoledo, *I teatri del Veneto: Venezia e il suo territorio. Imprese private e teatri sociali*, Venice: Corbo e Fiore

Mignosi Tantillo 1996
A.M. Mignosi Tantillo, 'Domenichino a Grottaferrata. La decorazione della Cappella dei Santi Fondatori', in *Domenichino 1581-1641*, eds. C. Strinati and A. M. Tantillo, exh. cat. (Rome, Palazzo Venezia 10 October 1996 - 14 January 1997), Milano: Electa, pp. 197–223

Peppiatt 1996
M. Peppiatt, *Francis Bacon: Anatomy of an Enigma*, London: Weidenfeld & Nicolson

Rossi 1996
F. Rossi, ed., *Ritratti lombardi e veneti dalla Accademia Carrara*, exh. cat. (Luxembourg, Palais Cercle Municipal, 24 May–9 June 1996), Milan: Skira

Schulze Altcappenberg 1996
H.-Th. Schulze Altcappenberg, *Giambattista Tiepolo (1696–1771) und sein Atelier: Zeichnungen und Radierungen im Berliner Kupferstichkabinett*, exh. cat. (Berlin, Kupferstichkabinett, 30 November 1996–2 March 1997), Berlin: Kupferstichkabinett and Sammlung der Zeichnungen und Druckgraphik

Udine and Bloomington 1996
Giandomenico Tiepolo: Maestria e gioco. Disegni dal mondo, ed. A. M. Gealt and G. Knox, exh. cat. (Udine, Castello, 14 September–31 December 1996; Bloomington, Indiana University Art Museum, 15 January–9 March 1997), Milan: Electa

1996–1999

Ballarin 1996–1999
A. Ballarin, 'I cartoni con le teste di Cristo e degli Apostoli dal Cenacolo di Leonardo: la serie del Musée des Beaux-Arts di Strasburgo e quella già del Museo Granducale di Weimar (1996–9)', in *Leonardo a Milano: problemi di leonardismo milanese tra Quattrocento e Cinquecento. Giovanni Antonio Boltraffio prima della Pala Casio*, 4 vols, Verona: Grafiche Aurora, [2010] 2011, vol. II, pp. 734–852

1997

Agosti, Agosti 1997
B. Agosti and G. Agosti eds., *Le tavole del Lomazzo (per i 70 anni di Paola Barocchi)*, Brescia: Edizioni l'Obliquo

Kwakkelstein 1997
M. W. Kwakkelstein, 'Two Weimar Drawings Rediscovered', *Achademia Leonardi Vinci*, 10, pp. 197–8

Mazza 1997
A. Mazza, '"Il metodo d'una vera e lodevole imitazione": la fortuna di Simone Cantarini nella pittura bolognese della seconda metà del Seicento e del primo Settecento', in *Simone Cantarini detto il Pesarese 1612–1648*, ed. A. Emiliani, exh. cat. (Bologna, 11 October 1997–6 January 1998), Milan: Electa, pp. 359–96

Morel 1997
P. Morel, *Les grotesques: les figures de l'imaginaire dans la peinture italienne de la fin de la Renaissance*, Paris: Flammarion

Robertson 1997
C. Robertson, 'Annibale Carracci and Invenzione: Medium and Functions in Early Drawings', *Master Drawings*, 35 (1), pp. 3–42, fig. 19

1998

Bettagno 1998
A. Bettagno, 'Una data per i *Capricci*?', in *Giambattista Tiepolo nel terzo centenario della nascita*, ed. L. Puppi, conference proceedings (Venice, Vicenza, Udine and Paris, 29 October–4 November 1996), 2 vols, Padua: Il Poligrafo, vol. I, pp. 39–41; vol. II, pp. 25–6

Bora 1998a
G. Bora, 'Camillo Procaccini', in *Rabisch. Il grottesco nell'arte del Cinquecento. L'Accademia della Val di Blenio, Lomazzo e l'ambiente milanese*, ed. G. Bora, M. Kahn-Rossi, F. Porzio, exh. cat. (Lugano, Museo Cantonale d'Arte, 28 March - 21 June 1998), Milan, Skira, p. 204

Bora 1998b
G. Bora, 'Milano nell'età di Lomazzo e San Carlo: riaffermazione e difficoltà di sopravvivenza di una cultura', in *Rabisch: il grottesco nell'arte del Cinquecento. L'Accademia della Val di Blenio, Lomazzo e l'ambiente milanese*, ed. G. Bora, M. Kahn-Rossi and F. Porzio, exh. cat. (Lugano, Museo Cantonale d'Arte, 28 March–21 June 1998), Milan: Skira, pp. 37–56

Caroli 1998
L'anima e il volto: ritratto e fisiognomica da Leonardo a Bacon, ed. F. Caroli, exh. cat. (Milan, Civico Museo d'Arte Contemporanea, 30 October 1998–14 March 1999), Milan: Electa

Cogliati Arano 1998
L. Cogliati Arano, 'Tiepolo a Milano e a Brescia', in *Giambattista Tiepolo nel terzo centenario della nascita*, ed. L. Puppi, conference proceedings (Venice, Vicenza, Udine and Paris, 29 October–4 November 1996), 2 vols, Padua: Il Poligrafo, vol. I, pp. 423–30; vol. II, pp. 137–42

Lugano 1998
Rabisch. Il grottesco nell'arte del Cinquecento. L'Accademia della Val di Blenio. Lomazzo e l'ambiente milanese, edited by G. Bora, M. Kahn Rossi, F. Porzio, catalogue of the exhibition (Lugano, Museo Cantonale d'Arte, 28 March–21 June 1998), Skira, Milan

Marani 1998
P. C. Marani, 'Francesco Melzi', in *I leonardeschi: l'eredità di Leonardo in Lombardia*, ed. G. Bora et al., Milan: Skira, pp. 371–84

Milan 1998
L'Ambrosiana e Leonardo, edited by P. C. Marani, M. Rossi, A. Rovetta, exh. cat. (Milan, Biblioteca Pinacoteca Ambrosiana, 1 December 1998–30 April 1999), Novara: Interlinea

Rome, Milan and Florence 1998
Leonardo: la Dama con l'ermellino, ed. B. Fabjan and P. C. Marani, exh. cat. (Rome, Palazzo del Quirinale, 15 October–14 November 1998; Milan, Pinacoteca di Brera, 19 November–13 December 1998; Florence, Palazzo Pitti, 16 December 1998–24 January 1999), Cinisello Balsamo (Milan): Silvana Editoriale

Trutty-Coohill 1998
P. Trutty-Coohill, 'Bracketing Theory in Leonardo's Five Grotesque Heads, in Enjoyment: from Laughter to Delight in Philosophy, Literature, the Fine Arts and Aesthetics', ed. A.T. Tymieniecka, *Analecta Husserliana*, 56, pp. 185–202

Zava Boccazzi 1998
F. Zava Boccazzi, 'Pellegrini "privato" nell'epistolario di Rosalba Carriera', in *Antonio Pellegrini: il maestro veneto del Rococò alle corti d'Europa*, ed. A. Bettagno, exh. cat. (Padua, Palazzo della Ragione, 20 September 1998–10 January 1999), Venice: Marsilio, pp. 62–87

1999

Androsov 1999
S. Androsov, *Pietro il Grande collezionista d'arte veneta*, Venice: Canal

Lanzeni 1999
L. Lanzeni, 'Ancora su Carlo Lasinio e gli autoritratti di Galleria', *Mitteilungen des Kunsthistorischen Institutes in Florenz*, 43 (2–3), pp. 665–91

Loisel Legrand 1999
C. Loisel Legrand, '82. Study Sheet with a Man Bowling and the Head of Saint Gregory', in *The Drawings of Annibale Carracci*, ed. D. Benati, exh. cat. (Washington D.C., National Gallery of Art, 26 September 1999–9 January 2000), Washington D.C.: National Gallery of Art, pp. 258–9

Mazza 1999
A. Mazza, 'Per gli inizi di Donato Creti a Palazzo Fava', *Arte a Bologna: bollettino dei musei civici d'arte antica*, 5, pp. 182–99

Montecuccoli degli Erri and Pedrocco 1999
F. Montecuccoli degli Erri and F. Pedrocco, *Michele Marieschi: la vita, l'ambiente, l'opera*, Milan: Bocca

Venice 1999
Da Leonardo a Canaletto: disegni delle Gallerie dell'Accademia, ed. G. Nepi Sciré and A. Perissa Torrini, exh. cat. (Venice, Gallerie dell'Accademia, 24 April–25 July 1999), Milan: Electa

2000
Bucciarelli 2000
M. Bucciarelli, *Italian Opera and European Theatre 1680–1720: Plots, Performers, Dramaturgies*, Turnhout: Brepols

2001
Bellettini 2001
P. Bellettini, ed., *Biblioteca Comunale dell'Archiginnasio, Bologna*, Florence: Nardini

Guffanti 2001
M. V. Guffanti, 'Il conte di Caylus e le caricature di Leonardo', *Raccolta Vinciana*, XXIX, pp. 303–16

Marani 2001
P. C. Marani, 'Leonardo da Vinci: scheda', in *Un milanese che parlava toscano: Lamberto Vitali e la sua collezione*, exh. cat. (Milan, Pinacoteca di Brera, 1 June–9 December 2001), Milan: Electa, pp. 98–9

Py 2001
B. Py, *Everhard Jabach collectionneur (1618–1695): les dessins de l'Inventaire de 1695*, Paris: Réunion des Musées Nationaux

Rostirolla 2001
G. Rostirolla, *Il 'Mondo novo' musicale di Pier Leone Ghezzi* (L'Arte Armonica, Series IV, Iconografia e Cataloghi 2), Milan: Skira

Sadie 2001
S. Sadie, ed., *The New Grove Dictionary of Music and Musicians*, 21 vols, London: Macmillan

2002
Bettagno and Magrini 2002
A. Bettagno and M. Magrini, eds, *Lettere artistiche del Settecento veneziano*, vol. 1 (Fonti e Documenti per la storia dell'arte veneta 10), Vicenza: Neri Pozza

Clayton 2002a
M. Clayton, 'Leonardo's "Gypsies" and the "Wolf with the Eagle"', *Apollo*, 155, August, pp. 27–33

Clayton 2002b
M. Clayton, *Leonardo da Vinci: The Divine and the Grotesque*, exh. cat. (Edinburgh, Queen's Gallery, 30 November 2002–30 March 2003; London, Queen's Gallery, 9 May–9 November 2003), London: Thames & Hudson

Lévy 2002
L. Lévy, 'Quelques remarques sur la caricature à partir de Léonard de Vinci et d'Annibal Carrache', *Ridiculosa*, 9, pp. 129–57

Py 2002
B. Py, *L'Honneur de la curiosité: de Dürer à Poussin. Les dessins de la seconde collection Jabach*, exh. guide (Paris, Musée du Louvre, 17January–15 April 2002), Paris: Musée du Louvre

2002-2003
Rosenberg 2002–2003
P. Rosenberg, 'Parigi–Venezia o, piuttosto, Venezia–Parigi: 1715–1723', *Atti dell'Istituto Veneto di Scienze, Lettere ed Arti*, CLXI, 2002–3, pp. 1–30

2003
Bambach 2003
Leonardo da Vinci: Master Draftsman, ed. C. C. Bambach, with A. Cecchi, C. Farago, V. Forcione, M. Kemp, A.-M. Logan, P. C. Marani, C. Pedretti, C. Vecce, F. Viatte and L. Wolk-Simon, exh. cat. (New York, The Metropolitan Museum of Art, 22 Janaury–30 March 2003), New York: The Metropolitan Museum of Art; New Haven and London: Yale University Press

Bora 2003
G. Bora, 'Les léonardesques. Léonard de Vinci et les "léonardesques" lombards: les difficultés d'une conquête du naturel', in *Léonard de Vinci: dessins et manuscrits*, ed. F. Viatte and V. Forcione, exh. cat. (Paris, Musée du Louvre, 5 May–14 July 2003), Paris: Réunion des Musées Nationaux, pp. 311–34

Caroli 2003
Il Gran Teatro del Mondo: l'anima e il volto del Settecento, ed. F. Caroli, exh. cat. (Milan, Palazzo Reale, 13 November 2003–12 April 2004), Milan: Skira

Favilla and Rugolo 2003
M. Favilla and R. Rugolo, 'Dorigny e Venezia: da Ca' Tron a Ca' Zenobio e ritorno', in *Louis Dorigny 1654–1742: un pittore della corte francese a Verona*, ed. G. Marini and P. Marini, exh. cat. (Museo di Castelvecchio, Verona, 28 June–2 November 2003), Venice: Marsilio, pp. 37–59

Forcione 2003
V. Forcione, 'L'album du Louvre: les grotesques de Léonard de Vinci, originaux, dispersion, copies, estampes', in *Léonard de Vinci: dessins et manuscrits*, ed. F. Viatte and V. Forcione, exh. cat. (Paris, Musée du Louvre, 5 May–14 July 2003), Paris: Réunion des Musées Nationaux, pp. 206–16

Marani 2003
P. C. Marani, 'Leonardo's Drawings in Milan and their Influence on the Graphic Work of Milanese Artists', in *Leonardo da Vinci: Master Draftsman*, ed. C. C. Bambach with A. Cecchi, C. Farago, V. Forcione, M. Kemp, A.-M. Logan, P. C. Marani, C. Pedretti, C. Vecce, F. Viatte and L. Wolk-Simon, exh. cat. (New York, The Metropolitan Museum of Art, 22 Janaury–30 March 2003), New York: The Metropolitan Museum of Art; New Haven and London: Yale University Press, pp. 155–201

Nepi Sciré and Perissa Torrini 2003
G. Nepi Sciré and A. Perissa Torrini, eds, *Disegni di Leonardo e della sua cerchia nel Gabinetto dei disegni e stampe delle Gallerie dell'Accademia di Venezia*, Florence: Giunti

New York 2003
Leonardo da Vinci: Master Draftsman, ed. C. C. Bambach with A. Cecchi, C. Farago, V. Forcione, M. Kemp, A.-M. Logan, P. C. Marani, C. Pedretti, C. Vecce, F. Viatte and L. Wolk-Simon, exh. cat. (New York, The Metropolitan Museum of Art, 22 Janaury–30 March 2003), New York: The Metropolitan Museum of Art; New Haven and London: Yale University Press

Paris 2003
Léonard de Vinci: dessins et manuscrits, ed. F. Viatte and V. Forcione, exh. cat. (Paris, Musée du Louvre, 5 May–14 July 20013), Paris: Réunion des Musées Nationaux

Parma 2003
Parmigianino tradotto: la fortuna di Francesco Mazzola nelle stampe di riproduzione fra il Cinquecento e l'Ottocento, ed. G. M. de Rubeis and M. Mussini, exh. cat. (Parma, Biblioteca Palatina, 29 March–27 September 2003), Cinisello Balsamo (Milan): Silvana Editoriale

Sparti 2003
D. L. Sparti, 'Cassiano Dal Pozzo, Poussin and the Making and Publication of Leonardo's Trattato', *Journal of the Warburg and Courtauld Institutes*, 66, pp. 143–88

2004

Cassinelli Lazzeri 2004
Carlo LasinioI incisioni, ed. P. Cassinelli Lazzeri, exh. cat. (Florence, Gabinetto dei Disegni e Stampe delle Gallerie degli Uffizi, 28 July–30 November delle 2004), Florence: Olschki

Knox 2004a
G. Knox, 'Pulcinella in Arcadia', in *Tiepolo: ironia e comico* (Cataloghi di mostre, 62), ed. A. Mariuz and G. Pavanello, exh. cat. (Venice, Fondazione Giorgio Cini, 3 September–5 December 2004), Venice: Marsilio, pp. 97–99

Knox 2004b
G. Knox, 'Tomo terzo de caricature', in *Tiepolo: ironia e comico* (Cataloghi di mostre, 62), ed. A. Mariuz and G. Pavanello, exh. cat. (Venice, Fondazione Giorgio Cini, 3 September–5 December 2004), Venice: Marsilio, pp. 119–22

Loisel 2004
C. Loisel, *Inventaire général des dessins Italiens VII: Ludovico, Agostino, Annibale Carracci*, Paris: Réunion des Musées Nationaux

Mazza 2004a
A. Mazza, 'Gli artisti a Palazzo Fava: collezionismo e mecenatismo artistico a Bologna alla fine del Seicento', *Saggi e memorie di storia dell'arte*, 27, 2003, pp. 313–77

Mazza 2004b
C. Mazza, *I Sagredo: committenti e collezionisti d'arte nella Venezia del Sei e Settecento*, Venice: Istituto Veneto di Scienze, Lettere ed Arti

Pavanello 2004
G. Pavanello, 'Tutta la vita, dal principio alla fine, è una comica assurdità, ovvero "il segreto di Pulcinella"', in *Tiepolo: ironia e comico* (Cataloghi di mostre, 62), ed. A. Mariuz and G. Pavanello, exh. cat. (Venice, Fondazione Giorgio Cini, 3 September–5 December 2004), Venice: Marsilio, pp. 14–53

Pavesi 2004
M. Pavesi, *Cassiano dal Pozzo*, 'Nicolas Poussin e la prima edizione a stampa del 'Trattato della pittura' di Leonardo tra Roma, Milano e Parigi', in *Tracce di letteratura artistica in Lombardia*, ed. A. Rovetta, Bari: Edizioni di Pagina, pp. 124–33

Venice 2004
Tiepolo: ironia e comico (Cataloghi di mostre, 62), ed. A. Mariuz and G. Pavanello, exh. cat. (Venice, Fondazione Giorgio Cini, 3 September–5 December 2004), Venice: Marsilio

2005

B. Aikema, R. Lauber and M. Seidel, eds, *Il collezionismo a Venezia e nel Veneto ai tempi della Serenissima*, conference proceedings (Venice, 2003), Venice: Marsilio

Antichi disegni 2005
Antichi disegni dalla Collezione Ligabue, ed. S. Scarpa and P. Scarpa, Milan: Electa

Ciardi 2005
R. P. Ciardi, 'Lomazzo, Giovan Paolo', in *Dizionario biografico degli italiani*, vol. LXV, Rome: Istituto della Enciclopedia Italiana, pp. 460–67

Cogliati Arano 2005
L. Cogliati Arano, 'Un importante inedito leonardesco', *Raccolta Vinciana*, XXXI, pp. 285–98

Dell'Aquila 2005
G. Dell'Aquila, 'Intenti satirici e omaggio alla tradizione nell'onomastica pariniana del Discorso sopra le caricature', 10th conference proceedings, Onomastica & Letteratura (Pisa, 19–20 February 2004), *Il nome nel testo: International Journal of Literary Onomastics*, VII, pp. 31–47

Gealt and Knox 2005
A. M. Gealt and G. Knox, eds, *Giandomenico Tiepolo: scene di vita quotidiana a Venezia e nella terraferma*, Venice: Marsilio

Isella 2005a
D. Isella, *Lombardia stravagante: testi e studi dal Quattrocento al Seicento tra lettere e arti*, Turin: Einaudi

Isella 2005b
D. Isella, "I "Rabisch": Giovan Paolo Lomazzo e l'Accademia dei Facchini della Val di Blenio, in *Lombardia stravagante: testi e studi dal Quattrocento al Seicento tra lettere e arti*, Turin: Einaudi, pp. 75–101

Knox 2005
G. Knox, 'Le caricature dei Tiepolo', in *Antichi disegni dalla Collezione Ligabue*, ed. S. Scarpa and P. Scarpa, Milan: Electa, pp. 139–51

Pavanello 2005
G. Pavanello, ed., *I disegni del Professore: la raccolta Giuseppe Fiocco della Fondazione Giorgio Cini* (Cataloghi di mostre, 64), exh. cat. (Padua, Musei Civici degli Eremitani, 8 May–24 July 2005), Venice: Marsilio

Rosenberg 2005
P. Rosenberg, *Da Raffaello alla Rivoluzione: le relazioni artistiche tra la Francia e l'Italia*, Milan: Skira

Schnapper 2005
A. Schnapper, *Curieux du Grand Siècle: collections et collectionneurs dans la France du XVII*[e] *siècle*, rev. and updated 2nd ed., author's notes ed. M. Szanto and S. Mouquin, Paris: Flammarion, (1994)

Tomezzoli 2005
A. Tomezzoli, 'Una nota discorde nel giardino di Armida: la raffigurazione dei "Nani" nella statuaria veneta da giardino del Sei e Settecento', *Arte Veneta*, 61, 2004, pp. 124–77

Trabucco 2005
O. Trabucco, 'Il "corpus" fisiognomico dellaportiano tra censura e autocensura', in *I primi Lincei e il Sant'Uffizio: questioni di scienza e di fede*, conference proceedings (Rome, Accademia Nazionale dei Lincei and National Academy of the Lincei, 12–13 June 2003), Rome: Bardi, pp. 235–70

Wilson 2005
T. Wilson, 'Iconografie sessuali nella ceramica rinascimentale: un "intricamento" tra Leonardo ed Arcimboldo', *CeramicAntica*, 15(2), February, pp. 10–44

2006

Benati 2006
D. Benati, in *Annibale Carracci*, ed. D. Benati and E. Riccòmini, exh. cat. (Bologna, Museo Civico Archeologico, 22 September 2006–7 January 2007; Rome, Chiostro del Bramante, 25 January–6 May 2007), Milan: Mondadori Electa, cat. VIII.11

Biscarini and Nardelli 2006
P. Biscarini and G. M. Nardelli, 'Alcune Riflessioni sulla coppa erotica dell'Ashmolean Museum di Oxford', *CeramicAntica*, 16(10), November, pp. 48–50

Favilla and Rugolo 2006
M. Favilla and R. Rugolo, '"Il sommo onor dell'arte": Pietro Antonio Novelli nella Patria del Friuli', in *Artisti in viaggio 1750–1900: presenze foreste in Friuli Venezia Giulia*, ed. M. P. Frattolin, conference proceedings (Udine, 20–22 October 2005), Venice: Cafoscarina, pp. 191–226

Laurenza 2006
D. Laurenza, 'Figino and the Lost Drawings of Leonardo's Comparative Anatomy', *The Burlington Magazine*, CXLVIII(1236), pp. 173–9

Mehler 2006
U. Mehler, *Rosalba Carriera 1673–1757: Die Bildnismalerin des 18. Jahrunderts*, Königstein im Taunus: Ortensia Königstein

Melli 2006
ed., *I disegni italiani del Quattrocento nel Kupferstich-Kabinett di Dresda*, exh. cat. (Florence, Istituto Universitario Olandese di Storia dell'Arte, 15 September–5 November 2006), Florence: Centro DI

Milan 2006
Il Codice di Leonardo da Vinci nel Castello Sforzesco, ed. P. C. Marani and G. Piazza, exh. cat. (Milan, Castello Sforzesco, Sala delle Asse, 24 March–21 May 2006), Milan: Electa

2006–2007
Brumana 2006–2007
B. Brumana, 'Francesco Bartolozzi (1728–1815) incisore della musica', *Esercizi: Musica e spettacolo*, XX, n.s. 11 (2006-7), pp. 33–75

2007
Barone 2007
J. Barone, 'Poussin come costruttore della figura umana: le illustrazioni del Trattato di Leonardo', in *Leonardo: dagli studi di proporzioni al Trattato della Pittura*, ed. P. C. Marani and M. T. Fiorio, exh. cat. (Milan, Castello Sforzesco, Sala delle Asse, 7 December 2007–2 March 2008), Milan: Electa, pp. 99–119

Coccolini *et al.* 2007
G. Coccolini *et al.*,"La serie di ritratti di pittori celebri del Gabinetto Disegni e Stampe del Museo Correr: un problema di restauro, *OPD Restauro*, 19, pp. 49–66

Cogliati Arano and Spezzani 2007
L. Cogliati Arano and P. Spezzani, 'Da "Leonardesco" a Leonardo', *Raccolta Vinciana*, XXXII, pp. 197–208

Ferino-Pagden 2007
Arcimboldo 1526–1593, ed. S. Ferino-Pagden, exh. cat. (Paris, Musée du Luxembourg, 15 September 2007–13 January 2008), Milan: Skira

Gnann 2007
A. Gnann, *Parmigianino: Die Zeichnungen*, 2 vols, Petersberg: Michael Imhof Verlag

Milan 2007
Leonardo: dagli studi di proporzioni al Trattato della Pittura, ed. P. C. Marani and M. T. Fiorio, exh. cat. (Milan, Castello Sforzesco, Sala delle Asse, 7 December 2007–2 March 2008), Milan: Electa

Pavanello 2007a
G. Pavanello, ed., *Rosalba Carriera 'prima pittrice de l'Europa'* (Cataloghi di mostre, 67), exh. cat. (Venice, Galleria di Palazzo Cini a San Vio, 1 September–28 October 2007), Venice: Marsilio

Pavanello 2007b
G. Pavanello, 'Rosalba 1757–2007', in *Rosalba Carriera 'prima pittrice de l'Europa'* (Cataloghi di mostre, 67), exh. cat. (Venice, Galleria di Palazzo Cini a San Vio, 1 September–28 October 2007), Venice: Marsilio, pp. 56–79

Pavesi 2007
M. Pavesi, 'Milano, Firenze, Roma, Parigi: la diffusione del Trattato della Pittura di Leonardo', in *Leonardo: dagli studi di proporzioni al Trattato della Pittura*, ed. P. C. Marani and M. T. Fiorio, exh. cat. (Milan, Castello Sforzesco, 7 December 2007–2 March 2008), Milan: Electa

Pomian 2007
K. Pomian, *Collezionisti, amatori e curiosi: Parigi–Venezia XVI–XVIII secolo*, Milan: Il Saggiatore

Rancate 2007
Camillo Procaccini (1561–1629): le sperimentazioni giovanili tra Emilia, Lombardia e Canton Ticino, ed. D. Cassinelli and P. Vanoli, exh. cat. (Rancate, Pinacoteca Zust, 14 September–2 December 2007), Cinisello Balsamo (Milan): Silvana Editoriale

Romberg 2007
M. Romberg, 'Anonymous', in *Arcimboldo 1526–1593*, ed. S. Ferino-Pagden, exh. cat. (Paris, Musée du Luxembourg, 15 September 2007–13 January 2008), Milan: Skira (Eng. ed.), pp. 183–4, no. IV.36

Sani 2007a
Bernardina Sani, 'Note al carteggio di Rosalba Carriera', in *Rosalba Carriera 'prima pittrice de l'Europa'*, ed. G. Pavanello, exh. cat. (Palazzo Cini, Venice, 1 September–28 October 2007; Venice: Marsilio, pp. 4–49

Sani 2007b
B. Sani, *Rosalba Carriera 1673–1757: maestra del pastello nell'Europa ancien régime*, Turin: Umberto Allemandi & Co.

Selfridge-Field 2007
E. Selfridge-Field, *A New Chronology of Venetian Opera and Related Genres, 1660–1760*, Stanford, Cal.: Stanford University Press

Taglialagamba 2007
S. Taglialagamba, 'La rappresentazione del grottesco in Leonardo: ricapitolazione del problema', *Raccolta Vinciana*, XXXII, pp. 141–96

Toutain-Quittelier 2007
V. Toutain-Quittelier, 'Antonio Maria Zanetti à Paris: l'inspiration retrouvée', *La Revue de l'art*, CLVII (3), 2007, pp. 9–22

Wied 2007
A. Wied, in *Arcimboldo 1526–1593*, ed. S. Ferino-Pagden, exh. cat. (Paris, Musée du Luxembourg, 15 September 2007–13 January 2008), Milan: Skira (Fr. ed.), pp. 60–61, no. II.9

Zamperini 2007
A. Zamperini, *Le grottesche: il sogno della pittura nella decorazione parietale*, San Giovanni Lupatoto (Verona): Arsenale

Zava Boccazzi 2007
F. Zava Boccazzi, 'M.lle Rosalba très vertueuse pentresse', in *Rosalba Carriera 'prima pittrice de l'Europa'*, ed. G. Pavanello, exh. cat. (Venice, Palazzo Cini, 1 September–28 October 2007), Venice: Marsilio, pp. 15–25

2008
Marani 2008
P. C. Marani, ed., *I disegni di Leonardo da Vinci e della sua cerchia nelle collezioni pubbliche in Francia* (Edizione Nazionale dei Manoscritti e dei Disegni di Leonardo da Vinci V), Florence: Giunti

Milada 2008
J. Milada, 'I Denzio: tre generazioni di musicisti a Venezia e a Praga;, *Hudebni věda*, 45, pp. 57–114

Pavesi 2008
M. Pavesi, 'Giovan Paolo Lomazzo pittore milanese 1538–1592', PhD thesis, Università Cattolica del Sacro Cuore, Milan

Strohm 2008
R. Strohm, *The Operas of Antonio Vivaldi*, vol. I, Florence: Olschki

2009
Barcham 2009
W. Barcham, 'Rosalba Carriera e Anton Maria Zanetti tra Venezia e Parigi nella prima meta del Settecento', in *Rosalba Carriera 1673–1757*, ed. G. Pavanello, conference proceedings (Venice and Chioggia, 26–28 April 2007), Verona: Scripta, pp. 147–56

Berra 2009
G. Berra, 'Il ritratto "caricato in forma strana, e ridicolosa, e con tanta felicita di somiglianza": la nascita della caricatura e i suoi sviluppi in Italia fino al Settecento', *Mitteilungen des Kunsthistorischen Institutes in Florenz*, 53 (1), pp. 73–144

Guffanti 2009
M. V. Guffanti, 'Bibliography of Printed Editions of Leonardo da Vinci's "Treatise on Painting"', in C. Farago, ed., *Re-reading Leonardo: The 'Treatise on Painting' across Europe 1550–1900*, Farnham: Ashgate, pp. 569–605

Llewellyn 2009
T. D. Llewellyn, ed., *Lettere artistiche del Settecento veneziano*, vol. 4: *Owen McSwiny's Letters 1720–1744* (Fonti e Documenti per la storia dell'arte veneta 14), Verona: Scripta

Mason and Borean 2009
S. Mason and L. Borean, *Il collezionismo d'arte a Venezia*, Venice: Marsilio

Prosperi Valenti Rodinò 2009
S. Prosperi Valenti Rodinò, 'La caricatura a Roma nel Settecento', in *Il Settecento e le arti: dall'Arcadia all'Illuminismo. Nuove proposte tra le corti, l'aristocrazia e la borghesia*, conference proceedings (Rome, 23–4 November 2005), Rome: Bardi, pp. 261–5

Turner 2009
S. Turner, *Wenceslaus Hollar*, vol. 21, in *The New Hollstein German Engravings, Etchings and Woodcuts, 1400–1700*, 48 vols, Rotterdam: Sound & Vision Publishers

2010

Hattori, Leutrat and Meyer 2010
C. Hattori, E. Leutrat and V. Meyer, eds, *À l'origine du livre d'art: les recueils d'estampes comme entreprise éditoriale en Europe (XVIe–XVIIIe siècles)* (Cinisello Balsamo [Milan]: Silvana Editoriale

Mara 2010
S. Mara, 'Il *Libro di disegni* della Biblioteca Ambrosiana', *Arte Lombarda*, CLVIII–CLIX (1–2), pp. 74–118

Marani 2010
P. C. Marani, 'Collezionismo e filologia: a proposito dei disegni di Boltraffio, Solario e Luini dalla collezione Jabach al Louvre', *Artibus et Historiae: An Art Anthology*, 61 (XXXI), pp. 133–48

Pavanello 2010
G. Pavanello, ed., *Sebastiano Ricci: il trionfo dell'invenzione nel Settecento veneziano* (Cataloghi di mostre, 70), exh. cat. (Venice, Fondazione Giorgio Cini, 24 April–11 July 2010), Venice: Marsilio

Pavesi 2010
M. Pavesi, 'Una "Flagellazione" di Giovanni Antonio Figino al Museo del Prado', *Nuovi Studi: Rivista di Arte Antica e Moderna*, 15, 2009 [2010], pp. 189–213

Porzio 2010
F. Porzio, 'Lo "stile senz'arte" dei Rabisch e l'Accademia della Val di Blenio', in *Lombardia manierista: arti e architettura*, ed. V. Terraroli and M. T. Fiorio, Milan: Skira, pp. 195–209

2011

Berra 2011
G. Berra, 'L'Arcimboldo "c'huom forma d'ogni cosa": capricci pittorici, elogi letterari e scherzi poetici nella Milano di fine Cinquecento', in *Arcimboldo: artista milanese tra Leonardo e Caravaggio*, ed. S. Ferino-Pagden, exh. cat. (Milan, Palazzo Reale, 10 February–22 May 2011), Milan: Skira, pp. 283–313

Ebert-Schifferer 2011
S. Ebert-Schifferer, 'Quando mangiare fagioli fa una rivoluzione: considerazioni su realismo e "genere"', in *Nuova luce sui Annibale Carracci*, Rome: De Luca, pp. 21–39

Ferino-Pagden 2011a
S. Ferino-Pagden, ed., *Arcimboldo: artista milanese tra Leonardo e Caravaggio*, exh. cat. (Milan, Palazzo Reale, 10 February–22 May 2011), Milan: Skira

Ferino-Pagden 2011b
S. Ferino-Pagden, 'I mestieri e gli esordi della caricatura', in *Arcimboldo: artista milanese tra Leonardo e Caravaggio*, ed. S. Ferino-Pagden, exh. cat. (Milan, Palazzo Reale, 10 February–22 May 2011), Milan: Skira, p. 156-173

New York 2011
Infinite Jest: Caricature and Satire from Leonardo to Levine, ed. C. C. McPhee and N. M. Orenstein, exh. cat. (New York, The Metropolitan Museum of Art, 13 September 2011–4 March 2012), New York: The Metropolitan Museum of Art; New Haven and London: Yale University Press

Porzio 2011
F. Porzio, 'Arcimboldo: le Stagioni "milanesi" e l'origine dell'invenzione', in *Arcimboldo: artista milanese tra Leonardo e Caravaggio*, ed. S. Ferino-Pagden, exh. cat. (Milan, Palazzo Reale, 10 February–22 May 2011), Milan: Skira, pp. 221–53

Sapori 2011
G. Sapori, 'Risfogliando le "Arti di Bologna": Carracci, Agostini, Massani, Algardi, Guillain', in *Nuova luce su Annibale Carracci*, ed. S. Ebert-Schifferer and S. Ginzburg, Rome: De Luca, pp. 227–53

Tamburini 2011
E. Tamburini, 'I comici Gelosi e l'Accademia della Val di Blenio', in *Studi e testimonianze in onore di Ferruccio Marotti (III), Biblioteca teatrale*, 97–8, January–June, pp. 175–95

2012

Kowalczyk 2012
B. A. Kowalczyk, 'Bellotto and Zanetti in Florence', *The Burlington Magazine*, CLIV (1306), 2012, pp. 24–32

Riccòmini 2012
E. Riccòmini, *Donato Creti: le opere su carta. Catalogo ragionato*, Turin: Umberto Allemandi & Co.

Rossi 2012
F. Rossi, ed., *Simone Peterzano ca. 1535–1599 e i disegni del Castello Sforzesco*, exh. cat. (Milan, Castello Sforzesco, 15 December 2012–17 March 2013), Cinisello Balsamo (Milan): Silvana Editoriale

Signorini 2012
C. Signorini, in *Pinacoteca Civica di Vicenza: lascito Giuseppe Roi*, Catalogo Scientifico delle Collezioni, VI, ed. M. E. Avagnina, G. C. F. Villa, Vicenza: Fondazione Giuseppe Roi – Musei Civici di Vicenza, pp. 56–60, no. 22

Veronese 2012
F. Veronese, 'Politica e potere nella corrispondenza di Margherita Pio di Savoia (1670–1725)', in *Spazi e poteri: diritti delle donne a Venezia in età moderna*, ed. and, Bolzano: QuiEdit, pp. 107–15

2013

Marani 2013
P. C. Marani, 'Maniera Milano: 1513–1564 circa', in *Prima di Carlo Borromeo: lettere e arti a Milano nel primo Cinquecento*, ed. E. Bellini and A. Rovetta, conference proceedings (Milan, Biblioteca Ambrosiana, 7–9 November 2012), Studia Borromaica, 27, 2013, pp. 3–44

Pavesi 2013
M. Pavesi, 'Qualche riflessione sull'attività pittorica di Giovan Paolo Lomazzo', in *Studi in onore di Maria Grazia Albertini Ottolenghi*, ed. M. Rossi, A. Rovetta and F. Tedeschi (Quaderni di Storia dell'arte 2), Milan: Vita & Pensiero, pp. 155–61

Villata 2013
E. Villata, ed., *Intorno a Leonardo: rarità dell'Ente Raccolta Vinciana al Castello Sforzesco*, exh. cat. (Milan, Castello Sforzesco, 9 November 2013–2 February 2014), Milan: Raccolta Vinciana

2014

Borean 2014
L. Borean, 'Per il collezionismo grafico tra Venezia e Londra nel Settecento: il caso di John Skippe', *Studi di Memofonte*, 12, pp. 73–85

Boutin Vitela 2014
L. Boutin Vitela, 'Inscriptions and the Dynamic Reception of Italian Renaissance Maiolica', *Word & Image*, 30/2, pp. 168–76 (DOI: 10.1080/02666286.2014.912907)

Pedretti 2014
C. Pedretti, 'La bellezza secondo Leonardo', in *L'arte del disegno*, ed. and, Florence: Giunti, pp. 11–95

Pigozzi 2014
M. Pigozzi, 'Annibale Carracci, Giulio Cesare Croce e Agostino Carracci', in *Le arti e il cibo: modalità ed esempi di un rapporto*, ed. S. Davidson and F. Lollini, conference proceedings (Bologna, Università di Bologna, 15–16 October 2012), Bologna: Bononia University Press, pp. 231–43

Pedretti and Taglialagamba 2014
C. Pedretti and S. Taglialagamba, eds, *L'arte del disegno*, Florence: Giunti

Rinaldi 2014
F. Rinaldi, 'Bernardino Luini "Mediolanensis", Aurelio Luini e Giovanni Paolo Lomazzo: disegni firmati tra autografia e documento', in *Studi sul disegno italiano tra connoisseurship e collezionismo*, ed. F. Grisolia, *Horti hesperidum*, IV (2), pp. 5–57

Taglialagamba 2014
S. Taglialagamba, 'I disegni caricaturali', in *L'arte del disegno*, ed. C. Pedretti and S. Taglialagamba, Florence: Giunti, pp. 118–23

2015

Androsov 2015
S. Androsov, 'Giove ritrovato di Antonio Tarsia', in *Venezia Settecento: studi in memoria di Alessandro Bettagno*, ed. B. A. Kowalczyk, Cinisello Balsamo (Milan): Silvana Editoriale, pp. 189–95

D'Amelio 2015
A. M. d'Amelio, '"Lo Sposalizio di Marfisa": una raccolta di caricature di Giuseppe Piattoli', *Paragone*, LXVI, 120(781), March, pp. 50–60

Kowalczyk 2015
B. A. Kowalczyk, 'Il "prezioso" manoscritto della collezione Bettagno: l'*Indice* della Biblioteca di Anton Maria Zanetti', in *Venezia Settecento: studi in memoria di Alessandro Bettagno*, ed. B. A. Kowalczyk, Cinisello Balsamo (Milan): Silvana Editoriale, pp. 31–6

Lucchese 2015
E. Lucchese, *L'album di caricature di Anton Maria Zanetti alla Fondazione Giorgio Cini*, Venice: lineadacqua

Magrini 2015
M. Magrini, 'Anton Maria Zanetti e Dresda', in *Venezia Settecento: studi in memoria di Alessandro Bettagno*, ed. B. A. Kowalczyk, Cinisello Balsamo (Milan): Silvana Editoriale, pp. 229–37

Marani 2015
P. C. Marani, 'Scheda', in *Leonardo da Vinci 1452–1519: il disegno del mondo*, ed. P. C. Marani and M. T. Fiorio, exh. cat. (Milan, Palazzo Reale, 15 April–19 July 2015), Milan and Geneva: Skira, p. 556, cat. V.16

Milan 2015
Leonardo da Vinci: il disegno del mondo, ed. P. C. Marani and M. T. Fiorio, exh. cat. (Milan, Palazzo Reale, 15 April–19 July 2015), Milan and Geneva: Skira

Prosperi Valenti Rodinò 2015
S. Prosperi Valenti Rodinò, *Carlo Marchionni caricaturista tra Roma, Montefranco Civitavecchia e Ancona* (Studi e Testi 503), Rome: Campisano

Rosenberg 2015
P. Rosenberg, 'Les dessins vénitiens du XVIIIe siècle de la collection de Pierre-Jean Mariette', in *Venezia Settecento: studi in memoria di Alessandro Bettagno*, ed. B. A. Kowalczyk, Milan: Silvana Editoriale, pp. 111–29

Stefani 2015
G. Stefani, *Sebastiano Ricci impresario d'opera a Venezia nel primo Settecento* (Premio Ricerca 'Città di Firenze' 46), Florence: Firenze University Press

Zelen 2015
J. Zelen, 'The Venetian Print Album of Johann Georg I Zobel von Giebelstadt', *The Rijksmuseum Bulletin*, 63(1), pp. 2–51

2016

Debenedetti 2016
E. Debenedetti, 'Saggio introduttivo', in *Rossiano 619: caricature. Carlo Marchionni e Filippo*, ed. andb,Città del Vaticano: Biblioteca Apostolica Vaticana, pp. 7–37

Kowalczyk 2016
Bellotto e Canaletto: lo stupore e la luce, ed. B. A. Kowalczyk, exh. cat. (Milan, Gallerie d'Italia, 25 November 2016–5 March 2017), Cinisello Balsamo [Milan]: Silvana Editoriale

London 2016
In the Age of Giorgione, ed. exh. cat. (London, Royal Academy of Arts, 12 March–5 June 2016), London: Royal Academy of Arts

Lucchese 2016
E. Lucchese, 'Attorno alla Gallerie di Palazzo Clerici', in *Tiepolo a Milano: la decorazione dei Palazzi Archinto, Casati e Clerici*, ed. L. Finocchi Ghersi, Rome: Artemide, pp. 69–91

Marani 2016
P. C. Marani, *'Bella quanto l'originale istesso': la copia del Cenacolo della Royal Academy di Londra. Vicende, fortuna, attribuzione*, Vicchio (Florence): LoGisma

Tantardini 2016
L. Tantardini, 'On the Grotesque: Aurelio Luini and Leonardo', in *Il Rinascimento a Milano e in Lombardia: storia e storiografia dell'arte del Rinascimento a Milano e in Lombardia*, ed. A. Jori, C. Z. Laskaris and A. Spiriti, conference proceedings (Milan, Pinacoteca Ambrosiana, 9–10 June 2015), Rome: Bulzoni, pp. 215–24

Winner 2016
C. Winner, *Alberto Giacometti: A Line Through Time*, London: Bloomsbury

2017

Costa and Perini Folesani 2017
S. Costa and G. Perini Folesani, *I Savi e gli ignoranti: dialogo del pubblico con l'arte (XVI–XVIII secolo)*, Bologna: Bononia University Press

Loire 2017
S. Loire, *Peintures italiennes du XVIIIe siècle du musée du Louvre*, Paris: Gallimard and Louvre Éditions

Lucchese 2017
E. Lucchese, 'Nel segno della grazia: Antonio Balestra maestro di Anton Maria Zanetti di Girolamo e nella "Scuola del nudo" di Giambattista Tiepolo', *Valori Tattili*, 9, 2017, pp. 155–61

Mara 2017
S. Mara, 'Carlo Giuseppe Gerli e l'edizione dei Disegni di Leonardo da Vinci (1782–1784)', in *Le arti nella Lombardia asburgica durante il Settecento*, ed. E. Bianchi, A. Rovetta and A. Squizzato, conference proceedings (Milan, Università Cattolica del Sacro Cuore e Pinacoteca di Brera, 5–6 June 2014), Milan: Scalpendi, pp. 395–407

Marani 2017
P. C. Marani, 'Suggestioni leonardesche nella cultura e nelle caricature di Anton Maria Zanetti dell'Album Cini', *Arte Veneta*, 73, 2016 [2017]), pp. 187–96

Olmi and Tongiorgi Tomasi 2017
G. Olmi and L. Tongiorgi Tomasi, 'Giuseppe Arcimboldo tra natura, arte e artificio', in *Arcimboldo*, ed. S. Ferino-Pagden, exh. cat. (Rome, Gallerie Nazionali di Arte Antica, Palazzo Barberini, 20 October 2017–11 February 2018), Milan: Skira, p. 85

Razzall 2017
R. Razzall, 'Consul Smith and his Circle', in *Canaletto and the Art of Venice*, ed. R. Razzall and L. Whitaker, exh. cat. (The Queen's Gallery, London, 19 May–12 November 2017), London: Royal Collection Trust, pp. 21–33

2018

Barone 2018
J. Barone, 'Seventeenth-Century Transformations: Cassiano dal Pozzo's Manuscript Copy of the Abridged Libro di pittura', in *The Fabrication of Leonardo da Vinci's Trattato della pittura*, 2 vols, Leiden: Brill, pp. 261–99

Guffanti 2018
M. V. Guffanti, 'The Visual Imagery of the Printed Editions of Leonardo's Treatise on Painting', in *The Fabrication of Leonardo da Vinci's Trattato della pittura*, ed. C. Farago, J. Bell and C. Vecce, 2 vols, Leiden: Brill, appendix, pp. 373–411, 547–49

Haarlem 2018
Leonardo da Vinci: The Language of Faces, ed. M. W. Kwakkelstein with M. Plomp, exh. cat. (Haarlem, Teylers Museum, 5 October 2018–6 January 2019), Bussum: Thoth

Loisel 2018
C. Loisel, ed., *Éblouissante Venise: Venise, les arts et l'Europe au XVIIIe siècle*, exh. cat. (Paris, Grand Palais, 24 September 2018–21 January 2019), Paris: Réunion des Musées Nationaux

Lucchese 2018a
E. Lucchese, *L'album di caricature di Anton Maria Zanetti alla Fondazione Giorgio Cini di Venezia: indice analitico & errata corrige*, Venice: lineadacqua

Lucchese 2018b
E. Lucchese, 'Il Vedutismo, lo specchio di Venezia', in P. Di Loreto, ed., *Originali, repliche, copie: uno sguardo diverso sui grandi maestri*, Rome: Ugo Bozzi Editore, pp. 272–9

Melani 2018
M. Melani, 'Leonardo e Hollar in scala 1:1', in *Leonardo disegnato da Hollar*, ed. A. Perissa Torrini, exh. cat. (Vinci, Pedretti Foundation, 16 December 2018–5 May 2019), Poggio a Caiano (Prato): CB Edizioni, pp. 77–105

Pavesi 2018
M. Pavesi, *Giovanni Ambrogio Figino pittore*, Santa Palomba (Rome): Aracne

Perissa Torrini 2018
A. Perissa Torrini, ed., *Leonardo disegnato da Hollar*, exh. cat. (Vinci, Fondazione Pedretti, 16 December 2018–5 May 2019), Poggio a Caiano (Prato): CB Edizioni

Taglialagamba 2018
S. Taglialagamba, '"Molte teste di vecchi"', in *Leonardo disegnato da Hollar*, ed. A. Perissa Torrini, exh. cat. (Vinci, 16 December 2018–5 May 2019), Poggio a Caiano (Prato): CB Edizioni, pp. 157–70

2019
Bambach 2019
C. C. Bambach, *Leonardo da Vinci Rediscovered*, New Haven and London: Yale University Press

Costa 2019
S. Costa, *Dal magnifico concerto all'ordinato metodo: collezioni e musei d'Ancien Régime*, Bologna: Bononia University Press

Lucco, Humfrey and Villa 2019
M. Lucco, P. Humfrey and G. C. F. Villa, *Giovanni Bellini: catalogo ragionato*, ed. M. Lucco, Treviso: ZeL Edizioni

Lucchese 2019
E. Lucchese, 'Carnevale 1750: il cantante Gizziello per i Grimani ai Servi in una tela di Pietro Longhi', *Musica e Figura*, 6, pp. 97–114

Mara 2019
S. Mara, 'Il collezionismo di disegni nel tardo Cinquecento a Milano e le origini della raccolta grafica dell'Ambrosiana: il caso di Giovanni Battista Clarici', in *La donazione della raccolta d'arte di Federico Borromeo all'Ambrosiana 1618–2018: confronti e prospettive* (Studia Borromaica 32), ed. A. Rocca, A. Rovetta and A. Squizzato, Milan: pp. 345–81

Marani 2019
P. C. Marani, ed., *La Cène de Léonard de Vinci pour François Ier, un chef-d'œuvre en or et soie*, exh. cat. (Amboise, Château du Clos Lucé, 7 June–2 September 2019), Paris: Clos Lucé and Skira

Perissa Torrini 2019a
A. Perissa Torrini, ed., *Leonardo da Vinci: l'uomo modello del mondo da Vinci*, exh. cat. (Venice, Gallerie dell'Accademia, 17 April–14 July 2109), Cinisello Balsamo (Milan): Silvana Editoriale

Perissa Torrini 2019b
A. Perissa Torrini, 'Leonardo a Venezia', in *Leonardo da Vinci: l'uomo modello del mondo da Vinci*, ed. A. Perissa Torrini, exh. cat. (Venice, Gallerie dell'Accademia, 17 April–14 July 2109), Cinisello Balsamo (Milan): Silvana Editoriale, pp. 53–65

Pisot 2019
Goya, Fragonard, Tiepolo. Die Freiheit der Malerei, ed. S. Pisot, exh. cat. (Hamburg, Kunsthalle, 13 December 2019–1 June 2020), München: Hirmer, 2019

Rosenberg 2019
P. Rosenberg, *Les dessins de la collection Mariette: écoles italienne et espagnole*, Paris: Somogy

Sonetti 2019
A. Sonetti, 'La Città di Colonia a Livorno', *La Nuova Antologia*, 623 (2292), pp. 230–49

Urbini 2019
S. Urbini, 'Fortuna in Laguna: xilografie, letterati, editori e attori. A proposito dell'*Arboro di frutti della Fortuna*', *Engramma*, 162, January–February, http://www.engramma.it/eOS/index.php?id_articolo=3545

Zavatta 2019
G. Zavatta, 'Antonio Morassi, Federico Zeri e un falsario di disegni guardeschi: Giuseppe Latini alias "il prete romano" alias il Maestro del Ricciolo', *Storia dell'arte*, n.s. 2(150), 2018, pp. 127–35

2020
Alberti 2020
A. Alberti, 'Giovanni Ambrogio Brambilla: Poet, Painter, Draughtsman, and Printmaker between Milan and Rome', in *Lomazzo's Aesthetic Principles Reflected in the Art of his Time*, ed. L. Tantardini and R. Norris, Leiden and Boston: Brill, pp. 63–89, 178–83

Favalier 2020
S. Favalier, 'La lingua facchinesca o l'illusione della lingua bergamasca', *Italies:* Illusions et Chimères, 24, pp. 105–16

Jacobi 2020
C. Jacobi, *Out of the Cage. The Art of Isabel Rawsthorne*, London: The Estate of Francis Bacon–Thames & Hudson

Lucchese 2020
E. Lucchese, 'Zanetti, Anton Maria', in *Dizionario biografico degli italiani*, vol. C, Rome: Istituto della Enciclopedia Italiana, p. 507

Mara 2020
S. Mara, *Arte e scienza tra Urbino e Milano: pittura, cartografia e ingegneria nell'opera di Giovanni Battista Clarici (1542–1602)*, Padua: Il Poligrafo

Melani 2020
M. Melani, 'Hollar "copia" Leonardo: l'uso della carta lucida per incisioni in scala 1:1', *Incontri: rivista europea di studi italiani*, XXXV, pp. 21–31 (DOI: 10.18352/incontri.10331)

Pezzini 2020a
E. Pezzini, 'Lomazzo e i "Rabisch": status quaestionis e nuove prospettive', *Italianistica*, 49, pp. 177–212

Pezzini 2020b
E. Pezzini, 'Significato storico e lettura dei "Rabisch" di Giovanni Paolo Lomazzo', *Italique*, 22, pp. 81–105

2021
Barcham 2021
W. L. Barcham, 'The Issue of Copies: Three Drawings by Giannantonio Guardi in New York', *Artibus et Historiae*, 83(XLII), pp. 255–75

Eco 2021
U. Eco, 'La bruttezza' (2017), in *Sulle spalle dei giganti*, Milan: La Nave di Teseo

London 2021
Francis Bacon: Man and Beast, ed. M. Peppiatt, A. Testar and S. Lea, exh. cat. (London, Royal Academy of Arts, 19 January–17 April 2022), London: Royal Academy of Arts

Lucchese 2021
E. Lucchese, 'I pittogrammi nelle lettere', in *Lettere artistiche del Settecento veneziano*, vol. 6: *Anton Maria Zanetti di Girolamo: il carteggio, Fonti e Documenti per la Storia dell'Arte Veneta*, 17, ed. M. Magrini, Verona: Scripta, pp. 165–71

Luyckx and Leeflang 2021
J. Luyckx and H. Leeflang, *The New Hollstein. Dutch & Flemish Etchings, Engravings, and Woodcuts 1450-1700. The Liefrink Dinasty. Part A*, 2 vols, Ouderkerk aan den Ijssel: Sound & Vision Publisher

Magrini 2021
M. Magrini, ed., *Anton Maria Zanetti di Girolamo: il carteggio*, Verona: Scripta

Metz 2021
Face à Arcimboldo, ed. C. Parisi and A. Horvath, exh. cat. (Centre Pompidou-Metz, 29 May–22 November 2021; Paris: Éditions du Centre Pompidou-Metz

Resciniti 2021
L. Resciniti, ed., *Tiepolo: catalogo dei disegni del civico museo di Trieste*, Trieste: Comune di Trieste

Rossetti 2021
E. Rossetti, 'Il testamento di Aurelio Luini e la sua eredità leonardesca (1593)', in *Mitteilungen des Kunsthistorischen Institutes in Florenz*, LXIII, 3, 2021, pp. 358–75

Sani 2021
B. Sani, 'Rosalba Carriera', in *Lettere artistiche del Settecento veneziano*, vol. 6: *Anton Maria Zanetti di Girolamo: il carteggio*, ed. M. Magrini (Fonti e Documenti per la Storia dell'arte veneta 17), Verona: Scripta, pp. 1–22

Spadaccini 2021
B. Spadaccini, 'La pietra rossa nelle stampe che imitano i disegni', in *Disegni a pietra rossa: fonti, tecniche e stili 1500–1800 ca.*, ed. L. Fiorentino and M. W. Kwakkelstein, conference proceedings (Florence, Istituto Olandese di Storia dell'Arte and Dutch University Institute for Art History, 18–19 September 2019), Florence: Edifir, pp. 223–36

Stefani 2021
G. Stefani, 'La musica e il teatro', in *Lettere artistiche del Settecento veneziano*, vol. 6: *Anton Maria Zanetti di Girolamo: il carteggio*, ed. M. Magrini (Fonti e Documenti per la Storia dell'arte veneta 17), Verona: Scripta, pp. 187–210

2022
Bertolini 2022
L. Bertolini, 'L'estetica del grottesco nelle *Rime* di Giovan Paolo Lomazzo', *Fillide. Il sublime rovesciato: comico, umorismo e affini*, 24, pp. 1–15

Bodart 2022
D. H. Bodart, 'Il Braghettone e l'uccellino. Le sperimentazioni caricaturali di Aurelio Luini', in *Viaggio nel Nord Italia. Studi di cultura visiva in onore di Alessandro Nova*, ed. D. Donetti, H. Gründler and M. Richter, Florence: CentroDi, pp. 161-6

Lucchese 2022
E. Lucchese, 'Angela Carriera, Giovanni Antonio Pellegrini e Daniele Antonio Bertoli tra Venezia, Vienna e San Daniele del Friuli', in *Patrons, Intermediaries, Venetian Artists in Vienna and Imperial Domains (1650–1750)* (Storia dello Spettacolo 2), ed. E. Lucchese and M. Klemenčič, Florence: Polistampa, pp. 75–91

Stevens and Swan 2022
M. Stevens and A. Swan, *Francis Bacon: Revelations*, Glasgow: William Collins

Tassinari 2022
G. Tassinari, 'Collezionisti, committenti e incisori di pietre dure a Venezia nel Settecento', in *Collezionisti e collezioni di antichità e di numismatica a Venezia nel Settecento*, ed. A. Gariboldi, conference proceedings (Trieste, 6–7 December 2019), Trieste: Edizioni Università di Trieste, pp. 99–211

PHOTO CREDITS

© 2000-2022 The Metropolitan Museum of Art. All rights reserved. Gift of Harry G. Friedman, 1953: p. 64, fig. 4.

© 2000-2022 The Metropolitan Museum of Art. All rights reserved. Rogers Fund, 1937: p. 117, fig. 7.

© Albertina, Vienna: p. 102, fig. 8.

© Bibliothèque Nationale de France: p. 68, fig. 7.

© Christie's Images Limited 2022: p. 112, fig. 1.

© Civici Musei e Gallerie di Storia e Arte di Udine: p. 135, figs 4, 5.

© Comune di Milano. Tutti i diritti riservati, Archivio Storico Civico e Biblioteca Trivulziana: p. 21, fig. 1.

© Comune di Milano. Tutti i diritti riservati, Ente Raccolta Vinciana, Castello Sforzesco, Milano. Studio fotografico Luca Carrà: cats 37, 38, 43, 47, 49, 78, 79, 83, 84, 85 (p. 122, detail).

© Comune di Milano. Tutti i diritti riservati, Gabinetto dei Disegni, Castello Sforzesco: cats 22, 24, 56, 57, 58, 59, 60, 62; p. 156, fig. 2.

© Comune di Milano. Tutti i diritti riservati, Raccolta delle Stampe "Achille Bertarelli", Castello Sforzesco, Milano: p. 133, fig. 2 (p. 130, detail).

© Fondazione Giorgio Cini. All rights reserved: p. 27, fig. 8; cats 50, 53 (p. 25, fig. 4, detail), 54 (p. 26, fig. 5, detail), 55.

© Gabinetto Fotografico delle Gallerie degli Uffizi: cats 31, 32, 48.

© G.A.VE Archivio fotografico. Su concessione del Ministero della Cultura: cats 20, 30, 39.

© HLMD, Photo Wolfgang Fuhrmannek: p. 112, fig. 3.

© Nuova Fondazione Rossana e Carlo Pedretti: cats 44, 45, 46.

Photo Pernille Klemp © Designmuseum Danmark: cats 34, 35.

© Pinacoteca di Brera, Milano: cat. 17; p. 62, fig. 1.

© Rijksmuseum, Amsterdam. Purchased with the support of the F.G. Waller – Fonds – Public Domain CC0 1.0: p. 80, fig. 1.

© RMN-Grand Palais / Dist. Foto SCALA, Firenze. Photo Laurent Chastel: p. 26, fig. 7. Photo Adrien Didierjean: p. 101, fig. 6. Photo Thierry Le Mage: p. 28, fig. 9; cat. 29. Photo Michel Urtado: cat. 40.

Royal Collection Trust / © His Majesty King Charles III 2022: p. 22, fig. 2 (p. 18, detail); p. 26, fig. 6; p. 68, fig. 7 (p. 60, detail of the *Quaresima*); p. 102, fig. 6.

© Thaw Collection. The Morgan Library & Museum. 2017.253: p. 118, fig. 8.

© The Estate of Francis Bacon. All rights reserved / DACS / SIAE 2022: p. 198, fig. 1.

© The Estate of Francis Bacon. All rights reserved / DACS / SIAE / Artimage 2022. Photo Prudence Cuming Associates Ltd.: back cover; cat. 86 (pp. 202, 204, 205, details).

© The Morgan Library & Museum. 1996.58. Bequest of Miss Alice Tully: p. 114, fig. 5.

© The Morgan Library & Museum. 1966.133. Gift of Mrs. Rudolf J. Heinemann, in memory of Dr. Rudolf J. Heinemann: p. 120, fig. 9.

© Université de Montpellier: p. 116, fig. 6.

© Veneranda Biblioteca Ambrosiana / Gianni Cigolini / Mondadori Portfolio: p. 63, figs 2, 3; cats 1, 2, 3, 18, 19, 21, 25, 26, 27.

Collezione Ligabue. Photo Matteo De Fina: front cover; cat. 4.

Courtesy National Gallery of Art, Washington. Creative Commons Zero (CC0), Paul Mellon Fund: p. 67, fig. 6.

Firenze, Biblioteca Medicea Laurenziana. Su concessione del MiC. È vietata ogni ulteriore riproduzione con qualsiasi mezzo: p. 112, fig. 2; p. 113, fig. 4.

Gift of Dian Woodner. Courtesy National Gallery of Art Library, Washington: p. 28, fig. 10.

Herzog August Bibliothek Wolfenbüttel: p. 136, fig. 6.

Kupferstich-Kabinett, Staatliche Kunstsammlungen Dresden. Photo Herbert Boswank: cat. 23.

Photo Mark Smith: cat. 52.

Photo Matteo De Fina: cats 61, 63, 64, 65, 66, 67, 68, 69, 70, 71, 72, 73, 74, 75, 77, 80, 81, 82.

Photo Studio fotografico Luca Carrà: cats 33, 36, 42 (p. 96, detail), 51; p. 91, fig. 2; p. 96, figs 3, 4; p. 99, fig. 5; p. 132, fig. 1; p. 134, fig. 3; p. 142, fig. 1; p. 189, fig. 3.

Photo Vivi Papi: cat. 36.

Städel Museum, Public domain, via Wikimedia Commons: p. 25, fig. 3.

Stoccolma, Skoklosters slott. Photo Erik Lernestål. Public domain, via Wikimedia Commons: p. 66, fig. 5.

Su concessione di Fondazione Accademia Carrara, Bergamo: cat. 28.

The Devonshire Collections, Chatsworth. Reproduced by permission of Chatsworth Settlement Trustees: cats 5, 6, 7, 8, 9, 10, 11, 12, 13, 14, 15, 16, 41.

Wellcome Collection. Public Domain Mark 1.0: p. 137, fig. 7.

Reproduction and Printing
Opero s.r.l., Verona

For
Marsilio Editori® s.p.a., Venezia

Up to 15% of this book may be photocopied for personal use by readers provided they pay the SIAE fee as per art. 68, clauses 4 and 5 of Italian Law no. 633 of April 22, 1941. Photocopies for professional, economic, or commercial use or in any way different from personal use may be made, but only after obtaining specific authorization from the Centro Licenze e Autorizzazioni per le Riproduzioni Editoriali (CLEARDI), 108 Corso di Porta Romana, 20122 Milan, e-mail autorizzazioni@clearedi.org and web site www.clearedi.org.